Department of
Economic and Social Affairs

Internet Governance:
A Grand Collaboration

An Edited Collection of Papers Contributed to
the United Nations ICT Task Force Global Forum
on Internet Governance, New York, March 25-26, 2004

Opening Statement by **Kofi Annan**

Preface by **José María Figueres**

Edited with Introduction by **Don MacLean**

D1617352

.

Published by
The United Nations Information and Communication Technologies Task Force
One United Nations Plaza
New York, NY 10017
unicttaskforce@un.org

Acknowledgements

I would like to express my gratitude to the many individuals who worked to bring this publication to fruition. I sincerely appreciate the efforts of the staff of the UN ICT Task Force Secretariat, located in the Department of Economic and Social Affairs of the United Nations, who devoted many hours to the careful proofreading of this text. Serge Kapto, who adroitly coordinated communication between the contributors and myself and painstakingly compiled the copy, and Enrica Murmura, who skilfully oversaw the process from its inception, deserve special acknowledgement. Sirpa Hämäläinen and Cheryl Stafford demonstrated acute attention to detail as they drove the manuscript through copy-editing, design, layout and production. Industrious interns Anastasia Seliankina, Robert de Jesus and Emmanuel de Lange provided valuable assistance and technical expertise that enabled the book to be delivered by deadline. I would also like to recognize the Graphic Design Unit of the Outreach Division of the Department of Public Information for patiently working with us to deliver a cover design that captured visually the essence of the discussion within.

CONTENTS

Section 4: Public Policy Issues   181

OPENING STATEMENT AT THE GLOBAL FORUM ON INTERNET GOVERNANCE
Kofi Annan, United Nations Secretary-General

It gives me great pleasure to address this Global Forum on Internet Governance, organized by the United Nations Information and Communication Technologies (ICT) Task Force. This is a timely initiative, and it is very encouraging to see here today some of the key founders and leaders of the Internet community, along with government officials and representatives of the private sector and civil society. There is much for us to discuss. Even more importantly, there is much that we can do together as partners.

In only a few years, the Internet has revolutionized trade, health, education and, indeed, the very fabric of human communication and exchange. Moreover, its potential is far greater than what we have seen in the relatively short time since its creation. In managing, promoting and protecting its presence in our lives, we need to be no less creative than those who invented it. Clearly, there is a need for governance, but that does not necessarily mean that it has to be done in the traditional way, for something that is so very different.

The issues are numerous and complex. Even the definition of what we mean by Internet governance is a subject of debate. But the world has a common interest in ensuring the security and dependability of this new medium. Equally important, we need to develop inclusive and participatory models of governance. The medium must be made accessible and responsive to the needs of all the world's people. At present, its reach is highly uneven, and the vast majority of people have yet to benefit from it, or even to be touched by it at all.

As we all know, Internet governance was one of the most controversial issues at last December's Geneva phase of the World Summit on the Information Society (WSIS). I am glad that the keenly felt differences over the subject did not get in the way of overall progress. The Summit was able to produce results in our broader effort to put information and communication technologies at the service of development. Nonetheless, on Internet governance the differences were such that the Summit asked me to set up a working group.

But before I do so, we need to consult a broad cross-section of the communities involved. So I am glad that the ICT Task Force has decided to organize its Global Forum on this subject. Your views, and those emerging from other consultations, will help to frame the issues, find areas of complementarity and convergence among stakeholders, and identify issues for future consultations. Once these consultations have taken place, I will be in a position to establish the working group, which, I can assure you, will be open, transparent and inclusive of all stakeholders. To support the working group and to help me, I will be setting up a small secretariat in the near future.

These same principles of openness and inclusiveness will also apply to the task force on funding that the Summit asked me to create. This task force, which I plan to establish shortly, will review the adequacy of current funding approaches and consider new funding mechanisms that might strengthen our efforts to bridge the digital divide.

Important as it is to address the issues of governance and funding, let us not forget the larger task: implementing the Plan of Action in its entirety. Indeed, the Summit set very specific targets for access to information and communication technologies – in villages, schools, libraries, hospitals and clinics, government offices, and elsewhere – and this, too, will require us to muster all our creativity. Let me assure you of the United Nations' commitment to this effort.

In your talks over the next two days, I urge you to keep in mind the paramount goal of helping people everywhere build free and decent lives. That is the real backbone of your deliberations. Whatever you do must contribute to the cause of human development.

I wish you every success.

PREFACE

José María Figueres, Chairman, United Nations Information and Communication Technologies Task Force

We are witnessing the emergence of a new paradigm of global society. It is based on networking in pursuit of common interests, and on prevalence of non-hierarchical, multilateral and multi-stakeholder approaches. The Internet is perhaps the best embodiment of this new model, as well as its most potent tool.

As the Internet becomes part of the fabric of our lives and as its spread becomes increasingly global, harnessing its full potential may require a rethinking of how it should be governed. It is becoming increasingly important to think of inclusive, collaborative approaches that will enhance the Internet's impact on the achievement of our development goals, and thus improve lives of people everywhere. The Internet's potential to empower individuals, communities and countries needs to be effectively harnessed and become a tool for all peoples to extract value from globalization rather than watch globalization extract value from them. But in leveraging and harnessing the Internet's potential, we must remain true to its original principle of freedom.

The Geneva Phase of the World Summit on Information Society called for an international management of the Internet and a fuller understanding of the wide range of issues associated with setting up its governance mechanisms. It recognized that this task needs to involve all major stakeholders – governments, the private sector, civil society, and international organizations. To launch this process, WSIS requested the Secretary-General of the United

Nations to set up a working group that will investigate and make proposals for action on the governance of the Internet.

As a contribution to this important process, the United Nations Information and Communication Technologies Task Force organized a "Global Forum on Internet Governance" held in New York in March 2004. Attended by representatives of national governments, international organizations, the Internet community, the private sector, and civil society, this Forum served as a venue to facilitate the exchange of views and opinions on the technical, regulatory, public policy and development issues associated with Internet Governance. It was an open and inclusive dialogue, with sharing of perspectives, concerns and visions of the Information Society of the future.

This publication, *Internet Governance: A Grand Collaboration* is a compendium of papers submitted prior to the Forum as well as of presentations to the meeting itself. The book captures the substantive issues discussed and highlights the critical aspects of governance of the Internet. The diversity of views and approaches presented in this publication reflects the complexity of the problem. At the same time, a reader will clearly see certain important commonalities of views that we must build on.

I hope that this publication will prove to be a valuable reference for future dialogue on Internet governance and on ways to strengthen the development impact of the Internet.

INTRODUCTION
Don MacLean, Editor

The United Nations Information and Communication Technologies Task Force convened a Global Forum on Internet Governance in New York on March 25-26, 2004. In addition to the members of the Task Force, the forum was attended by more than 200 representatives of the private sector, civil society, national governments and international organizations. The purpose of the forum was to allow participants to exchange views on issues that should be considered by the United Nations Secretary-General's Working Group on Internet Governance, which will be established as a result of decisions taken at the first phase of the World Summit on the Information Society in Geneva in December 2003.

To help prepare the forum, the Task Force Secretariat invited written contributions from the international community. More than thirty papers were submitted in response to this request, by independent experts, Internet practitioners, and different stakeholder groups. Together, these papers cover a wide range of the most important technical, regulatory, public policy and development issues related to the general subject of Internet governance. The full text of all these papers is available on the web site of the United Nations ICT Task Force[1]. The aim of this collection is to present a selection of these contributions in relation to some of the main themes that emerged at the global forum and to highlight their essential messages.

To this end, contributions to the global forum have been organized into six sections, which deal with the following themes:

---

[1] See http://www.unicttaskforce.org/sixthmeeting/background.html.

- understanding the challenge;
- the evolution of the Internet governance debate;
- frameworks and definitions;
- public policy issues;
- technical issues;
- the way ahead.

In each of these sections, contributions are grouped into three categories:

- *background papers*, which provide comprehensive information and analysis in relation to the theme of the section;
- *comments*, which focus on a particular aspect of the theme and present the views of individual authors;
- *stakeholder perspectives*, which present the views of business, civil society, governmental, and intergovernmental organizations – either on the theme as a whole or on specific issues related to it.

Papers that deal with Internet governance issues in terms that are easily accessible to a wide international audience have been presented in their entirety. Papers that deal with issues other than Internet governance, that contain detailed technical information, or that present specific proposals for action by national or international organizations have been edited to highlight their most salient contributions to general discussions about Internet governance.

* * * * *

In introducing this collection, it is useful to begin by recalling the decisions made by the World Summit on the Information Society with respect to Internet governance.

The WSIS Declaration of Principles contains the following provisions:

48. The Internet has evolved into a global facility available to the public and its governance should constitute a core issue of the Information Society agenda. The international management of the Internet should be multilateral, transparent and democratic, with the full involvement of governments, the private sector, civil society and international organizations. It should ensure an equitable distribution of resources, facilitate access for all and ensure a stable and secure functioning of the Internet, taking into account multilingualism.

49. The management of the Internet encompasses both technical and public policy issues and should involve all stakeholders and relevant intergovernmental and international organizations. In this respect it is recognized that:

a) Policy authority for Internet-related public policy issues is the sovereign right of States. They have rights and responsibilities for international Internet-related public policy issues;

b) The private sector has had and should continue to have an important role in the development of the Internet, both in the technical and economic fields;

c) Civil society has also played an important role on Internet matters, especially at community level, and should continue to play such a role;

d) Intergovernmental organizations have had and should continue to have a facilitating role in the coordination of Internet-related public policy issues;

e) International organizations have also had and should continue to have an important role in the development of Internet-related technical standards and relevant policies.

The WSIS Plan of Action complements these provisions as follows:

13.b We ask the Secretary-General of the United Nations to set up a working group on Internet governance, in an open and inclusive process that ensures a mechanism for the full and active participation of governments, the private sector, and civil society from both developing and developed countries, involving relevant intergovernmental and international organizations and forums, to investigate and make proposals for action, as appropriate, on the governance of the Internet by 2005. The group should, *inter alia*:

i) develop a working definition of Internet governance;

ii) identify the public policy issues that are relevant to Internet governance;

iii) develop a common understanding of the respective roles and responsibilities of governments, existing intergovernmental and international organizations and other forums as well as the private sector and civil society from both developing and developed countries;

iv) prepare a report on the results of this activity to be presented for consideration and appropriate action for the second phase of WSIS in Tunis in 2005.

The Geneva phase of WSIS was not the first time that decisions about Internet governance had been made at the international level. In recent years, intergovernmental organizations such as the International Telecommunication Union (ITU), the World Intellectual Property Organisation (WIPO) and the World Trade Organization (WTO) have made decisions regarding specific aspects of Internet governance that affect the interests of the private sector and civil society, as well as the relations between governments. During this same period of time, international non-governmental organizations such as the Internet Corporation for

Assigned Names and Numbers (ICANN) and the Internet Engineering Task Force (IETF) have also made decisions that affect the interests of national governments and intergovernmental organizations, in addition to those of their private sector and civil society constituents. However, in all these cases decisions were made on a piecemeal basis, without benefit of an overall policy framework and without full participation by all affected parties.

Against this background, it is fair to say that phase one of WSIS marked a turning point in the development of international Internet governance arrangements, in several important senses. For the first time, the Geneva phase of WSIS:

- comprehensively addressed the technical, regulatory, public policy and development aspects of Internet governance;
- established a set of fundamental principles and objectives to guide the evolution of Internet governance arrangements;
- recognized that national governments, the private sector, civil society and international organizations have legitimate and complementary roles to play in Internet governance;
- put in place a process that will enable these different stakeholder groups to work together in developing an Internet governance agenda and action plan, for consideration at the Tunis phase of WSIS.

As well as being important "firsts" in the development of Internet governance arrangements, these decisions may help inspire innovation in other fields of international governance where success also depends on partnership and collaboration between governments, the private sector and civil society.

* * * * *

The members of the Secretary-General's working group, and all those involved in the second phase of WSIS, face a very significant challenge in implementing the decisions of the Geneva phase. What does the phrase "Internet governance" mean in concrete, operational terms? What public policy issues are relevant to Internet governance? What should be the respective roles and responsibilities of governments, intergovernmental and other international organizations, the private sector and civil society in the practical, day-to-day governance of the Internet? These are difficult questions to at least begin answering in a relatively short period of time, before the Tunis phase of WSIS in 2005. To help with this process, contributions to the Global Forum have been organized in the following manner.

Section One – Understanding the Challenge

Before beginning to think about governance definitions, issues and arrangements, it is essential to have a good understanding of how the Internet operates today and how it is likely to evolve in the future. Section One therefore presents three background papers intended to help readers understand the challenges involved in governing the Internet.

Participants in the Global Forum were privileged to hear Vinton Cerf and Robert Kahn, two of the principal inventors of the Internet, explain its origins, current structure, and future possibilities. As well as suggesting that Internet governance should be "a grand collaboration" among many different stakeholders, their presentations contributed a number of key concepts and principles to the forum's discussions – for example, by suggesting that different kinds of governance arrangements are appropriate at different Internet "layers", that the Internet evolves in much the same way as society does, and that care should be taken to avoid doing harm to governance arrangements that are working well.

In addition to the contributions of these Internet pioneers, Section One includes a paper by Daniel Karrenberg that explains in layman's terms how the Internet domain name system works. This is a very useful contribution, since the governance of the DNS has been the focus of much discussion and debate.

Section Two – Evolution of the Internet Governance Debate

With the workings of the Internet explained, Section Two proceeds to trace the evolution of the international debate about Internet governance throughout the WSIS preparatory process, and to situate the results of the Geneva phase in the context of broader discussions about global governance. Taken together, these papers show how a debate that was originally centred on a relatively narrow set of technical and regulatory questions rapidly evolved to include a much broader range of public policy issues and global development concerns.

Wolfgang Kleinwächter's paper "Beyond ICANN vs. ITU?" traces the development of arrangements for governing the DNS and analyses the debate about this topic that took place during the first phase of WSIS in order to highlight the emergence of two very different Internet governance models: the "industry self-governance" model represented by ICANN and the "intergovernmental governance" model represented by the ITU. In an accompanying background paper, Markus Kummer provides an insider's account of the negotiations that took place between proponents of these different points of view during the final stages of WSIS preparations, and proposes a process for moving forward. Although the debate about Internet governance continues, both Kleinwächter and Kummer suggest that the WSIS process may lead to the development of a new governance model that resolves the main contradictions between these competing visions, and fully engages all stakeholders.

This conclusion is supported in the papers contributed by Zoë Baird and Stefaan Verhulst, who argue that the Internet governance model developed by WSIS is applicable to other areas of international governance, and by Patrice Lyons, who draws attention to the links between more effective Internet governance and the achievement of the United Nations Millennium Development Goals.

Section Three – Frameworks and Definitions

Section Three presents a number of papers that address the first and third tasks facing the Secretary-General's working group – developing a working definition of "Internet governance", and developing a common understanding of the respective roles and responsibilities of the different stakeholder groups involved in Internet governance. The main messages of these contributions are that Internet governance is about much more than managing the Internet domain name and address systems; that a large number of institutions and organizations are already involved in Internet governance; and that the principal challenge facing the international community is to improve the functioning of existing arrangements, not to invent new structures. It is also clear from these analyses that it will be essential to set priorities among the many issues that could be considered as falling under the general rubric of Internet governance, in order to address those that are most critical for the future of the Internet and the many benefits it can bring to the peoples of the world.

In "Herding Schrödinger's Cats", the Editor provides a set of conceptual tools designed to help readers to think about the meaning of "Internet" and "governance" in practical terms, to map the issues and institutions that are relevant to Internet governance, and to identify the barriers to effective participation by developing countries in Internet governance arrangements. In "Making Sense of 'Internet Governance'", Milton Mueller, John Mathiason, and Lee W. McKnight take the reader to a higher level of analysis by proposing an operational definition of Internet governance, identifying the basic principles that underlie the operation of the Internet, articulating a set of norms derived from these principles, proposing a policy framework, and presenting a series of case studies illustrating how the Internet governance principles and norms they recommend could be applied to specific policy issues on the international agenda. In "Fifteen Baseline Propositions", William Drake first dispels a number of current myths about Internet governance and then goes on to provide a comprehensive framework for identifying the organizations involved in Internet governance and assessing their effectiveness, stressing in particular the need to find ways of including developing countries, civil society organizations, small- and medium-sized enterprises and individual users in an ongoing process of analysis, dialogue and consensus building.

These background papers are complemented by a paper from Raúl Echeberría commenting on a number of the key Internet governance issues facing the international community, as well as by contributions giving the perspectives of two very important stakeholder organizations: the International Chamber of Commerce, which has served as the *porte-parole* for the business community throughout the WSIS process, and the Internet Society, the umbrella organization for the global Internet community. Both of these stakeholder contributions emphasize the need to take a broad view of Internet governance, which encompasses technical standardization, management of Internet addresses and names, and relevant public policy issues.

Sections Four and Five – Public Policy and Technical Issues

Sections Four and Five present papers that address the second task facing the Secretary-General's working group – identifying the policy issues that are relevant to Internet governance.

Since this topic attracted the largest number of contributions to the Global Forum – in terms of the number of papers and the number of pages submitted – the contributions have been divided into two sections. Section Four includes papers that deal primarily with governance issues raised by the economic and social consequences of the Internet, while Section Five includes papers that deal primarily with governance issues related to the management and coordination of the Internet's technical resources. Although these differences in emphasis make it useful to distinguish between "public policy and development" issues on the one hand, and "technical management and coordination" issues on the other hand, the contributions demonstrate that these two dimensions of Internet governance are inextricably linked. Sooner or later, technical developments have policy consequences, and policy choices have technical implications.

Section Four begins with a discussion document on "Internet Governance" by George Sadowsky, Raul Zambrano and Pierre Dandjinou. This paper provides a comprehensive overview not only of public policy issues raised by the Internet, but of the full range of topics that are part of the current international discussion about Internet governance. It recapitulates many of points made in previous sections about the scope of Internet governance, and then moves on to identify the main public policy issues raised by the Internet for all countries, while putting special emphasis on the relevance of Internet governance for developing countries. This very useful survey is complemented by Norbert Klein's "Perspectives from Cambodia", which presents a case study of how one developing country has responded to the challenges and opportunities presented by the Internet. Although the paper mainly focuses on factors that are particular to Cambodia, it is clear that many of the lessons that can be learned from its experience are applicable to other developing countries.

The comments and stakeholder perspectives included in Section Four reinforce the importance of Internet governance issues for developing countries. In different ways, the papers by Veni Markovski, the United Nations Economic Commission for Africa (UNECA), the United Nations Economic and Social Commission for Western Asia (UNESCWA), and the United Nations Conference on Trade and Development (UNCTAD) make similar points. One is that in developing countries and regions, discussions about Internet governance must be situated in the context of discussions about achieving sustainable development, so that appropriate linkages are made at the levels of theory, policy and practice. Another is that government, private sector and civil society stakeholders from developing countries must be more effectively engaged in Internet governance processes.

Section Five begins with Karl Auerbach's "Questions and Answers about the Internet and Internet Governance", which sets out the technical parameters of Internet governance in simple, easy-to-understand language and distinguishes issues related to the technical governance of the Internet, IP addresses and domain names from issues such as copyright and trademarks that more properly belong to other domains. This is followed by two papers that examine different aspects of one of the currently most contentious areas of Internet governance – the management of domain names.

In "Internet Governance, National Interest and International Relations", Kenneth Neil Cukier argues that domain names are too important a resource to be left to the exclusive management of technicians, and that it is in their national interest for governments to become moderately, but not excessively, engaged in the domain name management process. Michael Geist's global survey of "Governments and Country-Code Top Level Domains" shows that many governments have heeded this message, at least with respect to the management of ccTLDs, although there are differences in the extent to which they have adopted "hands-on" management practices. These analyses are complemented by a paper from Carlos Afonso that examines issues related to the management of ccTLDs in Brazil.

Section Five also presents a number of papers that examine challenges for the technical governance of the Internet arising from the continuing development of the Internet naming and addressing systems, as well as from broader trends in the development of information and communications technologies (ICTs).

With respect to the evolution of Internet naming and addressing systems, Khaled Fattal outlines the challenges and opportunities involved in "Bridging the Digital Divide" and proposes an approach to making the Internet more easily accessible to the vast majority of the world's population who either do not know or are not comfortable communicating in English or the other languages that dominate the Internet today. In "e-Nations: The Internet for All",

Tony Hain, Patrick Grossetete, Jim Bound, and Latif Ladid demonstrate how the deployment of IPv6 – an improved version of the Internet Protocol – could correct disparities in the allocation of address space that currently exist between developed and developing countries.

With respect to the implications of ICT development trends, Rainer Händel argues that "Governance of IP-Based Next Generation Networks (NGNs)" should be treated as a new aspect of Internet governance, since these networks will merge the features of the current Internet and the Public Switched Telephone Network (PSTN) into a unified public network for IP-based electronic communications. The ITU's contribution on "Understanding Telecommunication Network Trends" expands this vision by analyzing the trends that are leading to the convergence of Internet, mobile and broadband communication technologies into the ubiquitous, IP-based networks of the future.

Section Six – The Way Ahead

The concluding section summarizes the results of the Global Forum. It presents comments from Faryel Mouria-Beji on the achievements of the Geneva phase and the challenges facing the Tunis phase of WSIS, and from Bertrand de La Chapelle on the views of civil society stakeholder groups.

* * * * *

As this collection of papers demonstrates – and the proceedings of the Global Forum made clear – there appears to be an emerging consensus about Internet governance. The main elements of this consensus include the recognition that many different organizations are already involved in governing the Internet and its effects on society, and that most of these arrangements, although not perfect, are working well. At the same time there is recognition that a number of important issues are not being addressed effectively, and that in some areas there is an urgent need to put in place new arrangements to counter real and present threats to the stability and utility of the Internet. The consensus also takes the view that all the major stakeholder groups – governments, the private sector, civil society, intergovernmental organizations and other international organizations and forums – should be involved in Internet governance, although the form and nature of their involvement is likely to vary according to the issue. One of the key contributions of the Global Forum to this consensus was to underline the absolute necessity of engaging developing countries in Internet governance, and of building their capacity to participate effectively in its institutions and processes.

This emerging consensus was largely captured in the Declaration of Principles and Plan of Action of the Geneva Phase of the World Summit on the Information Society. The Global

Forum, and recent similar events, have provided a useful "reality check" for the WSIS decisions with respect to Internet governance; they have helped to confirm that the summit process is on the right track; and have indicated areas where preparatory work for the Tunis phase might usefully concentrate. However, it will not be an easy task for the United Nations Secretary-General's Working Group on Internet Governance to discharge the mandate it has been given, and difficult discussions and decisions may still lie ahead on the road to Tunis.

Realizing the WSIS vision of constructing Internet governance arrangements that are multilateral, transparent and democratic with the full involvement of all stakeholders is a noble challenge. Meeting it will require goodwill among all parties, as well as good information on which to base decisions. The papers contributed to the United Nations ICT Task Force Global Forum on Internet Governance contain a lot of useful information and many interesting ideas. These contributions helped participants in the Forum begin the process of building a global consensus on Internet governance – a process that hopefully will continue throughout the second phase of WSIS and beyond. As a result of these contributions, the vision of a "grand collaboration" on Internet governance is a step closer to reality.

Section 1

UNDERSTANDING THE CHALLENGE

"FIRST, DO NO HARM"
Vinton G. Cerf, MCI

I thank you for the opportunity to offer a few thoughts on the term "Internet governance" and the task that Secretary-General Annan has set before the working group on that subject.

In his charge to this working group, the Secretary-General set out four goals, paraphrased roughly:

1. Develop a working definition of Internet governance;
2. Identify public policy issues relevant to the term;
3. Develop a common understanding of the roles and responsibilities of governments, intergovernmental organizations and other forums, as well as the private sector and civil society from both developing and developed countries;
4. Prepare a report as input to the World Summit on the Information Society that will meet in Tunis in 2005.

There is an old expression that was once used to describe the behavior of a governmental regulatory body: "If all you have is a hammer, everything looks like a nail." If we are not careful, we may fall into that trap by trying to develop overly simple definitions for what is really a very complex question.

It is fair to ask first whether the Internet needs governing. Celestial mechanics deals with the motions of the planets. Their orbits are said to be governed by the laws of physics. A great deal of what the Internet does is governed, in that sense, by the standard protocols that all players in the Internet environment agree to use. These are, practically speaking, the "technical rules of the Internet road". For the most part, the Internet has evolved openly, freely, and without a great deal of governmental or other oversight because these rules are developed openly and adopted voluntarily. Standards allow for interoperability, and that feature is a principal reason that the Internet has grown in scale and functionality. The very openness of the Internet design has contributed greatly to its evolution as participants in its use, operation and development have been able to contribute fresh ideas for new applications and functionality. When Robert Kahn first began thinking about the concept of the Internet, he began by listing attributes of what he called Open Network Architecture. That vision has surely been rewarded as we see what the Internet has become.

As this highly flexible communications infrastructure continues to evolve, it is beginning to subsume functions that have long been the subject of considerable regulation and this contributes, in part to the question whether the Internet needs more governing. Perhaps even more important than the functioning of the Internet is the use to which it is put. The Internet is, in some respects, like a piece of paper. The paper does not know what is written on it, and neither does the Internet. But like a piece of paper, the Internet accepts any digital writing and will carry it anywhere the network can reach. The Internet is unaware of the applications to which it is put. In fact, this very feature has contributed mightily to its flexibility.

If one does not like what is written on the paper, it is of little use to lecture the sheet of paper or punish it. Rather, one turns to the writer. This is an application of the layered approach to thinking about governance. Perhaps if we need to govern, our need should focus more on the use or abuse of the network, and less on its operation, except where the technical rules of the road dictate adherence to standards to assure the stability and integrity of the system.

Governance is sometimes thought of as a means of restricting what may be done. A much more positive perspective might be gained if one asks, "how can one use governance to facilitate access to and development of new uses of this medium". The Internet Society motto is that "the Internet is for Everyone". But we know we are still far from that goal. If we think of governance as the steps we collectively take to facilitate the spread and constructive use of the Internet, we may come to positive and constructive conclusions.

Perhaps a few concrete examples will be helpful. To facilitate the use of the Internet for global electronic commerce, it would be beneficial to develop international procedures for the use of digital signatures, mechanisms to resolve disputes associated with international electronic transactions, treatment of various transaction taxes in an international setting and the protection of intellectual property held in digital formats and distributed globally through the

Internet medium. These are not new problems; rather, they are old problems emerging in a new medium.

If one reflects on the objectives of the United Nations Information and Communication Technologies Task Force, it is readily apparent that the use of the Internet can contribute to the achievement of many of the Task Force's Millennium Development Goals. It was recognized in the Millennium Summit in 2000 that the Task Force should seek to use information and communications technology to reduce poverty, facilitate education and health care, improve the environment and seek gender equality and empowerment of women. It was also recognized that the means to these ends involved partnerships among the public and private sectors, academia and civil society.

I submit to you that this conference would contribute greatly, both to the goals of the ICT Task Force and to the charge given to the Working Group on Internet Governance, if we could weave together these objectives by asking how such partnerships can be applied to facilitating the positive and constructive use of the Internet. There are many existing players in the Internet space. We should build on the foundation they collectively form.

Engineers have a saying: "If it isn't broken, don't fix it." Doctors say: "First, do no harm." This is good advice and we should follow it. The technical aspects of the Internet seem to be evolving very openly and in forums to which everyone is invited to participate. Rules for the use of the Internet are less well developed and deserve more consideration. I would caution, however, that one should strive not to stifle the innovation and freedom to create that the Internet offers.

There are many places at the Internet table. It is a grand collaboration of many entities in all sectors. I think it is our task to assure that all who may benefit from the use of the Internet will have a seat at the table and an opportunity to contribute to the constructive evolution of this new medium.

WORKING CODE AND ROUGH CONSENSUS: THE INTERNET AS SOCIAL EVOLUTION

Robert E. Kahn, Corporation for National Research Initiatives

I am delighted to provide this statement, which touches on some of the underlying themes addressed in this Forum and provides my own perspective on how to address the subject of "Internet Governance".

First, I want to reiterate what I have heard from so many of the organizers of this Forum, whom I congratulate for their hard work, that the main purpose of these deliberations is to uncover relevant subject areas and issues and to open a dialogue involving knowledgeable persons, stakeholders and Government representatives, with the goal of raising the overall level of awareness. It has been helpful to share experiences as well as concerns about the Internet, and perhaps to provide a glimpse along the way of what it might be appropriate to do about these concerns.

The recent past has been one of rapid technological change. I never thought I would see, in my lifetime, the kind of testimonial to the impact of the Internet on Society as was presented at the WSIS, where representatives of virtually every government delegation extolled the importance of the Internet in the future of the Information Society. What started out as an exciting research activity for a few of us some thirty years ago has become a staple part of the fabric of our society, and will likely remain so for the foreseeable future. Yet, almost everyone who has looked seriously at the Internet to try to understand it, and to speculate on its future role in Society, has begun with one simple question. Who runs it? Simply stated, who is in charge?

I can say that the answer "no one is in charge" usually takes a while to fully digest. This is neither the expected answer nor an easy one to fathom. Yet, like the world economy, to name another critical activity, the Internet facilitates and indeed encompasses a myriad of activities of innumerable individuals and their computer systems, coordinated by a system of protocols and mechanisms that, taken together, constitute a global information system based on an "Open Architecture". In the parlance of Internet 101, a new system that adheres to the requisite protocols may become a part of the Internet by simply connecting to it. Using the packet network postcard analogy that Dr. Cerf has presented, all the postcards from the new system can now be delivered to any of the other participants in the combined system, and vice versa. The result is a kind of global connectivity limited only by considerations of available and affordable bandwidth, system reliability, quality of overall service, and of course computers and available applications software. As we have heard, this simple formulation makes many basic assumptions that some of us take for granted, such as availability of electricity, literacy (computer and otherwise), and suitable language skills to navigate the network.

Of course, Internet 201 would tell us that it starts to get a little more complicated if we look a bit more closely at what is actually happening. For example, what about the little gremlins in the system, equipped with scissors, who take the postcards and cut them into mini-postcards? And how exactly does the billion bit-per-second sender manage to control himself, when he is sending to a very slow speed receiving system? Does the net ever get congested, and can one really make use of all that diversity of network capability? And when things go wrong, as they will from time to time, it may not be our job to get it fixed, but can we find out where the problem is? Surely, most of the users have no clue, but only know they have a problem. With regard to the evolution of the Internet, my dream is that, one day, the networks of the world, and perhaps the computers connected to them, will be "cognitive systems" that know enough about themselves and what they are doing to fix problems when they detect them if they can, and to alert users or the system operators accordingly. This is currently the province of the research community, but it brings us full circle on the Internet journey we began several decades ago.

You all know that the Internet was born within the research community. It began in the early 1970s as an experiment to link together three experimental computer networks – the ARPANET (which was the world's first packet switched network); the packet radio network (which was an extension of packet switching to mobile data communications); and SATNET (which used a single 64 Kbps channel on Intelsat IV to provide connectivity to four countries in Europe) – and of course computers and users on those networks. For the first ten years of its then experimental existence, virtually every major decision about the Internet was made by me, or by Vint Cerf, who by then had joined DARPA and was working with me in the U. S. Government, or by the two of us. There were also a growing number of technical contributors from many organizations during this period. We had a pretty free imprimatur back then to proceed as we wished, as none of the major telecommunications or equipment stakeholders saw this experiment as going further than perhaps limited use for defense applications. Had this not been the case, it is likely we would have made far less progress than we did.

From the late 1970s onward, a great deal of our time was spent on devolving responsibility for the evolution of the Internet from government to the private sector. Of course we were helped along the way by a few key developments, which I like to joke about having been able to predict with precision and clarity when we started the work, such as the development of the personal computer, the introduction of competition in the US telecommunications industry, and the agreement by the US Government in the early 1990s to allow the private sector to use the NSFNET, which by then had become the backbone for much of the Internet traffic. I think it is fair to say that we succeeded in this process.

A critical part of this story is the way in which standards have been developed and, more specifically, the social structures that were needed to support them. While the Internet Engineering Task Force (IETF) has responsibility for certain key elements of the standards process, and has been remarkably effective for more than two decades, it is not the only contributor to standards used in the Internet. The most widely used individual network technology in the Internet is the Ethernet, which became an IEEE standard. The World Wide Web, having been created initially at CERN, is now the product of the Web Consortium. And, of course, many ITU contributions that are indigenous to the telecommunications industry underpin the provision of many services on the Internet.

Even more notable have been the contributions of the many individuals and organizations that have helped evolve the Internet. A critical aspect of the IETF over the years has been the ability it provides for virtually anyone to try out a new piece of technology on the net and to have it move from being an experiment to the standards track through a process that involves promotion by its developers, possible adoption by users if it meets a basic need, and a mechanism for generating consensus within the technical community. This is truly a bottom-up, grass-roots process different from the way standards are usually developed by other standards bodies. For a long time, the motto of the IETF has been "working code and rough consensus".

However, as the Internet has matured and reliance on it for all kinds of activities has expanded, as with all such maturing systems prudence and caution have dictated a more deliberative and perhaps conservative approach for the future. Things have arguably slowed down a bit, and efforts to reinvent the Internet around a new approach are occasionally made. This is not really a rejection of the past, so much as it is a recognition that faster progress for the future may depend on freedom from the need to maintain and not harm the basic infrastructure on which we have come to depend. We need only look to how many years it has taken IPv6 to be fully deployed to have a notion of what we are facing here. Among the stakeholders here, it is worth remarking how few members of the research community are among us. In connection with the WSIS, CERN held a sidebar event called the RSIS – "The Role of Science in the Information Society" – to remind us all that there needs to be a role for science and engineering to develop technology, and to bring it to everyday use. It feels a little strange to have come full circle, but I think it is time for the research community to once again have a central presence on the Internet stage, only this time to share it with others, such as those here at this Forum.

There will surely be issues that cannot be solved within the technical community alone, and others for which the choice of technology is not really relevant. Some of these will surely be potentially worldwide in scope. We have discussed the need for coordination on a broader scale within the international community to deal with issues surrounding cyber-terrorism, to name but one such issue. At the extreme, dealing with specific threats, not to mention actual incidents, may only be addressed successfully with the collaboration of all those involved around the world. This is one example where the convening power of the United Nations may be particularly helpful.

I expressed my view at the ITU workshop last month that we need to take several steps in order to meet the charge given to the United Nations Working Group on Internet Governance. It has surely become clear by now that the term "governance" defies easy categorization. Even developing a clear idea of the Internet landscape is not easy, as it does not admit of a simple 3-D topography or a linear taxonomy. And not all of us would agree on what should be included in the landscape and what should be left out. So we will have to struggle with the representation of ideas here. Nevertheless let me assert that this is step one. We should do the best we can under the circumstances. Given what I will call the resulting cartography, it would then be advisable to articulate the issues underlying each of the charted elements and those that span multiple (or even all) of the elements. Security comes to mind as something that may span all of the elements. Another issue, providing Internet access to all, while a central concern throughout the world is largely a financial issue that would surely not involve more than a few of the elements, if that. Given the spectrum of elements and issues, the third step would be to determine whether resolution of each issue lies with the private sector, or by governments, or by a combination of the two. The fourth step would be to attempt to resolve the issues, where practicable, or to identify approaches to resolving them, where possible. I think we may have our hands full on the first two of these items for quite a while.

To me, a natural way to start identifying the elements would be to categorize them into several possibly overlapping segments such as Operations, Financing, Technical Standards, Social Implications, and Conflicts/Threats/Attacks. I can easily imagine turning this into a more sophisticated matrix, or any other more complex representation, but let me not attempt that here.

I would close with an anecdote from early 1983 when I managed the transition from the old host protocols on the ARPANET (known as NCP) to the newer TCP/IP protocols. This was neither an instantaneous transition nor a simple matter to accomplish. I knew most, if not all, of the affected organizations and the key individuals personally. Indeed, we funded many of them to participate in the Internet and gave them more than a year to prepare for the transition. It took several weeks to get a critical mass of machines and their software converted from the old to the new, and perhaps six months before all those that had planned to change actually did so. Indeed, less than a week before the stated conversion date, people I knew well were calling to ask if we were really serious about making the change. These were among the folks that took the six months to cut over. During that entire period, we kept up both the old protocols and the new. I shudder to think how such a transition would take place today with hundreds of millions of users around the world. Probably, it could not happen and one would have to reinvent a new system around the old.

So I leave you with that architectural conundrum. We know what the Internet is about today, but how can substantive change in the system best be made to occur in the future?

Will we have in place the mechanisms to allow for rapid evolution in the technological sense, or even in the sense of social utility, and what might they look like? What will make governments around the world develop a sense of comfort in depending on something that is not totally under their control – indeed not under anyone's control? What are the public policy issues that need to be addressed in this regard? There are no clear answers here.

The integration of new, even revolutionary capabilities, including new architectural paradigms, into existing systems is difficult at best. The building of such capabilities around existing institutions has proven to be possible, the Internet being one such example, but with potentially disruptive impacts in the process. Perhaps this is the only way in which such changes can occur. But I am hopeful, if not actually optimistic, that it need not always be this way. I do not know what kind of social compact, if any, can help to make this kind of evolution happen within existing structures and organizations. The evolution of the Internet has many of the attributes of the evolution of society itself, providing connectivity and linkages, enabling interactions, stimulating collaboration and competition, and providing for the public good. We, collectively, may not have done a perfect job of evolving the society in which we live, but we have mechanisms that allow it to evolve. The Internet will also need to evolve along many different dimensions. So we are left with the need to understand, perhaps better than we do today, how best to achieve this objective for our inevitable shared future together.

THE INTERNET DOMAIN NAME SYSTEM EXPLAINED FOR NON-EXPERTS[1]
Daniel Karrenberg, RIPE NCC

Dear non-Experts,

This is for you, who always wanted or needed to know how Internet names really work. The Internet Domain Name System (DNS) is a fascinating technology; almost all Internet applications make use of it. After reading this you will not suddenly have become a DNS expert, but you will have an understanding of how the DNS works and you should be able to distinguish a real DNS expert from a pretender.

Dear Experts,

This is not for you. For the sake of explaining principles we will often generalize and do this sometimes to the point where our explanations are not strictly correct in every last detail. The relevant Internet standards are where you find the details.

Purpose of the DNS

The purpose of the DNS is to enable Internet applications and their users to name things that have to have a globally unique name. The obvious benefit is easily memorizable names for things like web pages and mailboxes, rather than long numbers or codes. Less obvious but equally important is the separation of the name of something from its location. Things can move to a totally different location in the network fully transparently, without changing their

---

[1] Also available in ISOC Briefing #16, http://www.isoc.org/briefings/016/

name. `www.isoc.org` can be on a computer in Virginia today and on another computer in Geneva tomorrow without anyone noticing.

In order to achieve this separation, names must be translated into other identifiers which the applications use to communicate via the appropriate Internet protocols. Let's look at what happens when you send a mail message to me at `daniel.karrenberg@ripe.net`. A mail server trying to deliver the message has to find out where mail for mailboxes at 'ripe.net' has to be sent. This is when the DNS comes into play.

The mail server transmits this question, called a 'query' in DNS terminology, to the DNS. Quickly it receives as answer:

```
ripe.net. 1800 IN MX 100 postman.ripe.net.
ripe.net. 1800 IN MX 150 postboy.ripe.net.
"Mail for 'ripe.net' should be sent first to the computer
called 'postman.ripe.net'. If 'postman.ripe.net' is not
available, try 'postboy.ripe.net'."
```

The mail server will now make a connection with '`postman.ripe.net`'. In order to do this it needs to know the numeric Internet address for '`postman.ripe.net`'. This numeric address is sufficient to send Internet packets directly to the computer called '`postman.ripe.net`' from anywhere in the Internet. Again the DNS is queried and it returns '`193.0.0.199`'.

```
postman.ripe.net. 172800 IN A 193.0.0.199
```

From here on, the mail server delivering your message can directly communicate with the mail server that receives and stores my mail for me to collect later on.

It is obvious that the information we just obtained in our example cannot come from a central list somewhere. This list would simply be too large, change too often and its repository would be quickly overwhelmed with queries.

So how *does* this work?
Let us follow the DNS query starting from your computer. Your computer knows the address of a nearby DNS "caching server" and will send the query there. These caching servers are usually operated by the people that provide Internet connectivity to you. This can be your Internet Service Provider (ISP) in a residential setting or your corporate IT department in an office setting. Your computer may learn the address of the available caching servers

automatically when connecting to the network or have it statically configured by your network administrator.

When the query arrives at the caching server there is a good chance that this server knows the answer already because it has remembered it, "cached" in DNS terminology, from a previous transaction. So if someone using the same caching server has sent mail to someone at 'ripe.net' recently, all the information that is needed will already be available and all the caching server has to do is to send the cached answers to your computer. You can see how caching speeds up responses to queries for popular names considerably. Another important effect of caching is to reduce the load on the DNS as a whole, because many queries do not go beyond the caching servers.

DETAIL - CACHING HIERARCHIES

Caching servers can also be arranged in a hierarchy. This makes sense in cases where the network capacity is limited and/or network latency between the DNS client and the rest of the Internet is high. When connecting a laptop to the Internet through a slow dial-up connection, it makes sense to run a caching server right on the laptop. This way each click on a hyperlink on the same web site will not cause DNS related traffic over the dial-up link. Such a local caching server is often configured to send all queries for which it does not have cached answers to the ISPs caching server in turn.

Sometimes corporate networks have local caching servers that in turn send queries to a corporate caching server before they are sent out to the Internet. This way the corporate caching server can build a large cache based on queries from the whole enterprise.

Beyond the Cache

If the caching server does not find the answer to a query in its cache, it has to find another DNS server that does have the answer. In our example it will look for a server that has answers for all names that end in 'ripe.net'. In DNS terminology such a server is said to be "authoritative" for the "domain" 'ripe.net'.

In many cases our caching server already knows the address of the authoritative server for 'ripe.net'. If someone using the same caching server has recently surfed to 'www.ripe.net', the caching server needed to find the authoritative server for 'ripe.net' at that time and, being a *caching* server, naturally it cached the address of the authoritative server.

So the caching server will send the query about the mail servers for 'ripe.net' to the authoritative server for 'ripe.net', receive an answer, send that answer through to your computer and cache the answer as well.

Note that so far *only* your caching server and the authoritative server for 'ripe.net' have been involved in answering this query.

Redundancy – Many servers with the same answers

Now, what if either the local caching server or the authoritative server for 'ripe.net' is unreachable? Obviously your mail server would not get an answer and could not immediately deliver your message. It would simply queue the message and try later. However if your web browser needed to find the address of 'www.ripe.net' when you clicked on a hyperlink to that site, things are different. The browser would appear to be stuck while waiting for the name 'www.ripe.net' to be resolved to a numeric address because it would not be able to contact the web server without knowing that numeric address. Either you would tire of waiting and do something else, or your browser would give you an error message after timing out the DNS query. This does not happen very often because there is a lot of potential for redundancy in the Internet architecture, especially in the DNS.

To ensure high availability the DNS has multiple servers all with the same data. To get around the problem of the *local caching server* not being available your computer usually has a number of them configured from which it can choose. This way one can make sure that there always is a caching server available. But how about the authoritative servers?

To improve availability of *authoritative name servers* there always are a number of them for each domain. In our example of 'ripe.net' there are five of them, three of which are in Europe, one in North America and one in Australia.

```
ripe.net.  172800  IN  NS  ns.ripe.net.
ripe.net.  172800  IN  NS  ns2.nic.fr.
ripe.net.  172800  IN  NS  sunic.sunet.se.
ripe.net.  172800  IN  NS  auth03.ns.uu.net.
ripe.net.  172800  IN  NS  munnari.OZ.AU.
```

Our caching server does not get one place to look up authoritative information about 'ripe.net' names, but five of them, all being equally authoritative. It is entirely free to choose any one of these based on its own preference as they all hold the same information; the choice could either be made entirely randomly or based on previous response times of those servers. The important point to remember is that *any* choice is a valid one.

This mechanism provides the potential for pretty strong redundancy covering both server and connectivity problems since the servers can be located anywhere on the Internet. Of course the level of redundancy actually achieved depends on the design and placement of the servers. A rather large corporation discovered this a few years back when all of their two authoritative name servers located in the same computer room became unreachable from the Internet because of a network problem that "could not happen".

ENTERING INFORMATION INTO THE DNS

Information is entered into the DNS by changing the databases which the authoritative name servers use to answer queries. How these databases are maintained and transmitted to the servers is a local implementation matter fully transparent to DNS clients and outside the scope of this description.

For smaller domains often a local text file is changed on one of the authoritative servers and then transferred to the others. In this case the authoritative server on which the file is maintained is called the "master" server and the other authoritative servers are called "slave" servers. However this distinction is invisible to the rest of the DNS since all of the servers are equally authoritative.

Rising in the Hierarchy

Now let us consider the situation when our caching server has just been started and has an empty cache. Consequently it neither knows the answer to your query nor does it know where the authoritative servers for 'ripe.net' are. However it *does* know that it is possible to ask questions for 'ripe.net' to an authoritative server for 'net' because dots separate different parts of a domain name. This knowledge is part of the DNS protocol itself which says: "In case authoritative servers for a name are not known, strip off the leftmost part of the name including the first dot and send the original query to an authoritative server for that name."

In our example an authoritative server for 'net' does not know the answer to a query about 'something.ripe.net', because the 'ripe.net' servers hold that information, but it *does* know which servers are authoritative for 'ripe.net' queries. So instead of an answer to the query, the 'net' server will answer with the list of authoritative servers for 'ripe.net', a referral in DNS terminology. The caching server will receive the referral to the 'ripe.net' servers. Just as in the earlier example it now asks its question to an authoritative server for 'ripe.net', obtains the answer and sends it back to the client that asked for it. In addition, being a caching server, it will cache both the answer and the list of authoritative servers for 'ripe.net' for further use. Simple enough.

But hold on, we assumed the cache was empty in the first place, so how does our caching server know where the authoritative servers for 'net' are? In other words what happens once we have stripped off all parts of a domain name and still do not know where to go for an answer?

For this case there is a special set of authoritative servers, the DNS root servers. They know the addresses of all authoritative servers for names that do not have a dot in them, the Top Level Domains (TLDs) such as 'org', 'com', 'ch', 'uk'.

Root servers are the only DNS servers that have to be found without any other information being cached. To solve this bootstrapping problem all caching servers have a pre-configured list of numeric addresses for all root servers. When starting up, a caching server will send queries for the *current* list of root servers to each of these addresses in turn until it obtains an answer. Once it has obtained the current list, it knows where to send queries for names without dots. This may sound needlessly complicated but it ensures that a caching server will keep working when the addresses of root name servers change but its pre-configured list is not updated; these addresses change infrequently but they do change from time to time. A caching server will be able to use all current root servers as long as it can reach just one of the pre-configured addresses.

DOMAIN NAME

The dots divide domain names into different parts. This division in turn divides the set of all names into different domains where the same part of a name can be re-used, e.g. 'ripe.net' is entirely different from 'ripe.org'. More importantly those domains can be administered totally independently. The administrator of 'net' names does not need to know anything about the 'org' names. The 'org' domain is independent of the 'net' domain. Due to the hierarchical structure administrators of sub-domains within a domain can also act independently, e.g. "isoc.org" does not need to coordinate anything with "nanog.org" or even know about it.

One Last Example

So once more, here is what happens when a caching server that just started receives a query for the address of www.isoc.org. After it started, the server obtained a list of root servers and their addresses. When the query arrives it will not find the answer for 'www.isoc.org' in the cache, nor will it find the address of an authoritative server for 'isoc.org', neither the address of an authoritative server for 'org'. Having no other choice it will then ask a root server for the address of 'www.isoc.org'; the root server will answer with a referral containing the list of all authoritative servers for 'org'. Our caching server will send its query for 'www.isoc.org' to one of them and get another referral with the list of all authoritative servers for 'isoc.org'. When sending the query to one of them it will get the answer. All this typically happens in less than a second.

From here on the caching server can answer the same query again and again from the cache without asking another server. It can also send any query for 'something.isoc.org' directly to an 'isoc.org' server and send any question for another name ending in '.org' directly to a server authoritative for 'org'. Only when the next query ends in something different from '.org' does it have to ask a root server again. Quickly the cache will contain lists of authoritative servers for all popular domains, especially for all popular TLDs; usually our caching server will not have to query for this information again for several days. This design ensures that only a tiny fraction of all queries will have to be processed by the root servers or by authoritative servers for TLDs.

MANAGING CHANGE

What about the case when information at authoritative servers is updated but caching servers all over the world have still cached the old possibly incorrect information?

This is where the DNS 'Time To Live' (TTL) comes into play. Each part of DNS information that may be cached separately has a time to live associated with it. Once this time expires, the cached information must be discarded and has to be obtained from an authoritative server again if it is needed. The TTL is not configured locally in the caching server but is set in the authoritative server and passed along with the information itself. This way the administrator of a domain can control how long it takes for any change to be known throughout the Internet. By carefully choosing values, one can set the trade off between being able to change things rapidly on the one hand and minimizing computing and networking resources needed by name servers on the other hand. If particular information is not expected to change in the near future one can have a high TTL and information known to change soon can be transmitted with a low TTL. It is standard practice to reduce the TTL transmitted with information that is scheduled to change in order to make that change visible rapidly throughout the Internet; once the change has happened the TTL is increased again.

This ends our tour of the DNS for non-experts. We hope that you have enjoyed it and gained a basic understanding of one of the underpinnings of today's Internet. Maybe you are now interested in some more explanations for informed non-experts about related subjects. We are currently preparing a similar briefing on how the DNS root name server system is currently evolving.

EVOLUTION OF THE INTERNET GOVERNANCE DEBATE

background paper

BEYOND ICANN VS. ITU: WILL WSIS OPEN NEW TERRITORY FOR INTERNET GOVERNANCE?

Wolfgang Kleinwächter, University of Aarhus

Internet governance became one of the most controversial issues in the WSIS process. While the subject was a marginal one at the start of WSIS (PrepCom1, Geneva, June 2002), it moved step by step from the periphery of the debate into its centre. After the series of five regional ministerial conferences (from Bamako, May 2002, to Beirut, February 2003) Internet governance appeared suddenly as one of the "hot items" at PrepCom2 (Geneva, February 2003). But neither PrepCom3 (Geneva, September 2003) nor PrepCom3bis (Geneva, November 2003) could reach an agreement. PrepCom3bis+ (Geneva, December 2003) finally "agreed to disagree", to postpone the debate and to ask the United Nations Secretary-General, Kofi Annan, "to set up a Working Group on Internet governance" with the mandate, "to investigate and make proposals for action, as appropriate, on the governance of the Internet by 2005".[1] The second Phase of the Summit is scheduled for Tunis, November 2005.

What is Internet Governance?

The term "Internet governance", while undefined, rather vague and partly confusing, stands mainly for the global technical management of the core resources of the Internet: Domain Names, IP addresses, Internet Protocols and the Root Server System. The question, which

---

[1] See: WSIS Declaration of Principles; Building the Information Society: A Global Challenge in the New Millennium; December 12, 2003, in: http://www.itu.int/wsis/index.html

arose in the WSIS process, was how these core resources, which constitute the basic material infrastructure of the global information society, should be managed.

Some governments, mainly the United States and the European Union, supported by the private industry, argued that the private Internet Corporation for Assigned Names and Numbers (ICANN), with its narrowly defined technical mandate, should continue to be the central organization in this field. Other governments, led by China and members of the "G20 group" like Brazil, South Africa and India, based their arguments on a broader definition. Their understanding of "Internet governance" included not only domain names and root servers but also other Internet related issues like spam and illegal content. They wanted to move the whole Internet management system under the umbrella of an intergovernmental organization of the United Nations, notably the International Telecommunication Union (ITU), which hosted the first phase of the summit. Civil society, while critical of ICANN, did not support an "intergovernmental solution" but argued in favour of a "decentralized mechanism" with different organizations having different core responsibilities.

The conflict between ITU supporters and ICANN supporters pulled the subject into the spotlight of global policy. The Washington Post asked the question whether WSIS would "hand over the control of the Internet to the United Nations". Next to the battle around the "Digital Solidarity Fund", the "ICANN vs. ITU" controversy became the main conflict of the final stage of the WSIS I process.

In the beginning it seemed that the controversial discussion was a debate on two not directly related levels: technicians discussed technical issues, politicians political issues. ICANN supporters argued that Internet governance is a technical question and can be better handled by a private corporation. The ITU supporters argued that Internet governance is a political problem and falls under the national sovereignty of the governments of United Nations Member States. But a "compromise" to separate technical and political issues and to give both organizations a number of responsibilities could not be reached because the question is not so simple.

The problem is that technical and political aspects of Internet governance are interwoven in such a way that they cannot be separated by cutting the issue into two pieces. The technical control of the root server system is linked to the stability and security of the Internet, which is a precondition for the functioning of the global economy. The introduction of new Top Level Domains, while basically a technical question of putting a zone file into the root, is like the creation of "new territory in Cyberspace" and has unavoidable economic and political implications. The marriage between mobile telephony and Internet communication (ENUM) and the emergence of Internet telephony (VoIP) leads to the convergence of the "Internet

Numbering System" and the "Telephone Numbering System" which creates conflicts between two different allocation procedures: top down under the sovereignty of national governments for telephone numbers vs. bottom up by global private networks for IP numbers. Issues that have been discussed and decided within ICANN, like Dispute Resolution for Domain Names or the election/selection of representatives for individual Internet users, have a political component.[2]

In Internet governance, there is no "policy (regulation) here and technology (freedom) there". Cyberspace, as Lawrence Lessig has argued, presents something new for those who think about regulation and freedom. "It demands a new understanding of how regulation works and what regulates life there. It compels us to look beyond the traditional lawyer's scope – beyond laws, regulations and norms. Lessig adds: "In real space we recognize *how laws regulate* – through constitutions, statutes and other legal codes. In cyberspace we must understand *how code regulates* – how the software and hardware, that make cyberspace what it is, regulate cyberspace as it is."[3] In Cyberspace "Code is Law", says Lessig. In other words, in cyberspace the "law makers" are the technical developers, the providers and users of Internet services themselves.

The WSIS Internet governance controversy is so far much more than a classical interest conflict among two or more governments. It is a fundamental conceptual and philosophical conflict among different stakeholders about the questions of how the global Internet should be organized, and how the global information society, which is based on the Internet as its main infrastructure, should be governed.[4]

Looking Back to IANA and the IAHC (1988 – 1998)
The controversy can only be understood by going back to history.[5] Since the 1970s the coordination and, where necessary, the management of the Internet's core resources have been developed bottom up, mainly by the technical developers, providers and users of Internet services themselves, without governmental involvement. In contrast to telecommunication and

---

[2] See Wolfgang Kleinwächter, ICANN between technical mandate and political challenges, in: *Telecommunication Policy*, No. 24, London 2000, p. 553 – 563.

[3] Lawrence Lessig, *Code and other Laws of Cyberspace*, Basic Books 1999, p. 6.

[4] See Wolfgang Kleinwächter, Global Governance in the Information Age, in: *Development*, Vol. 46, N. 1, London 2001, p. 17 ff.

[5] See Wolfgang Kleinwächter; ICANN as the "United Nations" of the Global Information Society? The Long Road towards Self-Regulation of the Internet, in: *Gazette*, Vol. 62. No. 6, p. 451 ff, November 2000; and Milton Mueller, *Ruling the Root: Internet Governance and the Taming of Cyberspace*, New York 2002.

broadcasting, where top-down government regulation channeled and framed the design of the media according to national political and economic interests, there was no similar legislative approach with regard to the Internet. The necessary standards were developed and adopted by non-governmental organizations like the Internet Engineering Task Force (IETF) on the basis of the principle "running code and rough consensus", and it worked to the benefit of all. The tremendous growth of the Internet is a proof that national or international legislation was not really missed.

The Domain Name System (DNS) also developed bottom up. It was coordinated by its father, Jon Postel, with one assistant in his California office in Marina del Rey until the early 1990s. He managed the zone files of a database and was not interested in being pulled into policy. His system for Top Level Domains (TLDs) was simple and practical: one basket for generic names (gTLDs) and one basket for country names (ccTLDs). For the gTLDs, he suggested three for the US – ".edu" for academic institutions, ".gov" for governmental bodies, ".mil" for the military – and three for "the world" – ".com" for businesses, ".org" for organizations and ".net" for all other networks. For the ccTLDs, he made it explicitly clear in RFC 1951 that his delegation of ccTLDs was not a decision and what a country is or not. He linked zone files to units listed on the ISO 3166 list of the International Standardization Organisation (ISO), the most comprehensive list with 243 countries and territories Postel could find at this time.[6] Technically, Postel could have delegated thousands of TLDs. But Postel wanted to keep the system easy and understandable for users.

Until the end of the 1990s, the majority of the governments of the world more or less ignored the Internet, including the management of their country code Top Level Domain. The global Internet system grew in the shadow of intergovernmental policy. When governments discussed the controversial subject of the "New World Information and Communication Order" (NWICO) within UNESCO, nobody mentioned the Internet. When the European Commission published its "White Book" on employment and economic development in 1993, the word "Internet" did not appear in the 250 pages of the report. Event the ITU Kyoto Plenipotentiary Conference in 1994 did not discuss an intergovernmental strategy for Internet policy.

---

[6] RFC 1951 "Domain name System Structure and Delegation" says with regard to Country Codes in Paragraph 4.2: "The IANA is not in the business of deciding what is and what is not a country. The selection of the ISO 3166 list as a basis for country code top-level domain names was made with the knowledge that ISO has a procedure for determining which entities should be and should not be on that list." (March 1994.) The ISO list includes 243 units, mainly countries, but also "territories" like the Isle of Man (.im), Guernsey (.gg) and the British Indian Ocean Territory (.io). The so-called "Reserve List 2" of ISO 3166 includes also the "European Union" (.eu).

Only the United States government, which financed Internet research first via the Department of Defense (DoD) and later via the National Science Foundation (NSF), developed something like a "soft Internet policy". The Reagan Administration (1980-1988) created with its "deregulation" philosophy a flexible and open legal environment for Internet developers. Only when the registration of Internet Domain Names grew to more than 100,000 in the late 1980s, the Bush Senior Administration proposed to institutionalize the management of the Domain Name System. In a contract signed in 1989 between the US Department of Commerce (DoC) and Postel's Information Science Institute (ISI) at the University of Southern California (USC), the Internet Assigned Numbers Authority (IANA) was established. IANA – a one-man organization – became the recognized coordinator of Internet resources. IANA managed the TLD databases and allocated IP address blocks to the Regional Internet Registries (RIRs).

In the early 1990s, when the number of Domain Name Holders crossed the one million mark, and the Internet, stimulated by Tim Berners-Lee's invention of the World Wide Web, became a commercial platform, the political and economic dimensions of the technical coordination of the Internet resources became more and more visible. In 1995, Postel, realizing the need for a more stable and comprehensive DNS management system, wanted to move the IANA function under the umbrella of the Internet Society (ISOC), a policy oriented network of Internet technicians established in 1992. However, his effort faced opposition both from the US government and parts of the private industry, which argued that "technicians" do not understand the political and commercial dimension of the ".com revolution".

In particular, Network Solutions Inc. (NSI), which operated, on the basis of a contract with the DoC, the A Root Server and managed the Registry and Registrar functions for the gTLDs .com, .org, .net and .edu., feared that Postel's ISOC plan to introduce 150 new gTLDs could undermine its fast growing multimillion dollar business in the registration of domain names. In 1995, the NSF stopped its financial support for the Internet and the DoC allowed NSI, one of the beneficiaries of the NSF support, to introduce an annual registration fee of 35.00 USD for Domain Names. In 1996 NSI already had more than 10 million registered names in its database.

A growing interest in something like an "Internet governance policy" was also developing in the trademark community. Numerous conflicts between holders of registered domain names and owners of registered trademark names made visible the need for a consistent dispute resolution mechanism that would protect trademarked brand names in cyberspace.

The European Commission discovered "Internet governance" as an issue in the context of its new Information Society Programme, started under Commissioner Bangemann at the EU Summit in Corfu in June 1994. The EU also opposed Postel's proposed ISOC solution. It wanted to see a greater role for both European governments and European businesses in the fast growing new sector of the Internet economy.

Postel, who wanted to avoid both governmental and commercial control of the DNS, tried to find a "third way". In the summer of 1996, he initiated the so-called "Interim Ad Hoc Committee" (IAHC). The IAHC was a network which linked together three "technical" organizations – IANA, ISOC and the "Internet Architecture Board" (IAB) – two United Nations intergovernmental organizations – the Geneva based International Telecommunication Union (ITU) and World Intellectual Property Organisation (WIPO) – and a business group – the International Trademark Association (INTA). The plan was to establish a "Policy Oversight Committee" (POC) composed by the six groups as the highest decision making body for the management of domain names; to introduce seven new gTLDs; to license 28 Registrars; and to move the A Root Server from Herndon, Virginia to Geneva, Switzerland. For Postel it was important that both governmental and business institutions were involved, but the voting majority in the POC was in the hands of the three technical organizations – IANA, ISOC and IAB.

The "Memorandum of Understanding on generic Top Level Domains" (IAHC gTLD MoU) was signed on May 2, 1997 and celebrated in particular by the ITU, which became its depositary. ITU Secretary-General Pekka Tarjanne qualified the MoU as the beginning of a new global Internet policy and a turning point in international law. The MoU was not an intergovernmental treaty. It was a legally non-binding recommendation signed by about 80 governmental and business institutions. The majority of ITU members did not participate in the IAHC negotiations.

This MoU faced substantial opposition. The United States government was not amused by the plan to move the A Root Server to Lac Leman. US Secretary of State, Madeleine Albright, wrote a critical letter to Pekka Tarjanne, arguing that the ITU Secretary-General had gone beyond his mandate when he had signed the IAHC gTLD MoU without any further consultation among the ITU Member States. NSI, which saw its monopoly in the Registrar and Registry business of gTLD Name Registration challenged, opposed the MoU fundamentally, and lobbied the US Congress to turn down the gTLD MoU. Furthermore, the registries of the ccTLDs, which were not included into the gTLD MoU, criticized their exclusion.

The Making of ICANN

Two months later, on July 1, 1997, the US government introduced an alternative plan. The report "A Framework for Global Electronic Commerce", published by the White House and signed by US President Bill Clinton and US Vice-President Al Gore, suggested a privatization of the DNS. The US report, which did not mention the IAHC gTLD MoU and the ITU with a single word, became the starting point for a process which led directly to the foundation of ICANN in November 1998.

A first conceptual "Green Paper" was published by the Department of Commerce (DoC) in early 1998. The proposal was to create a "new private, non-commercial corporation" (NewCo), to introduce competition into the domain name registration business, and to develop a mechanism for the solution of disputes over domain names. At the same time, the DoC announced that it would terminate its contracts with NSI and IANA by September 30, 1998.

The "Green Paper" provoked another wave of criticism, this time mainly from the European Commission. The EU criticized US domination and called for an "international representative body" for future Internet governance. "The European Union and its Member States would wish to emphasize our concern that the future management of the Internet should reflect the fact that it is already a global communication medium and the subject of valid international interests."[7]

Ira Magaziner, US President Clinton's Internet adviser and the main architect of what later became ICANN, replied to the European criticism in a Hearing before the US Congress that "the purpose of the Commerce Department proposal is to improve the technical management of the DNS only. The Green Paper does not propose a monolithic Internet governance system. Frankly we doubt that the Internet should be governed by a single body or plan."[8] Magaziner recognized that "the Internet has become an international medium for commerce, education and communication" and "has outgrown the legacy system of technical management". He accepted the idea of an "international representative body" and proposed, that the composition of a Board of Directors of a "NewCo"should be balanced and represent the functional and geographic diversity of the Internet.

A more moderate and balanced "White Paper", published by the DoC in June 1998, defined four guiding principles for a "NewCo":

---

[7] Reply by the EU and its member states to the US Green Paper on Internet Governance, Brussels, March 20, 1998. The EU called "to reach a balance of interests and responsibilities, so that the international character of the Internet is recognized with respect to the relevant jurisdictions around the world".

[8] Ira Magaziner, Written Statement to a Hearing on Domain Name Issues before the Sub-Committee on Basic Research of the Committee of Science of the House of Representatives, Washington, March 31, 1998.

1. stability of the Internet;
2. competition in the Domain Name market;
3. private bottom-up policy coordination; and
4. global representation.

DoC spokesperson Becky Burr added: "We are looking for a globally and functionally representative organization, operating on the basis of sound and transparent processes that protect against capture by self-interested factions and that provides robust, professional management. The new entity's process needs to be fair, open and pro-competitive. And the new entity needs to have a mechanism for evolving to reflect the changes in the constituency of Internet stakeholders."[9]

Within a couple of weeks the bylaws of the "NewCo" were drafted. Its design came mainly from Ira Magaziner, and the final text mainly from Jon Postel.[10] While the drafting process was rather open and transparent – all drafts were published on the Internet and included an open discussion period for public comment – the making of ICANN was seen as a "great conspiracy" by groups that were not involved in the final drafting, or which had no idea about the existence of such "virtual negotiations".

Postel, who died some weeks later, defended his approach when he presented the final result to the US Congress: "We listened to everyone who wanted to offer comments or suggestions, and we then tried to turn those suggestions into actual documents. Group discussion is very valuable, group drafting less productive." And he added: "This new organization will be unique in the world – a non-governmental organization with significant responsibilities for administering what is becoming an important global resource."[11]

ICANN was incorporated as a "private not-for-profit-organization" representing the "global Internet community" under California law. ICANN's design was based on the idea, that the providers and users of Internet services themselves should have the decision-making capacity, while governments should have only an advisory role. Consequently, the Board of Directors (BOD) was composed of 19 members chosen from three so-called Supporting Organizations for Domain Names, Internet Addresses and IP Protocols, representing the providers and

---

[9] Remarks by Becky Burr, DOC Press Conference, Washington, June 5, 1998.

[10] Other key players in the final negotiations has been, inter alia, Christopher Wilkinson from the European Commission, Marilyn Cade from AT&T, Roger Cocchetti from IBM and Don Telage from NSI.

[11] Jon Postel, Testimony before the Sub Committee on Basic Research of the Committee on Science of the House of Representatives, Washington, October 7, 1998.

developers of Internet services (the private sector), and nine members who would represent the public at large, that is individual Internet users. Government representatives were not eligible to be ICANN Directors. A "Government Advisory Committee" (GAC) for the 180+ governments of the world was invited to give "advice" to the BOD on issues of public interest. However, according to the ICANN bylaws, the recommendations of the GAC had no binding power for the ICANN Directors.[12]

The creation of ICANN made the IAHC gTLD MoU obsolete. When ITU had its Plenipotentiary Conference in Minneapolis in October/November 1998, the gTLD MoU was treated as a "non-existing paper". Even ITU Resolution 102, which referred to "Management of Domain Names and Internet Addresses", did not refer to the gTLD MoU with a single word. Instead, it invited the Secretary-General of the ITU, "to take active part in the international discussion and initiatives of the management of domain names and Internet addresses, *which is being led by the private sector*"[13].

"The Minneapolis Consensus" was reached by a classical "diplomatic deal": The US government withdrew its opposition to the plans of the ITU to prepare a world conference on the information society, and got in exchange a recognition of private sector leadership in Internet governance. Eights days later, the Interim ICANN Board of Directors (BOD) had its first meeting in Cambridge, Massachusetts, and on November 25, 1998, the DoC recognized ICANN as the "NewCo".[14] The "Memorandum of Understanding" between the DoC and ICANN was for a transition period only. After two years and on condition that ICANN would fulfill its functions, the DoC wanted to transfer its remaining responsibilities, including the control over the A Root Server and the IANA function, to ICANN.

During the World Economic Forum in Davos in January 1999, ITU Secretary-General Pekka Tarjanne blamed President Clinton's Internet Adviser, Ira Magaziner, for hypocrisy. The US government argued for self-governance of the Internet by the providers and users of services without governmental involvement, but reserved a special role for itself by making the DoC the final oversight body for ICANN. Magaziner defended his position by referring to the "two year transition period" and the foreseeable end of the special role of the DoC.

---

[12] See Wolfgang Kleinwächter, The silent Subversive: ICANN and the new Global Governance, in: Info - The Journal of Policy, Regulation and Strategy for Telecommunication, Vol. 3, No. 4, August 2001, p. 259 – 278.

[13] Resolution 102 on Management of Internet Domain Names and Addresses, ITU Plenipotentiary Conference, Minneapolis, November 6, 1998.

[14] Before the DoC decided to recognize ICANN as the NewCo, The EU Commissioner for Telecommunication Policy, Martin Bangemann, signalled in an official letter to William Daley, US Secretary of Commerce, that the European Union agrees with the bylaws of proposed new corporation.

The idealism of the founding fathers of ICANN did not work as originally intended. Although the Board was composed by representatives from all regions of the world with US directors in a minority, as a result of the economic realities in the Internet economy and the domain name market, ICANN became very US-oriented, with VeriSign (formerly NSI) as a main player. The idea that nine "At Large Directors", representing Internet users, should balance the interests of the private Internet industry was never implemented. And the US government continued to be an oversight body for ICANN. Clinton left the Oval Office without finishing his Internet governance business, and the "Bush Junior" Administration renewed the ICANN-DoC MoU and extended it until September 30, 2006.

After the bursting of the .com bubble and the terrorist attacks of September 11, 2001, the broader political and economic environment for Internet governance changed dramatically. To guarantee security and stability of the Internet became the first priority. ICANN turned from a project on "Cyberdemocracy" into an instrument for "Cybersecurity". ICANN started a reform process and re-designed its management structure. While the representation of Internet users was fundamentally reduced, the role of governments was strengthened. The original principles remained the same, but ICANN 2.0 became a little bit less a self-regulatory body and a little bit more a "public-private partnership" organization.[15]

WSIS and Internet Governance

The irony of history was that the "Minneapolis Deal" from October 1998 – to give ITU a world summit and to leave Internet governance in the hands of the private sector – backfired, when preparations for the first WSIS phase started with PrepCom1 in June 2002. At this time, ICANN was in the middle of its reform process and the ITU was preparing its next Plenipotentiary Conference for Marrakech, which had, *inter alia*, a re-evaluation of Resolution 102 on its agenda. Internet governance was not an issue at PrepCom1, but during the series of regional Ministerial WSIS Conferences, it got more and more attention.

The African Regional WSIS Conference in Bamako (May 2002) ignored the subject. None of the 14 content-related preparatory workshops for Bamako dealt with Internet governance. The nine pages of the Bamako Declaration do not include any word or paragraph on Internet governance.[16]

The European WSIS Regional Ministerial Meeting in Bucharest (November 2002) raised one aspect of the issue, the management of domain names, but with low priority. Principle 5 of the

---

[15] See Michael Froomkin, (ed.) ICANN Governance; Loyola Law Review of Los Angeles, Vol. 36, No. 3, Spring 2003.

[16] Bamako Declaration, May 30, 2002, in http://www.itu.int/wsis/preparatory/regional/bamako.html

Bucharest Declaration includes under the heading "Setting up an enabling environment, including legal, regulatory and policy frameworks", one sentence which says that "the information society is, by nature, a global phenomenon and issues such as privacy protection, consumer trust, *management of domain names*, facilitation of e-commerce, protection of intellectual property rights, open source solutions etc., should be addressed with the active participation of all stakeholders".[17]

The Asian WSIS Regional Ministerial Conference in Tokyo (January 2003) followed the Bucharest Declaration, but added to "domain names" the management of "IP addresses". The Tokyo Declaration said: "The transition to the Information Society requires the creation of appropriate and transparent legal, regulatory and policy frameworks at the global, regional and national levels. These frameworks should give due regard to the rights and obligations of all stakeholders in such areas as freedom of expression, privacy, security, *management of Internet addresses and domain names*, and consumer protection, while also maintaining economic incentives and ensuring trust and confidence for business activities."[18]

The Latin America WSIS Regional Ministerial Conference in Bavaro (January 2002) went one step further. Here, for the first time, the term "Internet governance" appears in a WSIS document. The relevant paragraph of the Bavaro Declaration says: "Establishing appropriate national legislative frameworks that safeguard the public and general interest and intellectual property and that foster electronic communications and transactions. Protection from civil and criminal offences ('cybercrime'), settlement and clearance issues, network security and assurance of the confidentiality of personal information are essential in order to build trust in information networks. Multilateral, transparent and democratic Internet governance should form part of this effort, taking into account the needs of the public and private sectors, as well as those of civil society."[19]

The final Regional WSIS Ministerial Conference for West Asia in Beirut (February 2003) took this one big step further by introducing ideas like "suitable international organization", "multilinguism" and "national sovereignty" with regard to Internet governance. Article 2, paragraph 4 of the Beirut Declaration stated that "the responsibility for root directories and domain names should rest with a suitable international organization and should take multilingualism into consideration. Countries' top-level-domain-names and Internet Protocol

---

[17] Bucharest Declaration, November 30, 2002, in:
   http://www.itu.int/wsis/preparatory/regional/bucharest.html

[18] Tokyo Declaration, January 15, 2003, in: http://www.itu.int/wsis/preparatory/regional/tokyo.html

[19] Bavaro Declaration, January 31, 2003, in: http://www.itu.int/wsis/preparatory/regional/bavaro.html

(IP) address assignment should be the sovereign right of countries. The sovereignty of each nation should be protected and respected. Internet governance should be multilateral, democratic and transparent and should take into account the needs of the public and private sectors as well as those of the civil society."[20]

It is worth noting that, in parallel to the WSIS Regional Conferences, the ITU had its own Plenipotentiary Conference in Marrakech (October 2002). During the Marrakech conference a bitter controversy about private sector leadership and the future role of ITU in Internet governance took place. In Marrakech, US and EU governments, supported by private ITU sector members, expressed their satisfaction with the ICANN reform process and argued in favour of a continuation of the leading role of ICANN in Internet governance. However, a growing number of third world countries had discovered the management of domain names and IP addresses as an issue related to their sovereignty and economic development. They felt underrepresented in ICANN and blamed the California-based private corporation for being US-dominated and deepening the "digital divide". They felt that they did not have adequate opportunities to participate in the bottom-up decision-making process in such a private corporation. And they criticized the control function of the US government for the A Root Server. Additionally, some governments came with the idea of regulating the Internet in general – in a way similar to telecommunication and broadcasting – to protect unspecified national economic or political interests in areas like content control, cybercrime or VoIP.

The controversy in Marrakech produced a renewed Resolution 102 where the relationship between private industry leadership and government involvement was re-balanced. The "key role" and the "leadership" the private sector got in the 1998 resolution was replaced by the recognition of a "very important role". On the other side, the sovereignty of national governments over the ccTLD space was strengthened. The resolution tried furthermore to separate technical from policy issues. It emphasized that "the management of Internet domain names and addresses includes technical and coordination tasks, for which technical *private bodies can be responsible*, and public interest matters (for example, stability, security, freedom of use, protection of individual rights, sovereignty, competition rules and equal access for all), for which *governments or intergovernmental organizations are responsible* and to which qualified international organizations contribute".[21] The ITU Secretary-General got the instruction "to take a *significant* role in the international discussions and initiatives on the management of Internet domain names and addresses" and "to encourage all Member States to participate in

---

[20] Beirut Declaration, February 6, 2003, in: http://www.itu.int/wsis/preparatory/regional/beirut.html

[21] Resolution 102, ITU Plenipotentiary Conference, Marrakech, October, 2002, in: http://www.itu.int/osg/spu/resolutions/2002/resplen5.html

the discussions on international management of Internet domain names and addresses, so that worldwide representation in the debates can be ensured".[22]

Additionally, the Conference adopted another Resolution 133 on the "role of administrations of Member States in the management of internationalized (multilingual) domain names". The Resolution says, *inter alia*, that "it is estimated that in the coming years the majority of Internet users will prefer to conduct online activities in their own language" and that "the current domain name system mapping does not reflect the growing language needs of all users". It emphasizes that "the future management of the registration and allocation of Internet domain names and addresses must fully reflect the geographical and functional nature of the Internet, taking into account an equitable balance of interests of all stakeholders, in particular of administrations, businesses and consumers". And it recognizes "the existing role and sovereignty of ITU Member States with respect to allocation and management of their respective country code numbering resources". The ITU Secretary-General is instructed "to take any necessary action to ensure the sovereignty of ITU Member States with regard to country code numbering plans and addresses will be fully maintained, as enshrined in Recommendation E.164 of the ITU Telecommunication Standardization Sector, in whatever application they are used".[23]

It is interesting to see that substantial parts of the Marrakech Resolutions incorporated the language proposed by the Beirut Declaration. In PrepCom2, which took place one week after Beirut, Internet governance suddenly became a major WSIS topic. The recommendation of the Beirut conference was like throwing a stone into a negotiation room, where so far the digital divide, human rights, cybersecurity and the establishment of a digital solidarity fund dominated the debate. In one of the expert Round Tables, organized by the Civil Society Internet ICT Governance Caucus during PrepCom2, representatives from governments, private industry and civil society exchanged rather controversial positions about how Internet governance should be included into the WSIS agenda. Immediately after PreCom2, the ITU hosted an expert seminar on ccTLD issues, which was aimed at creating more awareness among national governments on the issue.

During the following WSIS InterSessional conference (Paris, July 2003) governments created an "Internet Governance Ad Hoc Working Group" which became the main negotiating body until December 2003. According to the "multi-stakeholder approach", which was introduced

---

[22] Ibid.

[23] Resolution 133, ITU Plenipotentiary Conference, Marrakech, October, 2002, in:
http://www.itu.int/osg/spu/resolutions/2002/resplen5.html

by United Nations Resolution 56/181 (December 12, 2001) for the WSIS preparatory process, private industry and civil society were to be directly involved in the discussions from the beginning. During the first meeting of the Ad Hoc Group, non-governmental observers participated in the meeting and offered welcome special expertise. But during PrepCom3 (September 2003), when observers with their laptops started blogging live from inside the group sessions – as is common in ICANN meetings – some governments pushed the observers out of the room again. They got only the right to make a brief statement in the beginning of a session and could ask for a briefing by the chair after the end of the session. Also during PrepCom3bis (November 2003) and PrepCom3bis+ (December 2003), observers, including ICANN President Paul Twomey, had to leave the room. Ironically, some government delegates, who did not agree with the exclusion, informed privately in detail the observers, who were sitting outside the conference room.

The Role of ICANN's Governmental Advisory Committee (GAC)

The relationship between ICANN and ITU can be described as something like a "cold war". This had consequences for ICANN's Governmental Advisory Committee (GAC), the body for channelling governmental input into ICANN's policy development processes. ITU is a full GAC member and its Telecommunication Standardisation Sector (ITU-T) was also a member of ICANN's "Protocol Supporting Organisation" (PSO) under ICANN 1.0.

During the ccTLD Workshop, organized by ITU in March 2003, some governments from third world countries called for a special "Intergovernmental Internet Governance Organisation". Others proposed to bring the management of the DNS and IP Addresses under the umbrella of a Study Group of the ITU-T. In the workshop ITU offered its services to take over more responsibility in Internet governance, by presenting itself as "unique in being a partnership between governments and industry for information and communication technology. It is widely acknowledged that the ITU-T performs its tasks to the general satisfaction of industry, governments and the public at large using processes that are open, transparent and ensure accountability to all stakeholders."[24]

The ITU proposals were countered by the GAC Chair, Mohamed Sharil Tarmizi, who argued that with the GAC, governments already have a channel to participate in Internet governance policy development. In the ITU, governments would be mainly represented by the ministries for telecommunication, while the GAC members also represent ministries for economics and labour, for technology and development, and even foreign affairs. Sharil argued that within

---

[24] Review of Cooperation between ITU-T and ICANN and ccTLD issues, ITU-ccTLD Doc 30, Geneva, March 3, 2003, in: http://www.itu.int/itudoc/itu-t/workshop/cctld/cctld030.pdf

ITU Study Groups public policy issues would be seen through the narrow eyes of telcos. GAC, however, would take a broader view. He called for a better coordination within national governments, for the development of coherent national strategies, and for a broader engagement of third world governments in the GAC.

The GAC is open to all United Nations Member States, intergovernmental organizations and other invited units. But the GAC has a number of deficiencies. By February 2004, only 86 governments had been accredited as GAC members and in GAC meetings the average number of participants is substantially lower, very often not higher than about 40. According to its operating principles, the GAC is an advisory body which does not take decisions. An additional conflict point is that the government of China does not recognize the membership of Taiwan in the GAC.

But while the GAC is indeed *de jure* only an advisory body, after the ICANN reform the GAC is *de facto* an intergovernmental organization. It develops policies and agrees on positions. And the GAC has now something like a "veto right" against the ICANN Board of Directors. In cases where the ICANN Board rejects a GAC recommendation, the GAC can under ICANN 2.0 ask for a "consultation". If this consultation fails, ICANN is obliged to explain to the global Internet community why no consensus could be reached, and governments reserve their right to act on their behalf in the area of the controversial issue.[25]

Sharil's observation that national governments often speak with different voices via different ministries was proven by the practical political process. While governments supported ICANN reform in GAC meetings, the same governments opposed ICANN in WSIS.

The ICANN/GAC meetings in Bucharest (June 2002), one week before PrepCom1, were an important milestone. At this ICANN meeting, the governments evaluated in detail the ICANN reform plans and gave clear advice on a broad range of issues, including core values, the mission of ICANN, etc.

The GAC shared the view that "a private-sector/public-sector partnership will be essential to ICANN's future success". This view underlies a number of statements issued by the GAC and in particular the "Principles for Delegation and Administration of Country Code Top Level Domains"[26] of February 23, 2000. The majority of GAC members agree that "the GAC is the principal forum for the international discussion of public policy issues related to the ICANN

---

[25] See ICANN bylaws (latest Version of June 23, 2003), Article XI, Section 1,
http://www.icann.org/general/archive-bylaws/bylaws-26jun03.htm

[26] http://www.icann.org/committees/gac/gac-cctldprinciples-23feb00.htm

mission and the Domain Name System".[27] But for the first time in GAC's history that GAC Communiqué was not adopted by consensus. In a special statement the ITU disassociated itself "from portions of this document". Also two other GAC members, France and Germany, disassociated themselves from parts of the GAC Communiqué. The two governments stated that "due to the evolutionary nature of ICANN's mission, a different organization of government participation, on a different legal basis, may be contemplated in the future". [28]

Two weeks after the ITU Plenipotentiary Conference in Marrakech, ICANN and GAC had their next regular meetings in Shanghai. Although the renewed ITU Resolution 102 encourages the 185 ITU member states to participate more actively in discussions of Internet governance, fewer than 50 governments came to China. Even the Chinese government, hosting the ICANN meeting, showed only a small profile in the conference. The GAC Communiqué included no reference to the ITU Resolutions 102 and 133. The governments, present in the GAC meeting, gave a green light to the proposed new ICANN bylaws and its continuing leading role. ITU representative Richard Hill, in a special meeting of the ccTLD constituency, explained at length the spirit of the ITU resolution 102, and entered into a controversial discussion with Marylin Cade, a member of the GNSO Council also representing ITU Sector member AT&T. But no ICANN body took official note of Resolution 102.

After an extraordinary ICANN meeting adopted the new ICANN bylaws and created ICANN 2.0 (Amsterdam, December 2002), ICANN/GAC had their next regular meetings in Rio de Janeiro two weeks after the end of PrepCom2. A controversial issue of the Rio Meeting was the planned "Country Code Domain Name Supporting Organisation" (CNSO). A number of mainly European ccTLD managers made clear that they would not accept any top-down decision by the ICANN Board with regard to the management of their ccTLDs. They wanted to keep their full sovereignty and argued that even if they operate as private corporations, they have to respect the national legal environments of their countries. The GAC Rio Communiqué, again, had no reference to ITU Resolutions 102 and 133. With regard to the CNSO, that GAC recalled that "its role in providing advice on public policy, as described in the ICANN bylaws, includes policy issues to be addressed by the proposed ccNSO. To this effect, GAC has already issued policy advice in the form of the Principles for the Delegation and Administration of ccTLDs."[29]

---

[27] GAC Statement on ICANN Evaluation & Reform, Bucharest, June 26, 2002, in: http://www.gac-icann.org/web/meetings/mtg13/gac13statement.htm

[28] Annex I, Ibid.

[29] GAC Communiqué, Rio de Janeiro, March 25, 2003, in:
http://www.gac-icann.org/web/meetings/mtg15/CommuniqueRioDeJaneiro.htm

In the ICANN/GAC meetings in Montreal (June 2003), two weeks before the WSIS InterSessional in Paris, ITU did not participate. After the GAC adopted its regular communiqué, the ITU distanced itself openly from the final text. "The ITU has not participated in this ICANN GAC meeting and therefore dissociates itself from this Communiqué." ITU also had strong reservations with regard to GAC recommendations on IDNs, where the ITU dissociated itself "from this statement because it is not yet clear whether ICANN's decisions, taken as a whole, will facilitate or hinder deployment of IDN". With regard to the ccTLDs, the ITU dissociated itself "from the support for the proposed bylaws regarding ccNSO because the proposed bylaws may be inconsistent with fundamental principles such as national sovereignty, freedom of commercial actors, non-binding recommendations, and consensus decision-making".[30]

The following ICANN/GAC meetings in Carthage, Tunisia (October 2003), between PrepCom3 and PrepCom3bis, again saw no ITU participation. On the other hand, the Public Meeting of the ICANN Board did not have WSIS on its official agenda. Only a separate round table, organized by ICANN's "At Large Advisory Committee" (ALAC), discussed aspects of the relationship between ICANN and WSIS with regard to Internet governance. The GAC Carthage Communiqué avoided any reference to WSIS. With regard to one of the most controversial Internet governance issues in WSIS, the root servers, the GAC took note of "the efforts to date in deployment of Anycast to mirror the root servers and recognises the efforts undertaken by the root server operators to increase the security and stability of the root servers system for the benefit of the whole Internet Community. GAC encourages the root server operators to make more information available in order to increase awareness and understanding of these issues."[31]

In this context it is interesting to note, that two days after the start of PrepCom2 in Geneva the US Government renewed in Washington its MoU with ICANN for another three years until September 30, 2006.[32] WSIS II, which will get a report with recommendations for decisions on Internet governance from a new WSIS Working Group, is scheduled for November 2005.

---

[30] ITU Dissociaction from the GAC Montreal Communiqué, June 30, 2003, in: http://www.gac-icann.org/web/meetings/mtg16/Index.shtml

[31] GAC Communiqué, Carthage, October 28, 2003, in: http://www.gac-icann.org/web/meetings/mtg17/index.shtml

[32] Amendment 6 to the ICANN/DOC Memorandum of Understanding, September 17, 2003, in: http://www.icann.org/general/amend6-jpamou-17sep03.htm

The Governmental Compromise: Agree to Disagree and Postpone

The WSIS controversy over Internet governance is not settled. The issue remained unsolved until the last hour of PrepCom3bis+. The final compromise was to agree to disagree and to postpone the discussion until WSIS II. United Nations Secretary-General Kofi Annan is asked to establish a working group which will have the task of elaborating recommendations for the Tunis Summit in November 2005.

However, both the WSIS Declaration of Principles and the WSIS Plan of Action define a number of principles which constitute the framework for future actions. The WSIS Internet governance principles include both conceptual and procedural guidelines.

The conceptual guidelines can be summarized in four points. Articles 48, 49 and 50 of the WSIS declaration say that:

1. the "international management of the Internet should be multilateral, transparent and democratic, with the full involvement of governments, the private sector, civil society and international organizations";

2. Internet governance "should ensure an equitable distribution of resources, facilitate access for all and ensure a stable and secure functioning of the Internet, taking into account multilingualism";

3. the management of the Internet "encompasses both technical and public policy issues and should involve all stakeholders and relevant intergovernmental and international organizations"; and

4. "international Internet governance issues should be addressed in a coordinated manner".[33]

For two other controversial issues – ccTLDs and root servers – the WSIS Plan of Action gives more vague and general recommendations. Governments are invited to "manage or supervise, *as appropriate*, their respective country code top-level domain name (ccTLD)". And they should "*in cooperation with the relevant stakeholders*, promote regional root servers and the use of internationalized domain names in order to overcome barriers to access".

Furthermore, the WSIS declaration tries to distribute different responsibilities to different stakeholders, recognizing, that no stakeholder alone can "govern the Internet". Article 49 of the WSIS declaration states, that:

---

[33] WSIS Declaration of Principles, December 12, 2003, in: http://www.itu.int/dms_pub/itu-s/md/03/wsis/doc/S03-WSIS-DOC-0004!!PDF-E.pdf

a. "Policy authority for Internet-related public policy issues is the sovereign right of States. They have rights and responsibilities for international Internet-related public policy issues;

b. The private sector has had and should continue to have an important role in the development of the Internet, both in the technical and economic fields;

c. Civil society has also played an important role on Internet matters, especially at community level, and should continue to play such a role;

d. Intergovernmental organizations have had and should continue to have a facilitating role in the coordination of Internet-related public policy issues;

e. International organizations have also had and should continue to have an important role in the development of Internet-related technical standards and relevant policies."

Article 49 is a *de facto* recognition of the need for a "multi-stakeholder approach" for Internet governance. It reaffirms on the one hand the sovereignty of states, in particular for "public policy issues". And it recognizes on the other hand "the important role" of the private sector (in the technical and economic fields) and civil society (at the community level). The interesting point is that "intergovernmental organizations" like the ITU should have primarily a "facilitating role", while other (private) international organizations like ICANN, IETF, and W3C "should continue to have an important role", mainly in the field of "technical standards and relevant policies".

This description of the different roles of the stakeholders as (relatively) equal partners with different functions is not yet an answer to the questions of how the political implications of technical issues and, vice versa, the technical implications of political issues, should be handled, and who decides what. Article 49 says nothing on the distribution of functions, rights, duties, freedoms, responsibilities and power among the three main stakeholder groups and the two types of international organizations. To find out how an interactive and decentralized mechanism for cooperation, coordination and consultation among all the players can be developed will be the task of the "Kofi Annan Group".

The WSIS Plan of Action specifies the mandate, process and composition of the working group. According to Article 13, paragraph b of the Plan of Action the process should be "open and inclusive". Active participants in the working group should be "governments, the private sector and civil society from both developing and developed countries". Intergovernmental and international organizations should be "involved". And the mandate includes the formulation of "a working definition of Internet governance", the identification of "public policy issues that are relevant to Internet governance" and the development of "a common understanding of the respective roles and responsibilities" of the different stakeholders and organizations. The group has to "prepare a report on the results of this activity to be presented for consideration and appropriate action for the second phase of WSIS in Tunis in 2005".[34]

From the "Diplomacy of the Industrial Age" to a "Diplomacy of the Information Age"

It will remain to be seen how the WSIS Internet governance compromise will work. Will the new group be able to escape from the "ITU vs. ICANN" deadlock and create an innovative triangular governance mechanism which includes both the stability government organizations can offer and the flexibility private sector and civil society organizations can offer? Will we see the emergence of a new co-regulatory model for Internet governance which could become a blueprint for a governance mechanism for other key areas of the global information society from e-commerce to cybercrime, from privacy protection to content regulation, from IPR to trade in services?

One of the conclusions from the WSIS I process is that traditional diplomacy with mainly intergovernmental "horse trading behind closed doors" no longer functions as it did in the "Industrial Age". Internet related issues are more complex and need the inclusion of all concerned and affected groups, that is all the main stakeholders. Classical, exclusively governmental "top-down policy", often very general, and developed by hierarchies through closed and non-transparent processes, does not work anymore in borderless cyberspace. Policymaking has to be turned around and develop bottom-up as an inclusive, open and transparent process within and among networks. And it has to be very specific.

The challenge is to develop a "new diplomacy of the 21st century" which goes beyond the "diplomacy of the 20th century". "Industrial Age Diplomacy" was rather simple and mainly a bilateral deal among governmental representatives of nation states which allowed a more or less balanced "take and give" ("I give you some money for a fund and you give me some human rights"). "Information Age Diplomacy" has to be much more complex and multidimensional. There are more stakeholders than governments – private industry and civil society – and there are different interests not only among the stakeholders but also within the different stakeholder groups. And interests differ from issue to issue. There is no "black or white", no "good guys vs. bad guys" anymore. As a result of this growing complexity, we observe the emergence of numerous "rainbow coalitions". Private sector, civil society and some governments vs. some other governments with regard to DNS; third world governments and civil society vs. private industry and first world governments in IPR; liberal first world

---

[34] WSIS Plan of Action, December 12, 2003, in:
    http://www.itu.int/dms_pub/itu-s/md/03/wsis/doc/S03-WSIS-DOC-0005!!PDF-E.pdf

governments, civil society and some private industry vs. more restrictive governments and other parts of the private industry in Internet related privacy issues.

We live in a period of transformation where the "old governance system", rooted in the concept of the sovereign nation state, is complemented by an emerging "new governance system", which is global by nature and includes more actors than the 180+ national governments and their intergovernmental international organizations.

In a certain sense, WSIS is testing out how a new "multi-stakeholder approach", driven mainly by market needs and user interests, could work. Somebody – governments, private industry, civil society – has to be in charge. Bilateral relationships in such a triangular environment offer new opportunities for shared responsibilities among groups that have both common and divergent interests. Neither stronger government regulation nor industry or civil society self-regulation alone will deliver the solutions. Flexible co-regulatory systems, designed according to special needs on a case by case basis, combined with open, inclusive and transparent bottom-up policy development processes can produce workable frameworks for all parties – governments, industry and civil society – which combine in an efficient way stability and flexibility.

Four hundred years ago, after the beginning of the industrial revolution, the first "new industrialists" realized that the governance system of the time, based on kingdoms with an absolutist monarch at the top, did not satisfy the new needs of the industrial age. The search for a "new governance system" in the 17th century led to a historical and grand political compromise: the introduction of a "constitutional monarchy". The constitutional monarchy was to a certain degree a "co-regulatory system". While the king and the feudal institutions (the old system) had still some concrete power inherited by birth, new institutions that gained power and legitimacy through elections were established, like national parliaments and bourgeois governments (the new system).

The first constitutions of the 17th century, in which rights and duties of citizens and governments were defined, did not yet create a "republic" and a "representative democracy", but they opened the door for the emergence of a new governance system, and they enabled philosophers like Montesquieu, Rousseau, Madison, Jefferson and others to develop a more detailed system of governance with concepts like the "division of the branches of power" and the "social contract". Later on, organized efforts and input by trade unions and democratic parties paved the way for the "social welfare state".

The present system of governance in the 21st century with nearly 200 nation-states has functioned more or less satisfactorily over the last 200 years. But with globalization, the system based on the sovereign nation-state shows some cracks when confronted with trans-national challenges. Like in the early days of the "industrial revolution", the challenge is to make the system more flexible for a changing economic environment by balancing the legitimate interests, rights and freedoms of all involved and affected stakeholders.

New actors which create new institutions for new challenges will move into the new territory, filling emerging gaps regardless of whether there is a governmental order or not. National governments will not disappear in the next century, but they will become one actor among others, obliged to join into cooperative networks and consensual arrangements with other global actors and to share power with them. Government will become in some of the new areas less an actor on its own, and more a moderator and facilitator for other stakeholders. This will lead unavoidably to broader diversification of power.

It would be naïve to expect, that this power shift will take place without a struggle. In this coming power struggle, which will also overshadow the "Road to Tunis", the new emerging global actors, both the private industry and the global civil society (still in its infancy), have not only to prove their legitimacy; they have also to learn that the rights and freedoms they are fighting for are linked to duties and responsibilities.

THE RESULTS OF THE WSIS NEGOTIATIONS ON INTERNET GOVERNANCE
Markus Kummer, Federal Department of Foreign Affairs, Switzerland

I have been asked to address the "range of issues arising out of the Geneva phase of the WSIS". I will try to do this from my personal perspective as a diplomat who happened to be put in the chair of the negotiating group dealing with the issue of Internet governance towards the end of the process leading up to the Geneva Summit. Let me add that I did not seek this role and that I had never dealt with the issue of Internet governance before – I just happened to be at the wrong place at the wrong time. When Switzerland was asked to take the lead towards the end of the WSIS negotiating process, my Head of Delegation was too busy to take on the task of dealing with this issue, so he asked me to stand in for him.

When preparing this paper I realized that instead of addressing "issues", I should talk about the "modalities of the process ahead". I will try and explain why. Having lived through the negotiations, I have a fairly good idea of where we are coming from. This experience may help in guessing where we are going, and it certainly does help in understanding the importance of the modalities of the process. However, it is only of limited use as regards the identification of public policy issues. Indeed, it is easier to set a negative agenda than a positive one. In the end, we had a fairly good idea of what the Summit did not want rather than what the Summit wanted to happen.

To the modalities first. A brief look back at the history of our negotiations may help understand their importance. The draft text we had as a basis on our last stretch of negotiations was very confused. The main sticking point was a paragraph on how to coordinate "Internet issues of an international nature related to public policies". There were five different proposals that were mutually exclusive. It seemed obvious by then that we would not be able to resolve these fundamental differences. Delegations were firmly entrenched in positions that were diametrically opposed, and it would have been overly optimistic to find a far-reaching solution. The only way out was to establish a process to deal with these issues and, in order to reach agreement, we had to concentrate on the modalities of the process we hoped to initiate.

Drawing on this experience, I can read out of the documents the following three process-related priorities:

- First, it was not possible to agree on any single organization that would be in charge of Internet governance. This is the reason the Summit asked the Secretary-General of the United Nations to set up a working group to deal with the issue. The institutional independence of the working group is therefore of paramount importance. It cannot be affiliated with any existing body other than the United Nations.

- Second, equally important is the open and inclusive character of the group. The description "open and inclusive" has two aspects; one of them concerns the stakeholders and the other one the governments.

  - The issue of stakeholder participation is closely linked to the institutional aspect. It was one of the reasons why an original proposal we put forward – to set up a working group as part of the WSIS process – was not accepted. It was felt by a significant number of key players that the WSIS process had not proved satisfactory with regard to the inclusion of the private sector and civil society. It was hoped that the formula finally agreed on would give sufficient flexibility to be more inclusive. The multi-stakeholder nature of the United Nations ICT Task Force was specifically mentioned as a possible model in this regard. Whatever the format, all stakeholders and all relevant intergovernmental and other international organizations will have to be given equal access to the work of the group.

  - Furthermore, throughout the WSIS process we had a strong emphasis on open-ended meetings. Any attempt to create, for efficiency's sake, a group with limited membership was doomed to failure. The Working Group on Internet Governance of course is different. It is not a negotiating group, but a group with the task of gathering facts and drafting a report with recommendations for possible solutions. It therefore seems obvious that its membership will have to be limited. There is, however, a need for a compromise between efficiency and legitimacy. The working group will need to be sufficiently representative with regard to its governmental as well as its stakeholder members. Maybe a two- or a three- tier system could provide the answer to this dilemma.

- Third, developing countries need to be given the possibility of making their voices heard. Their full and meaningful participation in this process will be essential. This of course involves travelling costs, but other things as well. There is also a need for efforts aimed at capacity-building among developing countries, to allow them to defend their interests effectively.

We need to make sure that the process leading to Tunis reflects these priorities. Of course, this is only the starting point. But we will have to get the modalities right before starting the substantive work of the working group.

What are the issues with which the working group is supposed to deal? In Geneva we were not really ready to discuss what we meant by "public policy issues". In particular we were unable to spell out whether we were thinking about a narrow, technical definition, or whether we were referring to a broad definition, including issues such as network security, intellectual property rights, consumer welfare and data protection. All these issues are listed in both the WSIS Declaration of Principles and the Plan of Action. They are considered by many as falling under the term "Internet governance". However, I feel somewhat reluctant to read an interpretation into the final documents. It will be up to the working group to decide on the scope of its mandate. After all, this will be its main task, namely to come up with a working definition of Internet governance and identify the public policy issues that are relevant to Internet governance.

Furthermore, it is to be expected that the working group will have to deal with concerns that were already expressed during the negotiations. In particular, the two schools of thought that manifested themselves late last year are bound to resurface. On the one hand, there was a school calling for multilateral cooperation under the United Nations framework, and on the other there were those who are happy with the status quo (their motto is: "if it ain't broke, don't fix it"). Let me briefly sum up the reasoning behind these two schools of thought:

- The first group argued that at the national level, governments played a role in Internet governance and that they had a platform for a dialogue with the various stakeholders. They pointed out that at the international level, however, there was no such forum for interaction. They stressed the need to establish a multilateral mechanism, preferably with the legitimacy of the United Nations system. This would not replace any existing mechanism (ICANN was mentioned specifically in the regard), nor infringe on the work of any existing organization, but would be supplementary and deal with policy issues. Furthermore, these delegations felt that Internet governance related to national sovereignty.

- The other group highlighted that the present system worked well and that – before trying to solve a problem – it would be necessary to know what the problems were that needed to be addressed. On the whole, these delegations insisted on the importance of full and active involvement of the private sector and all stakeholders.

The discussion showed that there definitely was a perceived problem, whether or not it was real. On the whole, the misgivings related to what I would call a narrow definition of Internet governance and in particular the ccTLDs.

The terms of reference in the WSIS Plan of Action start with the definition of Internet governance and then follow with the identification of public policy issues; presumably the report will follow that order. This makes sense. In order to get there, however, it might be more productive to reverse the order of these tasks and start from the bottom up, with a description of "who does what", before proceeding to the definition of the issues to be dealt with. As I mentioned, discussions during the WSIS process so far have focused on a narrow definition of Internet governance, but there might be some merit in starting with a definition as broad as possible and then narrowing it down, and focusing on some priority issues. This might have the advantage of avoiding an early polarization or an undue focus on any single organization.

There might also be some merit in addressing issues that are of concern to all parties, such as security, consumer protection or spam. I share the scepticism of those who doubt that it will ever be possible to conclude a binding and comprehensive "cybertreaty". However, a soft-law approach, as practiced within the OECD, might prove easier. It might also have the advantage of yielding an early harvest in Tunis. Based on the work already carried out in other relevant organizations, WSIS could develop non-binding guidelines on these issues.

In Geneva we initiated a reflection process on how best to coordinate Internet governance with a view to finding a solution in Tunis. We focused on the modalities of the process and gave a broad mandate to the working group that is to be set up by the Secretary-General of the United Nations. This was the essence of the agreement we were able to reach and, all in all, it was the best we could hope for. At the same time it is a very sensible result. It makes sense to gather the facts first and then to try to agree on definitions before making recommendations for possible actions to be taken. However, it is also worth remembering that we were reminded in Geneva that the Internet on the whole functions well and that we need to be careful should we introduce any changes in the way it is governed.

I have one very simple conclusion to draw from the WSIS process so far: it seems clear that the working group can only be successful if all stakeholders will recognize themselves in its final report.

A NEW MODEL FOR GLOBAL INTERNET GOVERNANCE[1]
Zoë Baird and Stefaan Verhulst, Markle Foundation

It came and went quietly, but the recently concluded World Summit on the Information Society (WSIS) in Geneva may represent something of a watershed moment in the history of the Internet. For all their differences, governments coalesced around the need to define and develop some form of global governance for the Internet. The Declaration of Principles, agreed upon on the final day of the meeting, refers to the need for 'management of the Internet'. In addition, it envisions a major role for governments in this management. 'Policy authority for Internet-related public policy issues is the sovereign right of States', the Declaration affirms. 'They have rights and responsibilities for international Internet-related public policy issues.'

It was not so long ago that the Internet was cherished precisely for its lack of rules and for the absence of anything that could be called 'governance'. As John Perry Barlow famously put it in his 1996 *Declaration of the Independence of Cyberspace:*

> Governments of the Industrial World, you weary giants of flesh and steel, I come from Cyberspace … You have no sovereignty where we gather … We have no elected government, nor are we likely to have one.

---

[1] First published in "The Partnership Principle: New Forms of Governance in the 21st Century", edited by the Alfred Herrhausen Society for International Dialogue, the socio-political think-tank of Deutsche Bank.

Yet the residents of cyberspace did not rise up in protest at the declaration of the WSIS.

Calls for a new system of rules are signs of growing complexities and the mainstream reach of the network. The fact is that the former system, which emphasized self-regulation and laissez-faire, is not adequate for the task. The growing commercialization of the Internet, the proliferation of spam, identity (ID) theft, viruses, the violation of intellectual property rights and the remaining imbalance of access and connectivity are challenging the tremendous potential of the network. The creativity and innovation of the Internet need to be protected from those who would take advantage of chaos and abuse. In short, we are facing a worldwide crisis of governance on the Internet.

There are many underlying reasons for this crisis, of course. But we believe that the main reasons comprise the international decentralized nature of the Internet and the resulting insufficiency of traditional systems of regulation. The Internet clearly needs some rules. But attempts to develop a new system of governance are unlikely to succeed if they look for answers only to the nation-state, which by definition is limited in its centralized authority and effectiveness to the borders of a single nation or the parties to treaties.

The purpose of this article is therefore to argue that we not only need Internet governance, but that we need a new paradigm of rule-making. The crisis of governance forces us to develop a new model of governance. Some essential components of this model are that: it must be international, capable of operating across borders; it must be multi-sectoral, including a wide variety of voices and participants; and finally, in this search for multi-sectoral governance, civil society must be accorded an equal voice alongside governments and industry.

Of course these three components are only preliminary and represent just the outlines of a new model. We are only now beginning to understand what it will take to govern the Internet – to balance innovation with rules, and to reach the necessary compromise between order and creative chaos. This process of generating new forms of Internet governance is, moreover, part of a more general search around the world for new, international models of governance to manage trade, immigration, security, development and other pressing global concerns. Existing forums of global governance – the World Trade Organization (WTO), for instance, or the World Intellectual Property Organization – have both something to teach emerging models of Internet governance and something to learn from them. The discussion here can therefore be seen as a contribution to a broader and still evolving conversation.

The need for a new model of governance
In order to understand Internet governance, it is helpful to briefly consider the history of the network. Created by the United States Department of Defense in the 1960s, the Internet was

initially a creature of government. Nonetheless, a large part of its early success can be attributed to the absence of anything that could be called governance. From its inception, the network thrived on a culture of openness and of collaboration between industry, civil society and users. Deregulation and privatization emerged as dominant tropes; the attendant notion of 'self-regulation' was supposed to offer a more flexible and adaptable form of control.

Early on, the results of this culture were impressive. They included the consensus-based standards, including TCP/IP and HTML, which fuelled the Internet's growth and popularity. But as the Internet grew in complexity and as the number of users (and interests) on the network increased exponentially, cracks began appearing in the surface of Internet self-governance. The newly apparent commercial value of the Internet, in particular, began complicating matters. As the dot-com economy boomed, companies had less incentive to collaborate with their competitors and more incentive to steer the development of the network in a direction that served their own commercial purposes. As Lawrence Lessig observed so astutely in his 1999 book, *Code and Other Laws of Cyberspace,* the absence of government control of the Internet did not mean that there would be no control at all; it simply meant that others could exert control, primarily through the code and software programs they wrote. In addition, and partly as a result of this growing commercialization, the network became increasingly clogged with various forms of 'abuse': some analysts estimate, for example, that up to 50 percent of traffic on the network today consists of unwanted emails and other forms of communication (spam), while pedophilia websites rose by 70 percent in 2003; also in that year approximately seven million people in the US alone became victims of identity theft in the prior 12 months.

These problems have not gone unnoticed (as, indeed, is illustrated by the WSIS Declaration). Around the world, governments have woken up to the dangers posed by an unregulated Internet and have stepped up their efforts to respond. The US, for example, enacted an anti-spam law (CAN-SPAM Act) that contains punitive and other measures designed to limit unwanted emails. The European Union, too, has enacted a series of strict directives regarding privacy and electronic communications. More generally, recent months and years have witnessed a slew of laws to uphold (and update) intellectual property rights, to limit the proliferation of viruses, and to regulate online gambling, ID theft, piracy and pornography.

The limits of the state

Such laws are no doubt well-intentioned. They are unlikely, however, to prove sufficient to address the Internet's crisis of governance for at least two reasons. First, because freedom from state regulation has in fact been central to the Internet's success, regulation always poses the danger of overregulation, which could stifle the entrepreneurial and innovative spirit of the network, and mission-creep. Purely technological solutions, however, have similar problems.

While vigorous filtering, for instance, will purge spam from inboxes, it can also act as an unintended censor by suppressing any mention of the typical spam themes – and even references to spam itself – in legitimate personal emails. It is therefore essential that any attempt to impose order on the Internet sees government (and technology) as just part of the solution among many actors.

Second, and perhaps even more fundamentally, government control is not the answer for the simple reason that it is unlikely to work. The Internet is too dispersed, too decentralized and too international. It truly is beyond the reach of any single nation-state. This means that it is resistant to traditional forms of regulation. It requires us not only to exert some control, but also to develop a whole new method of control.

Consider, to begin with, recent attempts by the record industry to limit the flow of copyrighted material on peer-to-peer file-sharing networks. While several countries (including the US) have ruled in favour of the record industry, such rulings have little practical effect when the networks themselves transcend national boundaries and legal jurisdictions. One new file-sharing network, Earth Station 5 (ES5), vividly illustrates the point: currently operated from the West Bank and Gaza, the network operates in a legal no-man's land, safely beyond the reach of most state authorities.

Such difficulties can be found across a range of issues. But the difficulties, it is worth noting, are not just limited to challenges of enforcement: the international nature of the Internet also raises questions regarding cross-jurisdictional harmonization. Not every country has the same legal standards regarding free speech; likewise, not every country has the same protections for privacy. This means that even when nation-states (or groups of nation-states) are capable of exerting control, their efforts may be undermined by colliding legal norms and standards, leading to a possible Balkanization of the Internet.

A notable – and notorious – instance of such collision occurred in 2000, when a French court, citing that country's anti-hate speech laws, ordered Yahoo! to block the auctioning of Nazi memorabilia on its site. The order, which would have affected all users of the Yahoo! network, was inconsistent with American free speech traditions and laws. A French court was in effect assuming the right to dictate what Americans (or Indians, or Russians, or Brazilians) could view on the network. A similar collision of legal standards occurred last year, when an Australian court ruled that a Melbourne businessman could sue Dow Jones for libel in Australia even though the content in question originated from the US Both cases shed light on the weaknesses of existing, state-led systems of governance: it is difficult (even impossible) to govern a global resource such as the Internet when the global community disagrees on the legal (or other) norms that should form the basis for governance.

Towards a new model and the importance of civil society

Taken together, these examples effectively demonstrate the challenges of governance on the Internet. It is now clear that the absence or Balkanization of rules can challenge the potential of the network; but the nation-state, it should be equally clear, is not capable of realizing that potential on its own. What we need, as we have argued, is an altogether new model of governance – one that is capable of governing across borders, and capable of supplementing (although not replacing) the powers of the state.

Lessons from other attempts at governance

Fortunately, we can turn to (and build on) some existing examples of international, non-traditional regulation. The Internet Corporation for Assigned Names and Numbers (ICANN), for instance, provides one innovative model of decision-making. Although ICANN has had many teething problems, its management of the Domain Name System (DNS) nonetheless provides a valuable illustration of how an international resource can be managed by a multi-sectoral, non-governmental organization (NGO). Likewise, the Digital Opportunity Task Force (DOT Force), initiated by the leaders of the Group of Eight (G-8) nations in 2000, provides an interesting experiment of cross-sectoral engagement. Government-created and endorsed, but led by a mix of government, business and NGOs from the developed and developing world, the DOT Force successfully managed to create a global action and implementation plan to use information and communications technologies to support economic and social development. Its governance structure and multi-sectoral processes have since been applied to the United Nations ICT Taskforce.

Of course none of these organizations is perfect and their scope is limited. Their failings have as much to teach us as their successes. ICANN's many problems, for example, offer a useful set of lessons in developing a more effective system of rule-making for the Internet. Although the organization's recent reforms may have put it on a new path, ICANN remains dogged by perceptions that it has been insufficiently participatory and open. Developing countries and civil society groups, in particular, have felt left out of the decision-making process. This sense of exclusion has undermined ICANN's legitimacy and authority, and therefore limited its effectiveness: it provides a cautionary reminder that any system of international rule-making needs to include as wide a range of voices as possible. That is why, as we have repeatedly argued, Internet governance must be based on a principle of multi-sectoral participation.

This principle, as much as the need for international solutions, is essential for successful governance. Traditional regulation relies primarily on the coercive and punitive powers of the state. But effective Internet governance is likely to rely on a culture of mutual interest and deference. Its authority will therefore depend crucially on its legitimacy and that, in turn, will rely on perceptions of inclusiveness, a sense that actors representing various sectors and regions have a voice at the table of Internet rule-making.

The role of civil society

Certainly, governments and the private sector must be among these actors: each represents an essential pillar upon which Internet governance rests. But an equally important, if often overlooked, pillar is represented by civil society. Indeed, civil society – in the form of NGOs and public interest groups – has an equally important role to play in multi-sectoral Internet governance.

Representing the public interest

First, civil society is an important actor because it is often best placed to represent the public interest. As noted above, many of the problems we are facing on the Internet stem from its growing commercialization. But this is not necessarily against the public interest: indeed, commercialization is at the root of much of the innovation and creativity on the network. Inevitably, however, there are moments when private and public interests collide; and at such moments, civil society groups are ideally placed to represent the latter and to defend individual rights against the state.

Trust

Part of the reason that civil society can play this role is because it possesses significant capital in the form of trust. Unaffiliated with the state and the commercial sectors, civil society groups often are able to articulate an independent and reliable point of view. Indeed, a recent survey on trust, conducted with 36,000 people by the World Economic Forum, found that civil society, i.e. NGOs and advocacy groups, had the second highest ratings as trusted parties (after the armed forces); the institutions that were least trusted were governments (at the very bottom) and private companies. Another survey on Internet accountability conducted by the Markle Foundation showed similar results, with respondents reacting positively to the idea of NGOs having a role in developing rules for the Internet. The public assigns a positive score to this idea (a rating of 7.1) – a far more favourable rating than those received by technical experts (6.6), individuals (6.3) or state governments (5.0). Given the widely recognized importance of trust in facilitating economic, social and other interactions, such figures point to the important role played by civil society in promoting the health of the online environment.

International

Finally, civil society can play an effective role because it often is truly global (and increasingly so) in its reach. Given that Internet governance requires international coordination, it is of course essential that it should include groups with global reach. Transnational NGOs and other civil society groups, which have grown rapidly throughout the world in recent decades, are ideally placed to fill the role of an international actor representing all segments of the global community. Indeed, a significant proportion of international aid is already channeled through international NGOs, and they have also been at the forefront of international advocacy and rulemaking for a range of issues.

Such advocacy, it is worth adding, is particularly important as a means of including developing countries in Internet governance. The early failures of ICANN, as well as the recent problems encountered by the WTO at Cancun, clearly demonstrate the perils of multilateral governance mechanisms that fail to address the needs of the developing world. Without an inclusive process, international rule-making institutions will lack legitimacy and thus authority. Perhaps even more importantly, the failure to include developing nations in rule-making processes will lead to an imbalance in those rules, a systemic exclusion of nations and populations that will only become more pronounced as the network evolves. Ultimately, such imbalances will not only harm developing nations; they will also undermine the network itself, stunting its growth and limiting the number of new, innovative applications that may emerge from the user community.

Conclusion

We remain fundamentally optimistic that we can develop new models of governance that will help us overcome current difficulties with the network and allow people to benefit from its tremendous potential. The model we have argued for must have three essential components: it must be international in its reach and authority; it must be based on multi-sectoral and geographically inclusive participation; and it needs to include representatives of civil society.

If each of these three conditions is fulfilled, we believe that the benefits will extend beyond the health of the Internet. Certainly, we will see the network flourish.

But in addition, and partly as a result of this flourishing, the Internet can also become an instrument for greater global cooperation and harmony. At a time when so many of our conflicts are being driven by competing ideologies and ideas, a global and inclusive internet can play an essential role in encouraging healthy (and peaceful) debate and discussion of those ideas. So much is at stake – for the Internet itself, and more generally for the global community.

comment

THE WORLD MEETS THE INTERNET[1]
Patrice Lyons, Law Offices of P. Lyons

Representatives from a wide spectrum of government, intergovernmental, private and what was termed "civil society" organizations met at Geneva in December 2003 at the first phase of the World Summit on the Information Society (WSIS) to discuss the challenges and opportunities presented by information and communication technologies (ICT), in particular the Internet. A primary focus of the gathering was on use of the Internet in meeting the needs of the least advantaged and marginalized groups in society, but there may be more profound effects stemming from this endeavour. Policies adopted with an Internet agenda in mind may also have an impact on future national and international laws and policies in areas such as frequency allocations, intellectual property rights, learning environments and methodologies, provision of financial aid, cybersecurity, spam, privacy, trade, taxation, and, more generally, the management and dissemination of information.

Millennium Declaration
A starting point in an understanding of the goals and objectives of the WSIS is the United Nations Millennium Declaration that was adopted at New York in September 2000[2]. This is a grand document full of fundamental statements and commitments on the part of a large group of government and private sector representatives. Some key objectives set forth in the

---

[1] This paper is also available at http://www.dlib.org/dlib/march04/lyons/03lyons.html

[2] http://www.un.org/millennium/declaration/ares552e.htm; see also
http://www.unicttaskforce.org/mdg/default.asp

Millennium Declaration include: (a) strengthening respect for the rule of law, in international as in national affairs; (b) making the United Nations more effective in maintaining peace and security; (c) ensuring the implementation of treaties in areas such as arms control and disarmament, and of international humanitarian law and human rights law; (d) taking concerted action against international terrorism; and (e) creating an environment at the national and global levels alike which is conducive to development and to the elimination of poverty.

There was a special focus in the Millennium Declaration on meeting the needs of the Least Developed Countries, particularly in the areas of duty- and quota-free access for essentially all exports from such countries, debt relief and grant of generous development assistance. There was an expressed resolution "to halve, by the year 2015, the proportion of the world's people whose income is less than one dollar a day and the proportion of people who suffer from hunger; and also, by the same date, to halve the proportion of people who are unable to reach, or to afford, safe drinking water", and to ensure that, by the same date, "children everywhere, boys and girls alike, will be able to complete a full course of primary schooling; and that they will have equal access to all levels of education". There are many other resolutions in the Declaration, but suffice to say that the world community assembled at the United Nations in 2000 took a strong stand and set milestones for the achievement of wide-reaching goals.

As noted in paragraph 2 of the Declaration of Principles adopted by the first phase of the World Summit on the Information Society, the representatives assembled specifically recalled the objectives set forth in the Millennium Declaration and other relevant documents as a motivating factor in their efforts.

WSIS Declaration of Principles and Plan of Action

There was a general recognition at the first phase of the World Summit, and in the various preparatory meetings leading up to that event, that the rapid advances in information and communication technologies open up real opportunities for the least advantaged to attain higher levels of development. As set forth in the first paragraph of the WSIS Declaration of Principles, the specific focus of world attention should be on the needs of young people, women, marginalized and vulnerable groups of society, the poor living in remote, rural and marginalized urban areas, and indigenous peoples; and the World Summit drew up a list of targets to guide the ongoing development efforts.

The fundamental principle that "everyone has the right to freedom of opinion and expression", as outlined in Article 19 of the Universal Declaration of Human Rights[3], was specifically

---

[3] http://www.un.org/Overview/rights.html

reaffirmed as an "essential foundation of the Information Society". This basic foundation for the work of the World Summit was stressed on many occasions by the various representatives. It was also recognized that: "*Everyone, everywhere should have the opportunity to participate and no one should be excluded from the benefits the Information Society offers.*" The importance of information and knowledge development, including culturally diverse and multilingual materials, with open access to such knowledge for human progress and well-being, was a consistent theme throughout the World Summit, particularly in the programs organized by the United Nations Educational, Scientific and Cultural Organization (UNESCO)[4].

In many of the World Summit events, it was recognized that scientists and engineers have a vital role to play in the development and evolution of information and communication technologies, as well as the power of these technologies to reduce traditional obstacles to learning and knowledge. This was particularly stressed at an important World Summit event entitled the "Role of Science in the Information Society" (RSIS) that was organized jointly by the European Organization for Nuclear Research (CERN), UNESCO, International Council for Science, and the Third World Academy of Sciences (http://rsis.web.cern.ch/rsis).

There was a clear understanding among the representatives assembled at Geneva that new information and communication technologies hold out the promise of changing how people access information, and a determination to use these technologies, in particular the Internet, to improve the condition of millions of disadvantaged people throughout the world. How to get there was and is a continuing challenge.

Digital Solidarity Agenda

How to pay for all the recommended activities lead to some interesting proposals under the heading "Digital Solidarity Agenda". As part of the preparatory work leading up to the second phase of the World Summit in Tunis, a Task Force is to be set up under the auspices of the Secretary-General of the United Nations to review the adequacy of all existing funding mechanisms "in meeting the challenges of ICT for development". Based on the results of this review, "improvements and innovations of financing mechanisms will be considered, including the effectiveness, feasibility and creation of a voluntary Digital Solidarity Fund".

An Agenda for the Internet

In the days leading up to the start of the first phase of the World Summit, the preparatory negotiations had largely been completed with one important exception: how to deal with what was called "Internet governance" matters. In order to move forward, there was an agreement

---

[4] http://www.unesco.org/wsis/symposium

to postpone further discussion of this issue at the World Summit. It was recommended that the United Nations Secretary-General set up a Working Group on Internet Governance to explore relevant issues and make proposals for action, as appropriate, as part of the preparatory effort leading up to the second phase of the World Summit.

Once constituted, the United Nations Working Group on Internet Governance may initially want to review how the Internet was established, as background for its deliberations. A helpful article was written by a group of individuals who each played an important role in the establishment of the Internet entitled "A Brief History of the Internet". It is available at the Internet Society site[5]. Anyone interested in an understanding of what it means to be the Internet, and how it was developed, should find a wealth of information in this article. It is a useful starting point in an exploration of Internet governance, if indeed "governance" is the right concept to apply with respect to such a dynamic information system.

Specific aspects of what some might view as Internet governance-related activities were discussed in connection with the first phase of the World Summit. For example, in the Plan of Action, governments, and other stakeholders, were encouraged to establish "sustainable multi-purpose community public access points, providing affordable or free-of-charge access for their citizens to the various communication resources, notably the Internet". It may be argued, however, that such activities do not constitute or require Internet governance, but rather the coordination of financial, technical, legal and other resources to marshal the strengths of Internet capabilities to assist in the implementation of specific WSIS development goals. By clarifying what is meant by "governance" in this context, the United Nations Working Group could make a substantial contribution toward advancing the development goals set by the World Summit.

The United Nations Working Group may want to consider a constructive role for the United Nations, including each United Nations Specialized Agency within their respective areas of competence, in coordinating information about the Internet, particularly information that relates in some way to the achievement of development and educational efforts, as well as the linking of such information resources through a designated United Nations Internet site. Such coordination of relevant information would provide helpful guidance to the public on existing and, possibly, proposed initiatives, and serve as an educational resource to individuals, organizations and government entities seeking to get involved in or to stay abreast of Internet developments. Such information is often difficult to obtain.

---

[5] http://www.isoc.org/internet/history/brief.shtml

In many WSIS-related deliberations, there appeared to be a common misperception that a key to Internet governance is the control of Internet names and numbers. There was also some discussion of the desirability of viewing the Internet in terms of distinct layers. While the desirability of such a "layered" approach in the context of such an inherently dynamic, interoperable information system has yet to be established, certain issues associated with the technical provision of Internet services clearly require global coordination, such as the apportionment of IP addresses. This is currently handled through coordination of the various Internet address registries, which operate under the overall umbrella of the Internet Corporation for Assigned Names and Numbers (ICANN[6]). In this context, an article written by the first Chairman of ICANN, Ms. Esther Dyson, discussing issues relating to management of Internet names and numbers, may be of interest to the United Nations Working Group (see Release 1.0, September 2003[7]). This article also highlights some advances that have been made over the last decade in the whole area of identification, structuring and management of information in the Internet environment.

In the early days of Internet development, the domain name system (DNS) was adopted to facilitate the location of host computers on the Internet. The system has been quite helpful in this task and is expected to continue to be helpful going forward. However, a basic limitation of this system is that the identifiers denote specific named machines on the Internet (DNS names are also used in the web context as part of URLs).

It should be acknowledged that the time has come to move beyond this limitation, while continuing to support existing systems that restrict identifiers to specific locations.

An example of a system that moves beyond such constraints and provides a location independent approach is the "digital object architecture" developed by the Corporation for National Research Initiatives (CNRI), with support from DARPA[8].

At its essence, the digital object architecture introduces the notion of a data structure, known as a "digital object", that consists of two ingredients: data and metadata (a key element of which is a unique identifier). An implementation of this architecture that concerns the assignment, resolution and administration of such identifiers is called the Handle System[9]. This system has

---

[6] http://www.icann.org

[7] https://www.edventure.com/release1/abstracts.cfm?Counter=6805767

[8] http://www.cnri.reston.va.us/doa.html

[9] http://ww.handle.net

been operational on the Internet since 1994, and is being incorporated in many of the systems or architectures that are an intrinsic part of the Internet[10].

There will be many other ways to identify resources in the Internet. Innovations in the future from the technical community may produce capabilities whose utility can best be understood from practical applications and deployments. As an information system, the Internet should accommodate the evolving capabilities of computers and other computational facilities to identify, manage, access, locate and track information (and other resources) represented in various formats. The United Nations Working Group will be making a substantial contribution to furthering the discussions at the second phase of the World Summit, if it helps to clarify the role of the DNS along with other identifier schemes, so the focus can be on the substantive development and educational issues that may actually benefit from governmental involvement.

To attempt to pin down this evolving system in a traditional governance structure, at this stage of its development, might serve to undermine the dynamism and evolution of the very resource that is of such intense interest to the governments, individuals and organizations involved in the World Summit process. If the scope of issues can be narrowed to those that are known or expected to actually require global governance, it would greatly facilitate progress in arriving at workable conclusions. It is not apparent how a monolithic or centralized management strategy for the Internet would be workable. This is a crucial moment in the evolution of the Internet. It can provide the essential information infrastructure for all who wish to bridge the digital divide, if it is allowed to evolve and prosper for the benefit of the global community.

------

[10] See, e.g. www.doi.org

Section 3

FRAMEWORKS AND DEFINITIONS

background paper

HERDING SCHRÖDINGER'S CATS: SOME CONCEPTUAL TOOLS FOR THINKING ABOUT INTERNET GOVERNANCE[1]

Don MacLean, Independent Consultant

I. Introduction

The WSIS Plan of Action asked the Secretary-General of the United Nations to set up a working group to investigate and make proposals for action on the governance of the Internet. Inter alia, this group is expected to do four things:

a) develop a working definition of Internet governance;

b) identify the public policy issues that are relevant to Internet governance;

c) develop a common understanding of the respective roles and responsibilities of governments, existing intergovernmental and international organizations and other

---

[1] This paper was originally commissioned by the International Telecommunication Union (ITU) as the background document for a Workshop on Internet governance that took place in Geneva on February 26-27, 2004. It is reproduced with the kind permission of the ITU.

Author's Note: The expression "herding cats" refers to a task that is very difficult, perhaps impossible, to accomplish – a good description of the challenge of coordinating the Internet-related interests and activities of governments, the private sector, civil society, and international organizations. "Schrödinger's cat" was the subject of a famous thought experiment by an Austrian physicist, which can be read as demonstrating that absurd results can follow if principles that make sense in one context are applied to very different kinds of problems – a suitable caution for all those grappling with the complexities of Internet governance!

forums as well as the private sector and civil society from both developed and developing countries;

d)   prepare a report on the results of this activity to be presented for consideration and appropriate action for the second phase of WSIS in Tunis in 2005.

In addition to governments, the private sector and civil society from both developing and developed countries, the Secretary-General's Working Group will involve relevant intergovernmental and international organizations and forums.

The purpose of this background paper is to provide some conceptual tools to help workshop participants do two things:

a)   systematically address the three issues mentioned in the WSIS Plan of Action;

b)   identify any other issues that ITU members may wish to consider bringing to the attention of the Secretary-General's Working Group (i.e. *alia*).

The paper will take a broad approach to issues of Internet governance.

a)   Section II will explore the meaning of the two key terms for the exercise – the "Internet" and "governance" – alone and in combination, with a view to identifying the fundamental conceptual choices facing the Secretary-General's Working Group.

b)   Section III will attempt to map the main issues raised by the Internet at the global level, along with the principal intergovernmental and international organizations and other forums currently involved in the governance of these issues. It will also identify a number of gaps that appear to exist between issues and governance structures.

c)   Section IV will draw on previous research into international ICT decision-making to identify a number of key issues related to the capacity of intergovernmental and international organizations on the one hand, and governments, the private sector and civil society in developing countries on the other hand, to govern the Internet effectively according to the criteria established by WSIS.

d)   On the basis of the foregoing analysis, Section V will present a set of conclusions with respect to key issues of Internet policy and governance that the Secretary-General's Working Group may wish to consider.

In presenting tools for thinking about Internet governance, the paper will draw on previous work by the author that is directly or indirectly related to this subject. In particular, the author wishes to thank the Commonwealth Telecommunications Organisation and Panos London, as well as the editors of Information Technology and International Development for permission to use conceptual tools originally published in the report "Louder Voices: Strengthening Developing Country Participation in International ICT Decision-Making" and in the article "The Quest for Inclusive Governance of Global ICTs: Lessons from the ITU in the Limits of National Sovereignty".[2]

II. Internet Governance: What Are We Talking About?

The first task facing the Secretary-General's Working Group is to develop a working definition of "Internet governance". The results of this work will presumably determine the scope of three tasks that follow – to identify public policy issues that are relevant to Internet governance, to develop a common understanding of the roles and responsibilities of various stakeholders, and to propose action to WSIS-05 – plus any others that are added to the Working Group agenda. The success of this project will therefore depend on getting the working definition of Internet governance right in several different senses.

a) It should not be an abstract exercise, or an exercise in solving problems other than those posed by WSIS. In other words, the working definition of "Internet governance" should fit within the WSIS frame of reference – which is essentially about creating an inclusive global information society – and should lead to actionable results, beginning at WSIS-05. In this respect, it is worth noting that the WSIS Declaration of Principles and Plan of Action contain a surprisingly rich framework for thinking about Internet governance. We will examine this in Section III below.

b) Given the time frames involved in dealing with governance issues at the global level, it should be forward looking and not deal only with the problems of the moment.

c) Given the ground rules for the Secretary-General's Working Group (an open and inclusive process that ensures a mechanism for the full and active participation of the major stakeholder groups), it must be something that everyone can agree is a reasonable point of departure for identifying issues, analyzing roles and making proposals for action.

---

[2] See MacLean, D., Souter, D., Deane, J., & Lilley, S. (2002). *Louder Voices: Strengthening Developing Country Participation in International ICT Decision-Making.* London: Commonwealth Telecommunications Organisation and Panos London. See also MacLean, D. (2003). "The Quest for Inclusive Governance of Global ICTs: Lessons from the ITU in the Limits of National Sovereignty." *Information Technologies and International Development* 1: 1-18. The former document is available at http://www.panos.org.uk/resources/booksection.asp?ID=1002, while the latter is available at http://mitpress.mit.edu/catalog/item/default.asp?sid=FA046030-D668-492D-AE85-7DED926A585E&ttype=4&tid=59.

This task is demanding, in and of itself. It is further complicated by the following factors.

a) The debates that have taken place about Internet governance, not just in the WSIS preparatory process, but over the better part of the past decade have caused a tendency in some quarters to equate "Internet governance" with arrangements for allocating and managing Internet addresses and domain names, while in other quarters there has been a tendency to assimilate "Internet governance" to "telecommunications governance". Neither viewpoint is accurate or helpful to the task facing the Secretary-General's Working Group.

b) The fact that these debates have taken place against the backdrop of a broader discussion about the effects of globalization, and the roles of the private sector and civil society in international decision-making, have led some to see the Internet as the standard bearer for a much broader governance reform agenda, both positively and negatively. Although Internet governance in some senses is a 'wedge issue', progress will depend on not overburdening an already difficult problem.

c) There appears to be a lack of clarity and common understanding among WSIS participants on the meaning of the terms "Internet" and "governance", when used either alone or in combination. For example, the WSIS Declaration of Principles appears to use the terms "governance" and "management" interchangeably; as we shall see in Section II Part B, it is more helpful to think of them as categorically distinct activities, belonging to different domains. The Declaration of Principles also refers to the Internet as a public "facility" – when in fact Internet services and applications run on the facilities of telecommunications operators. In addition, submissions from the International Chamber of Commerce (ICC) and the Internet Society (ISOC) oppose "governance" and "coordination" as mutually exclusive terms. Many would consider coordination – particularly of the kind done by bodies like Internet Corporation for Assigned Names and Numbers (ICANN) and the Internet Engineering Task Force (IETF) – to be a form of governance.[3]

In a more stable, less complex environment, the task facing the Working Group could be seen as a relatively simple exercise involving the construction of a 2-dimensional matrix or spreadsheet arraying public policy issues against institutional responsibilities. However, as we will see in the following sections, the whole question of Internet governance is very unstable

[3] See the IIC contribution at
http://www.itu.int/wsis/documents/listing.asp?lang=en&c_event=wg|ig&c_type=co| , and the ISOC contribution at http://www.isoc.org/news/7.shtml.

and highly contestable on every dimension, ranging from the definition of key terms to the selection of appropriate forms of governance and institutional arrangements. The following sections propose an approach to working through these problems.

A. The Internet

The Working Group must begin with an understanding of what the Internet is and the ways in which it is similar to and differs from other electronic networks. There are different views on this, and it is helpful to begin by exploring them since they condition different points of view on the relationship between the Internet, governance, and the manner in which it should be conducted. One feature all of them should share, however, is that they focus on the public Internet, or public networks that use Internet technology, and not on the private "Intranets" that are found in many companies and other organizations. While it may be questionable usage, the reference in the WSIS Declaration of Principles to the Internet as a "public facility" clearly indicates that the Working Group should limit its consideration to the public Internet.

The traditional Internet view – the view from inside the Internet community, or the "Nethead" view – sees the Internet as different from other electronic information and communication networks (telecommunications and broadcasting). Rather than being a single, centrally controlled network designed to deliver one service to "dumb" terminals, it is a "network of networks" that is controlled from the "edge" by users on an "end-to-end" basis, using intelligent terminals across a dumb network to access and provide a wide range of services which, although functionally similar in some cases to the services provided by other networks and media, are inherently different for multiple reasons including technology, design, capability, control, and economics. On this view, there are things about the Internet that need to be governed – particularly the management of the Internet numbering and address systems and technical standards – but the institutional structures by which they are governed, like the Internet itself, should be completely different from those that govern other networks.[4]

The traditional telecommunications/broadcasting/media view – the view from the outside, particularly from some developing countries and regions, and from traditional information and communications media that are subject to competition from Internet based service providers (i.e. telecommunications, post, broadcasting, film and sound recording, publishing, etc). Proponents of this view would agree on the need to govern the Internet numbering and addressing systems and technical standards, but would see different institutions and processes as appropriate in at least some areas. In addition, on this view, there is a need to level the

---

[4] See Denton, T. (1999). *Netheads versus Bellheads*, available at http://www.tmdenton.com/pub/index.htm for a classic exposition of the differences between the Internet and the PSTN from the nethead point of view.

governance playing field between networks that deliver the same or functionally similar services that are subject to specific governance, on the theory that if it "looks like a duck walks like a duck, and quacks like a duck, it is a duck" – regardless of the underlying differences that may exist. This viewpoint is also justified in terms of the need to protect investments in existing infrastructure and services, particularly in developing countries; to maintain universal and affordable access to basic communication services; and on views of consumer and social welfare, and the appropriate relationship between government and the private sector, that in some cases differ substantially from those held by traditional "netheads".

The network transformation view looks at the Internet and issues of Internet governance within a more holistic perspective, in terms of past developments, present trends, and future possibilities. From this point of view the Internet is not unique, in terms of the patterns that have characterized the development of international governance arrangements. Other information and communication technologies – beginning with the telegraph and continuing with the telephone, wireless, sound and television broadcasting – were not born as single, centrally controlled networks. The need to standardize different systems so that they could interoperate was the driver behind the construction of national, regional and global governance arrangements – just as it is in the Internet today. Although other technologies functioned as centralized, one-service networks for a certain period of time, the developments of the past decade have changed them significantly. Looking forward, this viewpoint would note the migration of traditional PSTNs to IP-based networks, and the potential integration of telecommunications, broadcasting, publishing and other media functions into these networks.[5] This view might also hypothesize a future in which past divisions between "vertical" network structures would progressively be transformed into "horizontal" divisions between different network layers; in which a mixture of user- and centrally- controlled networks, providing different qualities of service, would coexist; and in which everything in the universe ultimately would be connected in ubiquitous, mobile, broadband networks. In this view, the traditional Internet would not necessarily disappear. It would likely have a similar relationship to the IP-based networks operated by telecom carriers as radio amateurs have to other wireless networks. (In fact, from a historical point of view, there appear to be similarities between the culture of radio amateurs and the culture of the traditional Internet.)[6]

---

[5] The "Report of the Secretary-General on IP Telephony" to the 2001 ITU World Telecommunication Policy Forum, which is available at http://www.itu.int/osg/spu/wtpf/wtpf2001/sgreport/index.html , provides a very useful overview of the migration that is underway to IP-based networks, and of the policy implications for different stakeholder groups.

[6] See http://www.itu.int/osg/spu/newslog/stories/2003/06/06/ubiquitousNetworksResources.html for a list of reference resources on ubiquitous networks. See also

Judging which of these views is likely to prevail in the global information society, and which should provide the foundation for the Working Group, is not an easy task. It involves the consideration of complex questions at the levels of technology, business planning, consumer preference, and political risk analysis. In this respect, it is important to consider the following factors:

a) the amount of work already underway in telecommunications standardization bodies such as ITU-T and ETSI, in some cases in cooperation with the IETF, to develop IP-based standards for telecommunications networks and to bridge Internet addressing and telecommunications numbering systems;

b) the plans announced by major telecommunications incumbents to transform their wireline networks into IP-based networks and to adopt IP as the platform for future generation wireless networks;

c) the increasingly aggressive approach of content industries and IP holders to traditional Internet services;

d) the adoption by the sound recording industry of Internet-based distribution strategies, the consideration of similar strategies by other content industries;

e) the difficulty providers of traditional Internet-based services (indeed, many competitors to incumbent telecommunication carriers) have had in developing successful business models – in spite of the fact that they have not had to invest in the very capital-intensive business of constructing transmission facilities;

f) the impact of spam, viruses, fraud, identify theft, etc. on consumer confidence and expectations;

g) the concern of governments about the impact of Voice over Internet Protocol (VoIP) on traditional telecommunication networks and services, as well as about network-based threats to national security (hackers, terrorists, cyber-warfare, and other forms of vulnerability).

B. Governance

In the English language, "governance" is an old term which, like "civil society", fell into disuse, but which has been revived, given new meaning, and attained widespread currency. Like

---

http://www.wired.com/wired/archive/3.05/dejavu.html for the cultural similarities between radio and Internet pioneers.

"government" and "governor", it is derived from the Latin word "gubernare" – the action of steering a ship. A popular definition reflects these ancient Roman roots by defining governance as "steering, not rowing".

This definition captures an essential feature of the current concept of "governance". In this concept, there is a distinction between the people, structures, and processes that do the "rowing" in any human system – and the people, structures and processes that establish general goals for the system and guide the "rowers" toward these goals, setting the tempo and changing course as necessary. On this view, it is the action of "steering" that constitutes governance, while the action of "rowing" might be variously described as "government" or "public administration" if it takes place in the public sector, as "management" if it takes place in the private sector, or as "volunteering" or "social action" if it takes place in civil society.[7]

Recent discussion in different policy domains illustrates the ways in which this concept can be applied to different kinds of systems.

a) With respect to the public sector, there has been a lot of discussion about ways of improving governance at the national level in some developing countries by instituting democratic values, structures and processes, as an essential precondition to economic and social development. At the same time, in many developed countries there has been discussion about the need to revitalize popular participation in democratic processes and institutions. In both cases, there is belief that better democratic governance will lead to better government and public administration.

b) With respect to the private sector, there has been much discussion of the need to improve "corporate governance" in order to ensure that the managers run public corporations honestly, in the interests of their shareholders, and with greater attention to their social responsibilities – instead of for personal gain and private interests.

c) With respect to international affairs, there has been extensive discussion about the need to include the private sector and civil society in structures and decision-making processes that traditionally have been the preserve of national governments. In addition, there has been considerable discussion about the need to develop new

---

[7] The Oxford English Dictionary defines governance in a similar sense as "controlling, directing, or regulating influence; control, sway, mastery". A more elaborate definition, which was developed for the second Global Knowledge Conference (GKII), is "the process through which … institutions, businesses and citizen's groups articulate their interests, exercise their rights and obligations, allocate human choices and opportunities, and mediate their differences".

structures and processes that include civil society and developing countries in the governance of the process known as "globalization".

There are a number of different ways in which systems can be governed or steered. These can be conceived as ranging on a continuum from "hard" forms of governance such as laws and regulations to "softer" forms such as standards, policy coordination and voluntary cooperation.

a) It is important to consider which form is appropriate to a particular governance problem and how it should be structured by asking such questions as: Who should have a hand on the tiller? What are their roles and responsibilities? How should these be carried out in terms of organizational structure and decision-making process?

b) Before asking "how" questions of this kind, however, it is important to ask "why" questions. Why does a particular activity need governance? What is the value that will be added? Why can't the rowers just get on with the job?

c) The answers to "why" questions of this kind typically involve reference to deeper levels of meaning – common goals, shared values, accepted principles – as well as to conflicts of interest and differences of opinion that need to be resolved in order to progress the work of the rowers, to the benefit of society at large.

In any society, no matter how free, almost every activity is subjected to multiple sources of "hard" governance in the form of generally applicable laws and regulations, as well as to multiple sources of "soft" governance in the form of normal business practices, cultural values, and social conventions. In addition to these general forms of governance, some activities are subject to "sector-specific" governance in the form of laws, rules and regulations, as well as to "softer" forms of social control that apply specifically to these activities and are tailored to their particular features. In the information and communications sector, the following are among the reasons that typically trigger "sector-specific" governance:

a) to make sure that systems work so that they can be used to communicate;
b) to allocate scarce resources among competing users;
c) to encourage and protect investment in infrastructure, services and content;
d) to prevent the abuse of monopoly/market power – in terms of prices, service quality and availability, freedom of speech and expression, diversity of view, etc.;
e) to ensure universal and affordable access to basic services;
f) to protect public order and national security.

In comparing the Internet with traditional information and communications media, such as telecommunications and broadcasting, there are clear differences in patterns of governance at the national and international/global levels.

a) Unlike traditional telecommunications, broadcasting and media, the traditional Internet has been subject to very limited sector-specific governance at the global level – most notably in the areas of technical standardization and the management of Internet addresses and domain names – and has been free to govern itself without the involvement of public authorities. In many countries, this has also been the case at the national level. However, this appears to be beginning to change, as governments beginning to adopt Internet-specific laws and regulations to address issues like spam.

b) In its first few years as a widely-available public network, the Internet to some extent escaped governance under the general laws and regulations that many countries apply to traditional information and communications media in order to protect privacy and intellectual property rights; prevent illegal activities (e.g. commercial fraud, child pornography, hate crimes, abuses of freedom of expression, destruction of property, theft); protect consumers (e.g. unwanted solicitation, false advertising); and promote linguistic and cultural diversity (e.g. language of communication, local information). Some saw this as evidence the Internet had created a new, borderless world where the power of government was significantly diminished, and users ruled for better or for worse according to the rules and remedies they devised. Clearly, there are difficulties in applying national laws and regulations in cyberspace – to entities whose whereabouts may be unknown, or which may operate in different countries under different laws. There are also bound to be difficulties in enforcing laws that target users (as in the case of file sharing) or service providers, rather than originators. However, from the point of view of government, these difficulties are challenges that require the development of new tools for enforcing laws and regulations. They may also be an argument for harmonizing national approaches through international governance arrangements.

The primary concern of the Secretary-General's Working Group is international Internet governance, rather than national Internet governance (although there are references in the WSIS Declaration of Principles and Plan of Action to governance actions that might be taken at the national level). However, national and international governance are clearly linked.

a) Historically, the need to harmonize differences between national governance régimes in the interest of communications efficiency and global development led to the development of international governance arrangements for telecommunications and other ICTs.

b)   It might be argued that the case of the Internet is different since – although it originated in one country – it was designed from the beginning to be operated as network of networks by a variety of different users, on a potentially global basis. The Internet grew to become a global medium without the kind of intergovernmental coordination that characterized the development of most previous communications media.

c)   However, the debates about Internet governance that have taken place in different countries and regions and in various international forums in recent years appear to have demonstrated that it is one thing to design a medium of communications that operates on a global basis from the ground up on a technical level, and quite another thing to design a governance régime for such a medium that is acceptable in all countries and operates on an efficient, harmonized basis at the global level.

d)   Today, it appears that the different approaches being taken to Internet governance at the national, regional and international levels may limit, or even threaten, the long-term viability of the Internet as a global communications and information medium. WSIS appeared to recognize the seriousness of these conflicts, by deciding to launch a process for examining Internet governance comprehensively at the global level, within a United Nations framework. In light of these developments, it is possible to conclude that the future history of global Internet governance may not be all that different from the past history of telecommunications and ICT governance – i.e. that there is a need to harmonize governance approaches on a global basis, in order to reap the potential benefits of Internet technology.

C. Internet + Governance = ?

In sum, three possible views of Internet governance appear to have emerged, which parallel the three different views of the Internet laid out in Section A.

a)   One, which corresponds to the traditional Internet view, is articulated in the WSIS submissions of the Internet Society (ISOC) and the Internet Corporation for Assigned Names and Numbers (ICANN), as well as in the paper on Internet governance published by the ICC following the summit. On this view, Internet governance should be limited to three areas: technical standardization, management of the address and domain name systems and some service related issues, and that this should be accomplished through existing mechanisms of Internet self regulation and policy coordination, rather than through harder forms of governance involving the adoption of laws and regulations at the national and international levels.

b) A second view, which could be called the traditional telecommunications viewpoint, was articulated by a number of developing countries during the WSIS process. This view sees a much wider range of issues as requiring global governance, and favours a wider use of both established and new international governance mechanisms at the technical level (e.g. ITU involvement in the governance of the Internet addressing and domain name systems); in relation to financing the deployment of and access to the Internet (e.g. through telecom-style settlement systems, technical cooperation and development assistance programs); and in relation to the international framework for governing the Internet (e.g. through amendments to existing treaties, such as the ITU International Telecommunication Regulations, or the development of a new convention).

c) A third view, which might be called the network transformation view, focuses on the transformation of traditional telecommunication networks that is currently underway through the migration from circuit-switched to IP-based networks, and the progressive convergence of traditional telecommunications, broadcasting, information, entertainment and Internet services in the ubiquitous, broadband, mobile networks of the future. This view sees the need to rethink the governance of the Internet and the governance of other kinds of communication networks in light of these developments.

III. Internet Govenance: Issues And Forums

Since one of the ground rules this paper has recommended for the Working Group is to orient its work to the needs of the WSIS process, before attempting to map Internet governance issues and institutions, it is worthwhile analyzing what sort of framework WSIS Phase I put in place to demarcate the Internet governance universe. Figure 1 does this by using a framework for analyzing governance models and arrangements that was developed for a project on "Governance of Global Electronic Networks" being sponsored by the Social Science Research Council.[8] This model distinguishes three levels in any set of governance arrangements:

a) <u>the institutional level</u> – in the foreground are the legal foundations, organizational structures, procedures and processes that make up the governance institution;

---

[8] See http://www.ssrc.org/programs/itic/ggen_book/ for information on this project.

b) <u>the policy level</u> – embedded in these and underlying them are the players that participate in governance processes, the goals they share and the principles that guide their interaction;

c) <u>the issue level</u> – at a deeper level of analysis are the interests in play and the general framework of values that shape the structure and operation of the layers above them.

Figure 1: The Internet Governance Universe – According to WSIS

Internet Governance Institutional Framework	Internet Governance Policy Framework	Information Society Governance Issues
"The international (governance) of the Internet should be: • multilateral • transparent • democratic • with the full involvement of governments, the private sector, civil society, and international organizations"	<u>Goals</u> • An equitable distribution of resources • Facilitate access for all • Ensure a stable and secure functioning of the Internet, with multilingualism <u>Roles</u> • <u>States</u>: public policy • <u>Private sector</u>: technical & economic development • <u>Civil society</u>: community development • <u>Intergovernmental orgs</u>: facilitating coordination of public policy issues • <u>International orgs</u>: development technical standards and relevant policies	• Partnership among all stakeholders • Access to infrastructure and services • Access to information and knowledge • Capacity building • Confidence and security in the use of ICTs • Enabling environment • Social and economic applications • Cultural and linguistic diversity • Freedom of communication media • Ethical dimensions • International and regional cooperation

The Internet governance universe demarcated in the WSIS Declaration of Principles suggests that the Working Group should take a broad view of its subject if it wishes to be faithful to the spirit of the summit.

a) The three specific goals mentioned – ensuring an equitable distribution of resources, facilitating access for all, and ensuring a stable and secure functioning of the Internet, taking into account multilingualism – constitute an ambitious agenda in themselves.

b) However, Internet governance, like any form of ICT governance, is not an end in itself, but is undertaken to achieve more general economic and social goals. In the WSIS context, it seems reasonable to conclude that achievement of the three specific, Internet-related goals are intended to support attainment of the eleven information society principles identified in the WSIS Declaration of Principles, and should be governed or "steered" with these ends in view.

c) Moreover, the range of governance instruments contemplated, the number of players assigned roles and responsibilities, and the procedural requirements envisaged combine to suggest a rich and complex governance web.

It is also worth recalling the mandate of the Working Group set out in the WSIS Plan of Action, after developing a working definition of Internet governance, is to "identify the public policy issues that are relevant to Internet governance" and to "develop a common understanding of the respective roles and responsibilities of governments, existing intergovernmental and international organizations and other forums as well as the private sector and civil society from both developing and developed countries". Read in isolation, this text suggests that the Working Group could discharge its mandate by filling in a matrix of the kind presented in Figure 2.

Figure 2: Internet Governance – A Simple View

	Government	IGOs, IOs, & other Fora	Private Sector	Civil Society
Issue 1				
Issue 2				
Issue 3				
Issue n				

While attractive in its simplicity, an approach of this kind seems unsatisfactory for two reasons: it does not appear to be coherent with the framework set out in the WSIS Declaration of Principles; and it fails to capture the central and most intriguing feature of the Internet governance debate – the fact that everything has changed as a result of the Internet, that everything is now contestable. A more dynamic approach is needed to be faithful to the breadth of governance issues mapped out in the WSIS Declaration of Principles, and to take account of what is happening in "the real world".

In this spirit, the following sections will use the matrix presented in Figure 3 to attempt to map some of the issues that arise on this broad view of the Internet governance universe, as well as the major governance forums. This "governance matrix" is a slightly modified version of a tool that was originally developed in order to map the entire universe of international ICT decision-making in the report "Louder Voices: Strengthening Developing Country Participation in International ICT Decision-Making". This report was originally done for the G8 DOT Force, and has been adopted as a working document by Working Group 1 of the United Nations ICT Task Force. It arrays governance tools, ranging from "hard" to "soft" on one axis of the matrix, and the main categories of issues that historically have attracted international governance on the other – i.e. the exchange of information and communications between countries, the use of common resources, the development of networks, and applications of technology for economic, social, cultural and political purposes. On the basis of these mapping exercises, the paper will assess current governance arrangements to see if there are gaps that need to be filled, and examine the extent to which current governance structures meet the WSIS test of being multilateral, transparent, democratic, and open to full participation by governments, the private sector and civil society.

Figure 3: Mapping International Internet Governance

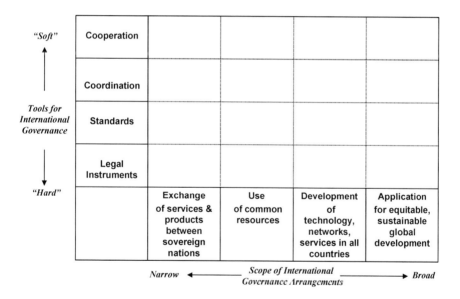

A. *Internet Governance Issues*

Figure 4: Mapping Internet Governance: Some Issues

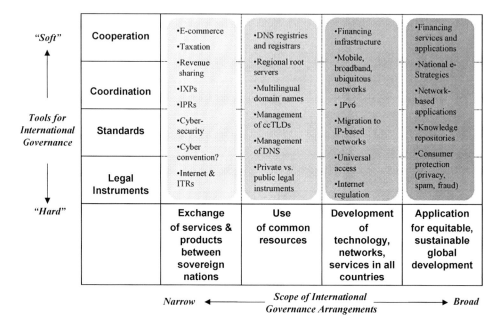

		Exchange of services & products between sovereign nations	Use of common resources	Development of technology, networks, services in all countries	Application for equitable, sustainable global development
"Soft"	Cooperation	•E-commerce •Taxation	•DNS registries and registrars •Regional root servers	•Financing infrastructure •Mobile, broadband, ubiquitous networks	•Financing services and applications •National e-Strategies
Tools for International Governance	Coordination	•Revenue sharing •IXPs •IPRs	•Multilingual domain names •Management of ccTLDs	•IPv6 •Migration to IP-based networks	•Network-based applications •Knowledge repositories
	Standards	•Cyber-security •Cyber convention?	•Management of DNS •Private vs. public legal instruments	•Universal access	•Consumer protection (privacy, spam, fraud)
"Hard"	Legal Instruments	•Internet & ITRs		•Internet regulation	

Narrow ← *Scope of International Governance Arrangements* → *Broad*

Figure 4 illustrates how it is possible to use this matrix to map out some of the main current subjects of Internet governance discussion according the categories on the horizontal axis. It also highlights questions about the potential match or mismatch between different issues and governance tools. For example:

a) If there is agreement that it is necessary to construct some new international arrangements to govern the flow of Internet traffic and services between different countries and regions, should this be done by a treaty or convention with the force of international law, backed up by agreed standards of conduct? Or is policy coordination sufficient – alone or in combination with cooperative assistance between developed and developing countries? If a treaty instrument is preferable, should the existing ITU International Telecommunication Regulations simply be amended? Or is a new Cyberspace Convention required, as some have proposed? If the latter, what should be its scope? Should it be general, or focus on a specific issue such as cyber-security?

b) Is it possible to resolve the issues that surround the management of the Internet numbering and addressing systems by improving the existing arrangements, which attempt to maintain the integrity and stability of the Internet by reconciling the interests of users, the private sector and government on a global basis through coordination arrangements based on private law within national jurisdictions? Will these arrangements only work if they are migrated to an intergovernmental organization? Or should the system be divided between private, public and possibly civil society governance arrangements?

c) What issues are raised for developed and developing countries by the transformation of traditional, circuit-switched public telecommunications networks into IP-based networks, the consequent replacement of the PSTN by VoIP and other forms of Internet telephony, the vast expansion of the IP address space that will result from the implementation of IPv6, and the introduction of truly ubiquitous networks? Should traditional telecommunications regulation migrate in the direction of traditional Internet regulation (i.e. less public, more self)? Or should traditional Internet regulation migrate in the direction of traditional telecommunications regulation? Do we need a new paradigm? What is the meaning of universal affordable access to basic service in the new network environment?

d) How can all of the preceding trends and developments be governed in order to achieve the Information Society goals laid out in the WSIS Declaration of Principles and Plan of Action? Are new laws required to protect consumers and secure human rights and fundamental freedoms, or will existing ones serve the purpose? What arrangements are required to apply new, IP-based network technologies and stimulate the development of services and content – in the economy, in society, in government, and in the public sector? Are new relationships required between government, the private sector and civil society?

B. *Internet Governance Structures*

Figure 5: Mapping Internet Governance: OGIs, IOs, and Other Forums

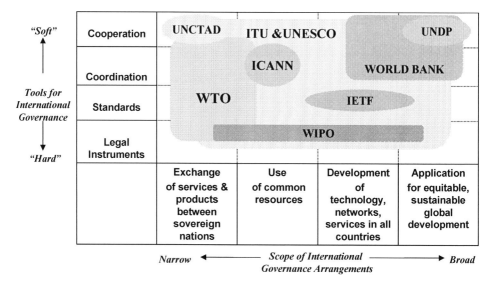

Figure 6: Mapping Internet Governance: Civil Society and the Private Sector

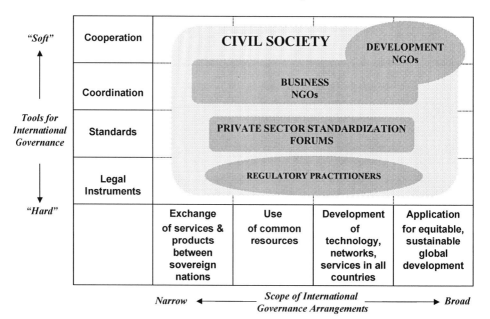

Figures 5 and 6 illustrate how it is also possible to use the matrix to map the roles of different actors (intergovernmental organizations, international organizations and other non-governmental forums, the private sector, and civil society) in relation to their areas of assigned or self-selected governance responsibilities, as well as in relation to the governance tools they have at their disposal. When read in conjunction with the issues map, this institutional mapping exercise helps to highlight areas of potential complementarity and cooperation between the different players in the Internet governance game, as well as areas of potential conflict, overlap and duplication. In this way, it can help give a sense of governance trends and the direction in which things are moving "on the ground". For example:

a) In discussions and debates about Internet governance, it is often assumed that the ITU and the Internet community are implacable enemies, representing as they do different philosophies of network design, different constituencies, different cultures, and different ways of doing things. In the past, it was not hard to find evidence to support this view. But is it still the case? As incumbent telecommunications operators transform traditional PSTNs into IP-based networks, the ITU Standardization Sector (ITU-T) is becoming increasingly involved in IP standardization issues, and appears to be liaising on a significant range of issues with the Internet Engineering Task Force (IETF). One particularly high-profile example is Electronic Numbering (ENUM), the critically important task of mapping IP addresses onto telephone numbers.[9]

b) While involvement of the ITU in the management of the Internet addressing and domain name systems remains a contentious issue, the relationship established between ICANN and the World Intellectual Property Organization (WIPO) through the Uniform Domain Name Dispute Resolution Policy (UDRP) is another interesting example of the possibility of cooperation between traditional intergovernmental organizations and self-regulating international organizations.

c) In spite of the wide range of governance turf covered by existing intergovernmental and international organizations, there are significant gaps in international governance structures in relation to some of the key issues that appear on the issues map. For example, there is no obvious home for a general convention on cyberspace or a more limited convention on cyber-security. In addition, there do not currently appear to be adequate means at the international level for protecting consumers from spam or the other problems that threaten the public Internet. Although some telecom traditionalists may be inclined to think that the ITU International Telecommunication

---

[9] See http://www.itu.int/ITU-T/studygroups/com13/ip/ietf-wg.html for a mapping of areas of common interest to IETF and ITU-T.

Regulations could provide a suitable platform for governing cyberspace, this is probably not a realistic view. Instead, a mix of new legal agreements, voluntary standards, and policy coordination likely will be required.

d) One obvious question, in light of the WSIS Declaration of Principles, is whether there is a need to construct a multilateral forum for discussing Internet governance issues that would engage participants from government, the private sector and civil society in developed and developing countries, through democratic and transparent processes. On the one hand, given the acknowledged importance of Internet governance issues to the global information society, it might be argued that such a forum is needed. On the other hand, given the range of issues and forums potentially related to Internet governance, it might also be argued that a general purpose Internet governance forum would, at best, add little value and might at worst duplicate work better done elsewhere. To help the Secretary-General's Working Group consider this issue, it may once again be helpful to take a long view of the problem.

C. The Big Bang and the Quest for Inclusive Governance

In the article entitled "The Quest for Inclusive Governance of Global ICTs: Lessons from the ITU in the Limits of National Sovereignty" that was previously referenced, the author of this paper advanced the following arguments:

a) Throughout the history of electronic communication networks, major technological innovations have led to the development of international governance arrangements with almost predictable regularity.

b) From a technological point of view, the history of global electronic networks can be seen as a series of relatively "short cycles" – typically of one or two decades duration – each of which begins with an invention, continues through the stages of application, innovation and diffusion, and ends with the construction of governance arrangements designed to ensure that that the technology in question is developed, deployed and operated in the common interest. This pattern began with the invention of the telegraph in the 1840s and continues today with the Internet, wireless, and broadband.

c) In addition to these technology-driven short cycles, the history of electronic communication networks suggests the intriguing hypothesis that there may be governance "long cycles", lasting sixty or seventy years, that alternate between periods of diversification and consolidation in international governance arrangements. Rather than being driven by specific technological innovations, these long cycles appear to be driven from the higher levels of policy and power, by sudden shifts in the perceived relationship between electronic communication networks on the one hand, and prevailing social and economic structures on the other.

d) The first of these long cycles, which began with the creation of the International Telegraph Union in 1865, was a period of institutional diversification that ended with the consolidation of the different governance structures that had been established for telegraph, telephone and radio technology into the International Telecommunication Union. During the second long cycle, which began in the early 1930s and ran until the late early 1990s, the ITU was effectively the single general-purpose forum for governing global electronic networks – a governance monopoly that reflected the monopoly enjoyed in most countries by incumbent telecommunications operators. However, the ITU governance model was blown apart in the first half of the 1990s, not just by the Internet and other technological innovations, but by a fundamental shift in thinking among all developed and many developing countries about the relationship between communication networks and economic and social development, and the models that would govern this relationship most effectively. This "Big Bang" brought a tidal wave of new issues, new players and new forums onto the governance scene – the World Trade Organization first and foremost among them.

The paper argues that the revolution in governance of global electronic networks that launched this third long wave has created "a global governance void within which a complex and confusing array of local activities take place without any overall coherence or 'top-down' coordination" of the kind formerly provided by the ITU. It goes on to suggest that in the new governance universe:

> The most powerful actors are able to exercise a significant degree of policy and regulatory control "from the bottom up" by pursuing national and/or regional interests across a wide range of forums, while the most powerful private actors are able to exercise an equally significant degree of market control by coordinating their activities through private forums, or through the exercise of raw market power. But what is often missing are opportunities for the less powerful to be engaged in discussion of global governance issues, to participate in decision-making processes, to understand the consequences of these decisions, and to adapt their policies, regulations and practices accordingly.[10]

---

[10] MacLean (2003: 7)

The paper postulates that *"policy, like nature, abhors a vacuum"* and notes that it was not long before a quest began to put some sort of order into the diverse arrangements that characterize the new governance universe. It argues that:

> It is important to be clear about the nature of this quest and how it differs from the goals that guided the earlier governance cycles. It is not a quest for a new overarching treaty or a new umbrella organization …. Instead, it is a quest with three ambitious but nonetheless challenging objectives. The first is to develop a policy vision, along with a set of goals and principles, that in some general sense applies to all of the diverse governance arrangements that characterize the new cycle, in order to provide a beacon for guiding and coordinating their activities. The second is to frame these overarching goals and principles in a way that addresses the needs and captures the interests of both developed and developing countries, so that no country is left out of the policy picture. The third is to include partnership between government, the private sector and civil society as a fundamental feature of this policy framework and of any coordinating mechanisms that are put in place to give it effect. In other words, the essential goal of this quest is to develop an inclusive policy and action framework, which brings together the diverse contributions of all players – not to establish a new institutional framework based on a new treaty agreement and featuring a new organizational structure.[11]

Although this analysis was undertaken with respect to the entire universe of global ICT governance, it appears to apply to the more limited domain of Internet governance, which is also characterized by a jumble of governance issues and institutions, and marked by tremendous disparities in the power of different participants in Internet governance processes.

If this is correct, the WSIS Declaration of Principles appears to be an important step in the quest for a new framework for governing not only the Internet, but also global ICTs in a more general sense. Whatever its weaknesses, it does set out goals and principles to guide governance that reflect the interests of all players – to a greater or lesser extent – and does establish participation and partnership between governments, the private sector, and civil society from developing and developed countries as the foundation of governance arrangements.[12] It does this with respect to Information Society issues in general and, as demonstrated in Figure 1, with respect to Internet governance in particular.

---

[11] MacLean (2003: 7)

[12] When the WSIS Declaration of Principles and the Civil Society Declaration to WSIS are compared, there appears to be substantial overlap at the level of principle, even if there are significant differences in vocabulary, tone and emphasis. The main area of disagreement, not surprisingly, is concerns the roles of the private sector and market mechanisms on the one hand, and public institutions and community initiatives on the other hand, in the achievement of development objectives.

IV. Governance Capacity

Even if the principles and goals embodied in the WSIS Declaration of Principles are a helpful first step, it would be a significant challenge to resolve even one major Internet governance issue, through the tangle of intergovernmental and international organizations likely to be involved, within the WSIS time frame. To resolve several of them would be exceptional. And to resolve any of them according to the governance formula embedded in the WSIS Declaration of Principles – i.e. in a way that is "multilateral, transparent and democratic, with the full involvement of governments, the private sector, civil society, and international organizations" – would be nothing less than heroic! As we set out on this particular stage of the global governance quest, there are many issues, a large number of governance forums – and not one that operates fully according to these principles. The issue of governance capacity should surely rank high in the list of *alia* that the Secretary-General's Working Group may wish to consider.

In 2002, the Commonwealth Telecommunication Organisation and Panos London undertook a research project to study developing country participation in international ICT decision-making, including participation by governments, the private sector and civil society. Three very different organizations were chosen for study – the ITU, the WTO and ICANN – and research was conducted from two contrasting perspectives: at the institutional level, by a research team that interviewed and observed developing country participants in meetings of these three organizations; and in six developing countries by local experts who studied national policy processes related to the governance agendas of these organizations.

The main output of this project was the *Louder Voices* report referred to previously. A number of its findings may be relevant to discussions of Internet governance.

There were clear differences between the three organizations that were the focus of the study – in terms of their purposes, histories, memberships, organizational cultures, structures, working methods, decision-making processes, etc. There were also clear differences between the six countries that were given detailed study – Brazil, India, Nepal, South Africa, Tanzania and Zambia – in terms of geography, demography and level of development. In addition, there were clear differences between the members of the institutional and in-country research teams, in terms of background, training and work experience. In spite of these differences, the study found that here was a high degree of coherence between "top down" and "bottom up" points of view on the obstacles facing developing country participants, and convergence on the actions required to strengthen their engagement.

The main obstacles to effective participation identified in the study were:

a) lack of awareness of the importance of ICT-related issues in relation to development goals;

b) lack of technical and policy capacity;

c) lack of easy, affordable and timely access to information;

d) weaknesses in governance processes;

e) financial barriers.

Study participants identified a number of actions that intergovernmental and other international organizations could take to help remove these obstacles – for example, by: providing better information on governance issues and processes to developing country participants; reforming governance structures; improving governance processes; and making more effective use of financial resources. However, there was consensus that the key to strengthening developing country participation in international ICT governance lies at the national and regional levels. Recommended actions included:

a) creating policy awareness among public and private sector decision makers of the links between ICTs and development, so that ICT governance becomes a key component of national e-Strategies;

b) building technical and policy capacity, with the assistance of international forums and development agencies;

c) strengthening national policy institutions and processes on both national and international governance issues by improving information flows, ensuring policy coordination between different agencies, promoting informed public discussion and debate, and including all relevant stakeholders in policy-making at the national and international levels.

As illustrated in Figure 7, international governance processes are complex. Many developing countries attend meetings and are present when decisions are made – but this is only a small part of the governance process. Effective participation requires the capacity to anticipate developments, identify interests, analyze issues, help set agendas, coordinate proposals, implement decisions, and evaluate their results. The Louder Voices report found that this capacity was lacking to a greater or lesser extent in the institutions and developing countries studied. The study concluded that building governance capacity in developing countries is a long-term challenge, and that developing countries will only succeed if they receive more effective capacity-building support from bi- and multilateral aid agencies, as well as from international organizations themselves.

Figure 7: The International ICT Policy Process

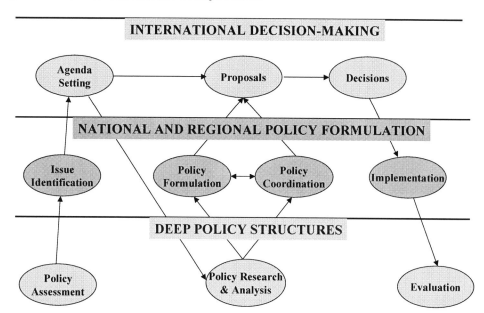

Conclusions

In attempting to apply some conceptual tools drawn from his previous research to the problems of Internet governance identified in the WSIS Declaration of Principles, the author has reached the following conclusions.

a)   If it is true that we are entering a third "long cycle" in the governance of global electronic networks – in which it is only possible to govern the Internet and other ICTs across multiple forums on the basis of guiding principles and inclusive processes, rather than on the basis of an overarching treaty and central institutional structure – then the WSIS Declaration of Principles and Plan of Action provide a workable point of departure in the quest for multilateral, transparent, democratic and inclusive governance arrangements.

b)   As a corollary to (a), this is of course only the case if all parties are truly committed to the WSIS framework – or at least sufficiently committed to continue to talk through their differences on specific points.

c)   The Secretary-General's Working Group needs to clarify the meaning of "Internet governance" within the WSIS framework as quickly as possible, in order to provide a foundation for building on the significant, but fragile, consensus among governments, civil society organizations and the private sector from developed and developing countries that appears to have been achieved through the WSIS process.

d) Growing this "fragile flower" will be a challenge. In addition to the differences of perspective on Internet governance outlined in this paper, underlying differences concerning the roles of the private and public sectors in the general governance of the information society could impede progress and rapidly render the Internet governance problem intractable. It therefore will be critical for the Secretary-General's Working Group to develop ways of managing these cleavages.

e) In the longer term, there will clearly be a need for widespread institutional reform, in order to actually implement the WSIS framework through the multiple intergovernmental and international forums involved in Internet governance. In this respect, competition between different organizations may be healthy. It is something of a myth that only Internet governance is driven from the "bottom up". All international organizations, including traditional intergovernmental bodies like the ITU, reflect the interests and wishes of their members. Any governance structure that becomes truly open to and inclusive of governments, the private sector and civil society from developed and developing countries is likely to become increasingly attractive to those who are doing the "rowing" – i.e. who are actually developing Internet technologies, networks, services and applications – if it is able to combine inclusiveness with efficient and effective governance in the relevant time frames (which may range from short- to long-term).

f) Efforts to develop inclusive governance structures at the international level will be ineffective unless initiatives are taken to build Internet governance capacity in developing countries and regions. In particular, it will be essential to build technical and policy capacity in relation to the migration to IP-based networks and the use of common resources – be they names, numbers, addresses or spectrum. In this regard, current initiatives to build broad e-Strategy, e-Policy, and ICT governance capacity may provide useful models.

g) While there may be no need to re-invent the capacity-building wheel, there is a need to identify good practices and to focus on key capacity issues. This should primarily be the work of governments, the private sector and civil society from developing countries and regions, although much can also be learned from the experience of those on the other side of the digital divide in many developed countries (e.g. aboriginal communities, rural and remote areas, urban core, etc.).

h) Even though it likely does not make sense to attempt to construct a new overarching Internet governance regime, there are clearly "holes" in the Internet governance universe that need to be filled. Issues relating to network security and consumer protection are leading candidates for immediate action. How large these holes are and how they should be filled depends to some extent on the view that is taken of the meaning and scope of "Internet governance". In some areas, it may be necessary to consider the adoption of treaty arrangements (e.g. cyber-security). In others, it is possible that holes can be filled through "softer" forms of governance – e.g. technical and operational standards, policy coordination, codes of conduct, etc.

i) In designing arrangements for Internet governance, it is important to bear in mind the architectural maxim that "form should follow function". In other words, the governance tools chosen to address a particular issue, and the decision-making structures designed to apply these tools to specific problems, should reflect and fully represent the balance of interests, capabilities and needs that exist in the 'real world' – and change as this balance changes. The history of global ICT governance demonstrates that some things are best left to the private sector, some are best left to governments, and that satisfactory arrangements have yet to be devised for including developing countries and civil society in either the public or private domains of governance. This experience has also shown that it is difficult, if not impossible, to become truly inclusive without fundamental recognition of the separate and complementary functions of public and private governance structures, the legitimate roles of different actors, and the need to create dynamic linkages between them.

As the title of this paper is meant to indicate, issues of Internet governance are difficult to analyze, discuss and manage – because of their novelty – because of their complexity – and because the differing points of view of different stakeholder groups are part of the problem, as well as part of the solution. However, in this respect as in others, the Internet may not be as unique as is sometimes thought. Even very mundane, mature technologies can generate controversy and sharp differences of opinion when issues of global governance are at stake. At this point WSIS seems – perhaps somewhat improbably – to have given all stakeholders a reasonable point of departure on their quest for inclusive Internet governance.

MAKING SENSE OF "INTERNET GOVERNANCE": DEFINING PRINCIPLES AND NORMS IN A POLICY CONTEXT

Milton Mueller, John Mathiason, and Lee W. McKnight, The Convergence Center, Syracuse University[1]

The World Summit on the Information Society's request to Secretary-General Kofi Annan to convene a working group on Internet governance provides an important opportunity to clarify roles in one of the most dynamic features of 21st century society. The Working Group has been tasked to:

i)   "Develop a working definition of Internet governance;

ii) Identify the public policy issues that are relevant to Internet governance;

iii) Develop a common understanding of the respective roles and responsibilities of governments, existing intergovernmental and international organizations and other forums as well as the private sector and civil society from both developing and developed countries;

iv) Prepare a report on the results of this activity to be presented for consideration and appropriate action for the second phase of WSIS in Tunis in 2005".

---

[1] Internet Governance Project: http://dcc.syr.edu/igp-home.htm

This paper surveys Internet governance issues as they are emerging and provides a context for the examination that the Working Group will have to make. The paper is intended to assist the Working Group process in the following ways:

It enumerates existing Internet governance regimes and shows where they intersect or overlap.

Applying regime theory, it attempts to identify some of the basic principles about the Internet and to articulate norms that can be derived from those principles.

It provides a framework for the examination of international Internet policy issues, and identifies some of the specific issues which the dialogue on Internet governance will have to cover.

The method we propose serves two purposes. First, it permits more precise analysis and understanding of existing Internet governance arrangements. Second, it provides a structured way to come to an agreement on whether new Internet governance arrangements are needed and if so, how they should be institutionalized.

I. Coming to Terms with the "G"-word (Governance)

The meaning of the term "Internet governance" needs to be clarified at the outset. The word "governance" seems to frighten many parties in the technical and business communities, who equate it with "government" or with the idea that "a single entity controls the Internet".[2] In contrast, the term is routinely used among scholars and practitioners in the fields of international relations, public administration and political science, who do not find it frightening at all.[3] The label "governance" at the international level was developed rather recently in those fields as a response to the fact that in an increasingly interdependent world there are administrative and organizational problems that transcend the boundaries of national sovereigns.[4] Governance in this context refers to the rules and procedures that states and other involved parties agree to use to order and regularize their treatment of a common issue. It does

---

[2] See e.g., "Issues Paper on Internet Governance," Prepared by the International Chamber of Commerce's Commission on E-Business, IT and Telecoms, January 2004. See also the Internet Society news release "Developing the Potential of the Internet through Coordination, not Governance," (December 9, 2003) http://www.isoc.org/news/7.shtml

[3] The word is also used in the business world frequently now in reference to "corporate governance;" i.e., the accountability and management arrangements used to supervise corporations. Since this usage applies to a single organization and the Internet consists of thousands of interconnected organizations, it is not appropriate to think of "Internet governance" and "corporate governance" as parallel concepts.

[4] The term was given particular importance by the Commission on Global Governance that issued its report *Our Global Neighborhood* (Oxford University Press, 1995).

not mean the same thing as "government"; in fact, the term was chosen specifically to differentiate (weaker) international ordering processes from (more binding) national ones. Within states, there can be "government", but in the non-sovereign worlds of international public organizations, civil society, and business organizations, there can be only "governance".

This leads to a fairly simple, if abstract, definition of "Internet governance". Internet governance can be defined as: *Collective action, by governments and/or the private sector operators of TCP/IP networks, to establish rules and procedures to enforce public policies and resolve disputes that involve multiple jurisdictions.*

The Internet is an international phenomenon, and determining the rules and procedures for its governance is neither simple nor obvious. But as we show in the next section, some forms of governance have already been adopted, and more may be needed if the institution is to achieve its full potential in contributing to the solution of the many problems confronting the international community. There are a variety of means by which governance can be secured, ranging from defining property rights and letting the forces of the market provide order, through action by national authorities, to responsibility for order being assigned to international public organizations. Which is most appropriate, as will be seen, depends on how the governance issues are defined.

II. Internet Governance Already Exists

Once the definition of "governance" is clarified, it becomes evident that international governance is already being applied to the Internet in several particular areas. Specifically:

- The Internet Corporation for Assigned Names and Numbers (ICANN) sets policy for domain name dispute resolution, engages in economic and technical regulation of the domain name supply industry, and controls the allocation and assignment of top-level domains and the top of the Internet Protocol address hierarchy. Efforts to portray this as mere "technical coordination" are mistaken. ICANN's main activity is to establish a system of rules, rooted in contracts, to order the global supply of domain names. These contractual rules are used to resolve fundamental public policy problems involving domain names and intellectual property rights, privacy, competition policy, and resource allocation. In other words, most of what ICANN does is "governance"; very little of its time and resources involve technical coordination.

- The Council of Europe's Draft Convention on Cybercrime deals with criminal offences committed through the use of Internet and other computer networks, such as copyright infringement, computer-related fraud, child pornography, and breaches of network security. Although not confined to the Internet, it certainly encompasses "governance" of important aspects of Internet use. The Council has also adopted a Declaration on "Freedom of Communication on the Internet".[5]

- The United Nations Commission on International Trade Law (UNCITRAL) has adopted a model e-commerce law and considers its purpose to "further the progressive harmonization and unification of the law of international trade", thus paving the way for Internet-based e-commerce. Likewise, the Hague Conference on International Private Law affects consumer protection and consumer-business and business-business transactions over the Internet. Harmonization of the rules and procedures governing transnational commercial transactions over the Internet is "governance".

- The World Intellectual Property Organization (WIPO) in December 1996 concluded two treaties updating copyright and related rights for digital media, which it promotes as "the WIPO Internet treaties". More recently, WIPO has proposed a treaty creating new forms of protection for broadcast content that could have profound implications for webcasting and Internet multimedia transmissions. WIPO also cooperated with ICANN in the development of domain name – trademark dispute resolution policies, and in 2001 proposed the creation of entirely new domain name rights with no basis in trademark law. This is "governance".

- The Internet's rapid international diffusion in the 1990s would not have been possible without domestic policies and trade agreements liberalizing the provision of "value-added" information services using telecommunication facilities. These agreements preceded the WTO, but were extended and institutionalized by the WTO's Basic Telecommunication Services agreements. The WTO also promulgated the TRIPS (Trade-related aspects of intellectual property rights) agreement, which treats copyright infringement as a trade barrier and requires WTO members to adhere to minimum standards of protection and enforcement. While not exclusively concerned with Internet-based intellectual property issues, the application of TRIPS standards could be applied to Internet-based infringers.

- International governance can also be achieved through the unilateral action of strong states. For example, the US Federal Trade Commission has proposed an "International Consumer Protection Act" focused primarily on transnational law enforcement involving Internet transactions. The US also passed the "Anticybersquatting Consumer Protection Act" globalizing some aspect of US legal jurisdiction over domain name disputes.

---

[5] Declaration on Freedom of Communication on the Internet and Explanatory Note. May 28, 2003. http://www.socialrights.or~/spip/IMG/pdf/Freedom of communication on the_Internet.pdf

Similarly, the European Commission's competition policy reviews have had and will probably continue to have transnational impact on the Internet. For example, before clearing the merger of two US companies, WorldCom and MCI, in 1998 the EU required MCI to divest its Internet service provider business. The same transnational impact characterized the EU's Data Protection Initiative. Is this "governance" or "government"? Perhaps somewhere in between.

There have also been proposals for governance regimes that have not succeeded, such as the global content classification regime proposed by the Bertelsmann Foundation,[6] proposals emerging from the Asia Pacific Economic Council (APEC) regarding an international settlements regime for Internet service providers, or the Council of Europe's "right of reply" proposal to regulate web site content.[7] Figure 1 diagrams some of the Internet-related international regimes and shows where they overlap.

The International Chamber of Commerce has prepared a more detailed matrix of issues related to the Internet and the organizations that are active in those areas.[8]

With all these localized regimes in place involving (or potentially involving) the Internet, why do we need to discuss "Internet governance" as a whole? Why not let international actors continue to respond to the problems posed by the Internet in a piecemeal fashion?

It is an important question – one that contains an implied critique of the WSIS mandate that is more legitimate and pertinent than the pretense that Internet governance does not or should not exist as an issue at all.

---

[6] "Memorandum on Self-regulation of Internet Content," Bertelsmann Foundation, Gutersloh, Germany, 1999.

[7] http://www.coe.int/T/E/Human Rights/media/7 Links/Right of reply hearing.asp#TopOfPage

[8] See http://www.iccwbo.org/home/menu_electronic_business.asp

Figure 1: (Some) Internet Governance Regimes

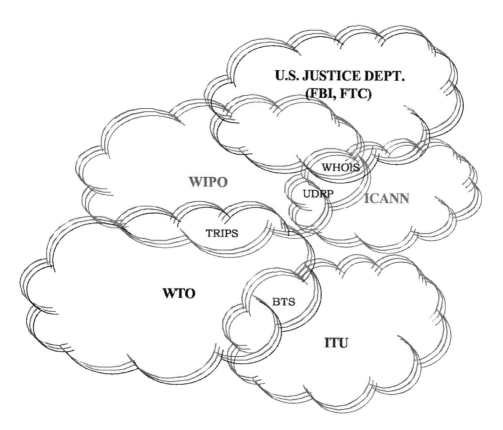

We recognize the possibility that the concept of "Internet governance" is too big for its own good. In a digitized communication-information environment, most electronic hardware, most software applications, and practically all information services can be linked to the Internet in one way or another. Thus, "Internet governance" has the potential to encompass virtually anything and everything that involves communication and information. Top-down regimes that attempt to comprehensively "order" such a large and complex space are likely to be less responsive to unique conditions in a particular policy domain – and possibly inimical to freedom, less efficient, and less effective.

Nevertheless, three reasons can be adduced why it is worth asking, at least, about the bigger picture. First, one cannot know whether a comprehensive governance regime is better or worse than what we have now unless one tries to sum the parts into a whole and assess what, if anything, is missing or not working effectively. There is, in other words, a need for agreement on fundamental conceptions about the nature of the phenomenon the international system is dealing with. In regime theory, these agreements about basic facts are called "principles". We elaborate on that concept in Section IV below. Secondly, localized regimes can be dictated by special interests, such as wealthy and well-organized industrial interests, powerful states, or some combination of the two. In smaller domains these special interests may have the clout to establish rules that, while congruent with their own immediate needs, are unfair or dysfunctional from a broader perspective. Third, even when the localized regimes are good on their own terms there may be overlaps, contradictions, or loopholes amongst them because they all evolved relatively independently of each other. Some of the policy issues related to these are discussed in Section V.

To conclude, a key issue for the United Nations Working Group is: How much unification or integration of the international governance frameworks pertaining to the Internet is needed? What are the dangers and potential benefits of a comprehensive approach?

III. Regime Theory

The Working Group will be discussing how to create an "Internet governance regime". The classical definition of a regime is "sets of implicit or explicit principles, norms, rules and decision-making procedures around which actors' expectations converge in a given area of international relations".[9] Put another way, a regime is a set of agreements on how to create and maintain order in a given area. In terms of Internet governance, it would be the agreements made by governments, civil society and international organizations about how critical elements of the Internet should be managed so that the Internet functions effectively and in an orderly manner for the benefit of all.

In practice, regime creation follows a sequence of agreements on central issues. First, the principles, defined as statements of fact, causation and rectitude, are agreed. Without an agreement about the nature of the problem or issue, no subsequent agreement can be reached on what to do about it. Then, there must be an agreement about the norms that apply. These are the standards and obligations that the parties to a regime agree should be followed. Once the norms are agreed, rules can be defined. These are prescriptions and proscriptions for action. As a final step, once the rules are agreed, the decision-making procedures and the institutions through which they are made can be agreed.

The United Nations ICT Task Force devoted a session to the discussion of principles in its March 2004 Global Forum. The discussion took two forms. First, many in the Internet technical community and the business community repeatedly called upon the United Nations

---

[9] Steven D. Krasner, "Structural Causes and Regime Consequences: Regimes as Intervening Variables," in Krasner (ed), *International Regimes,* Ithaca: Cornell University Press, 1983, p. 2.

process to "first, do no harm". In addition to that, there were calls for "transparency", "accountability" and "participation". All of these were put forward as "principles".

It would be more accurate to call these contributions *norms* rather than principles. That is because they describe desirable results but tell us nothing about how to accomplish those results or what other desirable goals we have to give up to achieve them. Unless normative appeals such as these are connected to fundamental statements of fact and causation about the Internet and the constraints governing its effective operation, they are just expressions of desired outcomes, like asking for fine weather and bumper crops. As such, they offer the United Nations Working Group little substantive guidance. It is unlikely that anyone, for example, could disagree with an aphorism such as "first, do no harm". It would be easy to obtain consensus that any new international governance arrangements should not make things worse than they are now. The real political accomplishments, however, will come when the involved community can come to an agreement about what constitutes "harm" and what actions make things "worse" or "better". A true *principle* would make a concrete and meaningful statement about that, and thus would help guide toward better governance arrangements. That is why this paper uses a more restrictive and "academic" definition of the term "principle". It is the only approach that will lead to any results.

The speed with which a regime can be set up depends on how long it takes to agree on each of the steps. Sometimes the first stage, agreeing on the facts and their implications, is easy, but more often it is the most difficult stage. For example, the agreement on the factual principle that human behaviour could alter the global climate was critical to further agreements on the climate change regime. In the case of the Internet, a key agreement will have to be reached about what the Internet is and its logical consequences.

All international agreements include statements of what should be expected of the parties involved. In the case of the Internet, these standards of behavior and obligations will have to apply to all of the actors: corporations and other businesses, epistemic communities, governments at all levels, and international organizations. They will define the contours of governance. As our analysis will show, there are many unresolved normative issues with regard to the Internet, but these can and should be resolved.

Agreement on rules, decision-making procedures and institutions is inevitably the last step in negotiating a regime. Partly this is because this step involves what are termed "financial implications" for the parties to the regime. Mostly, however, it reflects the fact that the rules, procedures and institutions have to be appropriate in terms of both principles and norms. To a large extent, the agreement on principles and norms will determine what rules, procedures and institutions will be needed.

IV. Principles for the Global Internet

In this section we begin the process of articulating basic principles upon which an Internet governance regime can be based. This particular set of principles should be considered provisional; its intent is to provide a basis for beginning the discussions and negotiations of the Working Group. The normative implications of each principle will be articulated in the next section.

A. The Global Commons Principle

The Internet is based on global, open and nonproprietary standards. The networking protocols upon which it is based can be freely adopted by anyone. They are published openly and can be used by anyone without paying a fee. Its core standards and practices are developed by a relatively open epistemic community, which while spearheaded by formal hierarchies such as Internet Architecture Board, IETF and W3C, really consists of a broad and informal conglomeration of technical experts located in universities, research institutes, small consultancies, large corporations and governments. This is in contrast to the older model of standardization, in which standards documents were developed by formally appointed representatives working in closed committees, and often sold as very expensive documents.

B. The Private Market Principle

The Internet is a decentralized network of networks. The networks connected by Internet protocols are owned and administered by autonomous organizations: the private networks of households, small businesses, large enterprises and nonprofit organizations as well as the (usually privately owned) public data networks, both large and small, of Internet Service Providers and telecommunication companies. This aspect of the Internet leads to privatization and decentralization of network operations and policies. By facilitating interoperability, Internet leads to privatization and decentralization of software applications and information content as well.

The private market principle has important infrastructural implications. As a software protocol, Internet can run on any available physical telecommunication infrastructure: wired or wireless, copper, fiber or coax. The Internet can aggregate large numbers of relatively small private investments in physical telecom infrastructure into an interconnected whole. Most of the investment is small scale and private.

This principle also means that the Internet's capacity for self-governance is great. Private networks or users can build electronic "fences" or adopt filters or practices that can, to some extent, shelter themselves from undesirable forms of communication while maintaining some form of compatibility and interconnection with the rest of the world. Whereas traditional notions of government and governance imply uniformity, Internet permits variation in policies adopted in response to the same problem.

C. The End-to-End Principle

The Internet was designed to follow, as much as possible, the "end-to-end argument," which is one of its few general architectural principles. End-to-end means that the design of the network is not optimized for any particular service or set of applications; the network provides basic data transport only, leaving applications and other forms of user specific information processing to the devices attached to the ends of the network.[10] This permits the network to serve as a relatively neutral and transparent platform for the widest possible variety of applications and services, including services that have not been anticipated by the designers. The end-to-end principle is believed to promote innovation, network growth and market competition, and a more rational, direct allocation of costs. When functions and applications are built into the network they have to be shared by everyone, regardless of whether they use them. Under an end-to-end regime, on the other hand, the users of new services and applications pay most of the additional costs associated with them, because most of the implementation costs of specific services and applications are borne by people at the endpoints.

Although we present commons, market and end-to-end as three distinct principles, it would be better to think of them as interrelated. At the endpoints, the free market and privatization rule; at the core standards level, a commons is in place. The end-to-end principle ensures that commons and market complement each other. The market in applications, content and networking requires neutral coordinating mechanisms that enable interoperation. With end-to-end, the sharing and coordinating mechanisms are deliberately minimized to provide maximum scope for initiative and innovation, and there is a clear separation between the parts of the system that are subject to private initiative and control, and the parts that are subject to global coordination and non-exclusive access.

D. Resource Bottlenecks Exist – and are Getting Worse as Scale Grows

The Internet standards, while open and nonproprietary, create resource spaces that cannot be governed as a commons. As the scale of the Internet increases and society's dependence on it grow, the value and stakes associated with the assignment and control of these resources

---

[10] Certain functions "can completely and correctly be implemented only with the knowledge and help of the application standing at the endpoints of the communication system. Therefore, providing [such] function[s completely] as a feature of the communication system itself is not possible." J. Saltzer, D. Reed and D. Clark: "End-to-end arguments in system design", *ACM Transactions on Computer Systems*, 2(4): 277-88, November 1984.

increases. Assignment and use of these resources must be exclusive and coordinated. We refer here to responsibility for DNS root servers, the assignment of top-level domain names, IP address allocation and assignment, and ISP routing tables. Control of these resources is concentrated, predictably enough, in the hands of the technologists and companies that developed the Internet first. There are legitimate grounds to investigate the technical, economic, and political impact of this legacy control. Some of the most difficult equity and distributional issues in Internet governance can be traced to this principle. These resource bottlenecks serve as a magnet for political intervention, much of which has the potential to be destructive.

E. Moral Neutrality

To those with the means to access it, Internet increases the transparency, speed and accessibility of information content and services. But this enabling power applies to "bad" as well as "good" information and communication behaviour. The same properties of the Internet that empower users to interconnect and interoperate create opportunities for criminal behaviour, theft, fraud, and misappropriation. The low cost of acquiring new accounts and new identities, the ease with which any infrastructure can be used to access the Internet, the delegation of significant amounts of control to the edges, means not only that all of societies' traditional problems (e.g., obscenity, terrorism) come in to the online world, but that new difficulties uniquely responding to the opportunities of cyberspace (spam, phishing, denial of service attacks, viruses) are created as well.

F. Multi-stakeholder Governance

The organizations with control of key Internet resources are highly distributed and multifarious and cannot be regulated in a top-down manner via agreements among states alone. Overlapping communities of technologists, educational and research institutions, private corporations, and civil society organizations constitute an informal and diverse "Internet community". Standards organizations affecting networking in particular are diverse and rely primarily on voluntary adoption. Moreover, information technology may empower companies and individuals to opt out of undesirable, burdensome or economically unsustainable institutional arrangements and to re-associate on new terms. There is always the possibility of system bypass; on the whole this is a healthy aspect of the world economy. This key constraint on international governance must be recognized and taken into account.

V. Norms for the Global Internet

The standards and obligations for parties that flow from these principles can be deduced as follows.

A. The technical model should be preserved

A future Internet regime must not interfere with the basic technical principles of the Internet (standards commons; decentralized responsibility for networks, content and services; end-to-end architecture). The basic model is not broken; in fact, it has an unparalleled record of success in facilitating communication, public access to information, adaptation to changing conditions, and making efficient use of available infrastructure.

B. Do not allow the commons to be privatized

Ownership of infrastructure, software or services should not become concentrated in the hands of commercial providers to the point that it threatens the open, nonproprietary status of the core Internet standards. Global competition policy initiatives should be guided by this norm.

C. Do not transform the standards commons into a basis for regulating the private market

This may be less of a threat in the short term, but it is equally dangerous. Maintenance of standards can become an excuse to engage in extensive regulation of business conduct. Overzealous applications of the end-to-end-principle may become an excuse to regulate conduct at the edges. At its worst, such regulation can change the essential character of the Internet from an association that adds value to all who are connected, to a compulsory compact that binds users in dysfunctional or suboptimal relationships. While action should be taken to prevent privatization of the internetworking process and standards themselves, the freedom of subsets of users to "secede" from the Internet's network federation in order to implement new technologies and new, possibly even incompatible standards should not be limited, so long as it does not technically harm the existing public Internet. Concepts of "harm" should not include so-called "economic harm" caused by end users adopting more efficient forms of communication.

The inherent tension between norms b) and c) is currently being faced in ICANN's encounter with VeriSign's Sitefinder initiative. This is an area where analysis yielding more precise definitions and criteria for intervention/nonintervention are needed.

D. Resource allocation and assignment rules and procedures should be consistent with the end-to-end principle

Insofar as is possible, resource assignment procedures should be uniform, objective, and impersonal, and facilitate the coordination of decentralized private activity at the endpoints. Discretionary, politicized merit assignment regimes are bad; objective mechanisms such as auctions or random selection are as a rule better, because they are more predictable, avoid costly investments in rent-seeking, and are more open to newcomers such as newly developing economies and smaller entrepreneurs. For an example of the application of this norm to domain name policy, see Mueller and McKnight (2003).[11]

E. Management of technical resources should not be overloaded with policy functions

This norm is intended to counter the growing temptation to use control of exclusive resources critical to the functioning of the Internet to exert leverage over areas of policy unrelated to the function of the resource itself. For example, the attempt by intellectual property owners and some law enforcement agencies to turn domain name registration data into a completely accurate form of public identification would convert a technical function into a law-enforcement function. The temptation by governments and other entities to grab on to any point of leverage must be resisted.

F. Regulation of the fraudulent and criminal aspects of Internet use must be directed at the responsible endpoints, not at the internetworking process itself

The idea that the content of Internet communication should be regulated through controls within the channel itself rather than sanctions on the sender or receiver should be resisted. Not only is it technically difficult to monitor communications over the Net, but efforts may make the functioning of the Net less effective or impose major externalities on innocent parties. There is an analogy with other efforts to deal with illicit activities where, as in the case of drug trafficking, the best approach is to address supply or demand rather than trying to interdict transportation.

G. Infrastructure development should be decentralized and competitive

Digital divide subsidies, if there are to be any, should go to users and not to centralized suppliers or governments. For most users, the main costs of the Internet are in terms of the equipment and software necessary to connect with the network (terminal equipment, access lines, access charges) rather than the costs of using the public network itself. The experience to date shows that competition among suppliers of that equipment and software has served to stimulate investment and growth, and reduce prices. Providing resources to end users, particularly in developing countries, to acquire those elements of end user infrastructure should serve to stimulate and encourage development while maintaining a maximum degree of choice and diversity in supply.

---

[11] M. Mueller and L. McKnight, "The Post-Com Internet: Toward Regular and Objective Procedures for Internet Governance." Telecommunications Policy (forthcoming). http://dcc.syr.edu/miscarticles/NewTLDs2-MM-LM.pdf

H. Multi-stakeholder governance should be encouraged, maintained, strengthened

More than most aspects of international life, the Internet involves governments, private business, civil society and international organizations alike. None of them, individually, can assure good governance of the Internet. As a result, governance institutions should be structured to involve all three parties based on their specific role in the aspects over which governance is sought. The rhetoric of tripartite representation is not enough, however; we must pay close attention to the details of representational structures and make sure that end users and individuals are adequately empowered. For example, many of the main application software products that power use of the Internet have been developed by private corporations with input from users – sometimes well-organized. The main parties to governance of this element should be those who produce and use the technology.

VI. Policy Issues in Internet Governance: A Framework

The political context for these principles and norms is reflected in a set of policy issues that have been suggested as requiring some form of Internet governance. Almost all are connected with the end-to-end principle but should be seen in terms of the norms that we have suggested. As the long list of existing Internet governance regimes above showed, there are now many issues: spam, domain name trademark conflicts, law enforcement surveillance activities, DNS root server system management, intellectual property, trade and security. As a start, some kind of classification scheme might be more useful than promulgating a long list of isolated and transitory "issues".

A. Policy Domains

We begin by identifying a set of policy domains, that is, areas where there is a common type of policy problem. In each of these domains, there is a recognizable type of activity that is the (actual or potential) subject of governance, and the various principles and norms used by national governments and international regimes to approach that type of a problem are understood. Such a list, which looks very much like a list of communication-information policy issues in a national/domestic polity, might look something like this:

1. Content regulation and Culture;
2. Data Protection, Privacy, and Surveillance;
3. Intellectual Property Protection and Fair Use;
4. Trade and E-commerce;
5. Competition Policy;
6. Security and Survivability of Public Infrastructure;
7. Subsidies and Wealth Redistribution.

Of course, policy issues don't fit into neat boxes. How the international system handles privacy rights on the Internet, law enforcement, and intellectual property have become closely interrelated. In domain name policy, all three of those areas have been linked to resource assignment rules and procedures, as we will see in our analysis of the WHOIS issue. Likewise, in our treatment of gTLD addition policy issue, we will see how a problem in global resource assignment can raise issues in competition policy, content regulation, and IPR. But while issues are not isomorphic to categories, a framework at least clarifies the common *types* of problems that are raised by any given Internet-related policy issue.

B. Meta-Areas of International Concern

There is another way of bundling or categorizing the issues. Regardless of the specific topic of the policy issue, one can look at why and how it creates a problem for an international system based on sovereign, territorial states. Thus, a meta-classification scheme can be defined based on three broad categories: how to apply national jurisdiction to activities that are global or cross-jurisdictional in scope; how to facilitate transnational law enforcement activities; and how to manage and interoperate technical infrastructure and resources that are global in scope. Each of the different policy domains listed above can each create one or more of these types of problems:

1. Jurisdiction application

For Internet users and suppliers, a great deal of ambiguity still exists about what particular national law might be applied to them. A content regulation issue, such as the France vs. Yahoo case on Nazi memorabilia, can raise important questions about how territorial laws are applied to multinational publishing of Internet content. The same is true of an Intellectual Property/Fair Use policy issue such as KaZaa. The Hague Convention on Private Law fits here, as does an analysis of the impact of the EU data protection law on other jurisdictions.

2. Law enforcement harmonization and cooperation

Even in cases when there is no ambiguity about *which* national law or international treaty will be applied, in order to actually enforce it, law enforcement activities may need to broaden their scope via transnational cooperation regarding identification, surveillance or law enforcement interoperability agreements (extradition, dual criminality, etc.). Law enforcement cooperation can span any number of policy domains; for example the Cybercrime treaty deals with security and survivability by criminalizing certain kinds of hacking; and it affects content regulation through its approach to child pornography.

3. Global resource management

This refers to the need for coordinated sharing, and/or exclusive assignment, of transnational resources related to communication and information, such as radio spectrum, satellite orbital slots, top-level domain names, IP addresses, and telephone numbering. When such management is best handled at the global level, international agreements might be needed, although it is always an open question whether these agreements should come from governments or from specialized self-regulatory arrangements in the private sector (e.g., Ethernet address assignment or root server operation).

Thus, as a first cut for the identification of policy issues, we suggest 1) asking what type of international coordination problem it poses (one of jurisdiction, law enforcement, or global resource management); and 2) mapping the issue to a policy domain, to clarify the principles, norms and regulatory techniques that might apply.

VII. Analysis of Specific Policy Issues

We turn now to a short analysis of four distinct policy issues in Internet governance that illustrates the problems that have to be addressed by governance. After describing the issues, we raise the question whether these issues should be handled via a localized governance regime or more comprehensive arrangements. Our intention is to raise that question, not answer it definitively. We use the cases mainly as examples of the kind of decisions an Internet governance regime would have to face, and while we have opinions about the answers that may be evident from the discussion, our main purpose is really to foster discussion.

Two out of the four specific policy issues discussed will be focused on ICANN-related issues. This is not because we think that ICANN is the only or the most important aspect of Internet governance, it is simply what we know the most about.

A. ICANN and the WHOIS database

The WHOIS protocol and directory are components of the Internet's domain name system (DNS) and its Internet Protocol address assignment registry. We will confine our attention in this discussion to DNS. WHOIS contains information about registrants of domain names and their name servers. In addition to the personal identity of the registrant, WHOIS contains extensive contact information, such as street address, telephone number, email address, and fax number. This information is available to anyone on the Internet who knows the domain name. The information for an entire set of registrants can also be purchased in bulk from domain name registration companies, according to rules and prices set by ICANN.

Created back in the days when the Internet was a closed network restricted to a few researchers and United States government contractors, the WHOIS protocol's original purpose was simply to provide technologists running an experimental data communications network with the off-network contact information they needed to notify each other when breakdowns and problems occurred. But when the rise of the World Wide Web after 1993 made domain names into valuable property, WHOIS was transformed. Trademark owners concerned about cyber-squatting found it to be an indispensable means of acquiring the information they wanted to issue legal challenges (or in US legal community terminology, "serve process") to domain name registrants. The influence of the IPR lobby pushed ICANN into adopting strict requirements to make WHOIS contact data complete and accurate, and require registrars to sell that data (basically, their customer lists) in bulk to any information service or IPR holder that wants it, as long as they do not use it for "marketing purposes". In short, WHOIS was transformed into a surveillance tool for law enforcement agencies (LEAs) and IPR holders.

WHOIS gives anyone in the world access to personal contact data in an indiscriminate, anonymous fashion, without need for any due process. Although you can do as much mischief with a telephone number as with a domain name, most countries do not require telephone companies to allow anyone in the world to type in your telephone number and see your name and home address, who your service provider is, etc. Because WHOIS capabilities emerged via a historical accident, however, and LEAs and IPR holders moved quickly to institutionalize these functionalities, established privacy and due process norms were bypassed. The mainly United States-based IPR interests have used their privileged access to United States lawmakers (and in turn US lawmakers' somewhat privileged role over ICANN) to push for harsh criminal penalties to make the WHOIS data accurate. These parties do not agree with the common argument that many registrants enter inaccurate data elements precisely because the information is exposed to anyone and everyone.

This unanticipated use of the WHOIS directory has created some benefits, it can be argued. Quite apart from the systematic exploitation of the WHOIS by IPRs and LEAs, many individual Internet users have come to appreciate being able to easily look up who or what is behind an Internet email address or web site; that function in some cases facilitates greater accountability on the net. But the availability of the information also causes problems. The information in the directory can be harvested by spammers. Registrars' WHOIS servers are pounded by scripted queries of data miners. Identity theft and stalking are facilitated. If larger and larger numbers of people acquire domain names and use them to participate on the Internet, one must ask whether they deserve the same levels of privacy enjoyed by users of the telephone or owners of license plates on automobiles. More fundamentally, the indiscriminate access to personal contact data violates established international norms regarding data protection.[12]

---

[12] See the presentation of George Papapavlou, European Union, before the ICANN Rome meeting, March 3, 2004. http://icann.org/presentations/papapavlou-whois -rome-03mar04.pdf

European registrars have voiced concerns about the applicability of the European Data Protection Directive, and are wondering whether they might be legally liable if they conform to ICANN's policies. Some countries have laws that require commercial entities with web sites to publish specific contact information about themselves on the web site; e.g., the German "Impressum" laws. Although these types of laws are often cited as a factor in support of ICANN's WHOIS policies, it proves just the opposite. If national laws can meet the needs of LEAs and consumer protection authorities with regulations requiring display of data, then there is no need for the WHOIS database to do it. In short, WHOIS brings international data protection/privacy principles and norms into conflict with ICANN's contracts governing domain name registration.

ICANN is now revisiting its WHOIS policies in a systematic way. But is ICANN the right place to resolve this issue? One can argue for either answer to this question, but anyone concerned with the consistency and fairness of Internet governance cannot fail to agree that it is an argument we need to have. Despite repeated efforts by privacy advocates to raise this issue within ICANN, for three years the ICANN regime has successfully fended off any attempts to consider the privacy issues inherent in the collection and publication of personal names and contact data.

In general, ICANN is dominated by IPR interests. Representation in the GNSO, its main policy development organ for domain names, is skewed such that business and IPR interests completely control 3 of the 6 constituencies, and registrars and registries control another two. There is no real representation within the system for individual domain name registrants and only one constituency for noncommercial users' interests. Within ICANN's Governmental Advisory Committee (GAC), national data protection authorities are not well represented relative to other governmental interests, such as commerce and law enforcement. In short, the ICANN regime is likely to generate a great deal of solicitude for those who want access and use the WHOIS data; those who are being subject to surveillance are pretty much left out of the discussion.

This case was chosen to illustrate how an Internet public policy issue can be situated at the intersection of multiple policy domains, but when responsibility for the issue is under the aegis of one particular localized international regime (in this instance, ICANN) it may bias the policy making process in a certain direction. In this case, a broader, more global perspective on the issue might result in a better outcome.

B. IPR - Music Downloading

The issue of large-scale exchange of digitized music files over the Internet also illustrates some of the problems for the various regimes that intersect. The corporate recording industry, through its associations in different parts of the world (RIAA in the United States), has tried to deter file sharing of copyrighted music by seeking civil and criminal penalties for individuals that they believe have been distributing music. They have also sought to compel Internet service providers to divulge the names of their customers, and to bring the developers of sharing software (like Kazaa) into court. They have also tried to prosecute programmers who have developed sharing or code-breaking software. The basis for these actions is found in intellectual property law. Counter-arguments are based on the "fair use" principle that is derived from both human rights and copyright law, and in common carrier law that absolves mere transporters of data from responsibility for illegal activities of its users. The matter has been complicated by the fact that some of the questioned servers are off-shore or in different countries (Kazaa's home corporation is chartered in Australia and its server is now off-shore as well). If it were just a matter of transnational law enforcement, the solution might be relatively simple. There is, however, no international consensus about what "fair use" means in an Internet context, nor about the degree to which Internet service providers can be required to assist in, or held responsible for, law enforcement. Moreover, the economic effects, positive or negative, of large-scale file sharing, whether done using proprietary software (like Apple's iTunes) or open system methods, are still in dispute. Here again, one could make a case for a broader international dialogue about what norms and rules we want to apply in this case. IPR enforcement will be more reasonably bounded, and more widely accepted as legitimate, if its standards emerge through such a dialogue.

C. gTLD Addition

The economic asset that keeps the ICANN regime afloat is its policy authority over the DNS root zone file. This gives ICANN the authority to decide which new generic top-level domains (gTLDs) will be created. GTLDs are potentially valuable resources; each top-level domain creates a new name space within which second-level domain name registration services can be registered. In terms of our classification scheme, gTLD addition is an international issue because it involves a need for globally exclusive resource assignment. In terms of policy domains, adding new top-level domain names can be connected to content regulation issues (Should certain types of content be "forced" into certain domains? Should obscene domain names be permitted?), competition policy issues (Do new TLDs create competition? Should new TLDs be awarded to incumbents? Should there be a vertical separation between registrars and registries?), and IPR issues (What kind of rights to names should be created or recognized within a TLD?).

The market for gTLD registry services is highly concentrated; the United States company VeriSign controls about 85% of the market due to its ownership of the ICANN contract to operate the .com and .net domains. A company closely affiliated with the ICANN regime,

Afilias, Inc., controls about 10% of the remainder due to its contract to run the .info and .org gTLDs. The rest is controlled by Neustar and a few other tiny players.

There has been tremendous controversy over how gTLD resources are assigned. The controversies began in 1995; at that time 100% of the gTLD market was controlled by one company (VeriSign's predecessor, Network Solutions, Inc.) and the Internet community was calling for hundreds of new TLD names and operators. That budding market was squashed, however, by debates over who had the authority to add TLDs and later by the concerns of trademark holders.

In principle, the ICANN regime possesses all the right ingredients to handle this issue well. It has close relationships to the Internet technical community and domain name registrars and registries, and makes some efforts to include domain name registrants in its policy formulation processes. Unfortunately it has botched the job. It has fostered artificial scarcity and kept the industry highly concentrated. Asked to provide "technical coordination" of the root zone file, somehow ICANN set itself up as arbiter of what TLDs sounded good and which did not, which TLDs had adequate customer demand and which did not (a guessing game it proved to be horribly bad at), and what business policies should be followed by applicants. ICANN's own board chair compared the TLD selection process to the vetting process of a venture capital firm. And of course, ICANN bent over backwards to ensure that user demand for new TLDs was subordinate to trademark interests, forcing registries to institute complicated and costly "sunrise" procedures to give trademark owners special claims. Thus, instead of setting up impartial and regular procedures for TLD additions that would allow anyone to play, such as auctions, random selection or fee-based application processes, it turned TLD additions into a politicized, expensive, unpredictable and discretionary process. After nearly six years of existence, ICANN still has no defined process for adding TLDs.

It seems clear that ICANN's *ad hoc* approach to TLD resource assignment has discriminated against entrepreneurs and applicants not well connected to ICANN or the Internet Society, especially those outside the United States and Western Europe. Advocates of multilingual domain names were not given a chance, and applicants from newly industrialized countries were thwarted by deeply complex legal requirements and the need for intricate United States-based political lobbying of ICANN staff and Board members. Of course, contention for TLD resources was exacerbated by the incredibly narrow – and completely arbitrary – supply restrictions placed on name space expansion by ICANN.

In this case, a more internationalized Internet governance process might be used to pressure ICANN to adopt more reasonable and inclusive TLD addition policies and procedures, while leaving the localized regime in place.

D. Spam

Spam represents a kind of Internet use that most email recipients find abusive, and which imposes major costs on the infrastructure. The United Nations ICT Task Force's Global Forum identified spam as a highly suitable topic for Internet governance, because it is a problem that is unique to the Internet, universally reviled, and trans-jurisdictional in scope. Many nations and sub-national governmental units such as states and provinces have already passed laws against various aspects of spamming. However, the sources of spam may not reside in the territory to which the law applies, or the problem of identifying and tracing the spammers may require international cooperation. Thus, in terms of our policy issue identification framework, it is primarily a coordinated law enforcement issue. The OECD has initiated discussions of spam that seem to be following this path.

While spam is usually approached as an issue of nuisance regulation or privacy, it is also a content regulation issue. Effective control of spam must distinguish between commercial and noncommercial communication, and make sure that regulations do not interfere with the basic right to communicate.

Spam can also be approached as an infrastructure management issue. If governments and international organizations possessed the consensus and political will to attempt strong interventions in the way Internet service providers function, they could attempt to rewrite protocols and implement authentication procedures that would facilitate spam control. Approaching spam as a technical issue, however, probably would lead to a far more intrusive policy with many more unintended consequences imposed upon innocent or borderline uses and users. Moreover, there are a variety of private, market-based technical responses that may yet prove to be the best way to approach spam. The growing market for software that filters spam is one example. Better authentication protocols and technologies might also have a major impact. Some of the more radical proposals involve economic and institutional arrangements that involve charges for the receipt of unwanted emails.[13] Those theoretical solutions, however, sometimes presuppose the existence of reliable global identification and accounting mechanisms that do not yet exist. The point is that in the spam case, as in many other Internet policy issues, "governance" solutions must be assessed against the dynamically changing alternatives posed by the technology itself. The United Nations process must guard against the assumption that any problem encountered on the Internet requires a solution that involves global governance.

---

[13] T. Lorder, M. Van Alstyne anmd R. Wash, "Information Asymmetry and Thwarting Spam," University of Michigan working paper, See also R. Wetzel, "Spam-fighting Business Models – Who wins, who loses?" *Business Communications Review* 34, 4 (April 2004) 24-29.

VIII. Conclusion

This paper is intended to contribute to the dialogue surrounding the United Nations Working Group on Internet Governance. It has proposed a definition of Internet governance and enumerated existing localized Internet governance regimes, showing the complex, overlapping relationships that exist among them. The paper provides a broad framework for pursuing the global dialogue on governance: a regime-theoretic framework that first identifies principles about the Internet and then derives norms from those principles. Once principles and norms are agreed, the next step is to develop rules and procedures that can implement the norms on a global basis. That aspect of the project will be taken up in the next paper in this series. The articulation of principles and norms in this paper is meant to be a first step; undoubtedly we have overlooked relevant items and we accept the inevitability and desirability of debate and discussion of the principles and norms we have proposed.

This paper has shown that Internet governance is already taking place in a variety of localized international regimes, each driven by a distinct politics. While any sweeping global governance regime for the Internet simultaneously raises dangers of intrusive over-centralization and irrelevance, we think that the problems, loopholes, and unsavoury politics associated with certain aspects of the existing evolution of governance makes it worthwhile to take a more comprehensive look at the system as a whole.

The paper also created a framework for the identification of public policy issues associated with Internet governance, and looked in greater detail at four specific areas of policy. That survey and examination supported the argument that some kind of broader dialogue about Internet governance at the global level is needed. The concept of "governance" in this regard need not be synonymous with "more intrusive governmental regulation"; it might also mean more just and efficient policies in those areas where current regimes are failing.

REFRAMING INTERNET GOVERNANCE DISCOURSE: FIFTEEN BASELINE PROPOSITIONS[1]

William J. Drake, International Centre for Trade and Sustainable Development

The global debate on Internet governance is in a liminal state. There is a total lack of consensus about how to define Internet governance, and about which issues and institutions are and should be involved in what manner. Similarly, there is a lack of agreement as to whether there are significant problems with existing governance mechanisms, and whether there are any pressing but unresolved issues that need to be tackled through international cooperation. Adding to the complexity of the situation, the technological and market environment is changing rapidly, making this a classic example of "shooting at a moving target", and some stakeholders' interests and policy preferences are in flux. Indeed, there is fairly widespread uncertainty about how best to proceed, and perhaps even some frustration and burn out among participants whose full engagement will be needed if the policy debate is to achieve anything significant.

These are not particularly propitious conditions in which to conduct a global dialogue and engage in collective problem solving. It is therefore entirely possible that all the energy that has

---

[1] Paper based on presentations at the *Workshop on Internet Governance,* International Telecommunication Union, Geneva, February 26-27, 2004; and the *United Nations ICT Task Force Global Forum on Internet Governance,* New York City; March 25-26, 2004

gone into the debate over the past few years will yield little in terms of mutual understanding and consensus, much less widely supported reforms. But if there is to be any chance of progress, at a minimum we need an open and inclusive policy discourse that facilitates the systematic and holistic assessment of both the current architecture of Internet governance and the potential options for improvement.

This paper suggests fifteen baseline propositions that could help advance the development of such a discourse. They are generally of a definitional and process-oriented nature, and are intended to be reasonably neutral with respect to the policy choices governments and other stakeholders may make about the substantive rules that define particular governance mechanisms. The propositions are grouped into three sections. The first section addresses some misconceptions and misrepresentations that arguably have worked against the establishment of the kind of discourse advocated here. The second section lays out some descriptive assertions about the current Internet governance landscape. Finally, the third section offers some prescriptive suggestions concerning unresolved analytical and institutional challenges.

I. Misframing Governance Discourse
1. Internet governance exists and is not inherently dangerous.
From the moment it entered into our collective lexicon, "Internet governance" became a heavily contested concept.[2] Indeed, the term seems to function like a Rorschach test, in which people see their hopes and fears in an abstract shape. A first style of argumentation that has arisen in the process can be labeled "Internet governance denial". Governance denial was especially prominent in the 1990s, when American techno-libertarianism was a driving force in the collective imagination of the Internet. Governance denial faded somewhat in the less heady and more grounded post-"dot.bomb" era, but it has recently been rejuvenated by prominent interest groups in the context of the World Summit on the Information Society (WSIS) process.

In general, governance deniers maintain that the concept of Internet governance is descriptively inaccurate and programmatically dangerous. They argue that to the extent that the Internet realm exhibits any behavioral and institutional organization, it emerges spontaneously, from the bottom-up, through the loosely or un-coordinated activities of technologically empowered netizens. Moreover, some add that the Internet cannot be governed because it is

---

[2] For some interesting illustrations, see the definitions of Internet governance offered by some leading American experts at, "The Debate Over Internet Governance: A Snapshot in the Year 2000", The Berkman Center for Internet and Society, Harvard University, http://cyber.law.harvard.edu/is99/governance/governance.html.

not a single network operated by one or even a few entities. Instead, it is vast array of heterogeneous networks and information resources that simply share a common technological foundation, i.e. the Internet Protocol (IP). At most then, what order there is in cyberspace involves a unique, highly distributed and semi-anarchistic "self-governance" that specifically rejects the top-down authority relations thought to be definitive of traditional forms of governance.

In addition, deniers argue that speaking of the Internet as having "governance" in any conventional sense could be dangerous. Doing so opens the door to governments and intergovernmental organizations to "meddle where they do not belong" and apply slow moving, bureaucratic, centralized, "old paradigm", state-centric approaches that would be fundamentally out of synch with and damaging to the Internet. Denying the applicability of the term is thus viewed as a way to keep the bureaucratic wolves away from the door.

The problem with these arguments derives from their limiting assumptions about the core concept, governance. This is not surprising, since governance enjoys a somewhat ambiguous status in our collective discourse. On the one hand, it is commonly employed in a wide variety of settings, and we generally have at least an intuitive sense of what we mean and what we think others mean when doing so. But on the other hand, if one probes a bit into the relevant scholarly and policy literatures and other public pronouncements, it becomes clear that peoples' understandings of governance can vary, sometimes significantly.

This is true even of social scientists who, because of the term's centrality to their work, might especially be expected to have settled on a consensual definition. Traditionally, scholars tended to equate governance either narrowly with government, or more broadly with authority relations and authoritative decision making at all levels of social organization – from the family unit or corporation up to the global polity. While some still hold these views, recent years have seen a shift in orientation. Many scholars now see governance as being fundamentally about shared or at least collectively recognized rules and procedures, irrespective of whether these are backed by the authority of one or a set of social actors over others. Process-oriented definitions of this sort are more generalizable to diverse social settings, in that they can accommodate situations in which governance emerges spontaneously or through negotiations, rather than through the top-down imposition of authority. Moreover, they highlight the behavioral content of governance – specifying and following shared notions of what is and is not acceptable in a particular context – rather than just who does the specifying.

Viewed from this contemporary perspective, governance is a generic concept that is neutral with respect to origins and institutional forms. It can rest on government authority, or on its absence; be established from the top down or the bottom up; arise spontaneously or be negotiated, or imposed; involve formalized or informal prescriptions and proscriptions; apply to centralized or decentralized systems (both social and technological); and can be done well or poorly. These are just some of the ways in which governance systems vary; others will be discussed below. The point here is that if there are collectively recognized rules and procedures in place that shape social actors' expectations, practices, and interactions in some realm of human affairs, then we are talking about governance. These conditions undeniably apply in the Internet environment with respect to both the underlying physical and logical infrastructure and to the transactions and content conveyed thereby.

Hence, I would define Internet governance as *the collective rules, procedures, and related programs intended to shape social actors' expectations, practices, and interactions concerning Internet infrastructure and transactions and content.* Without descending too far into the depths of conceptual minutiae, a few points about this definition should be mentioned. With respect to its terms:

- *Collective* means applicable to or acknowledged to be in force by a globally significant range of actors. Particularly at the global level, the term usually also means that those actors have actually agreed to the arrangement in question, but in some cases it is possible for a dominant actor to unilaterally impose governance mechanisms on others.

- *Rules* is used here generically to refer to both freestanding individual prescriptions and proscriptions and more complex "rule systems" – international and transnational regimes – comprising interdependent principles, norms, rules, and decision-making procedures.

- *Procedures* are simply particular kinds of rules but it is useful to list them separately in a definition so as to distinguish between substantive rules and decision-making/operational procedures and highlight the latter, which are of central importance in the Internet governance context.

- *Programs* are included in the definition to capture collective, purposive activities that impact social actors' expectations, practices, and interactions but may not consist of developing and applying rules regulating their daily conduct in a given arena. For example, much of international collaboration – such as developing and administering programs concerned with producing and disseminating information, monitoring events, managing shared resources and organizational facilities, providing technical and financial assistance to developing countries, etc. – is of this nature and may impact actors' capabilities and practices with respect to Internet governance.

- Finally, the phrase, *intended to shape social actors' expectations, practices, and interactions* is included to show how the collective principles, procedures and programs are meant to work. "Intended to" sounds a little wishy-washy, but it captures the notion of actors' goal-directed behaviour while acknowledging the reality that governance arrangements often do not work well or have much impact. Limiting the term's use to effective cases quickly would become cumbersome.[3]

Two other points conclude this definitional discussion. The first concerns the binary division of Internet governance matters into those pertaining to infrastructure and those pertaining to transactions and content. These categories are just heuristic ideal types; while distinguishing between carriage and content-related policies and practices has a long pedigree in communications policy, in reality technological and regulatory change often blur the boundaries between the two levels. Nevertheless, we need some way of distinguishing between issues that foreground one or the other dimension, and a stylized binary is easier to work with in this context than more differentiated technical descriptions like the four-layered model of Internet Protocol (IP)-based networks (applications, transport, Internet, and network access layers), the seven-layered Open Systems Interconnection model (application, presentation, session, transport, network, link and physical layers), etc.

The second concerns the merits of using the term, Internet governance, to refer to collective rules, procedures and programs pertaining to both levels. In the course of the WSIS process and elsewhere, some observers have argued that any such inclusive definition inevitably confuses matters. In their view, it is important to draw a sharp distinction between "Internet governance", which pertains to the infrastructure, and "governance on" or "governance of" the Internet, which pertains to the transactions and content conveyed over it. Others have gone further by arguing that measures involving the latter should be not be considered governance at all, but rather as just "public policy". In my view, these distinctions are more confusing than clarifying.

The "governance on" or "governance of" approach involves turning normal language into jargon that then requires explanation, is ill-suited to issues that blur the boundaries between the two levels, and detracts from our ability to view the governance terrain in an integrative manner. When it is necessary to distinguish, saying "infrastructure" or "transactions and content" is clearer than saying "governance" and "governance on/of". In addition, the collective rules, procedures and programs impacting transactions and content are by no means limited to "public policy", private sector practices are also very important sources of order in

---

[3] The points above are adapted from a longer discussion in, William J. Drake, "Defining ICT Global Governance", memo for the Social Science Research Council's Research Network on IT and Governance, 2004.
http://www.ssrc.org/programs/itic/publications/knowledge_report/memos/billdrake.pdf

this space, and will probably become more so in the future. This restrictive formulation would effectively take private sector governance of transactions and content off the table as a matter of concern to the global community. And since public policy is just a particular kind of governance, the distinction is anyway artificial.

In sum, Internet governance exists. It entails a heterogeneous and highly distributed array of prescriptions and processes that reflects the Internet's core features, rather than centralized, "one size fits all" control over a singular system. Viewing these governance mechanisms in an integrative manner would allow us to evaluate the full diversity of public and private sector practices that help to shape both the infrastructure and transactions and content; to systematically assess what works well and what does not, and what lessons can be learned from one domain that may be generalizable to others; and to consider whether there are any holes, tensions, or cross-cutting issues that have not been adequately addressed. And there is no *a priori* reason why a collective inquiry of this kind would necessarily point to dangerous conclusions. To the contrary, if properly structured, it could well build a stronger global consensus that would underpin the Internet's continuing growth as an open and vibrant medium. The discussion to follow elaborates on these and related points.

2. Technical and policy issues often cannot be neatly separated.

A second style of argumentation is related to but somewhat different from the first. Of course, objections to Internet governance discourse do not stem merely from libertarian ideology or organizational self-interest. Regardless of their politics or whether they work in the private, public or non-profit sector, many people in the Internet technical community are strongly disposed to view technical and policy issues as separate realms. Engineers, computer scientists and others who spend their days intensively focused on pushing the technological envelope often see the world of public policy as unduly messy and prone to decisions that are ill-informed and even counter-productive. These perceptions are especially prevalent with respect to intergovernmental policymaking, especially when it involves rapidly changing environments like the Internet. Hence, many technical people insist that issues concerning the constitution and management of the underlying infrastructure in particular should be insulated to the greatest degree possible from potentially troublesome policy discussions. Not surprisingly, people who are of this view readily find common cause with libertarians and businesses opposed to enhanced government involvement in governance.

While their perspective is entirely understandable, it presents at least two problems from the standpoint of developing an open global discourse on Internet governance. First, technical designs and processes frequently have clear socio-economic consequences. Standards, software code, Internet identifiers, interconnection arrangements, and many other nominally "technical" issues can have substantial effects on the competitiveness of markets, the prospects for social inclusion and individual empowerment, and so on. Many governments, civil society organizations (CSOs), and even segments of the business community rightly feel these issues cannot be ignored by public policy simply because they involve significant technical dimensions.

Second, the developing countries would be particularly unwilling to accept a sharp boundary line between the technical and policy realms. Throughout the WSIS process and in other global forums, many of these countries have expressed a strong sense of exclusion from effective participation in Internet governance processes. When those who have the lion's share of the expertise and related resources and control the technology and markets say that the technical realm should not be corrupted by extraneous policy deliberations, this sounds like they are being told to accept the status quo as a *fait accompli*. They would like to at least have an opportunity to move up the learning curve and come to clear views of their own about which technical matters may have which policy dimensions at the national and global levels. As such, they would be very reluctant to accept the proposition that such issues should be declared taboo and taken off the table at the outset.

Of less practical import to the current global debate, one might add that there are long traditions of social theory arguing that technical choices are embedded in and imbued by socio-institutional contexts and relationships, including power relationships. In these views, technology design may be heavily influenced by the organizations and objectives involved and hence have inherent properties that are properly the focus of social deliberation.

3. Internet governance involves much more than ICANN and Internet identifiers.

A third style of argumentation acknowledges the existence of Internet governance, but construes the concept very narrowly. The core proposition is that Internet governance consists of the collective management of Internet identifiers – IP address space allocation, protocol identifier assignment, generic (gTLD) and country code (ccTLD) Top-Level Domain name system management–and associated root server system functions. As one analyst concludes, "Internet names and numbers are resources…Internet governance [can be] characterized as the institutionalization of those resource spaces".[4] Since its creation in 1998, the Internet Corporation for Assigned Names and Numbers (ICANN) has played the lead role on these matters via a contractual/memorandum of understanding (MOU) relationship with the US Department of Commerce, which controls the Internet's root zone file. Hence, proponents of this view equate Internet governance with ICANN and its activities.

---

[4] Milton L. Mueller, Ruling the Root: Internet Governance and the Taming of Cyberspace. Cambridge, MA: The MIT Press, 2002, p. 58. Mueller now takes a broader view of Internet governance; see his chapter with John Mathiason and Lee McKnight in this volume.

It should be noted that ICANN's leadership at times has resisted this formulation. For example, in 1999, its former Chairman of the Board Esther Dyson famously argued that, "ICANN does not 'aspire to address' any Internet governance issues; in effect, it governs the plumbing, not the people. It has a very limited mandate to administer certain (largely technical) aspects of the Internet infrastructure in general and the Domain Name System in particular"[5]. Other ICANN leaders, including current President Paul Twomey, have made similar statements. ICANN's stance presents an interesting contrast with other organizations that have been quite willing to say that they have or should have an important role in Internet governance. It could be called an example of strategically applied governance denial, in that it reflects both the styles of thought discussed previously and a calculated desire to avoid being seen as having turf-building, regulatory aspirations. It seems fair to say, though, that these protestations have not convinced many stakeholders outside the ICANN fold or helped the organization to fly below the radar of public controversy.

Over the past six years, "governance equals ICANN" has become by far the dominant discourse in this arena. Indeed, it is now largely the standard practice for governments, international agencies, businesses, CSOs, the press, and the informed general public. The baseline reasons for this development are straightforward. On the one hand, when the Internet boom was taking off, many of the current rules, procedures and programs dealing with other governance issues were not yet in place. This was especially so with respect to intergovernmental policies and programs, but private sector practices were still in a fluid state of emergence as well. On the other hand, sorting out how the functions performed by the one-man Internet Assigned Numbering Authority (IANA) could be placed on a sounder organizational footing to handle rapid global commercial growth and related naming and numbering matters were extremely pressing and important concerns. It is therefore no surprise that the insertion of ICANN into the center of this mix, and the ensuing controversies surrounding its policies and decision-making practices, led many people to see it as the embodiment of Internet governance. And indeed, by any measure, the management of identifiers remains the most important and heatedly debated issue-area on the governance agenda today.

Nevertheless, the institutionalization of this dominant discourse has come at a price. It has filled up the intellectual and discursive bandwidth to such an extent that other rule systems by default get cognitively categorized as being something other than Internet governance. And it has fed into and reinforced the propensity of many stakeholders to focus their energies

---

[5] Esther Dyson, letter to Ralph Nadar and Jamie Love, June 15, 1999, at http://www.interesting-people.org/archives/interesting-people/199906/msg00028.html.

intensively on ICANN to the exclusion of other issues. Although they are also quite important and will become much more so in the future, processes and bodies dealing with Internet rules on intellectual property, trade, standardization, frequency spectrum, information and network security, privacy, jurisdiction, electronic contracting and authentification, development and so on typically attract far less press attention, "buzz" in Internet discussion forums, and engagement from CSOs. Conversely, also largely overlooked in governance discussions have been some important issues not yet subject to collective rules and programs, such as spam, competition policy, consumer protection, cultural and linguistic diversity, and the interconnection agreements linking the global North and South.

Ignored in parallel has been the aggregation of extant and emerging rule systems into a distributed architecture that can be productively analyzed as a whole. In the past this was perhaps a rather academic concern, and merely a source of minor frustration for those of us who have long argued for a broader view of governance in scholarly meetings and related settings. But now it is of much wider and more practical concern. Over the course of the lengthy WSIS preparatory process, many governments – and especially those from the developing world – often raised issues such as those mentioned above and suggested not only that perhaps these too should be viewed as Internet governance, but also that what is needed is a comprehensive review and assessment of governance issues and mechanisms. Similar views were expressed at the International Telecommunication Union's (ITU) February 2004 Workshop on Internet Governance, and at the United Nations ICT Task Force's March 2004 Global Forum on Internet Governance.

The desire for an integrative view also informed the Plan of Action agreed at the December 2003 WSIS in Geneva. The plan calls on the Secretary-General of the United Nations to set up a working group on Internet governance to, *inter alia*:

i)   develop a working definition of Internet governance;

ii) identify the public policy issues that are relevant to Internet governance;

iii) develop a common understanding of the respective roles and responsibilities of governments, existing intergovernmental and international organisations and other forums as well as the private sector and civil society from both developing and developed countries;

iv) prepare a report on the results of this activity to be presented for consideration and appropriate action for the second phase of WSIS in Tunis in 2005.[6]

---

[6] World Summit on the Information Society, "Plan of Action", WSIS-03/GENEVA/DOC/5-E, December 12, 2003, http://www.itu.int/wsis/documents/doc_single-en-1160.asp

In short, there now seems to be a growing recognition in some circles of the need for a more inclusive definition and approach. Even the United States government has made public statements along these lines. But the dominance of the "governance means ICANN" discourse up to now means that there is little on which to build and no agreement as to precisely what this may entail. The pending United Nations Working Group on Internet Governance (WGIG) and stakeholders willing to explore a broader view will therefore have to start from scratch on an intellectual and discursive terrain that is heavily pre-configured by the entrenched ICANN-centric view and the other misconceptions discussed in this section. Building international consensus around a new and rather different vision is possible, but it will require, as a first step, that a very careful and systematic case for doing so be made.

4. The United Nations is not scheming to control the Internet.

A final and more problematic style of argumentation holds that the core political dynamic at work in the emerging Internet governance debate is a power grab by United Nations bureaucrats and their supporters in the developing world. This discourse first began to take root when the ITU secretariat moved to carve out a leading role for the organization in the pending transition to an internationalized system for domain name management. In 1996, the ITU participated in the creation of the International Ad Hoc Committee which prepared a controversial Generic Top-Level Domain Memorandum of Understanding (gTLD-MOU) declaring name space a global public resource to be organized under a shared monopoly registry. ITU and the Internet Society then organized a signing ceremony in Geneva in early 1997, prompting United States Secretary of State Madeline Albright to fire off a cable criticizing the ITU for moving "without authorization of member governments" to hold "a global meeting involving an unauthorized expenditure of resources and concluding with the signing of a quote international agreement unquote"[7].

While the gTLD-MOU effort fizzled and was later superceded by the creation of ICANN and its contractual relationship with the US government, developing country governments and the ITU secretariat continued to push for an important ITU role in the management of Internet identifiers. Hence, the ITU Plenipotentiary Conferences of 1998 and 2002 adopted Resolutions calling on the Secretary-General to play an important role in international discussions and initiatives pertaining to Internet names and numbers. These and related ITU activities generated a good deal of controversy in Internet forums and on the conference circuit, with the ITU being denounced as an "old paradigm" cartel of government monopolists that would somehow over-regulate and ruin the Internet.

---

[7] Madeline Albright, "Domain Name MOU Request", April 23, 1997, US State Department cable at, http://www.gtld-mou.org/gtld-discuss/mail-archive/04644.html .

The 2003 WSIS preparatory process watered the roots of this discourse. In both the plenary sessions and intergovernmental Internet Governance Working Group sessions held during the Preparatory Committee meetings, a coalition of developing country governments sharply criticized ICANN and argued that the ITU should either take over its functions or otherwise be centrally involved in managing names and numbers. A sharp divergence resulted between these countries and the industrialized countries, business community, and the civil society coalition on the role of intergovernmental organizations in Internet governance. This split became the central source of conflict in the WSIS process, required intensive 12th hour negotiations in order to forge a compromise and save the December 2003 summit, and led to the abovementioned call for a WGIG that is to map out the issues and institutions involved in governance as an input into the second phase of WSIS that will extend to the November 2005 summit in Tunisia.

With the WSIS Summit of December 2003 and the United Nations ICT Task Force's Global Forum of March 2004, the on-line rhetoric about a possible "United Nations takeover" of the Internet sprang into full blossom. Reporting and opinion pieces by American libertarians and conservatives led the way, but even mainstream, professional media outlets picked up the issue framing of a prospective "United Nations takeover"[8]. Four themes in particular recur in this discourse. First, today's Internet governance discussion is driven by authoritarian governments seeking to wrest control over the Internet from democratic governments, and the WSIS and related dialogues are designed to advance that agenda and facilitate "Third World rants at the successful" countries.[9] Second, strategically joining in this quest are United Nations institutions, which are pursuing their own organizational turf objectives and coordinating to that end.

---

[8] A representative press example is, Jennifer L. Schenker, "UN Takeover of Internet? Some are 'Not Amused'", International Herald Tribune, December 8, 2003, http://www.iht.com/articles/120570.html. Even some serious scholars have bought into this sort framing, and taken it further: "At the first World Summit on the Information Society (WSIS) meeting, held in Geneva in December 2003, some countries called for the creation of an international government for the Internet....WSIS suggested the creation of a global authority by governments. Most of the governments that participated in the creation of a global operator might be expected to defer to it". David R. Johnson, Susan. P. Crawford, and John G. Paltry, Jr., "The Accountable Net: Peer Production of Internet Governance". The Berkman Center for Internet & Society, Harvard University, April 2004, pp. 4 & 18. http://papers.ssrn.com/sol3/papers.cfm?abstract_id=529022. While some developing countries argued that ITU should take over ICANN's naming and numbering functions, this falls far short of advocating an "international government for the Internet" or a "global operator".

[9] "UN Schemes to Take Over the Internet", *NewsMax.com,* December 9, 2003, http://www.newsmax.com/archives/articles/2003/12/9/121014.shtml . See also, Kelley Beaucar Vlahos, "Critics Balk at Efforts to Place Internet in Global Grip", *FOX News.com,* December 1, 2003, http://www.foxnews.com/story/0,2933,104413,00.html .

Hence, the Global Forum was organized by "a task force that intends to increase the United Nations' involvement with running the Internet", and "the United Nations has already made moves to position one of its agencies, the International Telecommunication Union (ITU), as a candidate for an ICANN takeover"[10].

Third, United Nations control would subject the Internet to the whims of wildly inefficient and corrupt bureaucracies and hostile, anti-American decision making, for instance in the United Nations General Assembly: "The United Nations is home to the world's most bloated bureaucracy, employing more than 56,000 people at salaries roughly twice what they would be paid in the private sector. What's more, the General Assembly, which had 191 members as of December 2002, has grown estranged from the United States in recent years and is hardly a place for enlightened political discourse. The United Nations makes ICANN look like a paragon of political perfection"[11]. And fourth, all this would fundamentally change the Internet, for the worse. "Although the United Nations process is still in its early stages, the result could dramatically reshape the way the Internet is run and put an end to some of the informal, collaborative processes that exist today".[12]

If all this were not scary enough, some observers go further and allege that more insidious and far-reaching plots are in the works. For example, noting United Nations Secretary-General Kofi Annan's statement to the Global Forum that "the medium must be made accessible and responsive to the needs of all the world's people", a leading conservative Internet helpfully explains:

> In United Nations speak, that means America better ready itself, once again, to relinquish a bit more of its free-market freedom and accompanying hard-earned dollars to support the policies and expenses of a socialist system that demands equality for all at whatever cost…. This is how the plot for global control will unfold. In its Plan of Action, the United Nations lists ten goals, most aimed at linking various

---

[10] Declan McCullagh, "U.N. Finds Net Governance Tempting", *CNET News.com*, March 25, 2004, http://news.com.com/U.N.+finds+Net+governance+tempting/2100-1028_3-5179122.html .

[11] Declan McCullagh, "Should the United Nations Run the Internet?" *CNET News.com*, March 30, 2004, http://news.com.com/Should+the+United+Nations+run+the+Internet%3F/2010-1028_3-5181327.html .

[12] Declan McCullagh, "United Nations Ponders Net's Future," *CNET News.com*, March 26, 2004, http://news.com.com/2100-1028-5179694.html . For similar contemplations, see also, "WSIS to Consider Internet Governance Under U.N.", *Slashdot*, December 5, 2003, http://slashdot.org/article.pl?sid=03/12/05/1447255; Jennifer Rast, "The U.N. Plan to Take Over the Internet", *ContenderMinistries.org,* January 10, 2004, http://www.contenderministries.org/UN/wsis.php; and, "UN to Take over the Internet?," *Geek.com*, December 2, 2003, http://www.geek.com/news/geeknews/2003Dec/gee20031202022877.htm

Internet users and records to one, single, master global system. Planned connections include "villages, universities, colleges, secondary schools and primary schools, scientific and research centers, public libraries, cultural centers, museums, post offices and archives, health centers and hospitals (and) all local and central government departments. Also planned is adapting "all primary and secondary school curricula to meet the challenges of the Information Society", ensuring world-wide access to television and radio and encouraging "conditions in order to facilitate the presence and use of all world languages on the Internet". This is United Nations language; in simpler terms, the principles and actions outline the goals and means for taking charge of the Internet at the international level. By their own statements, United Nations members want access to medical records. They want to know what's being taught in the schools, from elementary grades through college. They want to keep abreast of all scientific advancements. They want to know what's being mailed, what's being exhibited in museums and what's being discussed in town hall meetings. They plan to achieve these objectives by 2015. Once realized, our free-market system will surely crumble. Not only does the United Nations call for sharing technology with disadvantaged and possibly even hostile states, but this body will also be in position to impose whatever access and usage fees deemed necessary for the good of all, regulate business, and oversee all content placed on the Internet for public access.[13]

The United Nations takeover theme provides attention-grabbing headlines, raises the personal profiles its proponents, and cleverly plays on the fears of certain constituencies to promote ideological and political objectives. But while one has to admire the creativity and entrepreneurship involved, none of it makes any sense. The global South's varying concerns about Internet governance cannot be explained by the domestic political systems of certain countries; the WSIS process and other relevant global dialogues and activities reflect a wide variety of interests and considerations, not just the purported agendas of particular countries; international organizations are not autonomous entities whose secretariats can push through significant self-interested objectives entirely independent of or in opposition to powerful member states; the ITU is a rather independent specialized agency, and its activities with respect to naming and numbering do not stem from or even involve the United Nations' central organs and leadership; nobody is seriously contemplating any key role for those central United Nations organs, such as the General Assembly; a role for the ITU or some other intergovernmental body in naming and numbering would not constitute "control over" either the Internet or Internet governance, broadly defined; there is no logical basis for making the leap from the abstract notion of some sort of intergovernmental involvement in some undefined dimensions of governance to predictions of the Internet's radical reorganization and decline; and the WSIS targets for the expansion of global infrastructure and access are

---

[13] Cheryl Chumley, "UN Plan for Internet Control Tiptoes Forward", *FreeRepublic.com*, April 21, 2004, http://www.freerepublic.com/focus/f-news/1124384/posts .

normative and unlikely to be pursued through a singular or centralized process of collaboration, much less through the imposition of an all-powerful socialist world government.

It might be tempting to simply dismiss all this as fringe rumblings of no significance for the policy process. That would be a mistake; as with the other styles of argumentation discussed above, the United Nations takeover theme may resonate to varying degrees with a variety of constituencies in ways that constrain the political space for global dialogue and initiatives. In particular, it may reinforce attitudes amongst certain segments of the US government and business community that are already predisposed to suspicion of intergovernmental approaches generally and the ITU in particular. For example, impressionable young staffers on Capitol Hill and conservative activists could encourage the US Congress to press the Executive Branch in directions that even further limit the prospect of the United States agreeing to any changes involving an enhanced role for intergovernmentalism. Other parties to the process may be well advised to take that prospect into consideration going forward.

II. Descriptive Reframing
5. Internet governance involves a heterogeneous array of formalized public and private sector rules.
The distributed architecture of Internet governance clearly rests on at least three main pillars. The first consists of national policies and laws of powerful countries that in effect set broadly applied rules for the global community. The most obvious examples here concern the US government's control of the root zone file and its designation of ICANN to perform key functions regarding Internet identifiers. But one could also argue that the extraterritorial application of legislative and court decisions – e.g. on content-related issues like intellectual property and acceptable speech – also should be viewed as examples of global Internet governance. Obviously, taking this route would imply that the term covers a large and unwieldy set of decisions that could be difficult to map or address coherently in a world-wide policy dialogue.

The second consists of formalized rules, procedures and related programs that are collaboratively defined by the private sector, including both for profit and not for profit entities. Some business representatives appear to be uncomfortable with the notion that anything the private sector does can properly be labeled Internet governance, presumably in part because they worry that this opens the door to unwanted scrutiny and uncontrollable regulatory impulses. But if we view the question from a conceptual rather than strategic standpoint, it is not obvious what the argument against it would be in cases where industry groups set broadly applicable rules that shape the Internet and its use. This is especially so when those rules not only govern the interactions of the parties involved, but also directly impact third parties.

The third consists of negotiated intergovernmental regimes and related programs. Some of these have been designed specifically with the Internet in mind, while others are older agreements on information and communication technology (ICT) that are now expanding to apply to the Internet as well. Thus far, many of these regimes' impact on the Internet often has been limited or indirect. However, there are reasons to believe that they will have notably greater influence in the years ahead.

Below is a listing of some of more obvious examples of the second and third types of governance mechanisms. The list is by no means complete and is by definition highly schematic; the workings of these and other mechanisms will be analyzed in a separate project. And there is significant variation across cases in the extent to which they currently or potentially affect the Internet. The point here is simply to illustrate the diversity of regimes and organizations that could merit consideration in a systematic mapping of the Internet governance terrain.

INFRASTRUCTURE

Internet Addressing
Governance Mechanisms: Internet addressing regime based on US law, contracts
Organizational Settings: ICANN, APNIC, ARIN, CENTR, LACNIC, RIPE-NCC, VeriSign, global and country-code registrars, etc.

Technical Standardization
Governance Mechanisms: diverse rules and procedures
Organizational Settings: ITU, ETSI, Global Standards Coordination, IETF, IAB, W3C, MINC, ENUM Forum, XML Forum, EPCGlobal, ISO, ATIS, TTC Committee, APT, IEEE, CableLabs, TIA, CompTIA, ITAA, GSM Forum, WiMAX Forum, countless others

Network Security
Governance Mechanisms: diverse law enforcement and technical response agreements; guidelines, recommendations, standards
Organizational Settings: ILETS, Interpol, US Department of Homeland Security, COE, G-8, Wassenaar Arrangement, EU, ETSI, CERT/CC and the Internet Security Alliance, Microsoft, ITU, OECD, ENISA, APEC, ICANN, ISSA, CIS, ISC2, FIRST, IETF, W3C, IEEE, NATIA, etc.

International Telecommunications Policy/Regulation
Governance Mechanisms: treaty-based international telecommunications regime
Organizational Settings: ITU, OECD, CEPT, EU, APT, APEC, CITEL, ATU, ETNO, etc.

International Radio Spectrum Management
Governance Mechanisms: treaty-based international radio regime
Organizational Settings: ITU

Development
Governance Mechanisms: voluntary programs
Organizational Settings: World Bank, ITU, IADB, ADB, AFDB, ASEAN, UNDP, UNESCO, UNCTAD, Global E-Policy Resource Network, DOT Force, Global Internet Policy Initiative, etc.

TRANSACTIONS AND CONTENT

Intellectual Property
Governance Mechanisms: treaty-based international intellectual property regime, model laws
Organizational Settings: WIPO, WTO, US and EU laws, other regional bodies, INTA, MPAA, and other industry associations

Networked International Trade
Governance Mechanisms: treaty-based international trade in services regime; treaty-based international trade in goods regime
Organizational Settings: WTO, WCO, EU, NAFTA, OECD, UNCTAD

Electronic Commerce, Contracting, Authentication
Governance Mechanisms: model contracts, guidelines, programs
Organizational Settings: UNCITRAL, OECD, OASIS, DISA, EPCGlobal, UN/CEFACT, EDIFICE, ITU, UNCTAD, ICC, GBDe

"Information Security" and Surveillance
Governance Mechanisms: cybercrime treaty, law enforcement coordination, guidelines and recommendations
Organizational Settings: ILETS, NATIA, Interpol, ECHELON, US Department of Homeland Security, COE, OECD, G-8, EU, United Nations General Assembly, ENISA, APEC, TECF

Content & Information Flow
Governance Mechanisms: treaties, declarations, national/regional laws
Organizational Settings: ITU, OECD, United Nations General Assembly, UNESCO, courts, ICRA, Internet Quality Agency, etc.

Privacy Protection
Governance Mechanisms: convention, guidelines and recommendations, self-regulation
Organizational Settings: courts, COE, OECD, EU; APEC, TRUSTe, ICC, GBDe

Fraud and Consumer Protection
Governance Mechanisms: directives, guidelines, recommendations
Organizational Settings: OECD, EU, ICPEN, United Nations, WTO, APEC, ICC, GBDe

<u>Spam</u>
Governance Mechanisms: bilateral and plurilateral MOUs
Organizational Settings: national courts and agencies, EU, OECD, ICPEN, ASTA, ITU, IETF

<u>Jurisdiction and Choice of Law</u>
Governance Mechanisms: national/regional laws, draft treaty
Organizational Settings: courts, Hague Conference on International Private Law

<u>Taxation</u>
Governance Mechanisms: national/regional laws, possible plurilateral action
Organizational Settings: courts; EU, OECD, WTO

<u>Dispute Resolution</u>
Governance Mechanisms: national/regional/international laws, diverse binding and voluntary rules
Organizational Settings: courts, WIPO/UDRP, ICPEN, private sector alternative dispute resolution systems

6. The principal definitional ambiguities concern informal rules and the character of private sector governance.

A number of participants in the WSIS-induced debate on Internet governance have suggested that the main conceptual disagreement concerns the choice between narrow and broad definitions, i.e. between Internet governance viewed as just ICANN functions or as the wider range of relevant rule systems. My view is that the latter approach is the only logical option, and that this binary framing overlooks two greater sources of ambiguity that need to be overcome.

The first pertains to rule systems that are not negotiated or established in formal instruments. Should we consider customs or general norms to be governance mechanisms, even if they emerge spontaneously through uncoordinated action? There are many scholars in fields like law and political science that would argue in the affirmative. However, there also are many others who reply that custom and intersubjective understandings are very brittle and lack the weight and impact of formalized rules. One might add that from an empirical standpoint, it is not immediately obvious which customs are particularly consequential for the social organization of the Internet. As such, this is a matter that merits focused analysis.

Some theorists are even more expansive, and characterize as rules-generating patterns of behavior that are often rather diverse. For example, David Johnson and David Post have argued that, "de facto rules may emerge as a result of the complex interplay of individual decisions by domain name and IP address registries (regarding what conditions to impose on possession of an online address), by sysops (regarding what local rules to adopt, what filters to install, what users to allow to sign on, and with which other systems to connect) and by users (regarding which personal filters to install and which systems to patronize)"[14]. Recent scholarship on the "accountable Internet" takes the latter proposition about users as co-producers of governance further still. David Johnson, Susan Crawford, and John Paltry maintain that, "[t]he aggregation of numerous individual decisions about who to trust and who to avoid will create a diverse set of rules that most accurately and fairly serves the interests of those who use the online world. In other words, we can use 'peer production of governance' to address the collective action problems that arise in the online context"[15]. One suspects that millions of individual choices about email filtering, web form disclosures, and so on are too heterogeneous and lacking in prescriptive and proscriptive character to constitute shared rule systems, and the scope of governance problems to which this could anyway be responsive is rather limited. Nevertheless, these are important matters to consider if we are to come to some measure of consensus about the nature of Internet governance.

The second ambiguity concerns the production and enforcement of collective rules by the private sector. When companies work together in industry forums to establish shared rules that shape the Internet, this is clearly governance. But what about situations – parallel to the unilateral extension of national laws and policies, mentioned above – where concentrated market structures allow powerful firms to in effect set generally applied rules via their business strategies, rather than through collaborative decision making? If Microsoft's "code is law" and significantly shapes the security of networked systems, the privacy of users, the conduct of e-commerce, and much more, should this be viewed as a form of governance?[16] What about the decisions of Tier 1 backbone providers regarding operating agreements and interconnection prices, or other firms that have enough market power to set terms and conditions that others must follow? One can point to a number of firms whose decisions in the normal course of doing business have more rule-like impact on the Internet than much of what happens in ICANN, ITU, WTO, IETF, etc.

This is obviously a potentially contentious issue. Presumably, many private sector representatives would reject it outright as fuzzy headed and even dangerous. And certainly conceptual objections could be raised; it would be difficult to define principled criteria for

---

[14] David R. Johnson and David G. Post, "And How Shall the Net Be Governed? A Meditation on the Relative Virtues of Decentralized, Emergent Law", in, Brian Kahin and James Keller, eds., *Coordinating the Internet*. Cambridge: MIT Press, 1997, pp. 67-68. http://www.cli.org/emdraft.html

[15] David R. Johnson, Susan. P. Crawford, and John G. Paltry, Jr., "The Accountable Net", April 2004, p. 9.

[16] The phrase is from, Lawrence Lessig, *Code and Other Laws of Cyberspace*. New York: Basic Books, 1999.

distinguishing which types of business decisions by whom should be viewed as constituting governance, and the result could be a slippery slope toward a definition that is so broad that it becomes meaningless. Nevertheless, insofar as some analysts and stakeholders do seem inclined toward this line of thinking, one could argue that issues should not be taken off the table by fiat if there is to be an open and inclusive global dialogue. At a minimum, it seems reasonable to suggest that there is ambiguity here worth eliminating.

7. The boundary lines between Internet governance and the wider universe of ICT global governance will blur over time.

The Internet's growing technological and economic centrality will increasingly encourage governments to embed it in frameworks of public authority. As that process unfolds, the fairly limited or indirectly relevant intergovernmental regime rules that helped nurture both governance denial and the ICANN-centric alternative will give way to a more densely populated policy space. Mechanisms designed specifically for the Internet increasingly will be complemented by regimes of broader application that simply cannot pretend it is outside the scope of their subject matter. Defining exactly how that is to be done will be conceptually and politically difficult, as has already been demonstrated by the WTO's negotiations concerning the classification and treatment of both infrastructure access services and network-based transactions.[17]

The emerging national-level policy debates concerning Voice Over IP, IP-enabled services, broadband and convergence may be a harbinger of things to come. For example, in the United States, Canada, and the European Union, governments are launching intriguingly comparable efforts to think through the preservation of traditional regulatory objectives in an IP-based environment.[18] Issues like national security and law enforcement requirements, public safety, disability access, services reliability and reporting obligations, restoration after failures, call prioritization in emergencies, privacy and consumer protection, universal service obligations, service categorization, inter-carrier compensation, competition and more are coming under scrutiny, and over time more governments will be compelled to undertake similar assessments. Public policy issues will also arise with respect to related technologies, such as integrated Next Generation Networks, the ENUM system for mapping telephone numbers and Internet

---

[17] For a discussion, see, William J. Drake and Kalypso Nicolaïdis, "Global Electronic Commerce and the General Agreement on Trade in Services: The 'Millennium Round' and Beyond". In, Pierre Sauve and Robert M. Stern, eds., GATS 2000: New Directions in Services Trade Liberalization. Washington D.C.: The Brookings Institution Press, 2000, pp. 399-437.
http://www.ceip.org/files/projects/irwp/pdf/GEC_and_GATS.pdf

[18] For a good overview of some of the issues, see, Federal Communications Commissions, "In the Matter of IP-Enabled Services: Notice of Proposed Rulemaking", WC Docket No. 04-36, March 10, 2004.

domains, the Object Name System for identifying networked physical objects using the Electronic Product Code, and so on.

As technological convergence gathers momentum and becomes increasingly central to cross-border networking and transactions, governments will have to confront the implications for global governance arrangements. In some cases new frameworks may be needed, in others existing multilateral frameworks may require some adjustment. Either way, notions of the Internet as a pristine wilderness relatively free of intergovernmental authority will probably become even more antiquated. The challenge then will be to ensure that such authority is not exercised in an unduly inhibiting manner.

8. Internet governance mechanisms vary widely in their institutional attributes.

Governance mechanisms are diverse not only in their topical focus and substantive rules, but also in their institutional attributes. This variance is evident along a number a dimensions, three of which are particularly important.

First, Internet governance mechanisms vary by institutional form. This includes, *inter alia:*

Organizational setting: Some are linked to a formal organization, be it a particular business or national government, or an inter-organizational body that has a permanent staff and serves as a negotiation forum and/or operator of joint programs and facilities. Others are free standing policy agreements, contracts, and perhaps general norms that are not tethered to a single legal person.

Decision making procedures: In formalized settings, some utilize voting, whether weighted or equal, while others are based on consensus or hierarchical authority. Also variable are the rules on recognition and representation of participants in inter-organizational arrangements.

Agreement type: Some are intergovernmental frameworks in the form of treaties, recommendations, guidelines, declarations, MOUs, or even customs. Others may be private sector frameworks in the form of contracts, MOUs, recommendations, codes of conduct, or customs. Some are formalized as in texts, while others involve informal understandings reached through dialogue.

Scope: Some cover multiple issues of varying degrees of interdependence, while others are focused on one or a few issues.

Strength: Some are binding on their members, while others are voluntary. Some mechanisms may entail combination of these different approaches.

Distributional bias: Some allocate benefits – whether *de facto* or *de jure* – widely across participants, other do so more narrowly. Some allocate benefits via administrative authority to achieve desired outcomes, others set rules for the market-based determination of outcomes.

Monitoring and compliance: Some governance systems include centralized or decentralized mechanisms to monitor whether the parties comply, while others do not. In parallel, some have or set procedures to sanction noncompliance, others do not.

Second, Internet governance mechanisms vary by function. Here it is useful to distinguish between generic functions that are broadly common to rule systems or regimes and specific substantive functions. Regarding the former, governance mechanisms varyingly constrain actors from undertaking certain courses of action they might otherwise choose; empower actors to undertake other courses of action with community assent; reduce the transaction cost of forming agreements; reduce information costs related to acquisition, creation and distribution; establish liability rules; and generally, facilitate individual and collective learning, as well as organizational and national policy formulation. Regarding the latter, governance mechanisms may be designed or emerge *inter alia* to render technologies interconnected and interoperable; allocate and manage resources that are scarce, whether naturally or by design; establish economic terms and conditions for passing traffic from one system to the next; facilitate the commercial exchange of content; set rules on the substantive types of information acceptable for communication and exchange; promote the development of particular systems, organizations/countries and so on.

Third, Internet governance mechanisms vary by the domain of participants. One axis of variation concerns the character of the actors involved, i.e. (inter)governmental, private sector, or multistakeholder. In principle, at least three multistakeholder configurations are possible: actors may serve on teams led by others that control the process (e.g. business or CSO representatives serving on national delegations to intergovernmental meetings); directly participate and self-represent in processes controlled by others; or participate on equal footing with their counterparts. The other axis of variation concerns the number of players, i.e. unilateral, bilateral, plurilateral, regional, or broadly multilateral.[19]

---

[19] From a strict definitional standpoint, any process that involves more than two actors can be called multilateral. However, it has become common practice in the international organization environment to use the term "multilateral" to refer to broadly inclusive or even universal cooperation, "regional" to refer to regionally proximate countries, and "plurilateral" to refer to non-regional smaller-n groupings like the OECD. Of course, these terms are usually associated with intergovernmental rather than private sector cooperation.

Although necessarily a bit abstract, this brief discussion has descriptive and prescriptive implications. In WSIS and related forums there has been much talk about the need for a comprehensive listing of governance instruments, issues, and initiatives. While this is a necessary first step, simply listing these, as I did in discussing point 5, does not get us very far. What would be more useful is an information rich taxonomy that describes each governance mechanism in an internally differentiated manner according to these or other institutional attributes. In turn, this would facilitate comparative and holistic analyses of the governance architecture and, potentially, prescriptive assessments as well. I will develop these points a bit below.

III. Prescriptive Reframing

9. *Efficiency concerns suggest that form should follow function to the extent possible.*

In general terms, it is desirable to optimize institutional forms so that they match the issues to be managed. This overarching concern applies to both the substantive rules and institutional procedures embodied in governance mechanisms. If they are not designed to maximize efficiency and flexibility, they may not be functionally effective or politically sustainable. Over time, key players could become frustrated and redirect their energies to other arrangements, thereby leading to a downward spiral in performance and relevance. The result could be a governance landscape populated by legacy policy frameworks and organizations that remain in place due to inertia and residual support from other players, but that have little real significance in their nominal domain of activity. This is not an abstract concern; the history of global ICT policy offers a number of concrete examples of institutional arrangements that failed to adapt to changing circumstances in their operational environments, declined in effectiveness, and hence lost the political support necessary to remain vital.[20] In such cases, the less powerful stakeholders may end up the worst off, since their more powerful counterparts may have the means to pursue alternatives more suited to their interests.

With respect to the substance of rule systems, efficiency means devising frameworks that do not inhibit technological change, unduly constrain the development of markets, or make it difficult for governments and other stakeholders to reach agreements. With respect to their institutional forms and attributes, the meaning may be less immediately obvious and hence merits brief elaboration. In the previous section, we noted that global governance mechanisms,

---

[20] For a key example of this dynamic at work, see, William J. Drake, "The Rise and Decline of the International Telecommunications Regime", in, Christopher T. Marsden, ed., *Regulating the Global Information Society*. London: Routledge, 2000, pp. 124-177.
http://www.ccip.org/files/projects/irwp/pdf/draketelecom.pdf

including those pertaining to the Internet, vary along a number of dimensions, such as organizational setting, decision making procedures, scope and domain, and so on. These present us with a menu of design parameters from which to choose when evaluating current and potential governance mechanisms in terms of their fit with issues to be managed.

For example, some types of functional issues may call for a measure of institutional centralization, e.g. in intergovernmental or multistakeholder organizations. This might apply to what game theorists call, "collaboration problems", in which the parties have strong incentives to cheat on their commitments to play by the rules. In such cases, a shared formal organization could serve as a valuable forum for iterative consultation and problem solving, facilitate the monitoring of compliance and implementation, and provide robust mechanisms for dispute resolution and/or sanctioning. Similarly, such an organization may be optimal in situations involving especially high information and transaction costs, the allocation of scarce resources, or the operation of joint global facilities and substantial, ongoing programs.

In contrast, other types of functional issues may call for institutional decentralization, e.g. via networked cooperation or even independent rule-governed action. This might apply to "coordination problems", in which the parties do not have strong incentives to cheat on their commitments. In such cases, there may be correspondingly less need for ongoing consultation, or for strong monitoring and dispute resolution mechanisms. Decentralized approaches are also optimal for issues that can be addressed through localized action involving only baseline harmonization or mutual recognition; or for cases where an effective and broadly distributed community of practice is well established.

Other design parameters present similar choices. Some problems might be most efficiently tackled on a focused, single-issue basis, while others might be better handled by nesting them in a larger nexus involving substantive and tactical linkages across issues. Sometimes it may be most efficient to involve a wide range of actors so that rules are broadly applied and the value to each participant of agreements is increased. Other times it might be better to limit cooperation (at least initially) to those most directly effected or like minded, so as to increase the prospects of agreement and reduce the tensions associated with free riding. Sometimes strong and binding rules are optimal, and sometimes flexible voluntary agreements are preferable.

In short, when it comes to Internet governance, one size does not fit all circumstances. And adding to the complexity is the fact that optimal design choices cannot be mechanistically derived from these institutional attributes and issue characteristics due to contextual and related factors. While they can provide a basis for a first cut evaluation, further analysis is required that takes into account the specificities of difference governance challenges. But despite this caveat, it remains fair to say that Internet governance discourse and policy would be enriched by greater attention to the potential implications of alternative institutional configurations.

10. Equity concerns are equally important, and will become more so as the Internet becomes increasingly pervasive and thus affects a wider range of social interests.

While the match between form and function is a key design consideration, it cannot be the only one. Technology should serve society, rather than the other way around, and in some cases optimizing social institutions to promote efficiency alone could have unanticipated adverse consequences for other legitimate social objectives. Moreover, institutions designed in this manner may prove politically problematic as the range and diversity of relevant interests expands. What to first-movers seemed like a simple matter of efficiency may appear to latecomers to be an exclusionary *fait accompli* that they cannot support. And anyway, technology often does not point to singularly optimal institutional arrangements; there could be a number of viable ways to configure governance rules and procedures. The choice between efficiency and equity considerations is hence not a matter of black and white, but rather shades of gray along a continuum. The challenge is to properly calibrate that continuum and choose points that represent the best balance between competing objectives in the various domains of Internet governance.

In assessing or designing governance mechanisms, four equity concerns in particular merit attention. First, decision-making about rules of general applicability must be fully transparent. Complete and accurate information on all stages of governance processes should be freely available via the Internet and other means so that diverse stakeholders around the world can effectively evaluate the rules and procedures they are being asked to accept. The topics to be considered and the arguments for and against alternative solutions should be spelled out. Inputs should be solicited and made available to all, and the mechanics of subsequent decision-making should be explained. Whenever possible, there also should be mechanisms through which stakeholders can express their views in response to and, as appropriate, challenge the decisions taken.

A number of national telecommunications regulatory authorities follow procedures such as these, but the picture is more mixed with respect to global Internet governance. For example, the relevant intergovernmental organizations are generally quite selective about which documents are made freely available and to whom, and often those documents do not capture how decisions are actually reached. Some private sector bodies like ICANN, the regional registries, and the standards organizations are quite open, but others are not. Sometimes there is, or is alleged to be, a gap between the levels of formal openness "on paper" and actual openness in practice. In general then, transparency is an issue ripe for systematic analysis and potential reform.

Second, closely linked to transparency is the notion of democratic accountability. Admittedly, accountability is a somewhat problematic concept at the global level. As two leading international relations scholars have observed, "international institutions lack the essential feature that makes democracy possible and that, in democracies, facilitates accountability: an acknowledged public operating within a political community in which there is general consensus on what makes public decisions legitimate"[21]. Of course, governments are nominally accountable to their national citizens and businesses to their shareholders, but it seems fair to say that reporting and explaining their positions on Internet governance matters to constituents is hardly routine. Moreover, these constituencies leave out a great many other stakeholders around the world that may be directly or indirectly impacted by decisions. In consequence, CSOs and others argue that key Internet governance processes have a "democratic deficit" that seriously erodes their legitimacy. At a minimum, specifying to whom the various governance mechanisms should be held accountable and via what methods is a challenge that merits consideration.

Third, to the extent possible, there should be inclusive participation in governance decision-making. Obviously, there are limits to applicability of this norm. Internet governance involves many institutions and processes that have limited memberships for perfectly natural reasons, and it would be nonsensical to suggest that regional or plurilateral intergovernmental collaborations should become fully multilateral, that every relevant private sector collaboration should be open to all, etc. That said, in some cases there could be room for steps that would helpfully broaden the range of expertise and stakeholder support involved governance processes. For example, public and private sector initiatives alike often could benefit by ensuring that less powerful members are able to participate effectively and have their views given full consideration. In parallel, sometimes mechanisms could be desirable that would allow non-members to at least consult with or serve as observers in limited membership groupings. Particular attention should be paid to the participation of developing country governments and businesses, small and medium-sized enterprises (SMEs), and CSOs; I will expand on this issue below.

Fourth, and turning from process to substance, equity concerns also entail establishing rules that promote fairness and social justice. Governance arrangements that are skewed and unduly favor some stakeholders over others are both normatively problematic and subject to divisive political challenges that can limit their effectiveness and value to everyone. Rule systems should provide equality of opportunity and help to empower those who otherwise would struggle to

---

[21] Robert O. Keohane and Joseph S. Nye, Jr., "The Club Model of Multilateral Cooperation and Problems of Democratic Legitimacy", in, Keohane, *Power and Governance in a Partially Globalized World*. London: Routledge, 2002, p. 234.

take advantage of the openings provided. Address allocations that favour powerful firms and countries, lopsided and overly expansive trade and intellectual property rules, anemic privacy and consumer protections, and so on, do not fit this criteria.

11. In particular, the effective inclusion of developing countries requires much greater attention.

Some of the larger and relatively prosperous developing countries have become important players in ICT global governance. Nevertheless, the vast majority has experienced substantial difficulties participating in this arena, especially with respect to the Internet. This is a longstanding and widely noted problem that has bedeviled many of the international institutions involved. But over the past decade, two major trends have recast the problem in a new light.

The first trend is the dual transformation of ICT global governance that began in the late 1980s. On the one hand, the substantive character of ICT global governance has changed radically, with traditional international regimes based on state power and monopoly control giving way to new arrangements that facilitate the private sector-led development of competitive markets. These arrangements increasingly reach behind the borders of national sovereignty and require the adjustment of myriad domestic laws, regulations and practices to promote deep integration and globalization. As such, the stakes involved and the complexity of the issues have greatly increased. On the other hand, the architecture of ICT global governance has changed in tandem, with decision making in a limited range of multilateral institutions giving way to a heterogeneous array of intergovernmental and private sector collaborations. This has made it much more difficult for many developing countries to even track and understand, much less actually participate, in the full range of important forums and processes.

The second trend is an emerging shift in our collective understanding of the problem. Historically, the question of developing country participation had been viewed in a fragmentary manner. That is, participants in each of the relevant intergovernmental organizations assessed the issue and advanced solutions solely within these discreet environments. Now there is a growing recognition that many of the challenges faced are generalizable and evident across multiple governance arenas. For example, the widely noted "Louder Voices" report assessed the participation problem as manifested in the ITU, WTO, and ICANN and identified some common dynamics.[22] This sort of integrative approach has also been pursued in other research

---

[22] See, Commonwealth Telecommunications Organization and Panos London, *Louder Voices: Strengthening Developing Country Participation in International ICT Decision-Making*. London: Commonwealth Telecommunications Organization, 2002.
http://www.cto.int/publications/louder_voices_final_report.pdf

and advocacy initiatives, as well as in the international multistakeholder dialogues of the DOT Force, the United Nations ICT Task Force, the WSIS, and, potentially, the pending WGIG. Building on this momentum are new capacity-building initiatives designed to promote participation across ICT global governance arenas. A British-funded follow-up to the Louder Voices initiative has resulted in the launching of international ICT policy centres in Senegal and Uganda, and a similar body is to be set up in Asia. The challenge going forward will be to institutionalize this approach so as to help those developing countries that are struggling to cope with the substantive and architectural transformation of ICT and Internet governance.

Developing countries encounter impediments at both the international and national levels. Regarding the former, other than limitations on membership in regional and plurilateral bodies, intergovernmental organizations typically do not impose formal barriers to the participation of nominally equal sovereign states. Indeed, developing country representation in bodies like the ITU, WTO, and WIPO is actually quite good. Rather, the barriers are primarily informal, and pertain more to the ability to participate fully and effectively. ICT and Internet governance generally involves ongoing work programs comprising many meetings, some of which may be scheduled simultaneously. Developing countries usually send small delegations that may not be able to cover or otherwise keep up with all this activity. Sometimes countries can at best send an over-taxed representative from the local mission to pick up the documents and read a prepared statement sent from the national capital. For others, even this may not be an option; for example, at last count, thirty-six countries did not have a permanent mission in Geneva, home to the ITU, WTO, WIPO, UNCTAD, and other relevant organizations. That the issues are often very complex and require a high level of technical expertise presents additional problems. Moreover, the international organizations generally lack the resources to help developing country personnel attend, and what fellowships there are may be misallocated, resulting in "the wrong people attending meetings for the wrong reasons".[23]

These issues pertain to simply getting representatives in the room and able to engage effectively; translating participation into actual influence is an entirely different matter. International asymmetries in power capabilities routinely trump the nominal equality of states, and having a voice in meetings usually does not equate with being able to push through approaches opposed by more powerful nations. The concentration of wealth, power, technology, and expertise in the global North may mean that prior deals worked out therein pre-configure the actual agenda and the range of possible outcomes and thus make wider negotiations rather secondary. Power dynamics also can override the niceties of formal

---

[23] This was a frequent observation of developing country representatives interviewed for the Louder Voices report. Quoted in, *Louder Voices*, p. 24.

procedures, as when leading states opt to forge alliances and deals in small side gatherings, rather than to work through often slow and difficult to manage multilateral meetings.

Private sector governance presents even greater challenges. In the traditional telecommunications environment, many developing countries have struggled to cope with the reality that key rules are now set via business strategies and contracts rather than intergovernmental agreements. In the Internet environment, where much of the rule making has always been private, the challenge is even greater. Private sector bodies often do not provide for government participants or observers. Since relatively few developing countries have robust, organized, and internationally oriented private sectors with the requisite resources and interest in joining such bodies (when that is possible), they are often left without any sort of representation. And in the those cases where developing country governments can play a role, as in ICANN's Government Advisory Committee (GAC), they may have reasons not to. For some, the problem may be the cost of jetting around the globe to ICANN's far-flung assemblies, the difficulties of plugging into ongoing technical conversations, or a lack of perceived stakes in many of the issues, etc. For others, it may be more of a political choice between legitimating ICANN by participating in it or pushing for its functions to be performed in the ITU.

More generally, private sector bodies' number and diversity make it difficult for developing countries to keep abreast of rapidly changing developments. This is especially so when important bits of information are proprietary, or simply not made available. Private organizations' cultures and work styles are very different from what is familiar to developing countries used to intergovernmental forums, and are driven by what is sometimes perceived to be a semi-closed community of technical experts who have known each other for years. Their substantive approaches to the issues are also very different from what is common in intergovernmental settings, where concerns like national sovereignty, state authority, and development remain important undercurrents or explicit priorities. In sum, there is often a disconnect between the developing countries and private sector governance; this is an arena ripe for further consideration, in particular by the global business community.

But while impediments at the international level are important, domestic capacity constraints are a more pervasive limitation on developing country participation. Inadequate awareness of the issues and lack of training and expertise is common, both in terms substantive technical knowledge and bargaining/networking skills. So is the lack of high-level leadership commitment, coherent national e-strategies, forward-looking laws and regulations, deep policy making institutions, effective networks of government/business/CSO consultation, robust and organized Internet-related industries, access to and dissemination of information, and, of course, financial resources. Of particular concern is the fact that ministries (and their social constituencies) other than the ministries of communications are often not mobilized and engaged in either policy formulation or national representation in Internet governance deliberations. If the global community is to make significant progress toward establishing widely supported governance mechanisms that will contribute to the world wide development of the Internet and related economic and social objectives, tackling all these challenges will have to become much more of a priority than it has been to date.

12. *Similarly, greater attention is needed to the inclusion of civil society organizations, small and medium-sized enterprises, and individual users.*

These non-dominant stakeholders are a significant source of technical expertise, have made distinct contributions to the development of the Internet, have clear interests in governance activities that are not well represented by other actors, and could play important roles in ensuring that decisions taken therein are implemented in a functionally effective and politically legitimate manner. In particular, they could serve as vital partners to developing countries that want to promote both vibrant local Internet industries and socially beneficial applications and more open and inclusive governance processes. However, there are significant barriers that must be overcome in order realize this largely untapped potential.

In this context, the question of CSO participation in particular has generated the most extended and heated global debate. Over the past ten years, non-profit public interest advocacy and service organizations have become very mobilized and ardent in pressing their demands to participate in Internet governance. However, they have encountered a wide variety of obstacles. At the international level, the most fundamental of these has been the unwillingness of a great many governments to consider including them in any significant decision making activities.

Governments' various arguments in support of this stance are not terribly convincing. For example, CSOs are not "already represented" by national governments. Many of the relevant groups are multinational in character and cannot be represented by a single government; others are based in countries whose governments are not supportive of CSOs generally; and few are included in national policy formulation processes or delegations to intergovernmental meetings (and when they are, their views usually are not reflected in the positions taken). Inviting them to participate as observers, with a right to submit documents and at times take the floor, need not impose significant administrative and cost burdens or unduly complicate the search for intergovernmental agreement. And when it is really necessary, CSO participation can be limited to distinct stages in the process, e.g. allowed in agenda setting deliberations and monitoring/implementation, but not in the actual bargaining.

Allowing CSOs to participate is far from a radical or unprecedented idea. In fact, the practice is widespread in the United Nations system. For example, 2,418 CSOs have been granted consultative status by the Economic and Social Council, and 400 are accredited to the Commission on Sustainable Development alone.[24] In addition, many United Nations specialized agencies – the International Labor Organization, the Food and Agriculture Organization, the United Nations Conference on Trade and Development, the World Health Organization, and so on – operate their own accreditation programs for CSOs. But perhaps of even greater relevance here is the fact that at least one international organization involved in Internet governance – WIPO – is already quite open to CSO participation. While WIPO's liberal policy on non-governmental organizations was established with private sector entities in mind, CSOs also may apply for either permanent or committee-specific observer status. If accredited, they can participate in most meetings, including negotiations, and may be allowed to speak or submit informal position papers.[25] In neither the United Nations generally nor WIPO specifically has CSO participation led to unmanageable problems; to the contrary, it has broadened the pool of expertise deployed, enriched the dialogues, and enhanced the organizations' legitimacy.

These facts notwithstanding, other intergovernmental organizations involved in Internet governance have been far less forthcoming. In the ITU, CSOs cannot independently participate in key bodies like the plenipotentiary or regulatory conferences or the council meetings. They can apply to join one of the three sectors as an Associate, but this is subject to a payment of US $8,000 annually and the approval of member governments (waivers are technically available but do not appear to have been granted to any CSOs). In the WTO, CSOs can attend designated public symposia and the plenary sessions of the ministerial conferences, and they can submit position papers to the secretariat, but they cannot participate in the councils, working parties, or other meetings where issues are really discussed and decisions are made. In the OECD, CSO personnel have at times been invited to speak at selected seminars, but there is no general right to attend meetings, speak and submit documents. These are just three prominent examples; other relevant bodies impose similar limitations. Only in the two cases of government-initiated multistakeholder partnerships on ICT and Internet policy, the DOT Force and the WSIS, have CSOs been encouraged to participate, and in the latter they encountered a good deal of resistance from certain quarters and were periodically asked to leave the room.

---

[24] The framework for CSO accreditation is laid out in, United Nations Economic and Social Council, Resolution 1996/31, "Consultative Relationship between the United Nations and Non-governmental Organizations", July 25, 1996. http://www.un.org/documents/ecosoc/res/1996/eres1996-31.htm

[25] For an excellent overview of some WIPO issues and mechanics that includes a list of accredited CSOs, see, Sisule F. Musungu and Graham Dutfield, "Multilateral Agreements and a TRIPS-Plus World: The World Intellectual Property Organisation (WIPO)", TRIPS Issue Paper No. 3, Geneva: Quaker United Nations Office, 2003, http://www.iprsonline.org/ictsd/docs/WIPO_Musungu_Dutfield.pdf

Of course, if they had a right to participate in more intergovernmental bodies, many CSOs would face in accentuated form the same kinds of informal barriers discussed above with respect to developing countries. But there is every reason to believe that if political space were created, at least some of the leading groups would have the capacity to rise to the occasion and fill it effectively. Having the ability to participate undoubtedly would increase their ability to raise funds from foundations, build networks for knowledge and information sharing, formulate sound policy recommendations, cultivate relationships with policymakers at the national and global levels, and so forth. And stronger CSOs would make stronger partners for governments and business in the design and implementation of Internet governance agreements.

CSOs fare better in some of the leading private sector governance bodies – an interesting contrast with the developing countries. The most notable example here is ICANN, which has made explicit provisions for CSOs to participate and present their views via several avenues. In consequence, experts from advocacy and service CSOs (e.g. academia) have populated the Non-Commercial Users Constituency and made substantial contributions to the policy process. Further, ICANN has established an At-Large Advisory Committee that is supposed to advise the board and constituencies on the interests of individual users, and is encouraging the formation of "At Large Structures" around the world. In general, ICANN has been the subject of serious and sustained criticisms for failing to live up to its promises of inclusion and to heed much of the advice provided by CSOs, but the mere fact that they are able to participate at all certainly places the organization steps ahead of, say, the ITU. Beyond this, the picture in private bodies is somewhat mixed, ranging from open technical standardization groups at one end to closed industry associations and partnerships at the other.

Finally, the inclusion of SMEs and individual users is also important to the functional effectiveness and political legitimacy of Internet governance. However, national and international mechanisms to aggregate and represent their interests in this context are often weak to nonexistent, and the governments and large firms that set the global rules usually have not attempted to design processes that cater to their participation. In some cases where this has been attempted, the results have been mixed at best. Others, such as certain technical standards bodies, present a somewhat brighter picture, and it may be that there are lessons to be learned from their experiences that are generalizable. Either way, identifying the circumstances in which these stakeholders can be meaningfully brought further into the process is another task that should be part of the governance agenda.

13. A program of integrative analysis is needed and would reveal weaknesses, gaps and tensions in the governance architecture.

By integrative I mean an analysis that assesses the governance architecture as a whole and the parts in relation to both the whole and each other.[26] In points 8 and 9, above, I suggested that it would be useful to develop a rich taxonomy that describes each governance mechanism using a consistent set of key institutional attributes and performance indicators. If we could lay out and view the governance topography in this systemic manner, it would be easier to explore a number of potentially instructive comparisons and generalizations. For example: which issues have or have not given rise to what kinds of collective rules and programs, and why? When have mandatory or voluntary rules, broad or narrow agreements, centralized or decentralized monitoring, or other design attributes been used, and to what effect? More generally, which mechanisms have performed more or less well than the others in promoting technological innovation and new markets, or in terms of institutional efficiency? Which have done better or worse with respect to transparency, accountability, inclusion, and social justice? Which most effectively empower non-dominant stakeholders in terms of knowledge acquisition, negotiating capabilities, and national capacity building and implementation? Are there lessons that intergovernmental, private sector, and multistakeholder approaches could learn from one another? What would constitute best practices, or the key habits of healthy Internet governance arrangements?

Similarly, an integrative view of the whole might help us to identify weaknesses and gaps in the coverage of important issues. At least four sets of problems have not given rise to strong collective responses or "fall between the cracks" of existing mechanisms. The first pertains to users' trust in the Internet, e.g. spam, consumer protection more generally, privacy protection, and network security. The second involves boundaries and the organization of political space, e.g. the classification and facilitation of networked international trade transactions, e-commerce taxation, and the problem of applicable jurisdiction. The third concerns problems associated with market concentration, e.g. Internet interconnection pricing, competition policy, restrictive business practices, and the preservation of cultural and linguistic diversity. The fourth concerns development programs, e.g. technical assistance, financial support, and technology transfer, especially with respect to the least developed countries. Of course, whether some form of collective response to each of these challenges is really needed is a matter of debate, and there are undoubtedly important stakeholders who would argue that the status quo is preferable to

---

[26] For an initial effort to view the wider ICT global governance arena in this manner and to draw some generalizable lessons about it, see, William J. Drake, "Communications", in, P.J. Simmons and Chantal de Jonge Oudraat, eds., *Managing Global Issues: Lessons Learned.* Washington, D.C.: Carnegie Endowment for International Peace, 2001, pp. 25-74. http://www.ceip.org/files/pdf/MGIch01.pdf

any conceivable alternatives. In some cases that may well prove to be true, but building a consensus to that effect could require that the issues first be analyzed and debated in an open and inclusive manner.

An integrative approach also would help us to consider the merits of alternative solutions to outstanding issues in light of other experiences and general patterns. In the cases just mentioned, what would be most desirable: Intergovernmental agreements, private self-regulation, or some combination thereof? Where intergovernmentalism is preferred, should it be bilateral, plurilateral, regional, or multilateral? Which non-state actors should play what roles in what aspects of the process? Would harmonization via strong, treaty-based rules be best, or rather more limited MOUs on information sharing and cross-border enforcement? Would it be better to anchor any cooperative rules in a formal organizational setting, to distribute functions among networked institutions, or to have freestanding agreements? Should the rules cover a range of interrelated issues or be narrowly targeted? How should compliance be monitored and non-compliance sanctioned, as appropriate? How can procedural transparency and accountability and a good substantive balance between competing objectives be achieved? Examining proposals for new collaborations in relation to what has or has not worked under comparable circumstances in other issue-areas might help us to answer these and related questions more effectively.

Lastly, an integrative approach also would direct our attention to the possibility of procedural and substantive tensions between governance mechanisms. As the existing arrangements have been created in a piecemeal manner in response to individual problems, it is possible that some may at times clash a bit with others. This has certainly happened in the broader ICT governance environment where, for example, there have been contradictions between ITU and WTO instruments, between instruments concerning the free flow of information and national sovereignty, and so on. Similarly, in the Internet environment, there have been tensions between different technical standardization processes (e.g., between the ITU and the Internet Architecture Board), organizations and rules involved in managing identifiers, personal privacy and information security arrangements, and so on. Examining how well the various institutions mesh into a whole might allow the global community to not only avoid problems, but also unleash latent value through inter-institutional synergies.

It would be difficult to do the kind of analysis proposed here quickly or as a one-off effort. For example, were it to agree to try, the WGIG would be hard pressed to carry the approach very far due to its tight time constraints. The group could do an initial mapping of the terrain and identify some broad trends and implications, but probably it will need to focus in on a few institutions and issue-areas of particular interest in the WSIS debate. What would be needed is an ongoing, progressive program of research and dialogue in which the evidence is gathered and assessed and propositions are confirmed or rejected through careful analysis as the governance environment continues to evolve. Perhaps some academics, research institutions, CSOs and so forth will get interested in undertaking this kind of work, but the natural dispersion of intellectual agendas and orientations and the lack of consensus on a broadened definition and integrative approach to Internet governance would present obstacles to the formation of a well functioning epistemic community. Moreover, ideas generated from these quarters often do not percolate up into the debates among governmental and private sector decision makers. Hence, for this kind of approach to "take" and inform the policy process, it would probably be necessary to institutionalize it in a widely accepted global focal point, e.g. in a multilateral or multistakeholder organization.

14. The global community lacks an appropriate institution in which to pursue this integrative analysis and dialogue.

While issue-specific governance mechanisms must do most of the heavy lifting in Internet governance, this does imply some limitations. First, as was just noted, there are important issues that fall into the jurisdictional cracks between specialized mechanisms. Moreover, experience in the ITU, ICANN, UNESCO, and other settings indicates that when specialized groups do attempt to reach into such issue spaces, this can generate controversies and backlash on the part of stakeholders preferring narrower interpretations of their mandates.

Second, total reliance on vertically segmented organizations and processes can make it difficult to assess and respond effectively to issues that blur the boundaries between them. Viewing multidimensional issues from the single point perspective of a specialized arrangement inevitably foregrounds certain aspects and backgrounds others in ways that may prove functionally and politically problematic later on. Finding the right balances between, say, intellectual property and the public sphere, security and privacy, trade and digital development, domain name trademarks and freedom of speech or competition, and so on can be difficult if the issues are only tackled from one vantage point or the other.

Third, relying solely on segmented approaches may impede cross-sectoral learning and integrative responses. Expertise and interest in different arenas of Internet and ICT global governance are rather fragmented, with separate tribes of specialists following different issues, going to different meetings, reading and writing in different publications, etc. In consequence, there are not adequate incentives or opportunities to ask such the sort of comparative questions posed above, e.g. when is it better to rely on hard law vs. soft law instruments, or centralized vs. decentralized organizational models, etc.

Finally, as also was noted above, the distributed architecture of Internet governance poses significant challenges to developing countries, CSOs, and SMEs. Tracking and participating in a range of institutions and processes can be exceedingly difficult due to resource constraints, membership restrictions, and related impediments. Not surprisingly then, many developing countries in particular appear to desire some sort of universally accessible, "one stop shopping" forum that would be mandated to consider Internet governance and broader information society issues. Of course, a truly "one stop shopping" approach would be utterly unworkable given the frequent need for specialized, issue-specific expertise and collaboration. The point is simply that the calls for such an entity provide a political complement to the functional points above concerning the limitations of relying solely on distributed, specialized mechanisms.

Hence, it might be advisable to at least consider whether some sort of mechanism with an integrative mandate would be a useful addition to the governance landscape. This would provide a sort of horizontal overlay space that complements rather than replaces or overrides the important work being done in vertically segmented, specialized intergovernmental agencies, less formalized minilateral collaborations, or private sector coordination efforts. In functional terms, a potentially attractive model to build off of might be the OECD, or rather its Committee for Information, Computer and Communications Policy. Relevant elements of this model include: a small and expert research staff that produces highly regarded reports on Internet and related issues; ongoing dialogue and regularly scheduled meetings, rather than occasional one-off events with variable attendance; a single, convenient location for meetings, rather than world roaming assemblages; a broad mandate, continually reviewed and agreed; and normally, a reliance on "soft law" instruments such as declarations, recommendations, and guidelines.

A soft law approach might frequently be appropriate in a rapidly changing environment like Internet governance, where "hard" instruments like treaties can quickly be rendered problematic or obsolete. This approach would allow for collective learning, consensus building, and the voluntary and communally monitored mutual adjustment of national policies and organizational practices in light of shared objectives. Consensuses reached in this context could, in turn, feed into other, more specialized institutions and processes, just as OECD work has often proved useful to the WTO and other collaborations. Overseen by an institutionally light secretariat, such a mechanism could provide a place to take up issues that fall between the mandates of specialized groupings, analyze multidimensional issues from a multidimensional perspective, examine generalizable issues and dynamics that cut across disparate governance systems, and serve at times as a sort of coordinating node in an inter-institutional policy network. The main difference from the OECD, though, are that it would need to a) be a universal, multistakeholder collaboration in which developing countries and relevant CSOs and SMEs could take part alongside the industrialized countries and global business community; b) mainstream development considerations into all aspects of the work; and c) make heavy use of the technology to facilitate virtual collaboration and stakeholder input.

It is difficult to imagine the global community achieving broad-based agreement to develop such a mechanism from any of our existing institutions. To be sure, many developing countries clearly would like to see the ITU fill this gap in the governance architecture. In recent years they have repeatedly urged the ITU to play a greater role in policy matters concerning information society issues generally. The notion has even been floated of a new "ITU-I" sector for the Internet that would sit alongside the ITU-T (telecommunications), ITU-R (radiocommunications), and ITU-D (development) sectors. Given that the ITU is already incrementally expanding its involvement in Internet governance, especially with respect to technical standardization, proponents might argue that officially broadening its mandate would simply recognize the emerging reality and make it easier to do the work many member want done.

However, it is just as clear that a significant portion of the global business community, the US government, and to varying degrees other industrialized country governments would be firmly opposed to the ITU "expanding its turf" in this manner. They would rather see the organization stick to a narrow mandate concerning nominally technical issues, and perhaps even to shrink.[27] And while hundreds of corporations have become sector members, ITU procedures and financial requirements effectively preclude the inclusive participation of CSOs and SMEs. Similarly, governments are generally represented in the ITU by ministries of communications with close ties to dominant national carriers; other ministries that may have different views and social constituencies are largely marginalized from the process. For the ITU to gain widespread support and grow into the sort of open multistakeholder body that may be needed, it would have to undertake truly sweeping reforms that would fundamentally change the character of the institution. Since most of its membership would probably oppose such changes at present, there seems little prospect of the ITU filling the role discussed here.

Another idea that has been floated informally is to grow a new broad-range institution from ICANN's GAC. Yet a "GAC Plus" scenario seems equally implausible and problematic. The developing countries that have questioned ICANN's legitimacy and opted not to participate actively in its work would likely oppose building out one of its organs, especially as an alternative to the expanded ITU option they favor. Moreover, the fact that many other

[27] Some leading independent experts also advocate shrinking the organization, and more. For example, Donald MacLean–a former high-level official at the ITU–argues that the ITU should be broken up into a much looser structure, with its standards work fully devolved to the private sector and its development work moving to an independent agency, leaving only the radio frequency spectrum work still subject to intergovernmental authority and decision making. See his, "Sovereign Right and the Dynamics of Power in the ITU: Lessons in the Quest for Inclusive Global Governance", in, William J. Drake and Ernest M. Wilson III, eds., *Governing Global Electronic Networks: International Perspectives on Policy and Power.* Cambridge, MA: MIT Press, forthcoming, 2005.

stakeholders believe the GAC has a problematic record with respect to transparency, accountability, and inclusion would make it an additionally difficult sell. Nor it is easy to imagine any of the other specialized multilateral agencies or private sector processes populating the Internet governance landscape being well suited to the task and able to garner the necessary political support.

If the legacy arrangements in place are unlikely to fill the role, could an entirely new decision making arrangement be created? In today's political climate, the prospects do not seem good. For example, it has proven difficult to muster the financial support necessary to launch the WGIG that governments participating in WSIS said they wanted. If even a small, limited-term body with a bounded advisory mandate experiences problems getting off the ground, surely creating something more substantial would prove far more difficult. Accordingly, the most likely outcome is that we will continue to "muddle through" with a mix of arrangements that does not meet the full range of functional needs and political demands involved in Internet governance.

But if agreement cannot be reached on a multistakeholder process to promote dialogue and consensus (embodied, as necessary, in soft law), there could be a more minimalist and presumably digestible alternative. This would be to create a multistakeholder mechanism restricted to the monitoring, analytical, and information-sharing functions. By tracking developments across the Internet governance terrain, drawing attention to gaps and generalizable lessons, and providing the sort of multi-perspective assessment that is often lacking in more narrowly mandated arrangements, such a mechanism could enrich the dialogue and provide helpful inputs into other processes tasked with actual decision making. It would be especially useful to non-dominant stakeholders like developing countries, CSOs, and SMEs that already have difficulties monitoring and assessing governance processes, but other stakeholders could find it to be value-adding as well. A small, nimble, and well-connected secretariat supported by virtual networks of organizations and individuals could perform these tasks effectively. This was more or less the approach recommended by the civil society declaration released at the 2003 WSIS summit, which included a section on governance stating, *inter alia,*

> We need public-interest oriented monitoring and analysis of the relevant activities of both intergovernmental and "self-governance" bodies...As a viable first step in this direction, we recommend the establishment of an independent and truly multistakeholder observatory committee to: (1) map and track the most pressing current developments in ICT global governance decision-making; (2) assess and solicit stakeholder input on the conformity of such decision-making with the stated objectives of the WSIS agenda; and (3) report to all stakeholders in the WSIS process

on a periodic basis until 2005, at which time a decision could be made on whether to continue or terminate the activity.[28]

15. The WSIS process is unlikely to profoundly affect Internet governance.

The highly politicized WSIS debate on Internet governance apparently has raised hopes and fears in various quarters that significant, near-term changes could result from WSIS in general and the United Nations Working Group process in particular. In consequence, there has been a great deal of pushing and hauling, much of it behind the scenes, by various stakeholders seeking to influence every decision remotely related to which organizations and issues will be involved under which terms of reference. While these reactions are perfectly understandable, a reality check may be in order. As a general matter, powerful stakeholders that have been indifferent at best about the WSIS enterprise are unlikely to agree to outcomes they oppose. Given the configuration of interests and the distribution of power, incremental change seems far more likely than some sort of non-consensual "big bang".

More specifically, with respect to governance of the infrastructure, leading companies and industry associations have made clear their opposition to shifting ICANN's responsibilities into the ITU. For its part, the United States government is undoubtedly concerned about ICANN's weak support in much of the developing world, and will have to carefully weigh the options when its relationship with ICANN comes up for renewal in 2006. Nevertheless, even if the Executive Branch were to dramatically change its mind and actively consider alternatives (e.g. after the presidential election), there is no politically salient constituency on Capitol Hill – not even among ICANN's harshest critics – for adopting an intergovernmental approach, especially at the behest of certain developing countries. The same would be true with respect to any proposals to bring the zone file and root server system under some form of international authority. Nor is there broad support for dramatic change among the other industrialized world, France's interesting statements and more widespread disenchantment with certain ICANN practices notwithstanding.

What about other aspects of infrastructure governance? The interconnection charging issue will probably come in for closer scrutiny, with the developing countries justifiably complaining about being forced to pay the full cost of North-South circuits. However, the imposition of an accounting and settlements mechanism based on traffic measurements seems unwise and unworkable and has already been rejected in the ITU by the United States and global carriers.

---

[28] WSIS Civil Society Plenary, *"Shaping Information Societies for Human Needs"*, Civil Society Declaration to the World Summit on the Information Society, December 8, 2003. http://www.itu.int/wsis/docs/geneva/civil-society-declaration.pdf. The author participated in the drafting of this text on behalf of the civil society Internet Governance Caucus. Wolfgang Kleinwächter suggested the "observatory committee" formulation.

Increased development assistance for backbone deployment might be a possibility, especially if it could be linked to policy reform commitments in the global South. This would be worthy achievement, but hardly a revolution.

Network security is already attracting a lot of interest from governments in the industrialized world as an arena ripe for enhanced international cooperation. One could imagine an effort to move toward broader multilateral instruments that would put teeth into the "global culture of security" that has already been endorsed by the United Nations General Assembly and the December 2003 WSIS Summit. But on current trends, the WSIS process would probably play a supporting rather than a leading role in catalyzing any such activity.

With respect to governance of transactions and content, here too rapid, WSIS-induced change seems unlikely. Relevant and potentially important international regime negotiations are underway in forums like the WTO, WIPO, and the Hague Conference, but their prospects are rather unclear and in any event are unrelated to the WSIS process. A multilateral agreement to combat spam, such as a global MOU on information sharing and enforcement or a stronger regime under the aegis of the ITU, seems a distant possibility. There might be more hope for an OECD MOU, but this would do little for developing countries struggling with the epidemic. The WGIG and the 2005 WSIS Summit in Tunis might want to consider calling for significantly increased technical assistance to help the global South cope. More generally, an agreement to increase development assistance for other purposes is at least conceivable, although the disagreements to date on the proposed Digital Solidarity Fund and related matters are not encouraging. On other outstanding issues – such as privacy and consumer protection, competition policy, restrictive business practices, and the preservation of cultural and linguistic diversity – WSIS is unlikely to make significant headway.

In light of these considerations, it may be advisable to follow a two-stage approach. In the near-term, governments could focus on improving some of the procedural weaknesses of Internet governance, e.g. inadequate transparency, accountability, inclusion, and the lack of an appropriate, "light" global venue in which to analyze and maybe even debate governance policies. Such procedural reforms would no doubt be hotly contested, but they probably offer greater space for normative pressure and compromise than substantive issues that more directly touch on divided interests. Similarly, a push to increase development assistance for infrastructure, spam, security, and so on would run up against the usual donor fatigue, but should still be less controversial than deeper changes to rules and institutions. That said, if progress could be made on the near-term agenda, the global community might be better positioned to tackle the substantive challenges later on.

Conclusion

As I suggested at the outset of this paper, we are in a liminal moment. There is widespread disagreement on the most basic definitional questions, as well as on the issues at stake and the proper roles of the relevant institutions and stakeholders. Some players believe that there are significant functional and political shortcomings to the existing global order, while others maintain that everything is basically working fine and there is no need for change or even debate. Under these circumstances, a standard United Nations style call on the parties involved to roll up their sleeves and demonstrate political will would ring a bit hollow. Nevertheless, a real commitment to an open and inclusive dialogue is needed, particularly on the part of those who feel comfortable with the status quo. To secure the Internet's future as an open and vibrant global medium for communication and commerce, it would be better to engage, exercise soft power, and try to build a lasting and widely supported consensus than to let any problems and disgruntlements metastasize. Also needed, as a first step, is a reframing of the terms of policy discourse so as to facilitate the identification of reform options and collective problem solving. This paper has offered some suggestions in the hope of advancing that process.

INTERNET GOVERNANCE: WHAT ARE WE TALKING ABOUT?

Raúl Echeberría, Latin American and Caribbean Internet Address Registry (LACNIC)

It has been several years since the discussion of different Internet governance models began, and this discussion gained strength during the course of the World Summit on the Information Society (WSIS). In the end, at the World Summit meeting held in Geneva in December 2003, no significant resolutions were adopted in relation to this subject, and major decisions were postponed until the second phase of the Summit which will be held in Tunisia in November 2005.

Surprisingly, this became one of the most controversial issues during the preparation of the Summit, and for this reason this article attempts to clarify the different positions that exist in relation to the matter, while at the same time trying to contribute to a better understanding of the meaning of the extremely ambiguous and imprecise term that has been used up to now, namely "Internet governance".

What is Understood by Internet Governance?

A term more inappropriate than Internet governance could not have been chosen. It is impossible to affirm that all persons involved in the discussion attribute the same meaning to this expression, and I personally believe that the opposite is true. There is obviously no Internet government, nor is the Internet "governable" as a whole. There are numerous and extremely diverse aspects related to the Internet, some of which are discussed at different levels and by different organizations, while others are determined by local legislation and regulations.

A brief summary of some of the diverse aspects related to the Internet might include e-commerce, intellectual property, e-government, communications, human rights, education, and privacy, among many others.

There is no single organization or forum where these issues are discussed and channeled, and there is no single body where all decisions are made and all standards established, and, therefore, the much renowned Internet governance does not exist.

However, the term "Internet governance" has acquired an existence of its own merely through its constant repetition. For this reason, whether or not many of us believe that this is a slightly old fashioned expression, the term is used to reference the technical administration and coordination of Internet resources.

In other words, when people speak of Internet governance, they are referring fundamentally to the administration and management of domain names, of Internet addresses (IP numbers and autonomous numbers), the coordination of technical aspects and the definition of the technical parameters necessary for the operation of the domain name system, and root servers.

Current Situation

Now that we have clarified this matter we can focus on the matter under discussion.

Since the beginnings of the Internet, some organizations have assumed active roles in the administration and coordination of the aforementioned Internet resources.

The fact that the Internet was born as a project that depended on the United States government resulted in many of the functions necessary for what we could call the "Internet system" being performed by organizations under government contracts, and in many cases funded by United States government agencies.

Such is the case, for example, of IANA (www.iana.org), which is the organization responsible for the administration of the root of the domain name system and the administration of the unallocated space of Internet Number Resources (basically IP addresses).

Other organizations, such as the Internet Engineering Task Force (www.ietf.org) have operated independently, in an open and participatory manner, from the outset. The IETF is the forum where the standards for Internet architecture and operation are developed. Neither the IETF nor its related organizations (e.g. IAB, IESG.) depend directly or indirectly on any government.

Another relevant issue is that of root servers. There are thirteen similar servers, identified with the letters A to M, which constitute the basis, or rather the root, of the domain name system. There is no hierarchy among these thirteen servers; they are all at the same level. Ten of the thirteen root servers are located in the United States (http://www.root-servers.org/) and, of these ten servers, three are controlled by government organizations. Of the three root servers that are not located in the United States, two are in Europe and the other is in Japan. The selection of the organizations that operate the root servers is based on historical reasons, not on geographical diversity. These organizations are not under contract with the United States government.

In 1996, a global discussion process began with the aim of reforming the "Internet System". This process culminated in October 1998, with the creation of ICANN (www.icann.org). The idea was to build an international non-profit organization, with participation and representation of all interest groups related to the Internet. The United States government temporarily transferred to ICANN the functions that were under its control, through a contract. In theory, when a set of requirements established by the United States government are satisfied, these functions will be transferred to ICANN permanently. The current contract between ICANN and the United States government expires in the year 2006, and it is expected that at that time the transition will be finalized and that the functions currently performed by ICANN under the terms of the contract will be permanently transferred to this organization.

Internet Governance and the Summit
During the preparatory process prior to the summit, to the surprise of many, a debate on Internet resource administration models arose – that is to say, as we explained earlier, a debate on Internet governance. Some national governments stated the need for governments to have a greater degree of control on this matter, specifically the need for the functions that are currently in the hands of ICANN to be transferred to an intergovernmental organization. Some believe the ITU would be the appropriate organization, while others think some other organization within the framework of the United Nations would be better (although they do not specify which organization, or even if it should be a new organization).

The debate has always focused on the wording of certain paragraphs of the WSIS Declaration of Principles and Plan of Action, and it was never really clear what each national government understood by "Internet governance" and what the absorption of these tasks by an intergovernmental organization implied.

For example, would this imply replacing ICANN by an intergovernmental organization? Or is it the intention that ICANN's current Governmental Advisory Committee (GAC) be replaced by an intergovernmental organization? As to the functions that would hypothetically be transferred to this intergovernmental organization, what is their scope? Do they include, for example, the current role of the IETF? Would the new organization have only policy supervision functions or would it also have operational functions?

It would seem that, even among the countries that promoted the idea of assigning a significant role to an intergovernmental organization, there are many and quite varied answers to these questions.

The Alternatives

The Internet system is much more complex than it sometimes may seem. Frequently the discussion is simplified by mentioning only ICANN, but there are many organizations involved, such as those we have already mentioned (IETF, IAB, IESG, ICANN), in addition to Regional Internet Registries (RIRs) and country-code top-level domains (ccTLDs), among others. The current Internet resource administration model is obviously perfectible, but it is participatory, it is efficient, and it is admirably balanced. The public often demands greater transparency and participation within ICANN's structures, but it is clear that the levels of transparency and participation that have been reached are significantly greater than those of any intergovernmental organization.

The idea of an intergovernmental organization in charge of the abovementioned functions has not gained supporters among those persons and organizations more closely related to Internet operation. The most reasonable model seems to be to maintain these functions in participatory organizations where all stakeholders may express their interests, where the private sector and civil society organizations maintain a major role, and obviously where governments also have an appropriate level of participation.

However, it is necessary to attend to some of the claims asserted by these governments, in some cases because they are fair and in others because, although they are not priorities, they have been placed in the spotlight and will remain there until answers are provided.

It is difficult to envision that the plan whereby the transition from the United States government to ICANN is to be completed in 2006 will be maintained. This would be very risky, given the timing of the second phase of the Summit in November 2005. It is at least necessary to generate facts that are convincing and will allow governments to clearly see, before the second phase of the Summit, that the transition will end and to clearly predict when this will happen.

ICANN needs to become more international, something on which it appears to be working. We need information in more languages, simultaneous translations during meetings, to continue with the process of opening regional offices in order to enhance communications with the stakeholders from each region, and processes that enable a higher degree of participation on the part of the public.

The root server issue is an Achilles' heel of the current system. Although the root servers that are located in the United States are operated by different organizations and the possibility of a plot or conspiracy is absolutely minimal if not non-existent, and although technologies have been developed that allow the cloning of these servers and their multiplication in different parts of the world (there are currently 35 copies of different original root servers and this number is constantly on the rise) thus eliminating the problem of the geographical concentration of the root servers, it is difficult to justify that ten of the thirteen original root servers are located in the same country. In the near future, ICANN, working jointly with other system organizations such as the IETF and the IAB among others, will probably have to prove that it is willing to review the current geographical distribution of these root servers, obviously in a responsible manner so that the stability of the network will not be compromised.

Are there any other important elements and factors that could justify transferring these functions to an intergovernmental organization? If someone believes there are, then it will be necessary for them to specify which things are currently not working and which could function better within the framework that is being proposed. Today it is not possible to have a clear picture of what these elements might be. It will be the responsibility of national governments to clearly establish what requirements they wish to see satisfied and what changes should be implemented, so that it is possible to consider whether solutions may be achieved through the current structures.

Conclusions

- A better alternative to the current system and structures is not envisaged, one which could originate from an intergovernmental organization taking control of Internet resource administration.

- Within the framework of the current model, both third-world countries and the sectors that usually have the least influence on power structures have had active participation and influence, something that would have hardly been possible in an alternative model such as the one that is apparently being proposed.

- There is always much room for improvement, but the correct path appears to be to continue working on improving the current model.

- There is an agenda that has been imposed from outside this area but is now a fact of life, and some of the issues that have been set forth will have to be solved sooner than we were planning to deal with them. The existence of the second phase of the Summit together with its entire process of preparation, which includes the formation of an Internet Governance Working Group for following up on this issue, inevitably implies new schedules and working times.

INTERNATIONAL CHAMBER OF COMMERCE (ICC) BACKGROUND PAPER ON INTERNET GOVERNANCE

ICC Commission on E-Business, IT and Telecoms[1]

Introduction[2]

At the close of the first phase of the World Summit on the Information Society (WSIS), December 2003 governments called upon the United Nations Secretary-General to create a multi-stakeholder Working Group on Internet Governance.

The text from the WSIS states:

---

[1] February 2004

[2] This issues paper has been prepared by the ICC Commission on E-Business, IT & Telecoms (EBITT). Business leaders and experts drawn from the ICC membership establish key business positions, policies and practices on e-business, IT and telecoms. With members who are users and providers of telecommunications and information technology goods and services from both developed and developing countries, ICC provides the ideal platform to develop global voluntary rules and best practices for these areas. Dedicated to the expansion of cross-border trade, ICC champions liberalization of telecoms and development of infrastructures that support global online trade. For further information on the EBITT Commission, please visit our web site at: http://www.iccwbo.org/home/menu_electronic_business.asp. We acknowledge there are other activities and positions of concern to business worldwide with respect to these issues and these are being and will be addressed separately by ICC.

997366779695

The WSIS Declaration of Principles and Plan of Action

Declaration of Principles

"50 International Internet governance issues should be addressed in a coordinated manner. We ask the Secretary-General of the United Nations to set up a working group on Internet governance, in an open and inclusive process that ensures a mechanism for the full and active participation of governments, the private sector and civil society from both developing and developed countries, involving relevant intergovernmental and international organizations and forums, to investigate and make proposals for action, as appropriate, on the governance of Internet by 2005."

Action Plan

"13 b) We ask the Secretary-General of the United Nations to set up a working group on Internet governance, in an open and inclusive process that ensures a mechanism for the full and active participation of governments, the private sector and civil society from both developing and developed countries, involving relevant intergovernmental and international organizations and forums, to investigate and make proposals for action, as appropriate, on the governance of Internet by 2005. The group should, inter alia:

i)   develop a working definition of Internet governance;
ii) identify the public policy issues that are relevant to Internet governance;
iii) develop a common understanding of the respective roles and responsibilities of governments, existing intergovernmental and international organizations and other forums as well as the private sector and civil society from both developing and developed countries;
iv) prepare a report on the results of this activity to be presented for consideration and appropriate action for the second phase of WSIS in Tunis in 2005."

The following is a short summary of the discussions during WSIS regarding Internet 'governance' issues:

• Some governments were calling for a role to be played by an inter-governmental organization on "Internet governance" matters. However, our experience indicated that such governments varied as to what part of "Internet governance" they felt should be addressed by an inter-governmental organization. Some included ICANN's functions while others did not. It was a confused debate.

- It seems that several of these governments were from countries where government has primary or majority control over many infrastructures, but where teledensity may remain a challenge, and Internet access may be limited.

- Many governments from developing countries are seeking a one-stop-shop for advice on Internet policy matters. Many of these governments believe strongly that such a body should be within the United Nations framework.

- Some governments raised concerns that ICANN's Governmental Advisory Committee, as an advisory body, is not an adequate forum for their input into matters related to the technical management of the Internet.

- Other governments opposed the creation of a one-stop-shop under the United Nations framework; opposed an increased or changing role in these areas by the International Telecommunication Union (ITU), supporting continued private sector leadership particularly on technical; and supported the GAC as an appropriate forum for government advice into matters related to the technical management of the Internet.

This issues paper is meant to provide background information and spur discussion among businesses worldwide regarding its views on these important issues.

The Phrase "Internet Governance"

The first subject for discussion is the phrase "Internet governance" itself. Business has long maintained that this phrase has been part of a confused international debate, which has misled some to believe that a single entity controls the Internet.

The Internet consists of tens of thousands of networks that are interconnected and operated by different entities including businesses, universities, governments and others. All of these entities contribute to its proper and efficient functioning through a system of open network standards that ensure that all networks can communicate with each other.

The phrase is often mistakenly used to identify only the management of the Internet's names and numbers system. That system is not one of governance but rather coordination, administration and allocation through a cross-stakeholder, self-regulatory mechanism called the Internet Corporation for Assigned Names and Numbers (ICANN). ICANN will be discussed later in this paper.

The phrase "Internet governance" also implies that there is a need for the Internet to be governed in some way, a view that ICC does not support. We need to work on a definition of "Internet governance" and seek broad support for that definition.

The second subject for discussion is that in reality there are three components of Internet governance, and it is important to clearly distinguish each component from the others. Those components are:

i)   the technical engineering function that allows different components of the Internet to interact;

ii)   the technical coordination of the key protocols and addresses and names that underpin the technical functioning of the Internet, ICANN's functions, which in shorthand is simply, a sophisticated directory system that allows people to accurately contact a web site or other people on the Internet.

iii) the handling of public policy matters that should be discussed openly among governments, business and civil society.

The first two components are handled by numerous non-governmental organizations through open and transparent processes that ensure effective coordination and collaboration among the broad set of stakeholders. These processes are typically open to governmental attendance and participation. The third component is the traditional domain of governments through regulatory and legislative processes after effective consultation with all stakeholders. Each component is discussed in more detail below.

It is essential to ensure that all parties participating in this debate recognize the three components and differentiate among them. This will help to limit the confusion and ensure that all stakeholders, including governments, clearly articulate their views on each component separately. This will hopefully lead to greater clarity of the views of all stakeholders.

I. Technical Coordination of the Internet

As noted above, the Internet is a collection of networks that are joined together to form a global communications medium. The networks that make up the Internet have many different properties, but are based on technical protocols, numbering and naming systems, based on widely accepted standards that enable the transport of information across the multiple sets of interconnected networks. Internet users demand a unique and predictable result in domain name resolution anytime and from anywhere in the world as well as a high degree of reliability and stability in the operation of the networks themselves. As a result, the Internet's infrastructure and operation is a highly collaborative activity.

The technical coordination of the Internet includes:

•   the development of Internet protocol (IP) standards;

- the administration, coordination and allocation of IP addresses;
- the delegation of domain names;
- the coordination of the root server system;
- the coordination of procedures related to the technical coordination of the Internet.

The organizations involved in the technical coordination of the Internet depend on constant input from and interaction with relevant experts to keep the Internet and its related technologies developing in a robust and global manner, providing a platform for business-led innovation and communication for users from around the world.

Several private-sector-led organizations play a critical role in the technical coordination of the Internet, including technical security and stability. These organizations include:

- the Internet Architecture Board (IAB)
- the Internet Engineering Steering Group (IESG)
- the Internet Engineering Task Force (IETF)
- the Regional Addressing Registries (e.g. RIPE, ARIN, APNIC, LANIC and AFRINIC)
- the World Wide Web Consortium (W3C)
- the Internet Corporation for Assigned Names and Numbers (ICANN)

These forums involve experts and interested participants from all around the globe. They play an important role in ensuring that the Internet functions properly. They have demonstrated their ability to respond to an ever-changing environment.

Technical Engineering

This is done through network infrastructure development, including hardware and software, based on open network standards developed by several of the organizations noted above. A very brief explanation of each of these technical engineering standards bodies follows.

IAB is responsible for the strategic technical direction of the Internet, including architectural oversight of Internet protocol and procedures, and standards development oversight and appeal of the IETF (described below). Members of the IAB are solicited through an open process and selected by a nominating committee following open, published procedures. There are no restrictions on who may volunteer. Decisions are reached preferably unanimously, but they may also be reached by seven members assenting with no more than two dissents.

IESG manages IETF's activities and Internet standards process. It administers the IETF process by initiating working groups and either ratifying or remanding its output for further work. IESG members are selected according to the same nominating process of the IAB, and are either confirmed or rejected by the IAB. There are no restrictions on who may volunteer for IESG membership.

IETF is the principal body that develops Internet standards specifications with its work, including ENUM, Instant messaging and internationalized domain names through a widely participatory process, open to all interested parties. IETF's work is guided by IESG and IAB, and it functions through a wide participatory process based on open consultations open to all interested parties.

W3C develops interoperable specifications, guidelines, software and tools to promote the evolution and interoperability of the World Wide Web, including html, portable network graphics and web accessibility guidelines. W3C is open to vendors of technology products and services, content providers, corporate users, laboratories, standards bodies, and governments. Decisions are by consensus.

For more detailed information regarding several of the organizations involved in the technical coordination of the Internet, please refer to ICC's "Information paper on organizations involved in technical coordination of the Internet" updated version, September 2, 2003[3].

Coordination of the Internet Names and Numbers System

ICANN[4] is responsible for coordinating and managing the domain name system, a key technical function that underpins the Internet, ensuring universal resolvability of Internet communications so that all users can find a valid Internet address.

ICANN's responsibilities are limited to:

- the administration, coordination and allocation of IP addresses and domain names[5];
- the administration and coordination of the root server system[6];

---

[3] http://www.iccwbo.org/home/menu_electronic_business.asp

[4] ICANN is a not-for profit organization headquartered in Marina del Rey, California. Its location is a result of historical circumstances. ICANN's Board and its Policy Councils are required by their By-Laws to be regionally diverse.

[5] Each domain name (www.iccwbo.org) has a corresponding Internet Protocol address, which is a series of numbers separated by periods. The domain name system was devised to create an easily identifiable addressing system of words rather than a long series of numbers for communicating with others over the Internet.

[6] The root server system is an address book for the Internet. It indicates the IP address for TLD servers, which then route Internet traffic.

- the coordination of relationships with other entities, such as the regional addressing registries and the ccTLD registries;
- promoting competition within generic top-level domain name space (.com, .org, .net, etc);
- matters related to these functions such as a system for domain name dispute resolution.

Many people believe that ICANN does much more than these basic technical functions, and there is much work to be done to raise greater awareness of how the Internet functions and to correct this misunderstanding.

ICANN functions in an open and transparent manner through an interactive decision-making process. All ICANN meetings are open to whomever would like to attend in person and via webcast. All decisions are fully vetted by the global Internet community through a public comment process. The decisions by the ICANN Board are endorsements of recommendations developed by experts in an inclusive decision-making process after the above-noted procedure of public comment.

Prior to the creation of ICANN, the United States Government had been responsible for these functions. ICANN and the United States Government are in the final stages of completing a memorandum of understanding that will separate the United States government from any role in ICANN's functions, other than its participation as a stakeholder government in ICANN's deliberations. Governments provide advice to ICANN through the Governmental Advisory Committee (GAC). All governments and inter-governmental organizations are welcome to join the GAC.

The administration of the domain name system has been the subject of significant public debate. There are two types of top-level domains:

- generic (gTLDs - .com, .org., net, .info., .biz., .museum, .aero, etc.);
- country-code (ccTLDs - .fr for France, .us for the United States, .jp for Japan, .br for Brazil, etc.).

ICANN has sub-bodies, called supporting organizations:

- for gTLDs, the Generic Names Supporting Organization (GNSO), consisting of constituencies that span the stakeholder community;
- for ccTLDs, the Country-code Names Supporting Organization (ccNSO), now completing its self organization, consisting of the ccTLD administrators that choose to participate;
- The Addressing Support Organization, comprised of the regional addressing registries.

The GNSO and ccNSO are responsible for developing recommendations related to their respective sphere for acceptance by the ICANN Board. ICANN's responsibilities for gTLDs and ccTLDs are different and this is reflected by the supporting organization's functions. The gNSO is responsible for consensus recommendations related to gTLDs. The ccNSO is not yet operational, but it will provide a process whereby the actual administrators of ccTLDs will share information and develop any needed global recommendations that ccTLDs will abide by. ICANN's processes recognize that first and foremost, the ccTLDs are subject to the laws of their respective national governments. Therefore, ICANN will not be imposing policies and practices on ccTLDs. Rather, it will endorse policies developed by the ccTLD administrators themselves.

Given its responsibilities, ICANN plays an important role in ensuring the technical stability of the Internet. Its work ensures that Internet communications are properly directed. Therefore, every domain name holder, an individual, business or government, must follow certain procedures for domain name allocation, designation, etc., to ensure that Internet communications are not disrupted.

It is important to note that ICANN is not responsible for general public policy issues, but only technical coordination and matters related to its core functions.

ICANN is led by the private sector including technical, commercial and non-commercial experts with the advice and support of governments through the Government Advisory Committee.

II. Public Policy Matters

Public policy matters are, in general, the responsibility of governments. However, policy discussions must include the active participation of business and other stakeholders.

A public policy can result in governments regulating a particular activity, allowing business to self-regulate or any combination thereof. Therefore, a public policy might be to refrain from regulating where not essential, which we believe to be a wise strategy in an area of rapid change and technological development.

A small sample of public policy matters related to the information society include:

- intellectual property protection
- taxation
- privacy / protection of personal data
- trade
- security

- consumer protection / empowerment
- education
- spam

Some of these issues require international cooperation and action. There are international bodies such as WIPO and the WTO with authority and jurisdiction for some of these issues. Other issues require international coordination of national policy. A number of bodies exist such as the OECD, United Nations ICT Task Force, APEC and CITEL, where these issues can be discussed and coordinated.

DEVELOPING THE POTENTIAL OF THE INTERNET THROUGH COORDINATION, NOT GOVERNANCE

The Internet Society (ISOC)

The Internet has come of age

In many countries, the Internet has become a mass medium. This has brought with it reflexive pressure on policy makers to regulate it as if it were radio, television, or other mass media. While governments naturally seek to address their citizens' interests regarding online privacy, spam, Internet security, intellectual property protection, the price of Internet access, and the digital divide, our position is that better use of technology, and broad participation in today's Internet coordination processes, not government regulation, are the most effective and appropriate ways to satisfy these concerns.

The biggest barrier to the Internet fulfilling its immense potential could turn out to be misinformed and inappropriate intervention in the way in which the Internet's technologies, resources and policies are developed, deployed and coordinated. The Internet Society can help provide guidance here.

What is the nature of the Internet?

The Internet is a modern distributed communications medium. No one is in charge of the Internet and yet everyone is in charge. Unlike the antiquated system of national telephone network monopolies, the global Internet consists of tens of thousands of interconnected networks run by Internet Service Providers, individual companies, universities, governments, and other institutions. Some of these are global in scope, others regional or local. Hundreds of different organizations and thousands of different companies make decisions every year that contribute to how the Internet develops.

These varied entities, together with the users of the Internet and the developers of Internet technologies and applications, have specific needs for coordination. Collaborative processes that are critical for the future stability and evolution of the Internet, and which should not be modified arbitrarily or abruptly, satisfy these needs.

Coordination, not Governance

It is misleading to use the term 'Internet governance' when the Internet is clearly not a single entity to govern. It is more useful to refer to 'Internet coordination'. The multiple facets of the Internet require different types of coordination, each calling for specific competences and sensitivities to balance the needs of the Internet user community globally and locally.

Specific Internet coordination activities are taking place globally at three levels:

- Coordination of the definition of Internet standards
- Coordination of the availability and assignment of Internet resources
- Coordination of the policies preventing misuse of the Internet

This coordination is best performed by the existing set of organizations using proven processes. Because of the diverse nature of these activities, it is unrealistic to expect a single body - government or otherwise - to take on all these roles effectively.

Coordinating Internet standards

The Internet Engineering Task Force (IETF), under the umbrella of the Internet Society, is one of the oldest and most successful Internet coordination processes. Other organizations are also involved in Internet related standards, including the IEEE, the W3C and the ITU.

Many of the protocols at the heart of today's Internet (e.g. TCP, IP, HTTP, FTP, SMTP, Telnet, PPP, POP3, the DNS protocol etc.) were developed through IETF standards activities. The results of the IETF are well engineered and practical open protocol standards that are trusted and open to global implementation with little or no licensing restrictions - they are freely available on the Internet, without cost, to everyone.

The strength of the IETF process lies in its unique culture and talented global community of network designers, network operators, service providers, equipment vendors, and researchers. They all openly contribute their individual technical experience and engineering wisdom in an environment that fosters innovation and the open exchange of ideas.

This process, which is open to anyone, helps quickly identify and articulate problems of common interest. It also helps build the trust required to make the further investments necessary for a protocol to be usefully implemented and deployed. Ultimately, however, it is the Internet users themselves that determine whether or not a protocol is valuable and useful enough for widespread use. Here the IETF track record of producing useful, widely deployed protocols is unrivalled.

Coordinating Internet resources: The Internet registry system

There has always been a need to manage the allocation of Internet resources such as the unique addresses that identify devices connected to the Internet (IP addresses), generic top-level domain names (e.g. .org), country code top-level domain names (e.g. .ch), domain names (such as www.isoc. org), and the systems that translate domain names into IP addresses (e.g. the Domain Name System or DNS).

This coordination activity has been handled by long-standing, not-for-profit membership organizations such as the Regional Internet Registries (RIRs) and top-level domain (TLD) registries.

More recently, coordination at a global level has been supported by ICANN (the Internet Corporation for Assigned Names and Numbers). Established in 1998, ICANN is also a not-for-profit organization.

Business, technical, non-commercial, academic, governmental and end-user communities participate in ICANN.

These organizations are a meeting point for bottom-up, consensual, industrial self-regulation by the groups and individuals that use their services and resources.

Coordinating policies preventing misuse of the Internet

As we have seen, organizations such as the RIRs, TLD registries, ICANN and the IETF all have very specific roles. It is neither within their charters, nor within their capabilities, to take on responsibility for all areas of Internet coordination – particularly that of preventing inappropriate use of the Internet. For example, areas such as 'cyber crime' (e.g. fraud and child pornography) require coordinated global attention by lawmakers – and not by those responsible for the equitable coordination of the underlying Internet infrastructure. Security matters also need to be addressed by organizations providing Internet access (not only by standards developers), and intellectual property issues may best be handled by organizations such as WIPO.

In discussions about these broader Internet policy issues there is cooperation between all the organizations mentioned above. ICANN for example works with WIPO to implement its Uniform Domain Name Dispute Resolution Policy (UDRP). And the Internet Society, with technical advice from the IETF, works with governments and policy makers to explain the effects and possibilities of new Internet technologies.

The way forward - Make your voice heard

Existing consensus-based processes have given us the Internet and have successfully coordinated its phenomenal growth: thousands of new networks, new policy procedures, new top-level domain names, new protocols etc. All of them constantly balance the needs and stability of today's Internet with future demands.

An open debate is now needed to move towards common, globally acceptable policies, processes and technologies to prevent misuse of the Internet. Governments have a vital role to play here as a concerted effort on the part of the Internet community, non-governmental organizations and governments can help strengthen and extend today's successful coordination processes.

The successful continued development of the Internet for the benefit of everyone can be ensured by participation in these proven processes rather than by attempting to create new untested mechanisms that are inappropriate to the unique characteristics of the Internet.

The Internet Society remains dedicated to providing information and orientation about Internet structures and processes. We encourage broad participation in the activities of each of the organizations involved in Internet coordination.

Section 4

PUBLIC POLICY ISSUES

background paper

INTERNET GOVERNANCE: A DISCUSSION DOCUMENT

George Sadowsky, Global Internet Policy Initiative and Internews Network
Raul Zambrano and Pierre Dandjinou, United Nations Development Programme (UNDP)

1. Introduction

1.1. The WSIS Mandate on Internet governance

Discussions on Internet governance have been taking place for several years and predate the World Summit on the Information Society (WSIS) process. To a large extent, the many global debates on the subject grew in volume due to the technology boom of the late 1990s and the heavy involvement and interest of the ICT private sector in the process. The boom not only suggested the apparent emergence of a new economy but also the enormous social and political transformation power that the Internet and related new technologies could deliver into the hands of citizens throughout the globe.

Recognizing the importance of ICTs generally, and the Internet in particular, for the development of the Information Society, the WSIS process focused, inter alia, on the issue of governance mechanisms for the ICT sector. This issue was one of the more contentious that consumed the preparatory work for the Summit, in part because of widely differing viewpoints held by specific sectors, individual countries and by groups of countries. In addition, the uniqueness of the Internet's development, characterized not only by extraordinary rapidity and success of its diffusion, but also by bottom-up participatory and transparent decision making spurred by the not-for-profit and private sectors, provided no precedent upon which to rely. The existing governance structures were both questioned and defended, and consensus was reached only on the relevance of the issue.

These and other issues were addressed in the many WSIS preparatory sessions and at the summit itself. However, no short-term agreement was feasible before or at the Geneva Summit itself and, as a result, WSIS set out a follow-up process on Internet governance with the WSIS-2 Tunisia Summit in November of 2005 as a target for obtaining an acceptable position on this subject.

The World Summit permitted people from government, business, international organizations, and non-governmental organizations to discuss, inter alia, the Internet and the policies, standards, and organizations that are affecting its operation and evolution. Particular attention was focused on ways that developing countries can better exploit the Internet, on the allocation of Internet names and numbers, on cyber-security, on intellectual property rights, and on how to better support e-government, education, and health.

"Internet governance" was one of several major themes that were discussed. One motivation for the discussion was a challenge, made by several developing countries, to the role of the Internet Corporation for Assigned Names and Numbers (ICANN).[1] ICANN's role is to exercise technical coordination functions with respect to the Internet, and in particular, to coordinate the management of the technical elements of the domain name system (DNS) to ensure universal resolvability so that all users of the Internet can find valid addresses.[2]

The Summit participants included the following point in the Plan of Action produced by the Summit:

---

[1] The proposals presented by this group of countries at the various WSIS meetings included: (1) a request for a United Nations body or a truly inter-governmental and international organization to assume a key role on Internet governance issues; (2) the start of work on moving/creating regionally-based DNS root servers; (3) full internationalization of Internet domain and host names; and (4) larger involvement in the above processes by country registries and country stakeholders.

[2] The creation of ICANN (Internet Corporation for Assigned Names and Numbers) in 1998 by the US government, through a Memorandum of Understanding (MoU) between the United States Department of Commerce, provided a global forum to which all stakeholders involved in the process could contribute to the various issues. This same action created a quasi-global governance process with open and bottom-up participation to specifically deal with a mainly technical issue — the management and administration of Internet names and numbers. The most recently issued version of the MoU is intended to be the last and sets out a series of goals for ICANN that, when achieved, will result in a fully independent ICANN organization.

"13. To maximize the social, economic and environmental benefits of the Information Society, governments need to create a trustworthy, transparent and non-discriminatory legal, regulatory and policy environment. Actions include:

…

b) We ask the Secretary-General of the United Nations to set up a working group on Internet governance, in an open and inclusive process that ensures a mechanism for the full and active participation of governments, the private sector and civil society from both developing and developed countries, involving relevant intergovernmental and international organizations and forums, to investigate and make proposals for action, as appropriate, on the governance of Internet by 2005. The group should, *inter alia*:

i) develop a working definition of Internet governance;

ii) identify the public policy issues that are relevant to Internet governance;

iii) develop a common understanding of the respective roles and responsibilities of governments, existing intergovernmental and international organisations and other forums as well as the private sector and civil society from both developing and developed countries;

iv) prepare a report on the results of this activity to be presented for consideration and appropriate action for the second phase of WSIS in Tunis in 2005."

As an initial step, the United Nations ICT Task Force has assumed the initial responsibility of preparing the ground for the implementation of the above request. The Task Force has requested a series of background papers on Internet governance and the policy options associated with alternative concepts of the governance structure. A global forum on this subject facilitated by the United Nations ICT Task Force was held in New York during March 25-26, 2004.

1.2. Objective of this document

The goal of this background paper is to provide a framework that can contribute to sorting out and understanding the issues surrounding the term "Internet governance". It is our belief that this term has been used to represent a variety of different aspects of the operation and use of the Internet and the manner with which it interacts with society. Since one of the purposes of this paper is to delineate what is meant by "Internet governance", we will use the term in quotes until the point at which we can arrive at a definition of it.

We would like to make it clear at the outset that this paper is aimed primarily at those issues that are of importance and relevance to developing countries. A good portion of what has been discussed using the label "Internet governance" is perhaps of little relevance to countries that have larger problems than, for example, how top level global domain names are chosen or implemented. Issues of education, health, employment, and entrepreneurship, among many others, are central to developing countries and directly related to the achievement of the Millennium Development Goals (MDGs). ICTs, including the Internet are important to developing countries to the extent that they can be key contributors in helping to achieve those goals. The issues of governance, policy and implementation vis-à-vis developing countries matter because they allow for harnessing the new technologies in a more effective fashion in targeting social and economic goals.

In writing this paper, we hope to add clarity to the discussion by presenting a framework that provides certain fundamental delineations between different aspects of the activities surrounding the Internet. Such a framework should provide for a more informed and efficient discussion of the real policy issues and differences of opinion that deserve to be considered in this context. Our goal is that this framework should be useful and perhaps even compelling conceptually, rather than to attempt to be comprehensive in detail.

We provide a short history of the evolution of the Internet and the parallel evolution of administrative mechanisms needed for its efficient and effective functioning. Within the province of "Internet governance", we then sharpen a fundamental distinction between, on the one hand, the technical administration and coordination of the Internet, including the policy choices introduced to implement this administrative regime and their governance implications, and on the other hand the myriad of issues caused by the introduction of new ICTs into our existing social, economic and governmental environment.

We then describe how the Internet is now administered and coordinated, followed by a review of the broader set of ICT governance issues and the organizations and institutions that today have full or partial responsibilities for addressing them. In addition, we provide some observations and conclusions with respect to an understanding of what Internet and ICT governance are, as well as some views regarding how such governance issues might best be viewed.

1.3. Analytical framework for addressing the issues

1.3.1. Understanding governance

One of the reasons why the issue of "Internet governance" has been the subject of so much discussion and considerable debate is the lack of a clear and common understanding on the concept of governance itself. In this respect, it is possible to find at least two levels that need to be differentiated: (1) the distinction between government and governance; and (2) the relations between governance, policy and implementation of policy.

Governance is a relatively new concept that has been used in relatively wide variety of ways.[3] In general terms, governance refers to the rules, processes and procedures, and specific actions that impact the way in which power is exercised on a specific area of concern. It can thus be said that an organization has a governance responsibility for an issue, area, or activity. Note that this general definition of governance applies to any sort of organization and it is not intrinsically limited to governments. Governance is in fact a broader concept than government in that government essentially has "governance" responsibilities limited to specific areas (constitution, judiciary, legislative, etc.).[4]

It is perhaps important to stress this last point. Governance does *not* rely on the existence of any form of organized government structure. Non-governmental organizations and the private sector can self-organize and assume governance responsibilities on issues that are not necessarily related to their own internal operation or corporate structure.[5] This is in fact the case for many of the existing organizations that have been involved in Internet governance. Furthermore, it is *not* necessarily the case that government or governments decide what the governance structure or the scope of governance responsibilities are to be for an organization.[6] In fact, it is quite possible that a government may be prohibited from exercising a governance responsibility by virtue of restrictions on its involvement contained in the country's constitution.

Nor should it be assumed that restrictive governance, in the sense of control over policies and/or modalities of implementation, is necessarily better than a permissive governance model offering maximum degrees of freedom. In particular and of substantial importance for this discussion, much of the success of the Internet to date has been due to decentralized

---

[3] In effect, governance has been used in the context of: the minimal state; corporate governance; the new public management; good governance; ICT networks; and self-organizing networks. See "*The new governance: governing without government*", R.A.W. Rhodes, Political Studies, 44 (4), 1996.

[4] Although governance in itself does not include any normative considerations, it is possible to assess it effectiveness by using concepts such as openness, participation and accountability among others.

[5] It should be noted that the emergence of the Internet and new ICT have provided very powerful and effective tools to promote bottom-up governance organizations that can operate on a national, regional or global scale in ways that were not possible 20 years ago.

[6] In other words, who decides "who" (in the structure posited above) can have many different answers, and there can in fact well be a number of organizations that make such decisions in some fashion. The process of how that governance responsibility is assigned and/or legitimized, i.e. how and by whom that authority is conferred upon an organization of any type, is inherently a political or social question and is not explored in this document.

development and the absence of controls on either its expansion or the services that have evolved that use it.

Many "Internet governance" issues have a global scope and thus seem to require resolution on a global scale. From the point of view of governance alone, it is thus pertinent to distinguish between international governance and global governance. For our purposes here it will suffice to say that the latter, in contrast with the former, is characterized by an increased involvement of transnational and non-governmental actors at all levels vis-à-vis governments and a broader geographical scope that includes regional, sub-regional and local levels in addition to countries[7]. Thus, any suggestions or recommendations as to the type of organization that should or could address "Internet governance" should take this difference into account.

1.3.2. Governance, policy and policy implementation

Based on the above understanding of governance, we would like to introduce the following operational way of looking at the relationship between governance, policy, and implementation. With respect to issue areas, whether in the broad ICT sector or specifically with respect to the Internet:

- Governance responds to the "who" question, i.e. who has the authority to make decisions with respect to a specific set of issues or problems, and therefore, who takes the responsibility for the issue area, i.e. who has the mandate;

- Policy responds to the "what" question, i.e. what policies are to be put into effect to deal with a set of issues or problems; and

- Implementation responds to the "how" question, i.e. once the policies are in effect, how shall they be implemented and enforced.

It is our sense that a considerable amount of ongoing discussions of "Internet governance" mix elements from all these three categories into one, and this has confused many of the issues, including the role of a number of institutions, including ICANN. Second, this is probably the result of the fact that these three issues are closely related and a number of the issues at stake are seen to cut across them. A key point is that stakeholders involved in the ongoing Internet governance discussion should adopt a more "holistic" approach to the issues on the table before moving to specific recommendations on the governance of any aspect of ICT or the Internet.

---

[7] For a detailed discussion on the subject see for example "Global Governance and the United Nations System", United Nations University, 2002.

1.3.3. Proposed framework for approaching Internet governance

This paper proposes the following framework for discussing the issue of governance in relation to ICT and the Internet. The first part of the model is based upon three conceptual groupings, each of which is a superset of the grouping below it:

1. ICT governance issues, which contain as a subset:
2. Internet governance issues, which contain as a subset:
3. Administration and coordination of Internet names and numbers

One can visualize the relationships between the groups spatially as a set of concentric circles, with circle 1 containing circle 2, which in turn contains circle 3. It should be noted that each of these groups contains a variety of pure technical activities as well as governance and policy implications.

The first grouping above and the largest in scope relates to the emergence of the so-called information society triggered in large part by the emergence of new ICTs (including the Internet) which have brought forward a series of new issues (and some old issues now recast in a global scope) that require the attention of both governments and stakeholders.[8] We define this series of issues under the "Global ICT Governance" umbrella. The second grouping has been perhaps the most well referenced and most heavily discussed in the last several years. It is the "Internet governance" issue, which is indeed a subset of the first with an exclusive focus on the Internet. The third grouping is the more basic and perhaps even "simpler" issue of the administration and coordination of the assignment of Internet names and numbers — one of the components of broader Internet governance for which ICANN has taken the lead and the initiative — as well as the governance implications of these functions, at the global level.

A second and important component of the framework is the geographical dimension. The assignment of governance functions in each of the above categories depends on the geographic dimension under consideration — global, regional, national or local. Once we move from one geographic level to another, issues of institutional readiness, local capacity, ICT use, etc. vary tremendously from country to country. This is particularly true for developing countries. These differences must be taken into account if the issues of ICT governance are to be addressed and

---

[8] It should be noted that there are other new ICTs that are emerging, most notably second and third generation cellular phone services and other wireless networking technologies. The key point is that the convergence of information in digital form, combined with the Internet's ability to transmit it effectively, has changed the landscape both of ICT-base services and the regulatory and policy models that are appropriate to harness the technologies effectively.

implemented across the globe. Global and local tensions do exist today on many of the issues[9], and this seems to indicate that a 'one size fits all' solution is not at all feasible. On the other hand, the notion of "one country, one solution" should also be avoided.

1.3.4. Scope of the framework

This paper will focus on both Internet and ICT governance, but does not aim at providing a comprehensive view of the latter. Rather, the focus will be on highlighting the key issues and priorities in these areas while drawing from some of the lessons learned. Our goal is to provide a simple structure for the issues involved, abstracting what seems important to us and neglecting what we believe to be detail, without being simplistic in doing so.

In this context one can now speak of "ICT Governance", consisting of a broad set of issues and a corresponding set of organizations that can provide a policy framework for ICTs to be deployed to promote the emergence and strengthening of the Information Society. While the main focus of this paper is the Internet and "Internet governance", we need to keep in mind that the Internet is just one instance of a number of technologies, each of which has resulted in a set of existing understandings of varying strength and a set of existing institutions that over time has been shaped to guide the use of the technology.

The widespread use of the Internet and new ICTs now affects many aspects of the inner workings of society. These effects need to be confronted by an examination and possible alteration of policy, including legal and regulatory changes, required to address such changes. On the one hand, ICTs can impact areas and problems that previously existed in a way that may well require new governance mechanisms, continued policy dialogue, and innovative policies. Like previous emerging ICTs, the Internet's presence has changed the nature of the problems in such a way that existing policy, laws and regulations may no linger address them adequately or comprehensively. On the other hand, the introduction of ICTs may also raise new issues and thus create a governance and policy vacuum that did not exist before and that requires prompt attention by the various stakeholders involved in these processes.[10] [11]

---

[9] This in fact relates to the ongoing discussion on the character and scope of Global governance and its relation to development. See as an interesting example "The Global Governance of Trade: As If Development Really Mattered",
http://www.undp.org/mainundp/propoor/docs/pov_globalgovernancetrade_pub.pdf

[10] One example is provided by criminal behavior. Theft, fraud, invasion of privacy, and destruction of property have existed since the beginning of time, and governments and international agencies have established national legislation and international frameworks and institutions to address these problems. These laws and institutions exist on a local, national, regional and global scale. The introduction of the Internet has permitted new manifestations of criminal behavior, so that the ability of current legislation

2. History of ICT and Internet Governance Issues

2.1. Background

To a large extent, the continuous global debates on Internet governance have grown in volume because of the recognition on the part of governments and societies worldwide that the Internet is becoming a crucial component of global commerce and human development. The technology boom of the late 1990s and the heavy involvement and interest of the ICT private sector in the process of developing predictable, transparent rules, has contributed significantly to this recognition.

In addressing the issue of Internet governance, it is important to regard the development of the Internet in historical perspective, and within a context of the many and diverse technologies that are grouped under the rubric of Information and Communication Technologies (ICTs). In the last 100 years, and more prominently in the last 50+ years since World War II, ICTs have evolved from a relatively primitive state to one characterized by rapid technological progress and a multiplicity of services that would have been considered in the realm of science fiction at the beginning of the period.

At the beginning of the 1950s, direct dial telephony was in its infancy. Long distance and international direct dialing were practically non-existent, and long distance circuits were based upon noisy copper wire analog transmission. FM radio broadcasting was a relative novelty, and black and white television was just beginning to find a consumer market. Postal airmail was an expensive alternative to ordinary mail transported by land and by sea. Facsimile transmission (fax) was not known. The first artificial earth satellite, Sputnik, was several years away from its launch. Telegrams and cables were the workhorses of international communications; telex represented the first truly international email service. Cellphones were almost completely a

---

and institutional capabilities may be insufficient to cope. Therefore, a re-examination of what is needed to cope with this new manifestation of old behavior may be required. This is an example of an Internet public policy issue.

[11] Another example is provided by "spam", or unwanted bulk electronic mailings. While it has always been possible to send unsolicited mail, faxes, or other forms of messages to many recipients, previous technologies have imposed both costs and speed limitations that have kept the level of annoyance of recipients to acceptable levels. The Internet, however, allows the distribution of unsolicited material to millions of people at a much lower cost, the result being that by current estimates such spam accounts for well over half of the email sent on the Internet. This imposes aggregate costs for ISPs, which are in the long run passed onto users. More insidious is that such behavior imposes enormous aggregate costs on the user population in coping individually with such messages. It further globally threatens the attractiveness and utility of the medium, and in excessive cases, becomes a de facto tool for denial of service. While the problem existed before the Internet, the introduction of the Internet has transformed the problem into one where existing responses and policies are no longer adequate to deal with the threat.

speculation of science fiction. The transistor, a fundamental building block of today's ICTs, had just been invented and had not yet been incorporated into commercial products. Electronic calculators did not exist. Computers, both huge in size and primitive in capacity, had just been introduced into commercial service, and cost millions of 1950 United States dollars.

The inventions referred to above have clearly changed our world irrevocably. Just as the automobile disrupted prior patterns of life and made possible entirely new patterns of working and living, ICTs such as cellular telephony, direct dial digital telephony, television, communications satellites, worldwide courier service, satellite television broadcasting, computers and finally the Internet have further shrunk our world and have provided is with a capability to communicate, almost anytime, almost anywhere, with almost anyone, with a quality and types of services unimaginable to our ancestors. Needless to say, the spread of ICTs is far from uniform both across and within countries and to a large extent reflects existing socio-economic differences.

Each new use of technology has posed its own challenges in terms of how the deployment and use of the technology should be guided or regulated, if at all, to have a clear impact and benefit at the country level from the perspective of economic and social progress and development. These challenges have been met over time by the establishment of institutions on multiple levels — provincial, national, and international — to deal with issues raised by the introduction and exploitation of new technologies. Perhaps the best-known example of this in the last 15 years is the deregulation of the telecommunications sector in many countries.

The manner of dealing with each new technology and its commercial manifestations varies from technology to technology. The important thing to note is that as technologies have appeared, most nations both individually and collectively have created and changed institutions to address the issues that they have presented. A partial list of such institutions dealing with issues raised by ICTs at the global level would include, *inter alia*, IOS, ITU, OECD, UNCITRAL, UNCTAD, WTO, WIPO, G8, COE, APEC, European Union and the World Bank. In addition, many ICT governance issues are adequately handled by non-governmental bodies, such as industry associations and standards bodies, without recourse to intergovernmental involvement.

Thus there exists a broad variety of both issues and of existing institutions that have evolved to address the appropriate deployment of ICTs and the effects of their introduction on societies. This collection of organizations and institutions includes, *inter alia*, intergovernmental institutions, professional societies, industry trade groups, as well as voluntary associations of various types. For some issues, it has been decided that they are best left to private markets, requiring no institutional intervention, guidance, or regulation. This is particularly true in developed countries where internal markets are large and efficient. The fundamental question regarding the imposition or of such guidance should ideally be what form of guidance, if any, is best suited to ensuring the effective deployment of the technology for the public good.

2.2. Governance of ICTs and the Internet and the relevance for developing countries

New ICTs and in particular the Internet are in some respects remarkably different from previous ICTs, and offer a new range of powerful services that combine access to information and the ability to communicate. Like any other new technology, they have the capacity to be well used or misused according to societal norms. What kind of an environment of governance surrounding them will maximize their potential in the various important areas of human endeavour? What will their effects be on society and what policies, if any, need to be instituted to cope with them? Of great importance, how can they be best employed to assist developing countries to achieve their full potential in the global economy? These are the important questions that emanate from WSIS as well as from other concerned bodies and people.

The rapid development of the Internet has led to the emergence and quick deployment of new services that have *de facto* contributed to the creation of a global economy in which networks of all sorts and networking have become the salient features. Examples of this include the rapid growth of wireless technologies and networks as well as the increasing convergence of the various new technologies.

However, the full promise of the new ICTs and the Internet has not been reached. This is perhaps best reflected in the recent discussion of the so-called "digital divide" both between and within countries. Although some observers are now suggesting that the ICT gap between countries is closing[12], the same cannot be said about access to ICT within countries, particularly in developing countries. In fact, not only do most people in developing countries have limited or no access to the new technologies but they also have more pressing individual needs.

Does this mean that developing countries should not be concerned with the issues emerging from the deployment and widespread global use of ICTs? Certainly, the participation of developing countries in emerging ICT global issues, including the ICANN process, has been minimal by any standard. Moreover, when participation has occurred, generally only government representatives have been involved. Without doubt, most developing countries have been oblivious to the process, missing critical opportunities to bring their views and needs to relevant global forums.

---

[12] See *"Canyon or mirage?"*, http://economist.com/printedition/displayStory.cfm?Story_ID=2367710

In addition, our experience to date indicates that the new ICTs are disruptive technologies, with the capacity to affect many if not most aspects of our lives. New technologies bring new challenges with them, especially when they are capable of operating on a global level and disregarding national boundaries. Developed countries are generally rich in institutions that can capitalize upon the benefits of the Internet, and they are also generally well endowed with governmental and non-governmental organizations that address the issues and problems that the Internet brings. The corresponding institutions in developing countries, on the other hand, often do not exist, and when they do they often lack the knowledge and the resources to cope with significant issues.

To be effective players and key actors in the new global society, developing countries must build both the awareness of "ICT governance" and the capacity to respond to the new challenges. As it is today, the "ICT governance" agenda has been essentially driven by developed countries that are pressed to confront the issues and have ready solutions at hand. However some aspects of governance will require global and international action, and developing countries need to get involved and be active participants in order to fully reap the benefits of the new technologies and exploit them to support their development agendas.

2.3. Distinction between administration and governance of ICT public policy issues

We believe that there is a fundamental difference between certain functions that we label as the *Internet administration* part of Internet governance — the third innermost circle in the model presented above — and other functions that we include in *Internet governance*. Internet administration involves the operation of the network, ensuring that it is interoperable, functional, stable, secure and effective over the long run. It is concerned with functions that did not exist prior to the Internet, the most obvious being the coordinated cooperative management of a very large, global packet switching network based upon hierarchical, open, decentralized network administration. This is new territory for technologists, but one that is being successfully addressed by the coordinated efforts of a variety of groups.

The bifurcation of administration and policy is not as sharp as has been described above. Because of the malleability of the underlying software technology, approaches to policy problems as well as solutions often have both a technological component and a policy component. In most cases they are separable. Technologists can describe possible technological assists to problems, while policy makers need to determine what mix of technology and policy best satisfies the general good. In other words, it appears to be the job of the Internet governance apparatus (or the relevant arm of it) to make decisions regarding how a specific issue is to be addressed, using, *inter alia*, information from technologists and administrators that enhances the set of possible solutions. The technical community is then responsible for creating the best tools possible for implementing public policy — but policy considerations should drive the discussion regarding how the issue is dealt with.

Within this framework, the implications of Internet administration are quite important. In the next two sections, we focus upon each of these areas. The emphasis upon ICANN follows from WSIS' focus upon it because of its association in the minds of many (incorrectly in our view) with Internet governance, and *not* on its relative importance in Internet governance issues. To the extent possible, we believe that Internet administration should be policy free, and should be open, collaborative, consensus driven, bottom-up, reflecting the current operating culture that pervades the core Internet community. This approach has worked well up to now.

3. Management and Administration of Internet Space
3.1. Internet administration and coordination
The network research project that eventually became the Internet started in the late 1960s with funding from the United States government for a project known as the ARPANET. Over time, the ARPANET became the Internet, which now claims over 900 million users in all countries of the world.[13] During its formative years, Internet administration and coordination was a simple business, but the basis for it that was established during that time has allowed the Internet to scale rapidly and successfully. Annex 1 contains a brief history of the Internet and its governance prior to 1998.

It is very important to understand that no single person, organization or country manages the Internet. The Internet is managed by many entities, all of them working within an open, coordinated framework. The management model is one of distributed management, and is provided by groups of cooperating entities. These entities are both geographically and organizationally distributed, but their actions are coordinated by a commonly accepted set of standards and modalities of action. ICANN occupies a key role in that it provides, inter alia, central coordination at the global level of the addressing functions that allow the Internet to operate. Because of the bottom up orientation of the Internet's architecture and management model, such required coordination may be defined globally, but implementation is distributed and occurs at the local level in a bottom-up manner. This implies that governance models for the Internet are also likely to be distributed and cooperative in nature.

---

[13] "Population Explosion!", http://www.clickz.com/stats/big_picture/geographics/article.php/3347211. Note however that estimates of the number of users of the Internet, as well as definitions of what constitutes an Internet user, vary significantly. Furthermore, any estimate made rapidly becomes invalid because of the rapid growth of the user population. Suffice it to say that the number is probably about and possibly in excess of 15% of the total world population, and it is therefore a very important technology no matter what the actual number is.

Within the realm of Internet technical administration, ICANN is not the sole responsible institution. The technical management of the Internet is also directed by the following principal actors on the Internet stage, who are now responsible for the technical management of the Internet and related ICT functions:

- The Internet Engineering Task Force (IETF) is the Internet's standards organization, responsible for the development of tested standards upon which the Internet rests.

- The Internet Architecture Board (IAB), chartered by ISOC, provides oversight of aspects of the architecture for the protocols and procedures used by the Internet.

- The Internet Society (ISOC) contains the Internet Engineering Steering Group (IESG), which sets the general agenda for the work of the IETF. In addition, ISOC is the entity that provides the legal umbrella for the activities of the IETF and the IAB.

- The Internet Corporation for Assigned Names and Numbers (ICANN) is responsible for technical coordination of the Internet address space (IP numbers) and the Domain Name System.[14]

- The Computer Emergency Response Team (CERT) in the United States and the growing number of national CERTs in other countries that have banded together into the Forum of Incident Response and Security Teams (www.first.org), have responsibility for monitoring network-related threats to the integrity of the Internet and its attached computers.

- The Regional Internet Registries (RIRs) are responsible for the allocation of IP addresses in their regions of responsibility.[15]

- The Internet Assigned Numbers Authority (IANA) is responsible for various administrative functions associated with management of the Internet's domain-name system root zone.

- The root server operators maintain a synchronized set of distributed common databases of the directories for top level domains.[16]

- The World Wide Web Consortium (W3C) is responsible for standards pertaining to the World Wide Web.

---

[14] ICANN is also technically responsible for the assignment of numbers to specific protocols defined by the IETF. This is a purely technical function, and is delegated to the IETF.

[15] Regional Internet Registries will soon exist for every continent in the world. The African registry, the last to be defined, is currently being established.

[16] There are 13 root server operators, the majority of which are located outside of the United States. See http://www.root-servers.org/.

- The International Telecommunications Union (ITU) provides comprehensive standards at layer 1, (e.g. telephony) for communications technologies that carry Internet traffic. The ITU also provides international coordination of the allocation and use of the communication frequencies of the electromagnetic spectrum, among many other things.

- The network operator groups, including RIPE, Apricot, NANOG, APNG, SANOG, AFNOG, SilkNOG, and others, serve as important coordination points for the major operators.

- The approximately 100 companies that provide the core of the Internet[17] coordinate their activities through formalized network operators' groups, and have peering arrangements among themselves that provide connectivity to other ISPs.

The above list includes an intergovernmental agency, a number of professional societies, several operational entities, an administrative organization, and a meritocracy with no direct legal status. Voluntary cooperation and transparency of operation, a position publicly avowed by all participants, allows these organizations to work together.

The continuing involvement of the United States government in the administration of ICANN has been troubling for some countries. In effect, ICANN has operated under contract to the United States Department of Commerce, and is in theory subject to its direction. In practice, ICANN is more like an international organization, with a Board of Directors composed of more than 50% non-North American members. For all intents and purposes, the United States Department of Commerce has not made any attempt to overtly control any specific aspects of ICANN's activities. We believe that if the United States government were to relinquish control of ICANN, many issues of Internet governance would de-escalate somewhat.

3.2. A job of technical coordination and management

As we have noted, the Internet is a new form of communication. It shares characteristics with previous forms, but has attributes that set it apart from any previous form and make it unique. It rests on concepts that are technically elegant, and which have allowed it to scale to hundreds of millions of connected computers distributed over almost all countries. In the process of that evolution, however, its actual structure has become quite complex. Further, its fundamental architecture has had to evolve to meet some of the social issues that it has generated, most visibly the need to harden its infrastructure against individuals who want to cause it harm or use it to do harm to others. Such people were not part of the cooperative environment in which that architecture initially evolved, but are currently users of it.

---

[17] Technically, these companies provide the default-free routing zone.

The management of the Internet has the objective of maintaining the operation, the integrity and the interoperability of the global Internet. It is a new technical effort. Before the Internet there was no knowledge about how to manage large packet networks, what addressing structures would work, or what economic models of either cost sharing or economic sustainability would prove to be durable and effective in meeting an increasing demand for services offered. The early technical management of the Internet was helped by a clear and relatively scalable architectural vision and the very substantial input of many cooperative volunteers from multiple sectors through the Internet Engineering Task Force (IETF), which still serves as the formulating body for Internet standards even though it is essentially a body of interested and informed volunteers.

An essential aspect of the technical administration of the Internet has been that the administrative mechanisms that have evolved had little if any precedent, and that their creation and evolution have been essentially a technical task, invisible to the average user of the net. We believe that this is one of the two most important conceptual distinctions to make in the larger discussion of Internet governance. Internet administration concerns itself with the effective functioning of the network. In the execution of the administrative and coordination mandate, decisions have been needed that have governance implications. The set of Internet policy issues, discussed later in this report, concerns itself with the interaction of the Internet and a large set of public policy issues that preceded the Internet. In addressing these public policy issues, governance issues are prominent and diverse.

The technical administration of the Internet does involve some choices and the establishment of some policies by necessity. A discussion of these matters may be found in Annex 2.

3.3. Technical administration and coordination: An assessment

The current administration and coordination of the Internet's functions is a result of historical evolution. In general, given the pace of both technological change and growth of the Internet, the record has been quite good, particularly in industrialized countries. The policies that have been in place, combined with the informal and generally cooperative nature of the players in the Internet industry, have provided the flexibility and freedom for innovation that have fashioned the Internet into the ubiquitous and productive tool it is today.

The circumstances surrounding the Internet today are significantly different from the past, and it is reasonable to ask how a different set of policies and governance mechanisms for the administration and coordination of the Internet itself would assist in achieving certain goals. For the purposes of this exercise, the goal is certainly the rapid spread of the accessible and affordable Internet to as many people as possible, but with special reference to its availability and affordability in the developing countries, with the availability of useful and relevant content to assist in the development process.

Growth in companies and organizations inevitably requires change. The organizations in the Internet industry, including those listed above responsible for the operation and coordination of the network, have exhibited change over time. Alternative governance structures are certainly possible. However, in contemplating change, one should always consider the possibility of unintended consequences. Internet administration and coordination is a complex task in which there are many players, and the value provided by changes must clearly exceed the disruption and uncertainty that they may cause.

The situation in most developing countries is more complicated. First, although clear rules, guidelines and procedures have been established at the global level, their implementation and enforcement at the national level has been very uneven. It is still possible to find situations where users of the Internet are being asked to pay additional charges for the assignment of IP addresses. In addition, the price for domain names is usually higher, and ISPs often operate in a quasi-monopolistic market. As a result, users seeking domain names in their countries are often bypassing the use of ccTLDs. Secondly, in most developing countries there is little awareness of the existing rules and procedures for Internet administration and coordination. This is partly due to the fact that most of the population in these countries is usually not connected to the Internet, combined with the fact that there is no national organization or governance mechanism to oversee the implementation and management of existing procedures. Finally, many developing countries still lack the local capacity to address these issues, and insufficient effort has been made at the global level to promote national capacity development for this purpose. Contrast this with the now multiple capacity building efforts for telecom regulators supported by developed countries and bi/multilateral organizations.

4. ICT Governance and Public Policy Issues

The growth and increasing pervasiveness in the use of ICTs, including the Internet, has raised a large group of public policy issues, some new, some old now seen under a new light, which have acquired global relevance and require concerted action to be addressed in a successful fashion. These issues offer a considerable challenge, arising from the introduction and impact of the Internet into a sphere of activity that previously existed, but did not then have to contend with any of the disruptions that the Internet may have introduced. In addition, in many transitional and developing countries, Internet aspects of policy issues are arising at the same time that reforms are being undertaken in the underlying legal environment applicable to offline transactions.

For example, some countries eager to take advantage of the Internet's commercial potential do not have the legal rules and enforcement mechanisms that will support credit or debit cards even for face-to-face transactions. Similarly, the development of national and international rules for electronic funds transfers predated the Internet, but participation in that system will be necessary if the Internet is to be used for online commerce. Fundamental issues like transparency, the adoption and constant application of rules that are both predictable and flexible, and an efficient non-corrupt court system — all major objectives of law reform efforts generally — are also crucial to the development of the Internet.

We suggest that this distinction defines an area of policy concerns that we believe is appropriate to consider labeling as a separate group of issues, and to consider labeling the group as the domain of Internet-related policy issues that are not related to Internet administration, but come from the intrusion of the Internet into existing human activities. The issue areas involved are the same areas that presented issues prior to the introduction of the Internet, but the unique and distinguishing nature of the Internet, as described above, requires at the very least an examination of whether existing legal and other policy instruments suffice, or whether a more fundamental rethinking of the national and international policy environment is required to cope with new and different manifestations of those issues.

In particular, the relative elimination of distance by the Internet requires a rethinking of the geographic scope of policy instruments that may have sufficed in pre-Internet days. Policies that previously could be more or less successfully applied at the local or national level may now have to be coordinated at the national or global level, bringing into play the complexity of and interaction between different legal systems and the need for international resolution of issues that were previously more local in character.

If this framework is accepted, then it becomes clear that Internet-related public policy issues need to be addressed in a distributed manner, by multiple organizations at multiple levels. This conclusion derives directly from the fact that the responsibility for ICT policy, as well as implementation and enforcement, of those same issues in pre-Internet times was distributed throughout multiple organizations at multiple levels.

Furthermore, and of considerable importance, is the fact that there are existing institutions that already work at multiple levels and that currently address each of these problem areas, and they have the expertise and credibility that is crucial to the resolution of the Internet-related policy issues. These existing institutions include a mix of national governments, regional and international bodies, self-regulatory bodies, trade associations, and consensus-based voluntary standards bodies. Viewed in this light, Internet and ICT policy governance already spans a large range of issues, and this governance is shared among many institutions of significantly different types.

The policy issues within scope of ICT and Internet governance are, *inter alia*, described in the following sections.

4.1. Content issues

Content issues may be among the most difficult issues that the Internet affects in new ways. The question of what is acceptable content has always been a subject of debate. While it is recognized that different cultures and countries have different standards, there has been a worldwide commitment to freedom of expression and a movement in recent decades towards an expansion of freedom of expression. Article 19 of the Universal Declaration of Human Rights provides that "everyone has the right to freedom of opinion and expression; this right includes freedom to hold opinions without interference and to seek, receive and impart information and ideas through any media and regardless of frontiers." Similar language appears in Article 19 of the International Covenant on Civil and Political Rights (CCPR), in Article 10 of the European Convention of Human Rights (ECHR), and in Article 13 of the American Convention on Human Rights. In the age of the borderless Internet, the protection of a right to freedom of expression "regardless of frontiers" takes on new and more powerful meaning.

In the past, content has been regulated physically (censorship of indigenous publishers and border inspections to keep out objectionable materials from abroad) and in a very gross way by the jamming of television and radio signals and prohibitions on the ownership of receiving devices (satellite dishes). While Internet traffic is capable of being filtered, the process of filtering is much more complex due to the millions of sites of material and the ability of a site to add or change addresses of potentially objectionable material.

We see differences among different groupings of content types that may be useful in guiding public policy:

- content that is universally hateful and illegal – child pornography is in this class of content;
- content that is culturally objectionable and possibly illegal – often pornography, doubts about the established religion, and criticism of government fit into this category;
- content that is politically objectionable – generally criticism of government beyond tolerable limits (which may not exist);
- libellous content – content that causes injury to reputation;

- content that is objectionable not because of its substance but because of its means of transmission – such as spam, which increases transmission costs, places a burden on recipients, and degrades the on-line experience.

In this context it is important to note that while there are issues of "objectionable content", there is also the principle of the right of access to information, free of censorship.

Public policy needs to address all of these types of content, within the framework of cultural diversity, international human rights and the continuing relevance of the nation state. What may be objectionable in one place may not be objectionable in another, and vice versa. Despite the borderless nature of the Internet, nations still retain the authority to regulate their own nationals. France, for example, can still punish French citizens who access neo-Nazi material. The hardest issue, and one that remains unresolved, is the question of jurisdiction. There are a variety of ways in which content can cross national boundaries in such a way that laws or standards are violated, and there is no clean method of deciding the jurisdiction in which the case is to be considered. International human rights bodies, including the European Court of Human Rights and the United Nations Commission on Human Rights, continue to define the scope of the freedom of expression. These bodies have recognized that the scope of the freedom depends in part on the nature of the medium and that the Internet is entitled to the highest form of protection.

One of the most difficult issues concerning Internet governance is the question of jurisdiction. The Hague Conference on Private International Law has been drafting an international convention in an effort to set international rules for determining the court in which foreign parties can be sued and when countries must recognize the judgments of foreign courts.

Some argue that crafting a convention to address jurisdictional issues will take too long and that alternative dispute resolution may provide an interim solution. The World Intellectual Property Organization helped craft a policy instituted in late 1999 by the Internet Corporation for Assigned Names and Numbers, the organization charged with managing the Internet's domain name system, for resolving trademark disputes involving domain names. Others complain, however, that the ICANN process is one-sided in favor of business interests. WIPO has launched other initiatives aimed at addressing some of the questions surrounding applicable law and jurisdiction raised by the Internet, including draft guidelines for how the same trademarks in different countries can coexist on the Internet.

Meanwhile, national courts continue to exercise jurisdiction over their own nationals, and countries are seeking bilateral cooperation on matters of mutual interest.

Distinct from the question of what is illegal is the question of who is liable for illegal content. Generally, the more developed countries of Europe and North America have adopted a rule that holds the creators of content liable, but that does not impose liability on ISPs or other mere conduits of information. Under this approach, reflected in the European Union regulatory framework, an ISP is not responsible for monitoring traffic over its system. An entity hosting content it did not create is liable only if it is notified of the illegal content and fails to take it down.

4.2. Crime and cyber-security

The introduction of the Internet has brought with it new ways of committing illegal acts. These new ways depend upon knowledge of Internet technology, and often prey upon users who are not sophisticated or suspicious. A recent issue of *The Economist* introduced an apt term for some of these behaviors and actions: *e-hooliganism.*

Some examples of e-hooliganism follow. It should be noted that countries' legal systems vary widely regarding their defining any or all of these behaviors as illegal and criminal.

- Data interception - to intentionally intercept, without right, by technical means, non-public transmissions of computer data to, from or within a computer system. Deterrence of this crime constitutes an essential element of cyber-trust, for it protects the confidentiality of communications.

- Data interference - to intentionally damage, delete, degrade, alter or suppress data in someone else's computer without right. This would include, for example, intentionally sending viruses that delete files, or hacking a computer and changing or deleting data, or hacking a web site and changing its appearance.

- System interference - to intentionally cause serious hindrance without right to the functioning of a computer system by inputting, transmitting, damaging, deleting, deteriorating, altering or suppressing computer data. This would include things like denial of service attacks or introducing viruses into a system in ways that interfere with its normal usage.

- Illegal access: - intentionally accessing, without right, the computer system of another. It can be thought of as the cyberspace equivalent of trespass.

- Forging phony email addresses to avoid identification.

- Typosquatting, i.e. trapping the results of user mistyping and catching it with, e.g. a domain name containing the misspelling.

- Hijacking people's use of networked computers through the installation of hidden back doors.

- Spyware, such as hidden software in a computer that records keystrokes and/or screen information, which is then secretly transmitted to the party that installed the spyware.

- Display of material not requested, such as advertisements; these tools are often referred to as adware, pop-up windows, or pop-under windows.

- Increased ease of identity theft through increased availability of publicly available information on the Internet.

- Financial fraud through exploitation of financial data, most often attempted using credit card information.

A number of international institutions have undertaken efforts to harmonize national laws on cybercrime and address issues of cyber-security. The European Union has developed a cyber-security strategy in a series of Communications and proposals from the Commission. The APEC forum has adopted a cyber-security strategy drafted by its Telecommunications and Information Working Group. OAS has done regional work as well. OECD has issued a set of Guidelines that constitute a road map for governments and private enterprises in developing cyber-security strategies. One of the most extensive efforts was undertaken by the Council of Europe, which has drafted a convention on cybercrime.

4.3. Intellectual property issues (other than DNS issues)

Protection of intellectual property (IP) is crucial to many aspects of the information society, ranging from online e-commerce, to IT-enabled outsourcing, to software development. The Internet poses special challenges for the protection of intellectual property, especially as broadband services make transfer of large music and video files feasible.

The three main branches of intellectual property law are copyright, trademark and patents. There are more than two dozen international agreements concerning IP. The World Intellectual Property Organization (WIPO) is an international organization under the umbrella of the United Nations tasked with administering international IP treaties and assisting governments, organizations and the private sector with IP-related issues. Two of the crucial international treaties are the WIPO Copyright Treaty (WCT) and the WIPO Performances and Phonograms Treaty (WPPT), which came into force in March and May 2002 respectively.

Equally important is the Agreement on Trade-Related Aspects of Intellectual Property Rights (TRIPS), which nations must adopt in order to be part of the World Trade Organization (WTO). TRIPS sets a minimum standard for IP protection that all signatories must meet, based primarily on the Paris Convention for the Protection of Industrial Property and the Berne Convention for the Protection of Literary and Artistic Works. Countries that join the

WTO, and thereby agree to be bound by its rules, must amend their domestic law to conform to these conventions. TRIPS provides for the resolution of disputes between nations through the WTO.

4.4. The economics of interconnection for developing countries

Payments for international voice telephone calls are split between the connected countries and financial settlements are then computed for all countries. This has been a boon for developing countries, most of which maintain high international tariffs as a source of foreign exchange — although this has changed somewhat in the last few years due in part to increased competition among operators of voice services in developing countries.

This is not the case for Internet Service Providers (ISPs) who, to date, remain oblivious to geographic settlements. As a matter of fact, a globally agreed policy does not exist for this issue. As a result, ISPs settle payments among themselves. In this case, developing countries no longer have a subsidy and in fact often pay for the full cost of connecting to the global Internet. Tier 1 ISPs have argued in the past that this reflects the actual economics of the connection as most traffic from developing countries passes through them, regardless of its final destination. Although a thorny issue, the critical question here is both a lack of adequate empirical analysis to determine whether the current system is "fair", and the lack of a "governance" space to deal with the issue on a more systematic and complete fashion. As it stands today, the issue is not likely to be resolved in the short or medium run.[18]

4.5. Privacy and confidentiality of information

Privacy of communications and stored data is a critical element of consumer and user trust in an on-line environment and a necessary condition for the development of electronic commerce. Three international organizations have developed guidelines or rules that set forth a consistent set of basic consumer privacy protections: the Organization for Economic Co-operation and Development, which promulgated Guidelines on the Protection of Privacy and Transborder Flows of Personal Data in 1980 and has continued to monitor their implementation and to provide policy and practical guidance for implementing privacy protection online, addressed to member countries, business and other organizations, individual users and consumers; the Council of Europe, whose Convention for the Protection of

---

[18] It is not easy to understand why this issue has not been addressed by communications economists. Even though the situation changes continuously, it should be possible to study under some alternative sets of assumptions whether the real cost of providing the totality of transport services over the Internet is mirrored relatively accurately by the income paid to and accrued by the transport providers. The current situation of arguing about the fairness or unfairness of the current balance in the absence of any thorough analysis does not help the current governance discussions.

Individuals with Regard to Automatic Processing of Personal Data (1981) sets out the basic principles for data protection; and the European Union, which has issued a Data Protection Directive (1995). The OECD guidelines have been adopted by countries that are not members of the OECD, and the European Union Data Protection Directive has had an impact far beyond Europe.

Privacy is also widely recognized as a human right. Article 12 of the Universal Declaration of Human Rights states, "No one should be subjected to arbitrary interference with his privacy, family, home or correspondence, nor to attacks on his honour or reputation. Everyone has the right to the protection of the law against such interferences or attacks." Other international human rights instruments specifically recognize privacy as a right, including the International Covenant on Civil and Political Rights (Article 17).

At the regional level, various treaties make these rights legally enforceable, including Article 8 of the European Convention for the Protection of Human Rights and Fundamental Freedoms and Article 11 of the American Convention on Human Rights. International human rights tribunals and commissions have begun to define the meaning of this privacy right in the digital era. Concern with privacy is manifesting itself in public policy discussions around the world. For example, the Asia Pacific Economic Cooperation (APEC) group held a conference in February 2003 entitled "Addressing Privacy Protection: Charting a Path for APEC". The conference brought privacy advocates, businesses and government representatives together to develop a new approach to online data privacy for the Asia-Pacific Region.

4.6. Contracts and e-commerce

As commerce moved to the Internet, legal questions arose as to the validity and enforceability of contracts entered into by electronic means. Over time, many legal systems had given special significance to signatures as an expression of intent to be bound to a contract. This raised the question of what is a signature online. Similarly, evidentiary laws of some countries gave preference to the introduction of the "original" of a document. What is the original of a digital document?

The United Nations Commission on International Trade Law has addressed these issues, developing model laws on Electronic Commerce and Electronic Signatures. The Bank for International Settlements has promulgated a set of Core Principles for Systematically Important Payment Systems. The European Union has an extensive body of rules and procedures on electronic funds transfers, including a directive on electronic money institutions, and UNCITRAL has a model law on International Credit Transfers, i.e., wire transfers.

4.7. IP telephony (VoIP)

Voice over Internet Protocol (VoIP), in addition to video, is perhaps the best example of both the convergence of technologies and the recasting of an existing issue into our proposed 3-D space. Since its beginnings, the provision of telephone services has been the exclusive realm of telecom operators. Based on circuit-switching technologies, the provision of the service in developing countries, usually furnished by telecom monopolies until recently, relied on small markets with high profit margins and did not reach most of the population. The liberalization of the national telecom sector in many countries coincided with the emergence of VoIP. VoIP poses a tremendous challenge to existing telecom operators as new competition in the provision of phone services — in addition to cellular phone service — can undermine their core business. For our purposes, it will suffice to say the VoIP also poses a challenge to traditional telecom regulation as, being an Internet based technology solution; it also falls under the scope of ICT governance.

4.8. Universal access and service policies

Universal access refers to providing access to telecommunications facilities to all inhabitants of a country. Universal service refers to connecting every residence with telecommunications services. These concepts come from voice telephony, and generally involve policy issues of cross-subsidization between areas of low connection costs, generally cities, and areas of high connection costs, generally rural areas.

The concepts of universal access and universal service apply equally to ICTs other than voice telephony, including the Internet, although the services may be delivered in different ways provided by the technologies. The locations of service may be different for universal access, viz. telecentres may be appropriate for voice whereas libraries and schools may be equally appropriate for the Internet.

The more general issue is how to propagate the diffusion of the Internet as widely as possible in a country, in a manner that is financially sustainable and accomplishes the social objectives desired. Both intergovernmental agencies – the World Bank and the ITU among others – and bilateral aid agencies provide substantial assistance to countries in this area, directly and through non-governmental organizations.

4.9. Liberalization of telecommunications

In its early phases, the Internet operated on top of the telephone system. Important policy decisions in the telecommunications arena paved the way for the development of the Internet, especially the worldwide trend towards "liberalization": the introduction of competition and the privatization of telephone companies. With the convergence of wire line telephony, wireless communications and cable, the broad policy environment for ICTs is based on competition, interconnection, universal service obligations, and the elimination of many licensing requirements, among other policies. The major institutions driving these policy developments have been the World Trade Organization, through the GATS system and its Basic Agreement on Telecommunications, and the World Bank. The OECD and the European Union have also played important roles.

4.10. Consumer protection

E-commerce will flourish only if legal systems enforce both commercial and consumer contracts. Special protections are warranted in the case of consumers. For example, the protection of consumers includes laws prohibiting misleading advertisements, regulating consumer financial services and consumer credit, and concerning liability for defective products.

With regard to online contracts and other distance contracts, rules should ensure that, prior to the conclusion of any contract, the consumer is provided with clear and comprehensible information concerning key matters such as the identity and the address of the supplier; the characteristics of the goods or services and their price; and the arrangements for payment, delivery or performance. For major online transactions and other distance contracts, consumers should be afforded a right of withdrawal, which makes it possible to cancel credit agreements concluded in connection with a transaction. Unless otherwise agreed to, the supplier should be required to perform a contract within thirty days. Where the supplier fails to perform his side of the contract, the consumer must be informed and any sums paid refunded, unless the consumer agrees to accept an equivalent good or service. Consumers should not be held liable for amounts billed to them for "unauthorized transactions". In the event of fraudulent use of his payment card, the consumer may request cancellation of payment and reimbursement of the amounts paid. Vendors should promptly refund consumer payments for unauthorized transactions or sales transactions in which consumers did not receive what they paid for. Where unsolicited goods or services are supplied, the consumer's failure to reply does not constitute consent.

International bodies that have developed models on the protection of consumers in respect of distance contracts and e-commerce include the European Union and the OECD.

4.11. Taxation of goods and services on the Internet

Key principles for the taxation of electronic commerce were agreed to at the OECD Ministerial Conference in Ottawa in 1998. The OECD concluded that the taxation principles that guide governments in relation to conventional commerce should also guide them in relation to electronic commerce. The OECD framework provides that the present international norms are capable of being applied to electronic commerce, but that some clarifications should be given as to how these norms, and in particular the Model Tax Convention, apply. In the consumption tax area, the framework provides that taxation should occur in the jurisdiction where consumption takes place, and that the supply of digitized products should not be treated as a supply of goods. In the tax administration area, information reporting requirements and tax collection procedures should be neutral and fair, so that the level and standard is comparable to what is required for traditional commerce (although different means may be necessary to achieve those requirements).

Based on these principles, European Commissioner Frits Bolkstein stated in September 2000, "We have international agreement on the principle that for consumption taxes the rules should result in taxation in the jurisdiction where consumption takes place". The European Union endorsed three main principles drawn from the OECD framework. The first is that no new or additional taxes need be considered for e-commerce but that existing taxes – and specifically VAT – should be adapted so that they can be applied to e-commerce. The second principle is that, for consumption taxes, electronic deliveries should not be considered as goods. In the case of the European Union VAT system, they should be treated as supply of services. The third principle is that taxation should take place in the jurisdiction where consumption takes place.

4.12. Local content, languages and character sets

In order for information to be of use to people, they have to be able to read it. This implies that the content has to be in a language that is understood, and moreover, that the written characters that the language uses need to have a standard representation understood by all readers and writers of the language. This is often referred to as the multilingual issue, which is also implicitly a multi-alphabet issue.

The historical development of computing and networking in English-speaking countries has meant that most of the initial content of the Internet was expressed in the English language using a character set, ASCII, that did not include even common variants of the Latin alphabet. This situation is changing substantially as computer software is being adapted to use a much larger superset of characters, UNICODE, which is being increasingly adopted by the computing industry. Adoption of this standard is slower in the area of application programs (for market reasons) and in domain names (for technical reasons), but progress is being made.

Among the organizations working to achieve the penetration of multi-lingual, multi-alphabet capability into all aspects of the Internet are the IETF, the W3C, ICANN, and the various national standards bodies that have responsibility for defining their subsets of the character code tables.[19]

4.13. Enabling entrepreneurism and the private sector

The Internet and the information society in general are characterized by innovation, speed and flexibility. To support Internet development, legal and regulatory frameworks should be transparent, predictable and flexible. These are matters within the control of national and local governments. There is growing recognition worldwide that many policies that promote ICT development are the same policies that promote entrepreneurship in general. Entrepreneurs online and offline should be able to form a business and begin operations without having to satisfy unnecessary licensing requirements. The streamlining of regulatory burdens and the elimination of bureaucratic corruption can support all forms of business development including development of the Internet. Another key concern is redress, via an independent and efficient judicial system for the enforcement of contracts.

These legal reforms have been a major theme of international institutions, ranging from the World Bank to the United Nations, and are the focus of development aid initiatives both multilateral and bilateral in origin.

4.14. Organizations engaged in Internet governance and public policy

Summarizing the foregoing, it should be clear that there are many institutions engaged in Internet governance (even if they do not think of themselves as doing Internet governance), i.e. working in cooperation with countries to establish policies and implement them in order to contribute to their economic and social development:[20]

At the global level

- UNCITRAL (United National Commission on International Trade Law) – e-commerce and electronic signatures
- WTO – Basic Agreement on Telecommunications – telecommunications liberalization
- Organization for Economic Cooperation & Development (OECD) – guidelines on privacy, security, cryptography

---

[19] The issue of introducing multilingualism into all aspects of the Internet has been a difficult issue due to the initial environment in which the Internet evolved. The IETF in particular has spent a great deal of time and energy in constructing a phasing in of multilingual capabilities in such a way that the Internet remains completely interoperable and efficient.

[20] For a more comprehensive list of organizations involved in Internet governance, see the *Guide to International ICT Policy Making*, The Markle Foundation, 2003.

- World Intellectual Property Organization (WIPO) – intellectual property

At the regional level

- Asian Pacific Economic Cooperation (APEC) – cyber-security
- European Union (EU) – telecommunications, e-commerce, privacy
- Council of Europe (COE) – cybercrime, freedom of expression
- Regional Trade Agreements (NAFTA, Mercosur)

Other international organizations, including NGOs

- G8 – cybercrime and cyber-security, Okinawa Charter on the Global Information Society
- Human rights bodies

At the national level

- Government ministries
- Specialized organizations, e.g. universities, research institutions
- Private sector associations
- Not-for-profit organizations

5. The Relevance of ICT Governance for Development

5.1. The broad scope of ICT and Internet governance

Based on the discussion presented in the previous section, we can conclude that there are indeed a plethora of complex issues related to the subject of ICT and Internet governance. In addition, there are existing organizations that have been addressing some of the issues and could, in principle, tackle the ones that are emerging on a global scale. Unfortunately, there is no one-to-one correspondence between generic issues and institutions. Furthermore, each issue, either new or old — recast into new dimensions by the enhanced used of ICT and the Internet – now cuts across traditional policy sectors and the organizations that were created to handle them. In many instances for example, the new global issues that have emerge are challenging the competencies of existing organizations which *de facto* do not have the knowledge and expertise to address them alone.

Let us exclude from this discussion what we have labeled the pure technical administration of the Internet and other ICTs which, in any case, are required to ensure their continued proper functioning and operation. This does not mean that technical administration is not an important piece of the puzzle. Many developing countries, for example, still do not have such capacity to manage some of the key ICT issues at the national level and thus depend on external support to be part of the global ICT community. But this is certainly not a governance issue *per se*. The responsibility for this is clear: technical experts must do the task of technical administration.

Technical administration also implies the need for policy decisions and the establishment of specific policies to guarantee that those administrative functions proceed expeditiously and on a uniform standard. Perhaps the best example here is all the policies and procedures that ICANN has established for the proper management of the DNS. The same can be said for example of any of the other ICT issues described in section 4. However, it is not clear what the venue should be for these policy discussions and decisions associated closely with the technical administration of the Internet. There are indeed governance implications emanating from this technical coordination that need be addressed. This has in fact been one of the main issues confronting ICANN, and one that ICANN has tried to address using a bottom-up approach with global participation by all sectors. Fortunately for the developing countries, that class of issues is of little import when it comes to impacting countries' development goals, as is discussed in the following section.

Internet governance issues and policy implications that are of interest to the global community involved in the ongoing discussions on the subject have two distinct characteristics. First, they are truly new, and we are grappling with them now, trying to understand their visible and hidden consequences, both short and long term. If we have come more or less to terms with the effects of other ICTs in these areas, it is because the issues are at least familiar to us, and we have at least developed a context in which to regard them and some methods of dealing with them. Second, the manner in which the new ICTs and the Internet are impacting us now will be seen in retrospect, hindsight notwithstanding, as fundamentally different and more powerful than their predecessors. The Internet in particular defies easy classification and this is being complicated even more by the convergence of a wide variety of technologies into digital form. Thus, it should not be surprising that we somehow lack the ability to quickly respond to the new challenges in a manner that permits re-use of existing processes, institutions and solutions.

There is yet another dimension that needs to be incorporated into the analysis that relates to the global/local dichotomy. The Internet and new ICTs have greatly facilitated the creation of a "global community" in which stakeholders from most countries (those with access) can be part of and participants in relevant discussions and networks. In this context, national boundaries appear to be weak. However, national boundaries are still essential not only for the implementation of global agreements and policies, but also for setting up the local governance mechanisms needed to participate in the global discussions. Only a handful of developing countries have been able and/or have the capacity to do so. The enforcement of IPR on a global scale is a good example that, by the way, goes well beyond ICT-related issues (i.e., WTO and TRIPS).

5.2. Developing countries and ICT governance

To date, the involvement and participation of developing countries on most ICT and Internet governance issues and mechanisms has been scant and certainly not consistent over time. Needless to say, most of them are members of the various international organizations that have been set up to manage several of the issues — WTO is perhaps the most recent example here. But usually representation is limited to government officials and policy makers on the basis that most of these issues are in the realm on international governance where national governments make policy and promote its implementation on a national scale.

Although this is completely accurate, this is a sign of confusion between governance, government and policy making. Governance responsibilities are not necessarily held by government organizations. Policies can be designed and implemented on the basis of various governance models, including open and participatory processes that involve a wide variety of citizens and sectors, including businesses and NGOs. We describe these processes as 'Global Governance' processes, in which national governments are just one stakeholder among many others. This process is in fact further facilitated nowadays, and in contrast with say 20 years ago, by the increased use of ICT tools to create, support and enhance local, national, regional and global networks. Building bridges between governments and citizens on a global scale is probably easier now than at any other time in history.

The issues for developing countries are however more complex than the above. For starters, there is the issue of the "digital divide" — to a large extent a reflection of existing socio-economic differences between and within countries. Most of the discussions on the subject have focused on the gap between countries. Some recent studies now suggest that the gap is closing. However, for developing countries the news is mixed, since the internal "divide" is growing in size and scope. [21]

It is possible to find in many poor countries state-of-the-art technologies that are widely used in industrialized countries. In some developing country capitals for example, it is now feasible to get a fiber optic (100 megabits/sec, broadband) connection to the Internet for less than 70

---

[21] The issue of the "digital divide" and observations of its change are prone to misinterpretation. Once could also think of similar divides vis-à-vis health or education. Rather than decry the unequal diffusion of ICTs within developing countries, attention might instead be given as to how ICTs can help these countries achieve specific development goals and examine how public policy, at the national level backed up by assistance from the international community, can be shaped to fashion penetration rates that go along with local needs.

dollars a month, a service that is, by the way, not yet available in New York City. In this narrow context, we can certainly say that these countries are leap-frogging well into the 21st century. As it is now, however, the issue is that in developing countries the new ICTs are only available to a handful of users, usually the elites and/or those who can afford to pay for access.[22]

As mentioned before, many developing countries still do not have the human and institutional capacity to start addressing the emerging ICT and Internet governance issues in an immediate fashion. This is clearly a challenge — but also an opportunity in the sense that this set of countries do not have existing legacy institutions and organizations and thus could start the process from a clean slate. There are several issues here however.

First, we should understand that developing countries are not at all homogeneous. As examples, consider countries such as Haiti, Somalia, Brazil, India and South Africa, to name a few; all very different in multiple ways. Some of these countries do have capacity to work on the emerging issues and, in fact, some have been quite active in some of these areas. Poorer nations could certainly benefit from partnering and learning from the experiences of these countries, in addition to related experiences in industrialized countries. In other words, increased South-South cooperation and joint action could only be beneficial to all developing countries and thus lead to more informed global discussions on ICT governance issues – and beyond.

Second, discussions on the "digital divide" within developing countries must be linked to core development issues and agendas to be relevant for their citizens. The lack of relating one to the other has led to the now infamous and artificial debate on "PCs vs. penicillin". Governments and other stakeholders need to be fully aware of the opportunities that ICTs in general can provide in improving the delivery of basic services such as health and education, promoting government transparency and accountability, and fostering democratic governance.

With this in mind, developing countries need to do their part to kick-start the process internally to promote policies and programmes that involve the vast majority of citizens in terms of design, implementation and impact. It is only in this context that the broad issues found under the umbrella of ICT governance acquire real and critical importance for them. It is thus not a question of technology *per se*, but of using technology in a manner that furthers the economic and social development goals of a country.

---

[22] Note that for the average Least Developing Country (LDC), 70 dollars a month is about 2 times the average annual GDP per capita.

5.3. Institutional options for coping with ICT governance

As already mentioned, there are a large number of national, regional and global institutions and organizations whose mandate, at least partially, includes their involvement in one or more of the ICT and Internet issues described above. However, we also saw that, if the aim is to properly address those issues, it is clear that most of those issues go beyond the scope of any one institution or organization.

Does this imply a need to create a variety of new organizations? Or are current institutions in some combination sufficient for coping with the issues raised by ICT and Internet governance? What about developing country needs and development processes? Can one global institution alone take care of most of the existing issues? Is there an "institution gap" that needs to be filled? There is indeed no easy answer to any of these questions.

However, looking at the specific issue of the management and coordination of Internet names and numbers, the answer to this set of questions is clear: a new organization, ICANN, was created by a national government with the sole purpose of assuming full global responsibility on a very specific issue. Although the focus of this paper is not ICANN, it is perhaps interesting to take a quick look at the organization from the point of view of the institutional arrangements.

ICANN was the first ever organization whose functions were exclusively concentrated on the Internet — or to be more precise, on one of the technical aspects of the Internet. At the time, there was a clear global (in the Internet sense) need and even urgency to establish some sort of entity that could support, manage and coordinate the Domain Name System — or otherwise face chaos or collapse of the network.

The governance structure of ICANN quickly became one of the main issues, given both its nature and origin. The first ICANN board was chosen by Jon Postel and was then appointed by the United States government, which raised substantial controversy in Internet circles. To balance this, it was decided that approximately one half of the Board would be replaced by electing replacements in an open and democratic fashion. To a large extent, this concept does correspond to the inherent character of the Internet — essentially open and horizontal.

This contributed heavily to a shift in the public perception of the role of ICANN, from an essentially technical and administrative entity to one in charge of the first experiment in "Internet governance" in which all Internet users could vote (at least those connected, which did not then include many developing country stakeholders). The election of some board members through Internet voting provided additional elements that further contributed to the emergence of this dichotomy vis-à-vis ICANN which still persists today — in spite of recent efforts by ICANN itself. The dichotomy is characterized by whether ICANN should be "thin" and perform its original mandate in a narrow sense, or whether it should become "thick" and take on other Internet governance functions.

From the vantage point of the management and coordination of Internet names and numbers, it can be said that ICANN has been successful. Clear rules, procedures and related polices which guarantee the full operation of Internet space have been established. There is still a series of issues that remain to be solved, which are presented in some detail in Annex 1. There are also some governance issues that are regarded as unresolved and open, such as enhancing the participation of developing countries and the true internationalization and legal independence of ICANN from any national government among others. However, it should be clear that many other Internet and ICT related issues have also emerged, as we noted in section 4, that require the urgent attention of all countries and perhaps concerted efforts at the international level. Some of the issues that ICANN is facing today do require cooperation with other existing entities for addressing them in a satisfactory manner.

The "experiment" on "Internet governance" carried out under the ICANN umbrella had, in the eyes of many, mixed results and did not really yield the expected results. Nevertheless the important point here is to learn from this unique experience and determine if there is value in any similar process for addressing in an open and participatory manner the larger set of ICT governance issues. In this context, the ICANN process should be considered as a bottom-up exercise in global governance that made use, perhaps for the first time, of the new ICTs to include a variety of stakeholders from many countries. Clearly, these and other issues are fundamentally more important than the policy issues associated with the more detailed and technical issues of the management and coordination of IP addresses and names.

The existence at the international level of a variety of intergovernmental, non-governmental, and voluntary private organizations working on the various ICT and Internet issues seems to support the thesis that the creation of yet other specialized entities is not required. On the contrary, cooperation among national governments and these organizations spans all ICT-related issues, and it seems evident that the extension of this cooperation should be the primary direction for addressing the Internet-specific issues. The key question here is how this can be accomplished in an open and balanced manner.

There is an argument to be made that governments, especially developing country governments, would benefit from having a focal point within the government for overall coordination of policy with respect to ICT. It might be useful for countries to consider establishing a lightweight, nimble, coordination point within government that can distribute information, assist with problems, and ensure that government policy is informed and consistent. Such an entity could also serve as a 'first among equals' connection to organizations operating in the international space, and could in fact liaise with ICANN or any other technical administration organizations on matters of policy relating to their country's needs. For such a structure to be legitimate, however, such an organization must be inclusive and provide a meaningful voice for national non-governmental sectors and stakeholders. This possibility needs to be examined on a country-by-country basis, depending on specific local conditions and the particular issues at stake.

Finally, from the point of view of non-governmental stakeholders, there is ample room for creating and strengthening new and existing national and international networks. These networks can on the one hand promote not only South-South but also North-South cooperation and transfer information, knowledge and expertise to local stakeholders. They can also bring to the international discussion and processes, additional perspectives and views on various ICT governance issues and perhaps even serve as regional advocacy groups and increase national and local dialogue with national governments. Such a process is in fact quite feasible today due substantially to the Internet and the new ICTs.

6. Observations and Conclusions

The issues surrounding Internet governance are complex, and the ultimate decisions regarding the legitimacy of various governance structures are not a part of this paper.

We therefore have attempted to address the full set of issues raised by the evolution of ICTs and the introduction of the Internet and new ICTs that all countries are faced with, including the developing countries in perhaps special ways. These issues represent focal points for a re-examination of existing policy and/or its implementation. If governance of the Internet is to be meaningful, the structures must be those that best meet those needs.

We feel obliged to offer our views in a manner that responds to the framework defined by the WSIS process, since this was our starting point. However, as our conclusions indicate, we believe that this framing of the debate until now has been less than helpful in delineating the important issues with respect to the needs and interests of developing countries.

1. ICT governance, and Internet governance as a subset of it, encompasses a multiplicity of issues, some of which are in turn related to each other. Furthermore, most of these issues cut across traditional "sectors" and override national boundaries, and thus defy simple classification and classical solutions.

2. There are a variety of institutions and organizations that have already been involved in addressing the issues. These organizations include intergovernmental organizations, non-governmental organizations, professional societies, trade associations, and voluntary groups. Nevertheless, it is not always possible to map ICT governance

issues to existing organizations on a one-to-one basis. Thus, addressing and finding solutions for a rather large set of critical issues will probably require collaboration and cooperation between existing institutions and organizations. Being that as it may, the creation of new organizations or institutions does not seem to be a desirable option at this point in time.

3. Most developing countries still do not see ICT governance as critical, especially those poor nations where access to ICTs in general is limited to small segments of the population. The emerging issues that have become priorities in other countries do not seem to apply to them as more basic development issues still remain to be addressed.

4. The great majority of the public and technical policy issues that ICTs, including the Internet, pose for developing countries have a direct impact on their development agendas and goals. It is not just a question of technology, standards or compliance with international mandates. Developing countries need to be involved in the various ICT governance processes and to develop local capacity and policies to harness its benefits. Furthermore, the development of the information society requires that these issues be adequately addressed.

5. The principle of *participating globally* and *implementing locally* is a useful one in addressing ICT-related issues, including modalities of governance, national policies, implementation alternatives, and sources of assistance. Specific national, regional and international forums and the creation and strengthening of national and international multi-stakeholder networks can be very helpful in fostering cooperation between countries and enabling the transfer of knowledge and experience among them, especially when the underlying technologies provide a common base for discussion.

6. Internet governance is considerably larger than ICANN. ICANN's purpose in life is very detailed and narrow, and only includes a small subset of broader and emerging issues. ICANN's work is only about the management and global governance of domain names and numbers, which is not a critical priority for most developing countries. Thus, ICANN should not be the locus for the ongoing debates on Internet governance. This must be clear to all governments and stakeholders. ICANN is likely to be seen in a more favorable light to the extent that it becomes independent of United States government control.

7. ICANN should be assessed in this overall context. While it is surely possible to improve ICANN, calls for its demise should be considered vis-à-vis the relevance of its scope. Reforming or replacing ICANN with any other mechanism should be at a lower priority than the emerging ICT governance issues at the global and national

levels that have overtaken in importance and relevance ongoing DNS discussions. However, the management of DNS does include specific governance issues that still need to be addressed and solved.

8. ICT governance issues are not and should not be the exclusive concern of governments. ICT governance falls in the realm of global governance, and thus open participation and engagement with other sectors and stakeholders (in particular civil society organizations and the local private sector) are required to ensure that ICT issues are more closely linked to regional, sub-regional and local development needs and requirements. The emerging Information Society implies by definition more transparent and horizontal governance mechanisms and decision making processes.

9. The most effective direction that ICT governance can take is to concentrate specifically on the policy issues and prioritize them in such a fashion that developing countries are able to address their most pressing issues at national, regional and global levels. The prioritization should be strongly guided by the extent to which each issue impacts individual users living in their own countries. These are not simple issues, as the history of ICT governance indicates. However, many organizations of all kinds have already been involved for years, and have the responsibility of helping countries with such issues.

This document has tried to address the issue of Internet governance in a broad context, and with a special relationship to the issues of social and economic development. As is the case with most such documents, there is much more that could be said, and there is without doubt a rich set of ideas and opinions regarding this topic. We believe that this is a very important topic, and we encourage others to participate in the discussion.

Annex 1: The Internet and Internet Governance Prior to 1998

The network research project that eventually became the Internet started in the late 1960's with funding from the United States government for a project known as the ARPANET. Starting with electronic communication lines between four institutions in the western United States in 1969, the ARPANET grew as a tool for researchers in specific institutions (most of them working for United States government agencies or on research projects financed by the United States government) both to connect themselves to remote computing and information resources and to communicate among each other. Over time, the ARPANET became the Internet, which now claims at least 400 million users in all countries of the world.

The early environment surrounding the Internet was technical, research-oriented, practical, and cooperative, and until about 1985, the Internet was essentially a tool for people in the scientific and technical communities. During the period 1985-1995, commercial Internet providers emerged to provide Internet services to the commercial sector, and by 1995 they were fully integrated into an increasingly commercial Internet, a seamless network of TCP/IP networks connecting eventually all countries.

From its beginning, Internet development and operation have been characterized by bottom-up development, control decentralized down to individual networks, standards formulation through rough consensus and running code, and a system of coordination by multiple organizations, each having some responsibility for the Internet's operation. Its operation has been open and participatory, both by necessity because of its bottom-up orientation and through its initial culture strongly oriented to research, education, and sharing of information. The basic Internet protocols were developed in the 1970s and the 1980s and, to coordinate their development, called the TCP/IP protocol family, the Internet Engineering Task Force (IETF) was formed in the 1980s as a voluntary, unincorporated, non-governmental meritocracy open to anyone capable of contributing to their goals.

In the early days of the Internet, administration of addresses was a simple process. The early addressing function was located at the University of Southern California and eventually became formalized as the Internet Assigned Numbers Authority, or IANA. IANA undertook this activity as part of a grant agreement with the United States government, which funded the research work that created the ARPANET that later metamorphosed into the Internet.

Jon Postel, an Internet pioneer, administered the United States government grants to IANA to maintain lists of unique reference numbers for entities such as protocols and network addresses, which were used by everyone involved in the Internet to assure interoperability. Later, when the domain name system (DNS) was introduced, IANA took on the responsibility of creating and maintaining the root server, i.e. the server that pointed to servers for all second level domains, which included the global top level domains (gTLDs) and the country code top level domains (ccTLDs). IANA also took the responsibility to create additional root servers, distributed geographically, for redundancy, security, and efficiency of access. The United States National Science Foundation held initial responsibility for operation, or governance, of second level gTLD name service.

In 1993 the National Science Foundation, realizing that its control of the expanding Internet could not be sustained within a government body, transferred operation of its Internet-related administrative functions to three external non-governmental organizations. One of these organizations was Network Solutions, Inc., a private United States company, with whom NSF signed a 5-year contract for the administration of the Domain Name System (DNS). The impending termination of that contract in 1998 was one of the motivating factors for a reconsideration of Internet administration in 1997-98.

In 1998, as a result of the explosive growth of the Internet and serious concern regarding the scaling of both the Internet and the Domain Name System, the United States Department of Commerce (which had inherited the contractual relationship with ARPA) commissioned several studies of the problem. The United States government concluded that it should privatize the DNS functions, open them to competition, and bring them under some system of non-governmental but nevertheless global oversight. This process led to the creation of the Internet Corporation for Names and Numbers (ICANN), which has been concerned with managing Internet names and numbers since then.

Annex 2: Policy Issues Associated with Internet Technical Coordination

The material in this annex provides more detail regarding the major policy issues that arise out of necessity from the technical coordination and management of the Internet number and naming spaces.

This responsibility is currently in the hands of ICANN, which has held it from its inception in 1998. The governance structure of ICANN has itself been complex, with a currently self-perpetuating Board of Directors, Board of Directors and a number of constituent supporting organizations representing the major Internet stakeholder groups. Further, it depends upon cooperation with a significant number of other groups listed in this document, all of which have different governance mechanisms. As an example, the IETF depends upon an open, consensual process supported only by those participating in the process.

Technical management of the Internet has clearly involved some policy choices as the Internet has evolved and grown in size. In general, such choices have been necessary in order to build a viable Internet, and have been consistent with expectations at the time of the decision of the Internet's future use. Some of these decisions might be characterized as engineering design decisions as much as policy decisions, although they may have had policy implications. Governance implications stem from the non-technical aspects of this activity and the need to make choices when fashioning such choices.

A discussion of the major such issues follows. In some cases we believe that it would be possible and perhaps desirable to separate the policy issues and decisions from the technical administration and coordination function provided that there was an agreed upon governance mandate for an institution or institutions capable of exercising the policy functions.

Scarcity of IP address space. Decisions regarding address space and the allocation of Internet addresses, or IP addresses, have been part of the Internet engineering design process. An initial decision in the early 1970s to provide an address structure that allowed at most 256 hosts was soon found to be too restrictive. Work soon started on a new addressing scheme, IP version 4 (IPv4), which allowed a theoretical maximum of 4 billion IP addresses, although the structure of the address space and the manner of its allocation has been such that the actual usable number is less.

The assumption underlying IPv4 that an address space of 4 billion addresses would suffice was challenged by the growth of the Internet in 1990s, and in spite of increasing rationing by the Regional Internet Registries, address allocations had to become restrictive and other ways had to be found to provide addresses. One such method is the utilization of private address space, an extension that extended the availability of addresses although with some reduced functionality. Quite a few developing countries that connected to the Internet late in its development received only a few addresses relative to the number of addresses available in developed countries. While this was the result of an early low growth engineering estimate that seemed improbably high at the time, the result was that many developing countries were disadvantaged by it.

The Internet engineering community, in particular the IETF, has been quite aware of the situation and early in the 1990s started the design of IP version 6 (IPv6) that would very significantly increase the size of the address space to the point where no shortage would be perceived for many, many years and therefore there would be no scarce resource resulting in disputable allocation decisions. The particulars of the addresses in this version are primarily the result of engineering decisions, although significant features have been added to improve policy aspects of individual privacy and security, among others.

The technical underpinnings that will support IPv6 are spreading through the Internet now. The total number of addresses that will be available should provide an adequate supply for many years. The issue of address allocation across regions and countries is still a policy issue, and is independent of making the Internet IPv6-ready.

The remaining issue is the governance issue: who decides upon the allocation of this new address space. Is it regarded as sufficiently large so that the scarcity is not an issue, and therefore any reasonable allocation works? Or is there a case for specific intervention?

Domain name space: introduction of new generic TLDs. The original composition of the DNS contained 7 generic domain names (gTLDs) and country code TLDs (ccTLDs) as defined by the two letter ISO-3166 codes. The governance structure for this standard is maintained by and available from the German National Statistical Office, while changes to it are made by the authority of the United Nations Statistical Department.

Since before 1998, there has been a sense in the Internet community that the gTLD space was too small, and that it should be enlarged. ICANN's response has been to authorize the creation of a number of new sponsored domains for specific communities (e.g. .museum) and a number of unsponsored domains requested by private organizations (e.g. .biz). The domain requests have been coupled to their implementation by the specific organizations requesting them. The number of requests approved has been initially limited to ensure that the technical root server mechanisms continue to function well.

While some of the judgments made in this area serve the cause of technical stability, policy issues exist. What should be the balance between private and structured approaches to define which new TLDs serve the cause of Internet users, including the developed countries? Should choices of new TLDs be coupled to specific registries, or should they be independent? Where should the various responsibilities for registry viability lie, and what mechanisms if any should be in place for registry failures? And with respect to governance, who makes these decisions?

Name collision: Intellectual property rights. While the use of numbers such as IP addresses has little if any semantic content, names have been associated with specific rights for hundreds of years. Given the decentralized nature of the Internet, collisions in the space of domain names are inevitable and many have occurred. Realizing that the speed of judicial review was inconsistent with the rate of growth of the Internet and the felt urgency of implementation, a Uniform Dispute Resolution Process (UDRP) was rapidly established to provide a "fast track" resolution process that did not remove the rights of parties to nevertheless also invoke a standard judicial review process. The UDRP relies substantially upon the services of WIPO on a voluntary basis.

While there appears to be consensus regarding the need for such a "fast track" mechanism, the associated policy issue is how is it to be defined, and the associated governance issue is by whom? Both national and international mechanisms, governmental and private, for addressing and resolving intellectual property disputes have existed for a number of years. Is there a better mechanism than the UDRP? What mechanisms and organizations should be in place that have the authority to make the changes to the DNS that implements the decision? These decisions are independent of the technical coordination of the DNS.

Registry degrees of freedom. Within the operation of the DNS, registrars provide name service for their community, and have a position of stewardship and trust. To what extent is, or should the actions of registrars be governed by other organizations, and by whom? What criteria should be used for any such limitations, and how should they be determined? How should disagreements regarding such limitations be settled? Two significant disputes exist in this area now: Verisign's Site Finder service and Verisign's Wait List policy.

The single root. The structure of the DNS consists of a single root server, pointing to second level domain name servers for all TLDs. The accuracy and the security of the root server are crucial to the correct functioning of the Internet. The root server is replicated in a number of places around the world for both efficiency and security reasons. From the point of view of technical architecture, a single logical root server is believed by almost everyone to be essential, although there are a few isolated advocates of alternative architectures. Most Internet experts believe that departing from a single root server model would ultimately fracture the Internet.

Several policy and governance issues exist. Who should have administrative control of the root server system? Should there be any central control, including possibly escrow requirements, required of second level DNS registries? Should a different mechanism be used to modify the contents of the root files, or is the existing mechanism optimal, and how and by whom should such decisions be made?

Protection of Internet as critical infrastructure. In accordance with its goal of preserving the operational stability of the Internet ICANN has, with technical assistance from the broad Internet provider community, initiated a program of hardening the core of the Internet infrastructure. Such actions correspond primarily to conscientious technical administration of a valuable resource. It does raise the question, however, of who should be responsible for the integrity and security of the Internet and, if a different arrangement is preferred, how would the mechanism for ensuring these objectives differ from and improve upon what is currently being done.

International domain names. A consequence of the historical development of much of computing and networking in the United States was that the base alphabet for much of the standard setting in these fields was the Latin alphabet, without modifiers such as accents and umlauts to any characters. With the evolution and increasing acceptance of a Unicode format for text representation, other alphabets and languages can now be used to compose electronic documents. The internationalization of domain names has posed significantly more difficult technical problems, and the IETF has recently published a proposed standard for International Domain Names (IDNs), which is beginning to be implemented.

There is little disagreement regarding the desirability of implementing such a standard, but there may be policy and governance issues relates to its global implementation. If so, in which venues should such issues be discussed, and how should implementation of such decisions be governed?

ccTLD delegation. Historically, ccTLD responsibilities were delegated to individuals and organizations on a voluntary basis. The delegation was meant to be one of stewardship of the TLD for the good of the country rather than one of ownership. Given the global importance of the Internet, current policy requires, with some exceptions, the registry to be in the country, and a contractual relationship with the specific organization in order to provide assurance of continued viability and responsibility to the country. Redelegations are possible and may be requested, and are subject to the national government's support of the redelegation request.

The administration of such changes is straightforward, but requires vigilance to ensure the integrity of the database. Some redelegation efforts apparently have been made in the past with a view to hijacking country code domains. Policy and governance issues raised include the issue of whether the current rules for redelegation are appropriate, and who decides.

The WHOIS database. The WHOIS databases contain information regarding ownership and administrative and technical contacts of domain name holders. From the beginning of their existence, in a small and cooperative internetworking environment, these databases were declared to be publicly accessible for transparency and for administrative convenience. Today's Internet is large, impersonal, and populated by individuals with a variety of motives other than cooperative behavior, and the public availability of these databases is regarded as an invasion of privacy, with possible unacceptable consequences.

This conundrum is interlaced with some of the other policy issues raised in this section. The issue is further complicated by being the subject of various national laws that are not necessarily in agreement. The fundamental question remains: by what process, and with whose involvement, and in what manner, will a resolution to this issue be decided?

background paper

INTERNET GOVERNANCE: PERSPECTIVES FROM CAMBODIA
Norbert Klein, Open Forum of Cambodia

The invitation by the United Nations ICT Task Force Secretariat for me to contribute to the Global Forum on Internet Governance said: "We are especially keen on bringing developing country perspectives to the Global Forum" – and I was asked to assure that I "could present a developing country perspective". I will try to do this on the basis of our experiences in Cambodia. Every country has its peculiarities – but probably there are also enough commonalities to justify the assumption that the Cambodian experience is not unique.

The invitation to be at the Global Forum on Internet Governance was also issued, "taking into account the important role that your organization plays in matters related to Internet governance"; I therefore will draw heavily on the practical experience of the Open Forum of Cambodia, a Cambodian NGO where I have worked since 1994.

By way of background, let me mention briefly Cambodia's Internet history. The first connection to the Internet from Cambodia was established in early 1994 by an NGO – the Open Forum of Cambodia - using international phone lines at US$5 per minute to establish a regular store-and-forward dial-up connection for email. This service soon attracted many users, among them United Nations and Cambodian government agencies, NGOs, businesses, and individuals. This NGO operated system had over 1300 users when, only three years later, two commercial Internet Service Providers started to operate. By now, Cambodia has several ISPs, DSL and wireless broadband access, and probably eight times more mobile than wired phones.

I will reflect on our experiences by sharing information about the steps we took and our achievements, and relate them to the public policy issues that emerged and the roles and responsibilities of different stakeholders – in the hope that these landmarks are of wider relevance for other countries on the way towards an Information Society, and to the efforts underway to clarify what Internet governance implies.

Connectivity

The ITU Country Case Studies series states in its Cambodia edition "Khmer Internet – Cambodia Case Study":

> As with so much else in Cambodia, the international development community — bilateral and multilateral assistance agencies and non-governmental organizations (NGOs) — have played a critical role in introducing and nurturing the Internet in the Kingdom.

> For example, Norbert Klein of the Open Forum <www.forum.org.kh> was instrumental in introducing email to the country. The Forum has also been instrumental in promoting the usage and standardization of the Khmer font.

> Another networking pioneer was Bill Herod. Working with Canada's International Development Research Centre; he was involved in establishing Cambodia's first direct Internet connection.

> They have opened up the outside world to Cambodians as well as Cambodia to the outside world. These low profile organizations have done as much if not more than anyone else to launch Cambodia into cyberspace. They illustrate the constructive role that the international community can play in reducing the Digital Divide but also suggest that small, grass-roots initiatives are more effective than the larger aid organizations that tend to hog the headlines.[1]

The 2003 World Summit on the Information Society called, a decade after the Internet started in Cambodia, for "digital solidarity, both at national and international levels", because "building an inclusive Information Society requires new forms of solidarity, partnership and cooperation among governments and other stakeholders, i.e. the private sector, civil society and international organizations".[2]

In Cambodia, we went through the half cycle of this vision, because initiatives in civil society and the private sector offered an early use of the Internet – email services only – to the

---

[1] Published in January 2002, page 14 –http://www.itu.int/ITU-D/ict/cs/cambodia/index.html

[2] WSIS 2003: "Declaration of Principles" (from here on quoted as "Principles"), Point 17, http://www.itu.int/wsis/documents/doc_single-en-1161.asp

government and to United Nations agencies. The Ministry of Post and Telecommunications as well as a number of United Nations agencies used the connectivity provided by an NGO for their email services. But when the Ministry of Post and Telecommunications had established its own ISP, with substantial funding from IDRC/Canada in 1997, that Ministry intended to shut down the services of the very NGO which had supplied email connectivity to it free of charge over the years, since it considered this platform – the Open Forum of Cambodia – to be no longer necessary.

Civil society services were not considered, by the government, to be partners on the way to developing the Information Society, but only assistants substituting for an unfulfilled government and business task. Their service was to be closed down as soon as the government started to be active in the same field, on a fee basis. After lengthy negotiations, the Open Forum of Cambodia was permitted to continue its services, but was restricted to text services only – not Web services – at a monthly (!) license fee of US$ 200.

WSIS CHALLENGES - INCLUSIVITY

"We, the representatives of the people of the world... declare our common desire and commitment to build a people-centered, inclusive and development-oriented Information Society, where everyone can create, access, utilize and share information and knowledge, enabling individuals, communities and peoples to achieve their full potential in promoting their sustainable development and improving their quality of life."[3]

How can the global WSIS process assist national processes to be as all-inclusive and as multi-stakeholder-oriented as the representatives of the people of the world envisioned it in Geneva?

Internet Addresses

After establishing email connectivity for Cambodia since 1994, in 1996 the Open Forum of Cambodia established and administered the Internet country code address .kh – from "Khmer." At that time, there was consultation and no other entity was interested in doing this; and the same NGO continued to be the only email connectivity provider in the country. Two years later, in 1998, the Ministry of Post and Telecommunications requested to take over the administration of the Domain Name System [DNS]. There was an unwritten principle that IANA – the Internet Assigned Number Authority[4] - "the overall authority for the Internet Protocol Addresses, the Domain Names, and many other parameters used in the Internet" - would delegate the responsibility for the DNS of a country to a government agency, if so

---

[3] Principles, Point 1.

[4] http://www.iana.org

requested. In actual fact, in many countries the DNS service was performed by computer departments of universities, by Internet user organizations, or by private initiatives.

From the beginning, the Open Forum of Cambodia administered the DNS according to the standard "RFC 1591" document in use world-wide as the basis for delegating the administrative function for such services by IANA to a country top level domain administrator.[5] This document speaks about a delegation of responsibilities and duties and not so much about authorities and rights.[6]

It spells out a requirement for "a designated manager for a domain is that they be able to carry out the necessary responsibilities, and have the ability to do a … competent job… and have a duty to serve the community… However, it is also appropriate for interested parties to have some voice in selecting the designated manager… This includes… operating the database with accuracy, robustness, and resilience. … IANA…must receive communications that assure the IANA that … the new organization understands its responsibilities. It is also very helpful for the IANA to receive communications from other parties that may be concerned or affected by the transfer."

---

[5] ftp://ftp.rfc-editor.org/in-notes/rfc1591.txt

[6] A fairly long extract from RFC 1591 is given here, as a number of concerns and pitfalls are spelled out, for cases when the transfer of the administrative function is made not for technical reasons but because of other concerns, for example based on claims of authority.

"The major concern in selecting a designated manager for a domain is that it be able to carry out the necessary responsibilities, and have the ability to do an equitable, just, honest, and competent job

2) These designated authorities are trustees for the delegated domain, and have a duty to serve the community. The designated manager is the trustee of the top-level domain for both the nation, in the case of a country code, and the global Internet community. Concerns about "rights" and "ownership" … are inappropriate. It s appropriate to be concerned about "responsibilities" and "service" to the community… However, it is also appropriate for interested parties to have some voice in selecting the designated manager.

5) The designated manager must do a satisfactory job of operating the DNS service for the domain. That is, the actual management of the assigning of domain names, delegating subdomains and operating nameservers must be done with technical competence. This includes… operating the database with accuracy, robustness, and resilience.

6) For any transfer of the designated manager trusteeship from one organization to another, the higher-level domain manager (the INA in the case of top-level domains) must receive communications from both the old organization and the new organization that assure the IANA that the transfer in mutually agreed, and that the new organization understands its responsibilities It is also very helpful for the IANA to receive communications from other parties that may be concerned or affected by the transfer."

In Cambodia, after the official transfer of the function of the DNS administration from the NGO that had been providing this service to the emerging Internet community free of charge to the government, the only change for several years was that a fee for the registration of a domain was imposed by the Ministry of Post and Telecommunications – first of US$ 200 for the first two years, then - as this was criticized as being completely out of line with other countries – it was lowered to $160, and finally at present to $70 for the first two years. Despite the fees charged by the Ministry of Post and Telecommunications, the Ministry requested the NGO to continue to handle the technical aspects of the DNS system – without remuneration.

The service to the Internet community fell short, the community did not have a voice, and the high price of domain registrations combined with new special administrative requirements by the Ministry still keeps many from registering their names under the country code – including the National Assembly, the Senate, and Their Majesties the King and Queen of Cambodia[7] as well as ICT educational institutions, to give some examples.

The author has raised this situation repeatedly over the years with persons in the Government Advisory Committee [GAC][8] of ICANN, in view of the assumption that governments are always the natural guardians of public interest and that, as a consequence, governments must have the possbility to assert their priority to administer Internet resources for the public interest. But so far it has not been accepted that GAC could provide any friendly advice to a government, because it would be against the principle of non-interference in the internal affairs of a country.

WSIS CHALLENGES - COOPERATION

"We recognize that building an inclusive Information Society requires new forms of solidarity, partnership and cooperation among governments and other stakeholders, i.e. the private sector, civil society and international organizations. Realizing that the ambitious goal of this Declaration — bridging the digital divide and ensuring harmonious, fair and equitable development for all — will require strong commitment by all stakeholders, we call for digital solidarity, both at national and international levels."[9]

What forms of cooperation, fostering international harmonization of efforts, can be developed within the WSIS process that help to promote new possibilities for partnership within countries and thus better bridge the many non-economic gaps of the digital divides?

---

[7] http://www.cambodian-parliament.org, http://www.khmersenate.org,
   http://www.norodomsihanouk.info

[8] http://www.gacsecretariat.org/web/index.shtml

[9] Principles, Point 17.

Level Playing Field

Even before the WSIS process started, leaders of governments and international organizations have spoken about the crucial role of information and communication technologies for economic and social development. Nevertheless, the gap between the ICT rich and the ICT poor countries does not seem to be narrowing, as higher levels of technology often lead to an accelerated level of innovation and further advancement. The Geneva WSIS meeting did not achieve any broad agreement on economic measures which might address this growing gap.

However, another very important but indirect factor, the field of Intellectual Property Rights, in general and in the field of ICT, is increasingly exacerbating the gap and needs attention. How can it be expected that pirated software in poor countries will be replaced by commercial proprietary software, when a high school teacher would have to spend ten monthly salaries to buy one set of basic software for a computer?

WSIS CHALLENGES – GOVERNMENT INTERVENTION

"Connectivity is a central enabling agent in building the Information Society. Universal, ubiquitous, equitable and affordable access to ICT infrastructure and services constitutes one of the challenges of the Information Society."

"The rule of law, accompanied by a supportive, transparent, pro-competitive, technologically neutral and predictable policy and regulatory framework reflecting national realities, is essential for building a people-centered Information Society. Governments should intervene, as appropriate, to correct market failures, to maintain fair competition."[10]

It is obvious that the market will not lead to a universal, ubiquitous equitable and affordable people-centered Information Society. Can the WSIS process – facing the obvious - help to expose the international and national social reality that the market is not the appropriate instrument to address the divisions on the way to an ever more encompassing Information Society, and help to ensure that Open Source software development – one aspect of addressing the problem – receives strategic attention and support?

Cultural and Linguistic Diversity - and Local Content

In spite of the many controversies during the preparatory phase of the Geneva WSIS meeting, all stakeholder groups and regions of the world and political persuasions could easily agree on the point that linguistic diversity and local content are important. There does not seem to be any record of anybody not paying lip service to this noble cause.

---

[10] Principles, Points 21 and 39.

Cambodia has a unique writing system which has been developed over more than one thousand years. In the absence of national standards on how to implement the Khmer script on computers, the UNICODE Consortium[11] and the International Standards Organization (ISO)[12] solved this problem for Cambodia – with no Cambodian participation. After these two bodies, which do not have any[13] government basis, had decided how to handle the Khmer script on computers, the Cambodian National Information Communications Technology Development Authority (NiDA)[14] intervened. It was too late, as the UNICODE Consortium Policies state: "Once a character is encoded, it will not be moved or removed. Once a character is encoded, its character name will not be changed." After extensive efforts and negotiations which required participation in several international meetings, the only concession received was a letter from the president of the UNICODE consortium in April 2002, which said the "encoding approach taken… is not the preferred approach of the Cambodian National Body or of the Khmer linguistic experts, and it is at odds with the way the Khmer script is presented and taught in Cambodia… A number of symbols and other characters used in the representation of the Khmer script were overlooked in the encoding… This has resulted in the current unfortunate situation where all[15] interested parties now have to deal with a less-than-optimal outcome."

There are still about 5000 languages in the world; many of them are said to be dying out. Only about 50 languages have so far been encoded for the use on computers according to widely known standards. The majority of scripts without standard encodings are used in developing countries.

---

[11] Unicode provides a unique number for every character, no matter what the platform, no matt what the program, no matter what the language. The Unicode Standard has been adopted by such industry leaders as Apple, HP, IBM, JustSystem, Microsoft, Oracle, SAP, Sun, Sybase, Unisys and many others. Unicode is required by modern standards such as XML, Java, ECMAScript (JavaScript), LDAP, CORBA 3.0, WML, etc., and is the official way to implement ISO/IEC 10646." – Cambodia does not have any industry giants which would be members of the UNICODE Consortium. http://www.unicode.org/standard/WhatIsUnicode.html

[12] "ISO is a network of the national standards institutes of 148 countries, on the basis of one member per country, with a Central Secretariat in Geneva, Switzerland, that coordinates the system. - ISO is a non-governmental organization: its embers are not, as is the case in the United Nations system, delegations of national governments." – Cambodia, like many other developing countries, is not a full member of the ISO. http://www.iso.org/iso/en/aboutiso/introduction/index.html

[13] UNICODE 3.0, published in February 2000 - http://www.unicode.org/book/u2.html

[14] http://www.nida.gov.kh – created in August 2000.

[15] Digital Review of Asia Pacific ["Digital Review"], page 133, Encoding the Khmer script. – www.digital-review.org

---

WSIS CHALLENGES – LOCAL CONTENT

"The creation, dissemination and preservation of content in diverse languages and formats must be accorded high priority in building an inclusive Information Society... It is essential to promote the production of and accessibility to all content - educational, scientific, cultural or recreational - in diverse languages and formats."[16]

The complex process of creating international technical standards for different scripts needs careful attention and considerable financial support, if the call for local content in communication is to be made real. A clear commitment should be requested from the relevant standardization bodies that no further language standardizations will be established without the participation of representative organs of the affected language communities. As local content development has received almost universal verbal support, the WSIS process should actively care so that more scripts can be encoded without mistreating them in the same way as it happened to the Khmer language.

Technological Outreach and Innovation

The roughly 100 Internet cafés in Phnom Penh testify to the technologically innovative spirit and the entrepreneurship of people who developed these facilities, often without formal education in handling computers They provide publicly announced opportunities for many Cambodians to communicate internationally for about US$ 0.05 per minute with business partners or their overseas relatives, compared to the normal phone price of about US$ 1.- per minute for similar calls. Voice-over-Internet has helped many other countries to cut their communication costs considerably.

However, the web site of the Ministry of Post and Telecommunications[17] displays a "Declaration on Prohibition of Use of Voice Over Internet" dated December 30, 1998. "Any use of telephony via Internet or any business which offers telephony service via Internet is strictly prohibited. Any person who violates the above shall be penalized according to the law." It is not clear which law might apply. Until about half a year ago, this prohibition had never been enforced. Then a series of arrests of owners and operators who provide VoIP services started, reportedly along with the confiscation of equipment and even furniture. A number of Internet cafés have cancelled their high volume accounts with ISPs, and others have closed down completely, as they cannot maintain their businesses after not daring to continue offering their well used VoIP services.

---

[16] Principles, Point 53.

[17] http://www.mptc.gov.kh

A World Bank Consultancy had already warned in 2001 that "unless tariffs are brought closer to costs, other legal or illegal methods will be found to exploit the gap. Main threats are VOIP and illegal gateways."[18]

WSIS CHALLENGES - EMPOWERMENT

"We recognize that young people are the future workforce and leading creators and earliest adopters of ICTs. They must therefore be empowered as learners, developers, contributors, entrepreneurs and decision-makers."

"A dynamic and enabling international environment, supportive of ...international cooperation... are vital complements to national development efforts related to ICTs. Improving global affordable connectivity would contribute significantly to the effectiveness of these development efforts."[19]

What can be done practically to encourage the common WSIS vision of the assembled representatives of the people of the world - that young people, the leading creators and early adapters of ICT, be empowered as learners, developers, contributors, entrepreneurs and decision- makers who dynamically create global, affordable connectivity - not to discourage them through harassment, arrests, and confiscation of their ICT tools, when their entrepreneurship is seen as being in competition with government offered services, while they help to provide global affordable connectivity. What can be done to discourage limiting technically non-enforceable, and economically counter-productive prohibitions?

Are the WSIS Principles to be used only as a dream – or will there be procedures where the international community will actively attempt to promote the common vision against particular national or even more limited interests?

Internet Governance

Cambodia – like many other countries in the early stages of Internet use – does not have any consistent Internet governance.

Statements by the highest political leadership are encouraging: The Prime Minister, who chairs the Cambodian National Information Communications Technology Development Authority, declared in July 2003 at a National Meeting on the Formulation of National ICT Policies and Strategies, which was held with the support of the UNDP Asia Pacific Development Information Program:[20]

> Success in this regard will ensure that Cambodia will no longer be isolated or left behind the mainstream of the ICT revolution.

---

[18] http://www.dba.org.nz/PDFs/Cambodia%20Final%20Report.pdf, page 32.

[19] Principles, Points 11 and 40

[20] http://www.apdip.net

At the same time, we should note with pride that our liberal policies in education and the strengthening of partnerships with the private sector from both within the country and overseas, which I launched since a decade ago, has been quite fruitful... All Cambodians have open access to information from overseas for study and general knowledge, through the Internet and email without any restrictive controls as is the case in some countries in the region.[21]

Such words do not yet reflect present policy. When the first NGO based email system started to operate in 1994, there was no legal basis for it – but the NGO contacted and informed the Ministry of Post and Telecommunications, and the MPTC was happy to also get connectivity. However, until now, neither a National Telecom Act nor a National ICT Policy Framework has been defined, though both are under discussion since several years. There were rumors that the Internet would be censored, but a letter by a Secretary of State of the Ministry of Information declared that this would not be done.[22] VoIP has been prohibited by regulation since 1998, but continued to flourish publicly until violent crack-down actions started in 2003.

To impose a monthly licence fee of US$ 200 on a small email-only ISP operated by an NGO, which provides general ICT awareness and training activities and is the only institution offering special training in Khmer language use in communications, does not reflect any encouragement for the development of an Information Society.

The lack of predictability definitely has paralyzing effects. The regulatory environment still keeps Cambodian ICT developments behind the mainstream, compared to some neighbors in the Asia Pacific region. Internet penetration has moved ahead, not so much because of an encouraging regulatory environment, but in spite of its absence.

Broader conclusions to which this situation points may be useful as guidance for the international community in its struggle to find the best way forward for developing countries.

1a - The successful development of the Internet itself grew out of many different, interrelated cooperating initiatives.

1b - Successful Internet governance for "a people-centered, inclusive and development-riented Information Society, where everyone can create, access, utilize and share information and knowledge, enabling individuals, communities and peoples to achieve their full potential in

---

[21] http://www.nida.gov.kh/activities/summit/PMSpeech_English.pdf

[22] Digital Review, page 138, Note 32.

promoting their sustainable development and improving their quality of life"[23] can also only grow out of such multi-faceted cooperation.

2a - The Internet is a network without a center, of interrelated independent networks existing in different jurisdictions[24] - in differently self-determined cyber-spaces.[25] This is not only true between nations, but also within nations. Some of these cyber-spaces stretch beyond national borders.

2b - Internet governance can, therefore, not be established by organizing one over-arching governance structure. In the same way that the United Nations is not above its independent member states, but rather provides a coordinating platform, Internet governance cannot rule what happens in the different related cyber spaces.

3a - There is need for technical and policy coordination in order to maintain interoperability between the different cyber spaces.

3b - Internet governance is therefore only possible as an ongoing process of many processes of voluntary cooperation between different, independent stakeholders: all those who organize and maintain Internet spaces, and those who use it: governments, the business communities, civil society groupings, and individual end users.

The WSIS Challenge, on the way towards WSIS 2005 is to observe and advise, to organize and coordinate open ended multiple voluntary processes of technical and policy coordination, in order to increase understanding and acceptance of widely accepted best practices, where all stakeholders respect each others' different perspectives and interests – not imposing models from one space to another, but fostering open-ended communication, guided by the commitment to achieve a vibrant Information Society, composed of many independent spaces. The attempt to achieve ONE governance system would retard the steady progress in the growth towards an Information Society for all.

---

[23] Principles, Point 1.

[24] The continuing controversy about the scope of the WHOIS databases and the role of different privacy legislation in different countries is a pertinent example - http://gnso.icann.org/issues/whois-privacy/

[25] My acknowledgement on the fundamental implications of this aspect for Internet governance is due to Pindar Wong, an Internet pioneer from Hong Kong with long time involvement in international Internet governance issues - see http://www.icann.org/biog/wong.htm and others.

INTERNET INFRASTRUCTURE: DNS, IP ADDRESSES, OR MORE?[1]
Veni Markovski, Internet Society Bulgaria[2]

The Internet – General Comments

When people speak about the Internet, they usually start with the description "it's a network of networks, it's an electronic medium", but I'd like to draw your attention to the fact that it is also a tool for accessing and spreading information and knowledge, a means for interactive communications, and a way (in some countries) to enjoy freedom of speech.

Many people in the developed world take these features of the Internet for granted. In developing countries, where I come from, the problem is different. What is it?

We all know that the Internet is based on a protocol, created by Vint Cerf and Bob Kahn – the Transmission Control Protocol/Internet Protocol, or as it is known, the TCP/IP. It works in the following way: data is transmitted in packets, which are disassembled in the author's computer, and reassembled in the recipient's one. For packets to find the correct way, IP addresses were created. These are 32 bit numbers, like 193.200.15.187, and they are used to route data to the right computer. However, there are not that many of these addresses, also known as IPv4, – around 4 billion. The relative shortage of addresses was one of the reasons

---

[1] This article was made initially as a presentation, written with OpenOffice, at the United Nations ICT Task Force 6th meeting in New York, March 25-26, 2004

[2] The Internet Society in Bulgaria: www.isoc.bg.

for developing a newer version of addresses (among other reasons is security, but that is a different topic) – IPv6 was created, where the addresses are 128 bit.

Because it is difficult to remember so many numbers the Domain Name System, or the DNS, was created. The DNS uses names rather than numbers, so that instead of using 193.200.15.187, one can just use a domain name, e.g. veni.com.

The root servers are another important part of the Internet. There are 13 at the moment, fully redundant systems, that keep the zone files – the list of all top-level domain names.

The top-level domain names are basically of two types – generic (gTLD) and country code (ccTLD). The gTLDs are .aero, .arpa, .biz, .com, .coop, .edu, .gov, .info, .int, .mil, .museum, .name, .net, .org, and .pro. There are applications pending decision right now for nine new gTLDs.

The ccTLD are two-letter country codes, as defined in a document of the International Standards Organization, called ISO 3166.

The Internet – a Developing Country Perspective

These are all technical issues that anyone can read about in books or on the Internet. The key question here is: *what is important?* The DNS, the root servers, and the distribution of IP addresses – or the actual *access to the Internet?* In other words: what do we need for deployment and development of a free (of governmental control) and affordable Internet?

Our understanding at the Internet Society – Bulgaria is that we need to develop telecommunications infrastructure, wireless access and Internet Exchange Points first. This requires privatization and liberalization of the telecommunications market as well as free usage of 2.4 and 5.8 GHz frequencies for Internet access. Then we need lots of education, starting with educating the politicians.

Then we need good legal framework to encourage the spread of Internet services.

We don't need regulation of the Internet Service Providers. There's no economic or political need for that (you can find more about this at www.isoc.bg/kpd). We don't need domain names and IP addresses controlled by the government. *Bulgaria is a great example for liberalization of the legal environment,* as it became the first country to implement these rules in the latest Telecommunications Law, where IP addresses and domain names are deliberately left outside of the control of the government and the National Regulatory Authority.

We need an open environment for the development of the Internet. Civil Society must take the leading role in ensuring control over governments by means of legal systems, common practices, technical support, etc.

We need computers in schools, and not only in the headmasters' offices, but real computer labs, and a good program for educating both pupils and teachers. We need a legal framework ensuring freedom of speech and freedom of access to information. Again, the work of the Bulgarian Parliamentary Committee of Transport and Telecommunications with the Internet Society and the Global Internet Policy Initiative (www.internetpolicy.net) could be a good example for all developing countries that want to positively influence Internet usage.

These are the important issues, not the management of root servers and domain names. Developing countries that aim at ensuring Internet access, computerization of schools and software programming are far better at achieving their global aims – among them, to become modern, advanced states with increased GDP, better conditions for their people, and more democratic governments.

Therefore, the conversation about Internet infrastructure should not be limited to the technical resources, which are being quite well governed by organizations like ICANN, IETF, IAB, ISOC and others.

RESULTS OF THE AFRICAN DISCUSSION LIST ON INTERNET GOVERNANCE
United Nations Economic Commission for Africa (UNECA)

As part of its activities for the Tunis phase of WSIS and within the context of the United Nations ICT Task Force African Stakeholders Network[1] (ASN), the Regional node of the United Nations ICT Task Force, the United Nations Economic Commission for Africa[2] (ECA) organized a discussion list on Internet governance for contribution to the United Nations ICT Task Force Global Forum on Internet Governance. A summary of the discussions follows.

First Week: Issues Related to Global Internet Governance
Questions raised
How does the current management of the Internet affect the political, economic and cultural equilibrium of the world? What do you think are the advantages and drawbacks of an intergovernmental model - where several governments together on an equal footing would be in charge of defining the rules of Internet governance - and the multistakeholder model - where the governance players would be representatives from the private sector, civil society organizations or users association? What would be the "ideal" model?

---

[1] http://www.unicttaskforce.org/

[2] http://www.uneca.org/aisi

Contributions and comments

Some participants raised the importance of understanding the historical patterns to better understand the current shaping of the institutional and political framework of the current governance system.

The large range of actors intervening in the international management of the Internet does not simplify things.

Some participants noted that "The fruits of WSIS are being realized and the Internet governance contributions will definitely facilitate policy-making that will yield a better IT environment for tomorrow. We should have in mind that we need to cater for the future generation by making the policies sustainable".

With respect to the role of the different stakeholders, it was emphasized that governments have an important role in defining and establishing the enabling environment in which e-development can occur. A participant stressed that "[a]n enabling environment supports and encourages economic and non-economic activities that increase society's well-being. With the rise of the new economy, the enabling environment must be reviewed to ensure that progress within the new world setting can be achieved. Governments must remain focused on improving access levels and quality of telecommunication and electricity infrastructure and education".

From the perspective of a representative of the private sector, a participant emphasized that members of the Internet community and governments need to work together to gather the necessary conditions, in particular focusing on: "Lowest possible regulation level and enable competition, effective exchange of information between public and private sector, maintaining several technical possibilities to adapt to the Internet users' choice and last but not least the private sector must develop "services/content", that will interest Africans in order to create revenue from the Internet".

Second Week: Africa and Internet Governance

Questions and issues raised

How is Africa affected and/or is benefiting from the current Internet governance system? What are the other public policy issues that you think are priorities for Africa (IP matters on IP networks, cyber-squatting, consumer protection, cyberspace regulation, security and privacy concerns etc.). Do you think that these issues affect particularly the gender digital divide in most of our African countries? How best do you think African countries can tackle these issues? Can you give examples of how national e-strategies/ NICI plans have addressed

Internet governance- related issues? What would be the role of regional political platforms such as the NEPAD?

Contributions and comments

Participants noted the need for a broad understanding and definition of Internet governance, in order to proceed from there to determine what Africa's role should be.

A participant from a regional development bank suggested that Internet administration issues, technology management, regulatory environment and digital inclusion should be seen as the main elements of discussion for Internet governance.

Focusing on the technical administration/coordination of Internet and looking at how Africa is affected/or benefiting from current Internet governance system, participants pointed out that the un-preparedness of most African countries as far as Internet governance is concerned is mainly due to lack of access to the Internet itself and problems related to the management of domain names. Unavailability of local registrars in Africa and the lack of support for AfriNIC were mentioned as reasons for the domain names management problem. In this regard, it was noted that Africa should be offered the opportunity to have IP allocations that meet its needs, since the continent is the only one receiving its IP addresses from other regional registries, with limited size allocation.

On the other hand, participants noted the efforts of the South African Government to pass legislation to address the increased use of electronic communications in government and business environments, despite numerous challenges that may be considered of higher priority.

It was finally suggested to take stock of best practices in some African countries, like Kenya in ccTLD management, as a model to raise awareness and build the capacity of African governments and policymakers on this issue.

On the role of regional political platforms such as NEPAD, it was suggested that regional institutions should make sure that best practices in managing the ccTLDs are spread and that they should support capacity building activities for policy makers to efficiently organize African participation in and contributions to the international policy making forums.

Regarding public policy issues related to Internet governance, some participants suggested to look first at what was available in the areas of ICTs in Africa, at what changes are needed, and at how it would be possible to provide access to accurate and timely information and use that information for change.

Some participants noted that the two inseparable components of, "technical" and "policy" should be equally considered when the issue of Internet governance is raised. They also stressed that since ICANN welcomes working with the WSIS, this would be an opportunity to deepen our understandings of Internet governance and learn from the countries which are ahead in the process.

Regarding IPR related international regulation - bilateral and multilateral - it was mentioned that a number of political and diplomatic efforts have enabled the inclusion of IPRs in multilateral trade negotiations such as the Trade related Aspects of Intellectual Property Rights (TRIPs) agreement of the WTO. The TRIPs agreement has by far been a major turning point in the protection of IPRs at the international level by fixing standards in patents, trademarks, and protection of designs that affect the knowledge society... In the context of the current global knowledge based economy, African countries are indeed facing new challenges due to the strengthening of IPRs and its international regime. It was noted that ensuring an equilibrium between promoting innovation and knowledge on one side and ensuring access to information and knowledge on the other side is indeed a dilemma for a sustained African Information Society.

How can we strengthen the emergence of a software industry in Africa? It was suggested that ASN should consider hearing what the other players have to say on this.

An issue on proprietary software vs. open source was raised. Some participants discussed the importance of open source in Africa, which links to IPR-related issues. They promoted the use of open source by stating that open source will enable developing countries to develop capacity in ICTs and most of the other commercial applications.

Third Week: Recommendations

1. The United Nations ICT Task Force African Stakeholders Network (ASN) should devise ways of continuing the Internet governance consultation process formally or informally as it permits to create a continuity of ideas; and also as this would enable people to share experiences/views/comments to enable us to get sustainable solutions.

2. Internet governance as applied to developing countries, especially Africa is not only about Internet administration/coordination/policies, it is also about the ICT governance in general, and should be considered as such in a holistic approach.

3. The Working Group should insist on the necessity for a better knowledge and understanding of the ICT paradigm by decision makers, especially in their ability to help leapfrog if a conducive environment is created. In this regard, capacity building and

awareness raising programmes for policy makers are essential to enable them understand the stakes and challenges of Internet governance in order to act in an appropriate manner.

4. The Working Group should highlight the necessity of training for professionals in order to build in-house capacities for both technical and business aspects of Internet governance.

5. The Working Group should devise ways and means for an increased and informed participation of developing countries in global ICT policy-making forums.

6. National ICT policies should mainstream Internet governance issues in their activities.

7. All stakeholders must be part of the process at national, regional and international levels to make Internet governance a reality.

8. The WSIS regional preparatory meetings should organize workshops on Internet governance, whereby all stakeholders should be able to voice concerns and also share best practices on making Internet governance a reality within specific countries and regions.

INTERNET GOVERNANCE: MAIN DIRECTIONS AND PRIORITIES

United Nations Economic And Social Commission For Western Asia (UNESCWA)

I. Introduction

The Internet has evolved to become one of the most strategic resources essential for socio-economic development. Internet governance revolves around control and supervision of such a critical resource shared by the whole humanity. The debates related to Internet governance are another manifestation of the conflicts and contentions accompanying globalization, which will not be resolved without clear vision and proper strategy formulation.

The Internet governance contention is inflated due to the fact that the members of the global community are not in complete agreement as to what they want and what they do not want. Accordingly, the positions of the different stakeholders are in some cases oversimplified in the form of "with" or "against" the current system. To reach a rational problem formulation and accordingly an objective-driven strategy, "black-and-white" oversimplification should be avoided. Accordingly, in this document, a prudent analysis of the situation and the different available arguments and viewpoints is offered, followed by the introduction of a recommended strategy.

This document constitutes a contribution to the ongoing global discussions regarding Internet governance, in this instance the Global Forum on Internet Governance, in order to help reach an international consensus that would be beneficial for all. Accordingly, the document avoids repeating information that is well known to the participants, can be found in the literature, or is sufficiently covered by other contributors. It considers the issues from a high level perspective in the form of a problem, alternative strategies for tackling it and a proposed strategy. Efforts are made to simplify the presentation of points of agreement and others of disagreement, wherever relevant, while focusing on priority messages.

II. Analysis and Evaluation of Alternatives
What is actually the nature of the "current system"?

Since it was the United States of America that commercialized the Internet in the early nineties, it is only natural to see it playing a major supervisory role in the management and coordination system of the Internet. In this regard, the current system includes several technical organizations (i.e. IETF, IANA, IAB, etc.) and is coordinated through ICANN. The most important organization of the current system is IANA, which oversees the allocation of Internet resources (root servers, IP numbers, and addresses) through regional organizations. IANA is under the supervision of ICANN which is a non-profit organization that has been controlled by the United States Department of Commerce (DOC) through a Memorandum of Understanding (MOU) between DOC and ICANN since 1998.

Specifically, what is the nature of the contending viewpoints?

The complexity of the issue stems from amalgamating several dimensions of governance with several levels of opinions. For the purpose of this discussion, the different contentious positions can be categorized as follows:

(a) All contending parties seem to agree that issues involved in Internet governance (such as rights of access, user privacy, national sovereignty, content, security and unlawful use, etc.) need to be thoroughly studied for the benefit of the global community and with the purpose of lowering barriers to wider dissemination of the Internet.

(b) The majority of the global community views the current system of governance (policy-making and administration of resources) as being non-representative of the global community, and tightly controlled by the United States Government.

(c) Some view the system as being inefficient and/or unfair in terms of policy making.

(d) Few consider the system as being inefficient in administrative and operational matters, although it seems to be improving in terms of operations in spite of being sometimes unfair in its allocation of resources, banning one country or another.

Collectively, the two characteristics of "fairness" and "efficiency" are the main points of critique; these two parameters influence one another, and are believed to endanger the sovereignty of nations as well as to hinder further evolution of the Internet.

The symptoms of unfairness and inefficiency in the current system can be summarized as follows:

(a) The United States Government alone has a supervisory role over ICANN (and hence, IANA), which gives the United States a privileged position to direct and control the allocation of resources to certain countries;

(b) ICANN is not *clearly* accountable to the global community; it is mainly accountable to United States Department of Commerce. For instance, there is no MOU between ICANN and the United Nations entitling the latter organization to some sort of supervisory role;

(c) ICANN itself is a United States non-profit organization, which according to American laws cannot enter into relations with countries on the United States embargo list;

(d) The present supervisory mandate of ICANN as a coordination mechanism does not clearly tackle sensitive issues related to content (like pornography, child abuse, unlawful use of the Internet, etc.);

(e) ICANN does not only act as a coordinating body, but sometimes plays the role of a *regulator* as alleged by VeriSign in its recent lawsuit against ICANN[1];

(f) ICANN is not flexible enough with registrars, thus hindering innovation and delaying the introduction of new services – refer to Verisign lawsuit;

(g) The passwords for Country-Code Top Level Domains (ccTLDs) and management of the corresponding servers are not fully controlled by the respective countries;

(h) The response time for obtaining Internet numbers is sometimes very long[2];

---

[1] http://www.verisign.com/corporate/news/2004/pr_20040226_print.html

[2] Some ESCWA member countries complain about delays in getting IP address, and the position of ICANN related to the allocation of Domain Names. In other countries, the process of obtaining IP numbers and domain names is going on more smoothly than before; in fact, there is a perception that the service is getting better.

(i)   ICANN is sometimes reluctant to fulfill requests from country code managers before they sign an MOU with ICANN;

(j)   Very few countries in the world have agreed to sign such an MOU, thus hinting at ICANN's inability to extend its reach to all regions of the world.

What are the prevailing alternatives?

Due to the ambiguity of the whole issue, proposed alternatives vary widely[3]:

1.   Some continue to debate the need for and the structure of the sought-after governance: should it be "hard" governance or "soft" governance, or "no" governance at all?

2.   Others believe that the whole organizational system should be *replaced* by another system representative of the global community.

3.   Some think that ICANN should be *replaced* by another organization, preferably under the auspices of the United Nations.

4.   Others feel that the whole system should stay "as is" since any change will *disrupt* the operation of the Internet and lead to *instability*.

Valuation of the prevailing alternatives

The above-mentioned alternative strategies are not optimal for the following reasons – presented in the same sequence:

1.   Since there seems to be a consensus on the need for Internet governance, the debate should focus on *how to* achieve it in a fair and optimal manner, regardless of the structure of the sought-after governance. Flexibility should be a key characteristic of any emerging structure since any realistic changes to Internet governance should be gradual.

---

[3] For more details, the reader is referred to the following sources:

- Caslon Analytics cyberspace governance guide,
  http://www/caslon.com.au/governanceguide.htm .
- Issues paper on Internet Governance, Commission on E-Business, IT and Telecom, International Chamber of Commerce, January 2004
- http://computerworld.com
- Don MacLean, Background paper for the ITU Workshop on Internet governance, February 2004

2. Replacing the whole system by another one that represents the global community and fully abandoning the current system is not practical and may lead to market confusion, disruption of services, and disturbance of expertise in existing technical bodies.

3. Immediately replacing ICANN with another coordinating organization is also not advisable due to the fact that this move cannot be justified before the existence of an alternative competent body. Such a body cannot be competent enough to argue its right to replace ICANN without real on-the-ground expertise in coordinating Internet activities. Although this alternative cannot be completely ruled out in the long term, it is difficult to justify it in the short term.

4. Keeping the current system without any changes means unfair treatment to most countries and stakeholders, with many crucial issues remaining unsolved.

III. Proposed Strategy

There is a multitude of viable courses of action, whose prioritization needs to be conducted with clear objectives in mind. Only after prioritizing viable courses of action can a clear strategy be set. Based on the above rationale, this section presents the recommended strategy, summarized by:

> *"Full-fledged participation and balanced supervision are the main elements for achieving fair representation and enhancing efficiency."*

The proposed strategy is based on giving the issue of "unfairness" top priority in the context of problem and solution formulation. Accordingly, the global community – through a collective mechanism – should plan to immediately and fully participate in the existing bodies encompassed by the existing system, and in particular in the operations of ICANN and IANA. It should also create a vehicle to exercise supervisory role over the existing system in order to make it fully accountable to the collective will of the global community.

How to achieve full-fledged participation?

The current Internet status was achieved through existing committees or organizations and is acceptable from an operational perspective but not from a strategic perspective. Efforts exerted by the United States for Internet governance so far should be acknowledged. However, the following arguments need to be taken into account in order to achieve "fair representation" and accordingly be in a better position to achieve efficiency while maintaining stability.

(a) Despite the fact that almost all developing countries are currently not fully ready to participate in Internet governance, their right to participate should not be eliminated; in fact participation is a means of acquiring new rights.[4]

(b) As the involvement in the Internet governance process is contentious and would be debated for some time to come, the increased involvement of the global community in the technical management and coordination process will be a vehicle for participation in the high level functions of this governance.

(c) Multilingualization and decentralization should be a strategic aim to achieve regional empowerment, fair representation and full participation.

(d) Reforming accountability: instead of being restricted to one government, it is expanded to become accountability to the global community through balanced supervision.

Immediate actions with short-term impacts to achieve accountability of the current system to the global community and balanced supervision:

The vehicle through which global participation, fair representation, and balanced accountability may be fulfilled could be a new or existing body representing the international community. It is logical to assume that such an organization should be closely linked to the United Nations in order to induce and catalyze multi-regional participation in the whole process. The vehicle will be entrusted with negotiating a better position of the global community along the following two tracks:

(a) The first track considers that the most important document that needs to be immediately reviewed is the MOU between ICANN and the United States Department of Commerce. Accountability to the global community and global supervision can be achieved if another MOU is negotiated between the United Nations or one of its agencies and ICANN to make ICANN accountable to the global community.

(b) The other track aims at forging an MOU between the United Nations and IANA, through which IANA becomes accountable to the international community – via a certain vehicle to oversee the allocation of IP numbers and domain names – while ICANN continues to oversee IETF and IAB.

Intermediate actions only achievable after balanced representation is attained:
(a) An agreed upon "Internet Charter":

---

[4] "The limits and merits of participation" a paper by Paulo Vieira da Cunha and Maria Valeria Junho Pena.

Any proposed scheme for Internet governance has to be guided by an "Internet charter" based on the following principles:

- Broader participation of the global stakeholders and Internet community;
- A structure that distributes power instead of concentrating it, with one or two levels of hierarchy between the global community and those who have been entrusted with powers of governance;
- A mechanism for monitoring and controlling;
- Systematic and transparent procedures for the decision-making process;
- Better streamlining of existing processes for the allocation of resources;
- Balanced concern for content issues along with technical and administrative issues.

While the importance of formulating an "Internet Charter" is fully understandable, such a comprehensive document will naturally be debated for a long time before the great majority of countries agree to it. Even if a document of this sort is agreed upon, current "under-representation" of the global stakeholders in the mechanics of the existing system will remain a limiting factor hindering the enforcement of such an agreement on existing bodies that are not fully accountable to the global community or under its supervision.

Hence, the goal of "fair representation" will always be on the critical path towards achieving the ultimate goals of governance with or without a Charter. Therefore, it is better to direct efforts towards this priority objective of achieving fair representation and to avoid distraction by other detailed issues.

(b) Enhancing efficiency of Internet administration and policymaking:

Enhancing efficiency of Internet administration without ensuring proper representation will neither guarantee fair management by the global community nor would it guarantee the sustainability of such efficiency. Furthermore, inefficiency does not represent a real threat to sovereignty of countries as the issue of fair representation does.

After fair representation is achieved, an optimal structure will evolve; efficiency and effectiveness of this governance will be enhanced gradually on the different levels (policy making, management, etc.). In other words, the efficient structure of Internet governance cannot be initially decided before enough involvement in management and operational systems is achieved.

Immediate actions with long-term impacts:

To avoid conflicts in the future accompanying the creation and deployment of "tomorrow's Internet", the following actions are essential:

(a) The allocation of fixed shares of IPv6 numbers to the different countries should start immediately based on population and expected growth rates for the coming decade.

(b) The establishment of a multi-stakeholders mechanism that is supported by the global community to be more involved in research, development, deployment and policy setting of the "next generation" Internet.

IV. Conclusions

All stakeholders, through the proper channels, should be involved in the strategic planning and evolution of Internet governance. To unify the positions of the global community in reaching a common position, governments are expected to form national e-governance committees to coordinate representation of their local stakeholders in the process. Private sector and ccTLD bodies should encourage their technical experts to participate in the technical management functions of the Internet. Relevant organizations within the civil society should play a role in creating awareness of Internet governance issues on the community level.

ESCWA and other United Nations Regional Commissions can act as regional catalysts, by empowering all the stakeholders within their respective regions to assume their duties in implementing the "fair representation" strategy, through capacity building activities related to Internet governance on the regional level.

The subject of Internet governance is very contentious, with a broad scope that is expanding to involve controversial objectives, alternative strategies, and debatable priorities. This document attempts to maintain a sharp focus by identifying one high priority strategy, in order to define those immediate goals having a long-term impact. It is, however, fully understood that the final output of the global debate will result in a multi-dimensional strategy that is expected to represent the overall collective wisdom of the global community.

INTERNET GOVERNANCE
United Nations Conference on Trade and Development (UNCTAD)

The terms of the debate

Given the profound impact of the Internet on multiple aspects of social life, the debate about its future evolution and the role that different social players should have in deciding the direction it will take is bound to be an intense one. In such a debate, the technological implications of the issues involved are likely to be interpreted, to some extent at least, in the light of real or perceived conflicts of interests – political, economic and cultural – over the development of what has become a global resource.

Even though there is no agreement among the participants in the debate about the exact delimitation of the processes that the terms "Internet governance" designate, the discussions throughout the WSIS process made it clear that a majority of developing countries feel that the status quo does not serve their interests well and needs to be reformed. The establishment of some sort of intergovernmental mechanism has been proposed. Furthermore, the lack of satisfaction with current arrangements is not limited to the governments of developing countries, although the analysis of what is not working and the prescribed solutions may differ significantly among critics.

From another viewpoint, the rapid expansion of the Internet across the world, probably faster than that of previous technological revolutions and the phenomenal growth of its commercial applications would support the view that the structures that underpin the development of the Internet serve their purpose well. The argument goes on to say that given the evolutionary nature of such structures and the large extent to which they rely on coordination and cooperation among the members of the Internet community, the safest means to ensure the balanced growth of the Internet is to allow the evolutionary process to move on, avoiding in particular serious governmental involvement (interference). From this viewpoint some of the objections to the policy-making and coordination arrangements of the Domain Name System and the root servers system may concern more the processes through which these governance mechanisms operate than their outcome.

It may be true that there are not many examples of significant direct damage to developing country economic interests derived from the operation of such systems as they stand today (a partial possible explanation being that most developing countries have so far had a shorter and narrower exposure to the Internet). However, in order to be effective in the long-term, governance mechanisms must rely on their acceptance by the governed. Technical effectiveness alone does not necessarily provide legitimacy. While the very success of the Internet would point to the existence of a fundamental consensus among the original Internet community, such consensus is undergoing fast erosion. It is only a matter of time before a system lacking political support becomes a technically dysfunctional one. It is also important to keep in mind that the past is not always a reliable guide to the future, and that changes in both the demand and the supply side of the market for Internet services may well render obsolete the arrangements that were so useful during the earlier phases of the emergence of the Internet.

The concerns of developing countries

The weaknesses of some of the governance structures of core aspects of the Internet are not merely a matter of principle or perception. The dominance by one or a few countries over core Internet resources can generate concerns about the potential for discriminatory treatment of other countries. For instance, it has been pointed out that some universities in the developed world hold more IP addresses than many developing countries. Legal mechanisms based on the enforcement of private contracts (to be carried out essentially by the national courts of one country) are not necessarily the optimal way to settle international public policy issues. As the Internet penetrates almost every aspect of social life, Governments are justified in seeing it as a sort of a vital international public utility, the management of which cannot take place without regard to internationally accepted principles such as respect for the sovereign equality of States.

Also, measures intended to achieve desirable aims such as the empowerment of private players and the reduction of undue governmental control can overshoot, resulting in the extension of neo-corporatist approaches and the predominance of special interest groups that may seriously undermine transparency, openness and the democratic process. As the Internet plays a growing role in the implementation of national development strategies, governments as the only players in the development process that enjoy full democratic legitimacy have a clear interest in ensuring that the Internet evolves in a direction that is compatible with their development strategies and the protection of the public interest, for which – unlike any other actors – they are accountable to their populations. Unless globally endorsed responses are given to these demands, societies that feel that their political, economic or cultural interests are not considered or are even at risk might develop their own individual responses, thus jeopardizing the greatest potential of the Internet as a tool for development, i.e. its universal reach.

A first step that needs to be taken in order to move the discussion forward is to ensure that all participants share some fundamental understanding of the nature of the arrangements being discussed, and of the interests at stake. In this regard, it is important that the position of the proponents of change be articulated beyond matters of principle and process, so that a discussion can be established in terms of specific interests, problems and impacts on the ground, and an actionable agenda. From UNCTAD's perspective, the fundamental interest of developing countries is to ensure that their specific needs and concerns are taken into consideration in any decision-making that will affect the evolution of the Internet and in particular its application to development problems, including those that may affect the supply capacity and the competitiveness of their economies.

Governance "of" the Internet versus governance "on" the Internet

Once it is recognized that a political answer to these questions needs to be found, it is also necessary to admit that there are not many examples of concrete policy areas in which such responses require the development of new Internet-specific international institutions, especially from the viewpoint of economic competitiveness. In fact, given the political will to tackle the issues, existing systems of international coordination, cooperation or rule-making appear to be sufficient to deal with many if not most of the governance problems posed by the development of the Internet. It is important in this regard to distinguish "governance of the Internet" (that involves the physical and logical infrastructure of the Internet, and would probably be more appropriate to refer to as the management of the core resources of the Internet) from "governance on the Internet" (which concerns the activities that take place over the Internet, particularly the exchange of information, goods and services).

Of course, it is not possible to establish a clear-cut separation between all infrastructural/technological matters on one side and political and socio-economic questions on the other. Policy decisions very often have technological implications and vice versa. A crude device to categorize the public policy issues that need to be addressed and the responses that could be explored in each case could be to distinguish between the management of the Internet as a global utility and the international governance issues posed by the use people make of that utility.

Concerning the group of issues that could fall under the "governance on the Internet" category, the most commonly quoted include matters such as content regulation, intellectual property (although these are also affected by the operation of ICANN), jurisdiction, competition policy (in particular in connection with the question of Internet interconnection costs and the imbalances in the relationship between tier 1 backbone operators and developing country ISPs and smaller backbone operators), e-commerce taxation, consumer protection, security and spam. In most of these examples, international governance instruments already exist or could easily be devised. For example, UNCITRAL and the Hague Convention on Private Law provide forums that are suited to address legal issues raised by the conduct of commercial or private transactions on the Internet. In other cases, efforts have already been undertaken at the regional level (for example, the convention of the Council of Europe on cybercrime), and building on them, a global international framework could be devised without major conceptual difficulties. In other cases the nature of the problems is such that the optimal solution may involve a mixture of international law-enforcement cooperation and end-user awareness and action (for example, spam). In all these cases, the substantive character of the issue at hand, rather than the fact that the Internet is the medium through which the problematic activity is conducted, should be the determining criterion as to what level of "governance" (from consensus building and cooperation to rule-making) and what instruments should be applied.

The problem of the imbalances in the distribution of the cost of international Internet interconnection systems exemplifies the situations in which existing frameworks may not be fully satisfactory, while the creation of specific Internet-focused governance instruments may not be a better option. The case for intervention in this area rests on the possible existence of restrictive business practices on the side of large backbone operators, resulting in unfairly high costs for developing country ISPs and developing country Internet users, thus aggravating the international digital divide. The problem being essentially one of international competition policy, its treatment presents well-known difficulties, particularly when it is developing countries that are on the side that suffers the effects of the restrictive business practices and therefore stand little chance of benefiting from the activity of the competition authorities of the major players. In any event an improvement of this situation is more likely to result from measures that address the general trade and development issues connected with competition policy in a manner that is consistent with the interests of developing countries than from the establishment of a comprehensive Internet regulatory system. The issue in this case is therefore not so much the need for a new intergovernmental organization to deal with the issues raised by the Internet, but the inadequacy of some aspects of the multilateral framework of trade to deal with the concerns of developing countries.

Reform, stability and performance

The management of the DNS that is performed by ICANN and the operation of the root server system that is in the hands of a small group of public and private sector entities are at the core of the "governance of the Internet" in the narrow sense. Equally important are a number of mainly membership-based organizations that support the development of many of the standards and policies that provide the "logical" infrastructure of the Internet. Setting out their strengths and weaknesses and in particular those of ICANN is beyond the scope of this note; but the fact that many developing countries are not at ease with the limited influence of governments in ICANN and in particular with the purely advisory role of the Government Advisory Committee (GAC) must be recognized and addressed. In this regard, reaching a common definition of the interests of the international community that must be served by the system of Internet governance, and in the way in which governments should be involved in it is probably the most important aspect of the work to be accomplished before the second phase of WSIS. Although at this stage of the discussion it is too early to make concrete institutional proposals, some of the features that they should have can be distinguished.

First, it must be recognized that whatever the merits of the case for their reform, the loose constellation of organizations that have so far underpinned the development of the Internet have achieved remarkable success in ensuring the stability and unity of a highly decentralized network of networks, with no centre and no strong rule-making authority. In order for any reform proposal to be viable, not just technically but also politically, it must provide strong evidence that it will ensure the continued stability and quality of service of the Internet, prevent its fragmentation and maintain the "bottom-up" processes through which standards and policies have been developed so far.

Second, no one-size-fits-all solution is likely to emerge. In addition to the management of core resources (IP addresses, DNS, root servers, protocols), a number of questions in which technological and policy issues are particularly intertwined are likely to be best treated within a network of international frameworks (as opposed to a unified, structured organization) of cooperation and coordination for the development of the Internet. These include, for example, the regulation of the WHOIS database (in connection in particular with privacy protection concerns), security (from the viewpoint of the network and from the viewpoint of the user, which may sometimes enter in conflict), the dispute resolution system and the problem of multilingualism. In such a cooperative framework flexibility should be a paramount consideration: for instance, not all stakeholders need to play an equally relevant role in addressing every matter; some problems may require hard rules and formal structures while others may not. Structural flexibility and lightness are also needed in order to prevent governance solutions from being rendered obsolete by technological evolution.

Third, evolution is more likely to produce results than a voluntarist top-down approach. The current system of management of core Internet resources is the result of a process that has taken place over a remarkably short time. It is clear that this evolution has not yet reached a stage of maturity that is acceptable to all its stakeholders. It must also complete a process of genuine internationalization (which is not necessarily equivalent to full-fledged intergovernmentalization, but which implies representativeness requirements beyond the participation of individuals/organizations of various nationalities). In so doing it is essential to reconcile demands for change with the need to ensure the continued delivery of the critical services that ICANN and the root server system provide to the Internet community. If, as argued above, effectiveness alone does not confer legitimacy, ineffectiveness can ruin it.

Supporting the dialogue

The evolution of the governance framework towards a system that is more development friendly would be facilitated if developing country players (both governmental and non-governmental) would identify concrete policy issues (as opposed to broad policy areas) in which their concerns and interests are not being considered adequately. Developing countries need to assess the implications of different Internet governance models, including in terms of their impact on the capacity of their economies to benefit from the adoption of e-commerce and e-business practices. This is an undertaking to which UNCTAD could contribute within the limits of its mandate in the trade and development area.

A sustained effort of capacity building for Internet policy making is needed so that the majority of the developing countries can effectively participate in the management/governance systems that may emerge from the WSIS process. This is another area in which UNCTAD can make a contribution within an international framework in which the United Nations ICT Task Force could play an important coordination role.

Section 5

TECHNICAL ISSUES

background paper

QUESTIONS AND ANSWERS ABOUT THE INTERNET AND INTERNET GOVERNANCE[1]
Karl Auerbach, InterWorking Labs

This note is designed to address certain questions that commonly arise in discussions of Internet governance. It is anticipated that the contents of this note will expand and evolve over time. The latest version of this note may be found at http://www.cavebear.com/rw/igov-qa.html.

This note is divided into several sections:

- Definitions
- Internet governance
- Internet bill of rights
- Internet technology

Definitions

Q: What is the Internet?

A: The Internet is the open system that carries IP packets from source IP addresses to destination IP addresses.

---

[1] Updated: March 23, 2004

The Internet is a "layered" system. Services and applications are generally best added to the Internet at the edges of the net rather than by embedding them into the fundamental data carrying elements that form the lower layers of the Internet. This has been called the "end-to-end principle".

Many people consider services and applications such as the World Wide Web (WWW), Voice over IP (VoIP), and the Domain Name System (DNS) to be part of the Internet. One may, however, consider them as layered-on services and applications rather than mechanisms that are necessarily embedded into the core of the Internet. Clarity of thought regarding matters of Internet governance may be enhanced by considering these services as distinct applications and not part of the core Internet.

Background materials:

- Saltzer, Reed, Clark, 1981, "End-to-End Arguments in System Design", available online at http://www.reed.com/Papers/EndtoEnd.html
- David Isenberg, 1997, "Rise of the Stupid Network", available online at http://www.hyperorg.com/misc/stupidnet.html
- Karl Auerbach, 2004, "Deconstructing Internet Governance" available online at http://www.itu.int/osg/spu/forum/intgov04/contributions/deconstructing-Internet-governance-ITU-Feb26-27-2004.html - This was a submission to the recent ITU Workshop on Internet Governance (February 2004)

Q: Is "Internet" synonymous with "World Wide Web"?

A: No. The Internet is a system that can accommodate many applications. The World Wide Web is only one such application among many.

People often make the mistake of equating the Internet to the World Wide Web. That mistake can lead to misgovernance of the Internet when a policy intended for the World Wide Web is inadvertently applied also to other applications such as Voice over IP, email, file sharing, or remote medicine.

Q: What does the phrase "stability of the Internet" mean?

A: One useful definition is this:

In order to be considered stable, the Internet must demonstrate the following characteristics:

- *IP packets must move reliably and with dispatch from source IP addresses to destination IP addresses.*

- *IP address allocations and IP packet routing must mesh well.*

This definition of stability of the Internet is tied to the definition of the Internet proposed earlier in this note. It would be reasonable to create similar definitions of stability for the various applications that are layered onto the Internet. For example one could define "stability of the Domain Name System (DNS)" in this way:

In order to be considered stable, the Domain Name System must demonstrate the following characteristic:

- *DNS queries for the root and top level domain layers must be answered reliably, quickly, and accurately.*

These definitions exclude issues, such as the protection of trademarks or dispute resolution policies, that have no reasonable relationship to the technical behavior of the Internet.

Q: What is the nature of a country code top level domain (ccTLD)?

A: There is considerable ambiguity with regard to exactly what is this thing we call a country-code Top Level Domain (ccTLD).

Some observers consider ccTLDs to be something that is attached to, and derives from, a sovereign country. Under this interpretation the ultimate authority concerning operation of a given ccTLD would be vested in that country and in that country alone.

Other observers consider ccTLDs to be merely entries on a list or database that have nothing more than a circumstantial correspondence to sovereign countries. Under this interpretation, the ultimate authority concerning operation of a given ccTLD is not the country but rather some other body.

ICANN adheres to the latter point of view. ICANN considers that ccTLDs exist for and must be used for the benefit of the network users within a given country. Under that point of view, ICANN holds itself in a position superior to the government of each country regarding whether that country's ccTLD is being operated by the proper people or entities and whether that ccTLD is being operated in the best interests of the network users within that country. ICANN, under this point of view, is empowered to choose among multiple claimants for a ccTLD, a choice that, at least on the Internet, constitutes recognition of who is the legitimate government of a country. ICANN's position in this matter is made more complex by the role of the United States Department of Commerce in matters regarding what names are placed into the domain name system root zone.

Internet Governance

Q: Does the Internet require governance?

A: Yes. However, one must be careful to define with precision and specificity those matters that require governance and exactly how much. The danger of overbroad governance is real. And in many cases explicit governance may be unnecessary: the Internet operates to a large extent through voluntary cooperation driven by the self-interested desire to enhance connectivity. In many respects, the Internet imposes its own kind of regulation - those who are not willing to cooperate with others often will find that they have no means to communicate with others or even with third parties.

On the other hand, there are certain limited aspects of the Internet that do require one or more authorities to establish norms that range in force from voluntary recommendations to obligatory mandates. In some cases the exercise of authority is nothing more than the clerical designation of a protocol number (parameter) and the declaration that that number represents something. In other cases the exercise of authority involves the subjective balance of competing concerns and equities.

Here is a partial list of these aspects:

- Creation of policy for the assignment of Internet (IP) addresses.
- The actual assignment of IP addresses according to a policy for such assignments.
- Creation of a policy for the addition or deletion of top level domains (TLDs) from a DNS root zone.
- The actual addition, removal, and maintenance, according to a policy covering such tasks, of a TLD entry in a DNS root zone.
- Creation of a policy to decide among competing claimants for a country code top level domain (ccTLD).
- The actual application of ccTLD policy to decide among competing claimants for a ccTLD.
- Establishment of service criteria for the operation of DNS root servers, particularly the root servers that comprise the dominant system of root servers.

- Establishment of minimal levels of service for the end-to-end transport of packets across the Internet so that users and implementers can have a reasonable assurance (but not necessarily a guarantee) that new applications will be viable.

Q: Is a monolithic body of Internet governance necessary or desirable?

A: No. At the recent ITU meeting on Internet governance the consensus seemed to be that Internet governance would be best achieved through a variety of small regulatory bodies rather than one single large body. Many of the tasks of Internet governance are clerical in nature and many require little or no exercise of discretion. For example, the task of recording protocol parameters is a clerical task that could easily be assigned to an existing organization without coupling it to another unrelated task such as the delegation of IP addresses.

Background materials:

- Karl Auerbach, 2004, "Governing the Internet, A Functional Approach" available online at http://www.itu.int/osg/spu/forum/intgov04/contributions/governance-structureITU-Feb26-27-2004.html - This was a submission to the recent ITU Workshop on Internet Governance (February 2004)
- William Drake, 2004, "Framing 'Internet Governance' Policy Discourse: Fifteen Baseline Propositions" - This was a submission to the recent ITU Workshop on Internet Governance (February 2004)

Q: Are copyright and trademark matters appropriate for Internet governance?

A: No. Matters of copyright and trademark have no relationship whatsoever to the technical stability of the Internet. Although such matters have been introduced into ICANN, these are matters more appropriate for national legislatures and international agreements.

Q: Are Internet governance bodies immune from capture by those they purport to oversee?

A: Experience with Internet governance indicates that oversight bodies are very easily captured. Internet governance bodies are often directed by people who are primarily versed in the technology of the Internet and who, by education, experience, or predilection may fail to recognize the forces that create capture or the fact of such capture.

In addition, Internet governance bodies tend to be directed by people who view their role as a kind of part-time matter that they believe excuses them from fully engaging with the issues that come before the body. As a consequence, rather than directing the governance body they tend to relinquish their roles to a full-time secretariat or staff.

Certain industrial segments, such as the United States' intellectual property bar, have found it useful to assert that the desires of their industrial segments are essential to the "stability of the Internet". These assertions should be viewed with great scepticism and recognized for what they often are: attempts to create supranational laws without the benefit of national legislative processes or international agreements.

ICANN's UDRP is a case in point - it is a policy adopted by a private California corporation that had the worldwide effect of exporting onto the nations of the world, without their consent, a supranational law that expanded the protection of intellectual property beyond that enacted by any national legislature.

Internet Bill of Rights

Q: Is there a guiding principle to which Internet governance should aspire?

A: I have suggested the following as such a guiding principle:

> *The First Law of the Internet:*
>
> - *Every person shall be free to use the Internet in any way that is privately beneficial without being publicly detrimental.*
>
> - *The burden of demonstrating public detriment shall be on those who wish to prevent the private use.*
>
> - *Such a demonstration shall require clear and convincing evidence of public detriment.*
>
> - *The public detriment must be of such degree and extent as to justify the suppression of the private activity.*

Internet Technology

Q: What is the limit on the number of top level domains (TLD) that may be supported by the domain name system (DNS)?

A: Today the domain system has 258 top level domains (TLDs).

There is no firm upper limit on the number of top level domains that may exist. Analysis and actual experimentation have demonstrated that the DNS can support at least several million TLDs.

There is concern that before these technical limits are reached there will be administrative or procedural limits. It has been demonstrated, however, that it is possible to run large DNS zones containing millions of names, such as *.com* or *.org*, without there being administrative or procedural difficulties. That experience is directly applicable to the root itself and should eliminate the concerns that have been put forth regarding the risks of adding even a few hundred new TLDs.

The addition of new TLDs should be done conservatively. However, one should recognize that there is a difference between conservative growth and stasis. Even if the DNS root were to be expanded at a rate of one new TLD *per hour*, it would take several thousand years before the number of TLDs grew to the numbers that are routinely handled without difficulty today in *.com* or *.org*. This means that even an extremely conservative plan for growth ought to result in the addition of at least hundreds of new TLDs per year.

Q: What does a domain name actually represent?

A: There is a widespread belief that a domain name translates into an address of a website. That belief does not fully encompass the nature of a domain name.

A domain name is a key into a distributed database. A domain name leads to a collection of records in that database. There are many different kinds of records. Here is a very incomplete list of the kinds of records that may be represented by a single domain name:

- IPv4 addresses and IPv6 addresses
- Name server names (in order to delegate to a deeper level of the distributed DNS database)
- Aliases (i.e. to transform one domain name into another)
- Pointers (generally used to reverse translate IP addresses back into names)
- Email servers
- Geographic coordinates (latitude, longitude, elevation)
- Text (e.g. I have the text of the Magna Carta stored in DNS text records.)
- Regular expressions (a very arcane language used to translate telephone numbers into URIs for Voice Over IP)

Not only does a given domain name lead to potentially many types of records, but there may also be multiple instances of each type.

Thus, for example, a domain name such as *www.example.com* may lead to a collection of records containing multiple IP addresses, multiple email server names, geographic coordinates, anti-spam information, etc.

A given domain name can, and often does, lead to a rather multifaceted body of records. Consequently, what a domain name "means" depends on what actual records are requested by software and what that software does with those records.

To add to the complexity, even when a domain name does lead to one, and only one, IP address, the computer that responds to that address may itself be offering multiple kinds of services, not merely a World Wide Web server. Thus a computer that is found via the domain name *www.example.com* may offer email, relay-chat, VoIP, file transfer, time-of-day, and other services.

This complexity and flexibility of the domain name system represents a significant dissonance between Internet reality and Internet governance policies that try to impose content or business limitations based on the semantics of the words (usually English words) found in domain names.

Q: Will IPv6 bring new challenges or solutions to Internet governance?

A: From the point of view of Internet governance the main change brought by IPv6 is a significantly larger number of addresses. This will help relieve the already pent-up demand by ISPs and users for additional address blocks. IPv6, however, does not relieve the concerns about the increasing complexity of the IP packet routing system. Internet governance over IPv6, in the form of IP address allocation policies, will still have to be careful to ensure that the allocation of IPv6 addresses meshes well with the IP packet routing systems of the Internet.

Q: Does the Internet require there be one, and only one, root of the domain name system?

A: No, the Internet may have many domain name systems, each represented by a different root. From the point of view of users of the Internet, the main concern is that these different systems be consistent with one another - a name uttered by one person in one place using one domain name system ought to give the same results as that same name uttered by another person in another place. This is quite easy to achieve in practice and there are several root systems running today that are consistent. Users who find that a given DNS system does not provide satisfactory service or is inconsistent may quite easily choose to use another domain name system service.

Just as most users of personal computers use the Microsoft Windows operating system, most users of the Internet use one highly dominant domain name system that is overseen by the United States Department of Commerce, ICANN (a California corporation), and Verisign (a private California corporation.)

However, just as the Linux operating system provides an alternative to Microsoft Windows, competing roots offer alternatives to the DoC/ICANN/Verisign domain name root. Many of the arguments that have been used to justify the Microsoft hegemony have also been used in an attempt to deny the usefulness and value of competing DNS root systems.

Background materials:

- The Hush-A-Phone case available online at http://cyber.law.harvard.edu/filter/hush.html - This is an interesting case regarding a claim by a telephone monopoly, backed by the technical experts of a governmental regulatory body, that a benign attachment to telephones would damage the telephone system (the Internet of the day). The court rejected that claim. This case is raises an interesting parallel to the claims by an existing Internet regulatory body that competing DNS roots would harm the Internet.

- Open Root Server Network (ORSN) (http://www.orsn.net) - This is an example of a DNS root system that competes with that of the DoC/ICANN/Verisign.

INTERNET GOVERNANCE, NATIONAL INTEREST AND INTERNATIONAL RELATIONS[1]

Kenneth Neil Cukier, John F. Kennedy School of Government, Harvard University

Six long words. Three big concepts. One small idea. The title of this essay comprises things not normally associated together.

When one considers the Internet and foreign affairs, it is usually viewed in terms of cross-border regulations on content and usage, or the effect of the medium abroad (for example, regarding "soft power"), or the change in the process of diplomacy itself.

However, there is another dimension, which is the focus of this essay: who controls the network's operation and evolution? This is currently done by ICANN, the Internet Corporation for Assigned Names and Numbers. It was created by the United States in 1998 as an international, public/private-sector body to oversee the Internet's domain name system – a task previously managed by the United States Defense Department, which initially funded the Internet.

The one simple idea is this: *The Internet is a global resource whose control and allocation is a matter of political power; instead of doing away with geopolitics, the Net creates new areas of national interest and foreign policy concerns.*

---

[1] This essay, submitted as a background paper to the United Nation's Information and Communications Technology Task Force global forum in March 2004 in New York, is based on a seminar the author presented at the National Center for Digital Government at Harvard University on March 16, 2004.

This essay does not presume to offer a doctrine for foreign policy in the Internet age. Its more modest goal is to raise a number of empirical matters that governments collectively face regarding the network. Together, they reveal a new and mature way of understanding the medium.

The first part explains Internet governance, or "infrastructural coordination". Part two looks at it from the perspective of national interest, with an emphasis on US interests. Part three notes how these interests map to specific ICANN issues, which are concerns of international relations. The fourth part tries to explain why ICANN matters not just for students of politics and international affairs, but for ordinary individuals, companies and other stakeholders. Finally, the essay concludes by analysing current tensions concerning the Internet's institutionalization.

I. Internet governance

It is a regrettably misleading term (since "governance" sometimes presumes it is the sole responsibility of governments). A better term may be "coordination of Internet technical functions" though it may present public policy concerns, too. There are four aspects:

- **Names** (global ones like .com; territorial ones like .iq for Iraq). Who says who is a registry, a valuable economic asset that affects free speech? Who says who gets a country-code, an important way to establish presence online, and symbolically important?

- **IP numbers (e.g.** "255.255.255.0"). A valuable and finite resource that affects the types and number of devices that can connect seamlessly to the network. When the network was young, huge blocks of numbers were given to US companies and universities, so some benefit from abundance while entities outside the United States deal with relative scarcity.

- **Protocols** (TCP/IP, SNMP, etc.). Most communications standards have been set by national and intergovernmental bodies; the Internet's standards exist outside that process, which has historically led to tension with the ITU, among others.

- **Root servers** (1 master, 12 slaves, +30 mirrors). The computers match domains to their authoritative name servers for routing traffic. Currently, three are outside the US (Sweden, U.K. and Japan); the majority are under US governmental control. Mirror servers have been broadly diffused globally, providing advantages in routing, but meaningless in terms of internationalized political control.

These functions sound technical and arcane – and they are. That is one reason why many countries have been late to understand their geopolitical importance. Control over these aspects of the Internet is akin to a central bank's control over a nation's money supply. Names are the real estate of the Internet; numbers are the oxygen or oil of the network; the protocols are the utilities, or the legal system (from which the term intentionally derives); root servers are the central nervous system. Together, the system is important, and its daily operation as well as the influence over the substance of policy and institutional process represents important power in the modern age.

II. National interests related to Internet control

The question of what constitutes a national interest is a long-standing debate among scholars; this essay will not go there. Nor will it try to separate vital from secondary interests; that is for another time. Instead, it is meant for identification, not prioritization.

A few interests, along with where they fit in with the ICANN-related functions, include:

- Access to numbering resources (IP address space).
- Stability and robustness of the network (root servers and protocols).
- Access to improved media resources (domain names and content).
- Greater economic efficiency via new technology (protocol development).

These interests are not universal; in fact, in some cases they may conflict with interests of certain nations, for instance:

- An authoritarian regime would prefer a closed medium to control information flows.
- Greater technical efficiency may jeopardize the revenue of existing state-run firms.

But the interests correspond to objectives the Internet can support and fuel:

- Economic development.
- Openness, transparency, and accountability.
- Free expression and information sharing.
- Continuing technical innovation.
- Global political, economic and social stability.

Of course there is nothing about the Internet that inherently supports these goals – it must be shepherded in the right way. But the Internet, as a more open medium compared to all other communications technologies, can potentially further these goals by dint of its end-to-end design principle. This provides for its decentralization, lower cost, and openness.

III. How Internet governance interests dovetail with foreign affairs

There are pragmatic concerns facing Internet governance and nation-states that have escalated to the level of international relations. They include:

- National sovereignty over information infrastructure.
- Control over shared information resources.

- Influence over policy process and substance.
- Access to content and its restriction.

Each of these areas contains practical policy concerns, and merits closer consideration.

National sovereignty over information infrastructure

ccTLDs: Who is a country? – ICANN and its predecessor organization have always sought to avoid the issue of what is a state, yet is inherently unable to skirt it. For instance, in 2003 Chinese authorities raised the issue with US and ICANN officials of why .tw existed since it seemed to legitimize the island as an independent nation, which China regards as a province. Though China stopped short of asking its removal (there are a number of non-national territories in the ISO 3166 list, including .hk for Hong Kong), the incident is indicative of the offline politics that can easily enter domain name policy discussions. Secondly, in March 2000, ICANN established .ps to represent the Palestinian Authority, another example of how politics is implicit in Internet addressing.

ccTLDs: Who controls the domain? – There is a policy ambiguity over who has ultimate authority over county codes. In 2003, Singapore's governmental country-code registry withdrew its application for a trademark on its two-letter domain, .sg, after ICANN informed it that the country did not actually have rights to the domain; instead, ICANN controlled it. Rather than force the issue, the government acquiesced. The incident exposes the ambiguity of whether countries have sovereignty of their country codes, and why ICANN asserts it ultimately does when the United States government's 1998 statement of policy (White Paper) that established ICANN's principles indicated the contrary. At the United Nations World Summit on the Information Society in December 2003 in Geneva, Zimbabwe's President Robert Mugabe emphatically called this an example of neo-colonialism.

Control over shared information resources

International domain names – IDNs are a nascent technology that permits domain names in languages that do not use the Roman alphabet characters; it opens up Internet addressing to all the world's scripts. However, unlike country codes where there is normally one acknowledged entity that represents the nation, major languages often transcend one specific country, such as Arabic or Chinese. China initially claimed sovereignty over the language for the domain name system; it has since relinquished the stance. But the question of who decides what entity is legitimate to steward and set policies over a script is uncertain. Because the values and traditions of the speakers vary widely across cultures that share a language, the entity designated to register names can affect the degree of free speech or privacy online.

Internet Protocol numbers – The addresses represent important economic value and their access is vital for widespread deployment of Internet-enabled devices. Japan's consumer electronics industry is dependent on access to IP addresses; in 2001, the country's Minister of Industry travelled 40 hours round trip for a three-hour visit to an ICANN board meeting in California to make that point. China relies on access to IP addresses due to its huge population; for that reason it specifically obtained an unprecedented two seats on the executive council of APNIC, the regional Asia-Pacific IP number registry, so it has greater influence over the allocation process. Lastly, global mobile phone companies or handset makers will depend on access to IP numbers. These allocation concerns will remain despite an upcoming enhancement called IPv6, which increases the number of addresses exponentially.

Root servers – The constellation of 12 secondary root servers, capped at that number due to technical limitations, are managed by both private and public entities that are only loosely affiliated with ICANN, for historical reasons. Many countries have requested to operate a root server, including France and China. Global deployment is important for better regional traffic routing and quality of service, for network resiliency, for symbolism of internationalized Internet control and national prestige. It could potentially prevent any one entity from having a preponderance of control to unilaterally affect the addressing content that the rest of the Internet adheres to for universal interoperability. The use of mirror servers has led to better regional traffic routing, but confers no political control, and lacks the symbolic power that control infers.

Influence over policy process and substance

Process – The central intergovernmental debate at ICANN is over the role of the state versus private stakeholders, such as industry, technologists or civil society. ICANN's Governmental Advisory Committee has no formal policy-making powers, which some member states feel is inappropriate. ICANN itself is a creation of the United States government and lacks the formal legitimacy that international treaties confer. Moreover, the GAC exhibits classic politicization of offline disputes, such as when China walked out of a meeting in Melbourne in March 2001 when it saw "Taiwan" name cards for the island's representatives, rather than the traditional diplomatic word-play "Chinese Taipei."

Policy – ICANN has set policy in a few areas, either by action or non-action, that impact national law. For instance, one of the first acts the organization took was to establish a uniform dispute resolution procedure (UDRP) for generic, global domain names. This was a method of enforcing trademark rights globally, by adopting the procedure developed by WIPO. Secondly, ICANN has not changed the public nature of the WHOIS database for global domains, which makes openly available the name, address and phone number of registrants. It has been roundly criticized for violating norms of privacy. The reason it remains public is due to the influence of intellectual property holders who insist on having an easy way to contact Web site owners in cases of infringing content. These two examples underscore how the substance of ICANN decisions, by act or inaction, affect national policy matters and apply globally.

Access to content and its restriction

Protocol – The way the technical code of the Internet works makes identifying, tracing and monitoring traffic difficult. There is also an inherent trade-off between security that protects the integrity and confidentiality of communications needed for e-commerce with the potential for surveillance capability needed by law enforcement. In 1999, the United States Department of Justice sought to develop wiretap capabilities directly into the protocol of the Internet, via the standards body IETF, which is affiliated with ICANN. The initiative was rebuffed by the technical engineers, but underscores an area where national interests coincide with how the Internet operates, which matter for international relations.

These areas are of course not exhaustive. And the examples used are often just ones that stand for a number of similar incidents. Lastly, one of the most important aspects of the Internet relative to governments is network security, but this analysis has not included it as a point because, so far, there has not been a political dispute in that regard.

IV. Why ICANN matters

ICANN's actions affect how people use the Internet on a daily level. It does so because of its control over names, numbers, protocols and the root server system that holds it together. However, due to the idiosyncratic ways that the Internet evolved (informally, often non-governmentally, inherently internationally, etc.) its institutional structure remains largely outside the realm of classic national and intergovernmental control. Any entity that strives to "govern the Internet" in terms of the quasi-technical related functions will possess significant power, but also confront contentious issues.

Names

The power to decide the words that everyone in the world will use to communicate, identify content and interact online. This responsibility over the upper-most hierarchical terms is crucial for helping users navigate and give semantic meaning to the online world. That lets the institution delegate an enormous economic and political asset to an entity, to operate the domain registry.

The delegation permits it to influence the policies that the registry must follow concerning the appropriate use of words for domain names, which directly impacts freedom of speech and democratic dissent. It also determines the degree to which trademark holders are protected.

Oversight of registry operations and, as a result, the WHOIS database, gives it control over the degree to which privacy and anonymity exist at the most primal aspect of Internet communications – online identity, and entry-point of access.

Authority over the system lets it regulate the companies that sell domains, to ensure fair competition, consumer protection, and to a certain degree, the prices users pay. This power affects the visibility of individuals and companies on the Internet.

Numbers

The control of IP number assignments affects the way the Internet evolves in terms of its growth, cost, future services and openness to technical innovation.

Power to determine address allocations impacts the number of devices that can connect directly to the Internet, which affects how many people or machines are online. The policies determine the cost of IP addresses (one-time or annually-recurring fee), and affect the price that consumer and businesses pay to go online, as well as the economic model of businesses that rely on the deployment of network infrastructure. Power to control access to IP numbers impacts the types of services users are offered by affecting a company's ability to bring onto the network millions of devices or objects via embedded addresses.

Oversight of allocations can be used as a mechanism to achieve non-technical policy goals, such as, if implemented, positively identifying users and their precise geographic location for activities like surveillance, taxation, etc.

Controlling address availability impacts the openness of the Internet as a medium for technical innovation, by ensuring widespread address distribution so that devices can connect directly to other devices without the need for intermediaries that could act as a choke-point for network control. (Such control could entail prohibiting applications like Internet telephony or peer-to-peer file sharing, etc.)

Power over the network's openness assures the degree of user independence relative to the Internet service provider, which enables competition and usually lowers costs. The ability to preserve network openness affects democratic values of free expression; control of IP addresses could otherwise provide power over who may participate online.

Protocols

Control over the development of new protocols affects the degree of technical innovation that can happen online, and what users are able to do.

New protocols can be a means to remedy problems with the current design and operation of the network, such as devising service quality systems. That power can translate into control over code development to achieve mainstream policy-related objectives, such as privacy, censorship, surveillance, etc.

This control could also be used to prohibit certain activities such as content restrictions, or hobbling functional capabilities of the network, like file-sharing.

Root server system

Oversight authority ensures the stability and smooth functioning of the critical infrastructure of the Internet, so that traffic is routed efficiently and accurately, leading to quality of service for users and confidence in the network for new and sophisticated uses. Geographic distribution of root servers provides more efficient traffic routing (of address queries), which lowers cost and increases quality of network performance. This decentralized distribution, if coupled with control of the server, can risk a fragmented addressing system, if the entity decides to change any of the content in the zone file (adding or deleting a name, or changing the authoritative name server address). Contrariwise, decentralized distribution can act as an insurance policy to assure that no single actor holds so much control that it can unilaterally change the zone file in a way that other root operators have an incentive to unwillingly follow to prevent fragmenting the addressing system.

Control of a root server could be used for surveillance (albeit extremely inefficient) of Internet traffic connections (though not content).

Final thoughts: Institutions and governance

This analysis points to a paradox of Internet governance. It might be framed as the paradox of power and plausibility: the more horrific the scenarios of how Internet governance can be potentially abused, the less likely it will actually happen.

This should provide some relief. It injects a dose of reasonability and proportion to the debate, since it is not always big, abstract principles and hypothetical scenarios one considers, but practical questions of how to implement concrete policies in the real world.

Still, there are some fundamental tensions regarding the institutionalization of Internet governance. It is essential to balance:

- the need for openness with specialized expertise;
- representation with the naturally unequal influence of diverse stakeholders (and ability to continually add new ones);
- the application of the rule of law with the risk of politicization;

- established processes with flexible implementation for new circumstances;
- stability with experimentation to preserve continued innovation.

If there is an underlying conflict that drives the debate, it may be the question: "What is the Internet?" It is not a metaphysical concern, for the answer one gives effects whether one regulates/controls/manages/coordinates/oversees/ignores the medium. Questions about what constitutes the Internet include:

- Global public resource or common private good?
- Innovation at the core or at the edge?
- Commercialization of infrastructure or at higher layers?

Ultimately, we can hope there is more Internet governance or less of it; we can strive to centralize or decentralize the processes – and it seems appropriate to initiate a global discussion with ever-increasing numbers of stakeholders on these matters. But that is provided we are willing to do the harder work of agreeing on answers.

Conclusion

After having examined the specifics of Internet governance, it may be useful to return to the bigger picture – and the "one small idea" with which I began this essay. If a hands-off approach or watching (and, hopefully, learning) from the sidelines was an acceptable policy for governments in the 1990s, it clearly is not an option anymore. The Internet has become too important for governments to remain passive observers to its development, and the issues, this essay has sought to argue, has become an urgent matter of national interest, power, security and sovereignty. And thus, a matter of foreign policy.

As such, there are two extreme directions in which governments may go:

- Deviating in some way from the ICANN-sanctioned naming and numbering system.
- Becoming excessively engaged, seduced by ICANN's true or perceived power.

On the former, why one ought to care if a country decides to drop out of the ICANN addressing system is straightforward: the value of a network decreases for all parties if fewer users participate, albeit the effects are felt disproportionately more by the smaller group. For the United States, this disadvantage is borne economically in increased transaction costs of routing traffic and email, as well compliance with multiple technical standards. Most importantly, it sets back Western foreign policy interests for an Internet that can export the values of transparency, free expression and economic development.

However, from a practical standpoint, the key challenge facing ICANN is not a country dropping out, but countries being so enamored with ICANN that the Internet gets smothered in their embrace. Like the curse of Othello, the risk is not that of not loving enough, but too much. That governments try to become so involved that they harm the Internet's openness is a real risk.

As an observer of Internet governance for almost a decade, I take a moderate view. I don't think the issues surrounding Internet governance are so drastic that extreme positions are likely to seriously emerge for long. Instead, I believe that the world can settle these matters as it does in so many other realms – with difficulty, with discomfort, gradually and never perfectly. But eventually, well enough.

GOVERNMENTS AND COUNTRY-CODE TOP LEVEL DOMAINS: A GLOBAL SURVEY
Michael Geist[1], University of Ottawa, Faculty of Law

Background

The issue of Internet governance has gained increasing prominence in recent years as the importance of an effective and efficient domain name system becomes ever more apparent. While much of the focus has centered on the operations of the Internet Corporation for Assigned Names and Numbers (ICANN), the role of national governments has sometimes been overlooked. As the proportion of ccTLD domain name registrations continues to grow – recently reaching 38% of all domain names worldwide – the question of the role of national governments within the administration of national domain names has moved to the forefront.

In April 2003, Professor Michael Geist and the Telecommunication Standardization Bureau of the International Telecommunication Union prepared a circular to be distributed to all 189 ITU member states.[2] TSB Circular 160 was designed to increase global understanding of the role of national governments within their domestic top-level domain. It featured questions on the

---

[1] The author would like to thank Milana Homsi, a third year law student at the University of Ottawa, Faculty of Law, for her tireless effort and invaluable assistance with this project as well as the Canada Research Chair Program and the Social Sciences and Humanities Council of Canada Initiative on the New Economy for their financial support. The opinions expressed herein are those of the author and do not necessarily reflect the views of the International Telecommunications Union, the University of Ottawa, or Osler, Hoskin & Harcourt LLP.

[2] http://www.itu.int/md/meetingdoc.asp?type=sitems&lang=e&parent=T01-TSB-CIR-0160.

current legal role of ccTLD administrators, ccTLD policies, and governmental involvement in national and international Internet governance issues. An addendum to the policy was issued in July 2003, extending the deadline for return of the survey to October 30, 2003.[3]

The relationship between Professor Geist and the ITU on this project is properly characterized as one of cooperation for data collection purposes. The ITU agreed to use its large network of member states to distribute the survey and collect the data. Professor Geist and the ITU agreed to share the data to be used in their own respective ways.

This updated report, which includes additional survey results since the release of a preliminary report in November 2003, highlights the most significant findings arising from an analysis of the results of the survey. The opinions expressed herein are personal to Professor Michael Geist and do not necessarily reflect the views of the International Telecommunication Union.

Sixty-six countries responded to the survey as of February 2004. The respondents were primarily governmental or ccTLD representatives.[4] While a complete list of respondents is listed at Appendix One, it is noteworthy that the respondent pool features countries from every global region as well as a broad cross-section of developed and developing countries. Notwithstanding the wide array of respondents, it is possible that the governments that responded have ccTLD policies that are different from those governments that did not respond. Accordingly, given the roughly 35 percent response rate, non-response bias cannot be ruled out and the survey's findings should be considered as valid only for the respondents, not for all governments.

Key Findings
1. Governmental Role in ccTLD Oversight
The appropriate governmental role in the management and oversight of the domain name system is an increasingly contentious issue. At the global level, the domain name system is administered by ICANN, a California non-profit corporation. While ICANN enjoys support from the United States government as well as the governments of several other developed countries, many countries worldwide have begun to voice the view that all governments should share in the administration of the domain name system. Largely absent from the Internet governance debate in the late 1990s, they have awoken to its importance and have sought to place the issue firmly on the global agenda.

---

[3] Id.

[4] In addition to the 66 governmental responses, one ccTLD manager from Germany also provided a response. That response is not included in the overall statistical findings.

The push for greater governmental involvement in the domain name system has many critics, however. Reflecting the popular notion that the Internet's remarkable growth has come largely without governmental regulation, critics of increased governmental participation in Internet governance believe that the domain name system is best left to a decentralized self-regulatory approach.

The most significant finding of this global survey is that, at least at the national level, governments are currently deeply involved in domain name administration. In fact, contrary to most expectations, virtually every government that responded to the survey either manages, retains direct control, or is contemplating formalizing its relationship with its national ccTLD. This is true even for governments, such as the United States, that generally adopt a free-market approach to Internet matters. Given the near ubiquitous role of government at the national level, it should therefore come as little surprise that governments have begun to seek a similarly influential role at the international level where policy decisions may have a direct impact on their national domains.

Figure One illustrates the current role of governments at the national level. Forty-three percent of survey respondents indicated that they retain ultimate control in one of four ways. First, many governments directly operate the national ccTLD as part of a government ministry or agency. Second, some governments have established a subsidiary company of a government ministry or agency to manage their ccTLD. Third, several governments have enacted legislation granting themselves final authority over their ccTLD's operations. Fourth, a number of governments have entered into operational contracts with their national ccTLD manager in which they assert their ultimate authority over the ccTLD, but grant their approval to a non-governmental ccTLD manager.

A further 30 percent of survey respondents indicated that they had taken specific steps, including drafting legislation or creating a commission to consider legislation, toward asserting ultimate authority over their national ccTLD. An additional 19 percent of respondents indicated that they were considering formalizing their relationship with their ccTLD and expected that relationship to change in the future. In fact, only seven percent of respondents indicated no formal governmental role in their ccTLD with no plans to alter the present situation.

Figure 1: A move towards formalization

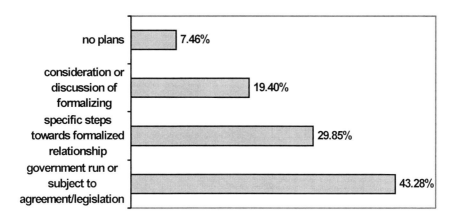

Figure 2: Organizational types

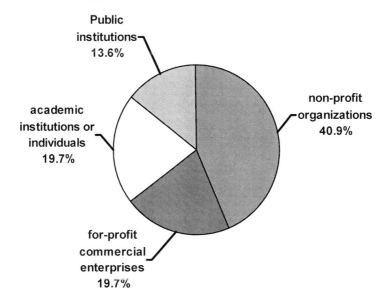

2. Differing ccTLD Priorities – Commercialization vs. the Public Interest

While the survey reveals increasing consensus on the need for national governments to assert a proprietary interest in their national ccTLD, it also uncovers striking differences in the commercialization of ccTLDs. These differences are manifested in the organizational structure of national domain name administrators. As illustrated in Figure Two, the survey found that among respondents 41 percent of ccTLDs are structured as non-profit corporations or organizations, 20 percent are structured as for-profit commercial enterprises, 14 percent are public institutions, and 20 percent are operated by academic institutions or individuals.[5]

The significance of organizational structure is illustrated by several additional findings that focus on:

- ccTLD priorities
- restrictions on domain name registration through presence requirements
- relative speed of ccTLD registrations
- emerging policy issues such as domain name dispute resolution and WHOIS policies.

a. ccTLD Priorities

One of the most difficult survey questions was a request for respondents to rank their ccTLD's policy priorities. Respondents were given nine priorities to consider and asked to rank the priorities from one to nine, with one being the most important priority and nine representing the least important. The nine priorities were:

1. Efficiency of the domain name system
2. Preservation of the public interest in the domain name system
3. Ease of domain name registration
4. Transparency and accountability in ccTLD management
5. Protection of intellectual property rights
6. Low cost of registration
7. Alignment with the government's general telecommunication policy or other policies
8. The local Internet community's cooperation in the ccTLD management
9. Registration size of the TLD

While several respondents declined to answer the question, 85 percent of respondents provided their rankings. The responses revealed significant differences in priorities depending upon organizational type. As Figures Three and Four demonstrate, countries with public ccTLDs consistently ranked the public interest and the protection of intellectual property rights as top priorities, while the number of domain name registrations was viewed as the least critical priority (the lower the aggregate number, the higher the priority). As the organizational type moved toward increasing commercialization, the data suggests that priorities begin to invert as the public interest and intellectual property protection diminished in importance, while the number of domain name registrations increased in priority.

---

[5] Statistics do not equal 100% as one country indicated that it is both a public and academic institution.

Countries with commercial ccTLDs were also collectively the least likely to answer the priorities question. While all countries in which ccTLDs are public organizations responded to the question, as did 94 percent of countries in which there are academic and individual ccTLD managers, only 64 percent of countries in which ccTLDs are commercial organizations specified their policy priorities.

Figure 3

Type	Size	Efficiency	Public Interest	IP
Commercial	6	3.6	4.6	5.4
Non-Profit	5.9	2.4	2.9	3.6
Academic/Ind.	6.1	3.2	2.9	3.9
Public	7.8	2.9	2.6	3.8

Figure 4: Priorities by organizational type

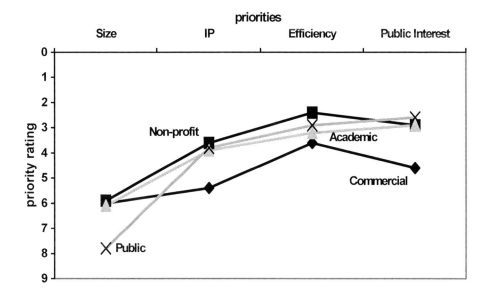

b. Public Interest and Presence Requirements

Survey respondents were asked whether their ccTLD actively pursues the public interest and whether the ccTLD has established restrictions on domain name registration that limit access to the domain to only those registrants who comply with national presence requirements.

The data in Figure Five illustrates noticeable differences between countries with public or commercial ccTLDs. While 77 percent of countries with public ccTLDs report that they actively pursue the public interest, only 54 percent of countries with commercial ccTLDs report a similar position. Moreover, the data suggests a direct correlation between the pursuit of the public interest and the imposition of presence requirements for domain name registration purposes. Eighty-eight percent of countries with public ccTLDs report imposing some form of presence requirements on domain name registrants, while only 54 percent of countries with commercial ccTLDs impose a similar requirement. These findings are consistent with the differing prioritization discussed above – the overwhelming majority of countries with public ccTLDs appear willing to forego larger registration numbers in favour of the protection of the public interest, with the public interest seemingly defined to include limitations on registrations designed to preserve the national character of a ccTLD.

Figure 5: Public interest by organizational type

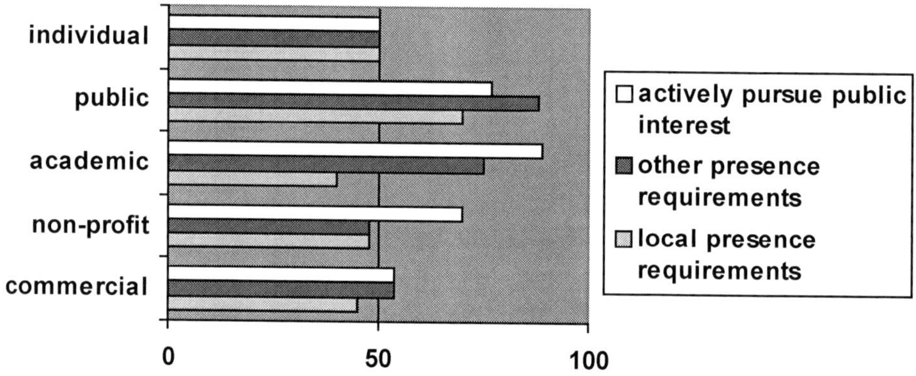

c. Speed of Registration

In keeping with their more commercial approach, it comes as little surprise to find that countries with commercial ccTLDs are more likely to offer immediate online registrations than their public counterparts. As Figure Six illustrates, 62 percent of countries with commercial ccTLDs compete with generic TLDs such as dot-com and dot-org by offering immediate online registrations, compared with only 22 percent of countries with public ccTLDs. Email registration is the favoured approach for 33 percent of countries with public ccTLDs, perhaps reflecting the more onerous registration requirements that may require manual or offline review.

Figure 6: Speed of registration by organizational type

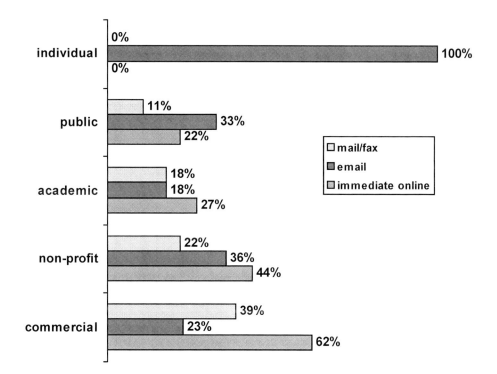

d. Cutting Edge Issues – Dispute Resolution and WHOIS

The survey asked respondents to report on whether their ccTLD had adopted a dispute resolution policy or a policy addressing WHOIS data. The results found no substantial correlation between organizational type and the adoption of these policies.

Countries with non-profit ccTLDs were the most likely to have adopted a dispute resolution policy (51 percent), followed by countries with commercial ccTLDs (39 percent), academic ccTLDs (36 percent), and public ccTLDs (33 percent). By contrast, 76 percent of countries with academic ccTLDs adopted a WHOIS policy, followed by both 63 percent of countries with public and non-profit ccTLDs and 55 percent of countries with commercial ccTLDs.

Appendix One – Survey Respondents

Australia
Botswana
Burkina Faso
Cambodia
Canada
Chile
China
Costa Rica
Cyprus
Czech Republic
Democratic Republic of the Congo
Denmark
Ecuador
Egypt
Estonia
Finland
France
Germany
Greece
Hong Kong, China
Indonesia
Iran
Italy
Jamaica
Japan
Jordan
Kenya
Kuwait
Kyrgyzstan
Lesotho
Lithuania
Luxembourg
Madagascar

Malaysia
Mauritius
Mexico
Monaco
The Netherlands
New Zealand
Niue
Norway
Oman
Pakistan
Peru
Portugal
Republic of Armenia
Republic of Korea
Republic of Macedonia
Republic of Singapore
Republica Dominicana
Romania
Seychelles
Slovak Republic
Spain
Suriname
Sweden
Switzerland
Tanzania
Thailand
Trinidad and Tobago
Uganda
Ukraine
United Kingdom
United States
Zambia

.BR: CCTLD AS ASSET OF THE COMMONS

Carlos A. Afonso, Information Network for the Third Sector (Rits)

What is a ccTLD really for?

Approval for the creation of the country-code Names Supporting Organization (ccNSO) at the ICANN Board meeting in Rome (March 2-6, 2004) has raised several (and some sensitive) issues regarding Internet governance at the country level.

In practice ICANN is focused on coordinating a complex system of management delegation (for profit or otherwise) of Internet domain names basically grouped in two large chunks: generic Top Level Domains (gTLDs) and country-code Top Level Domains (ccTLDs).

When ICANN was created, the United States government had already delegated to a private company (Network Solutions, now a subsidiary of Verisign) the registry function for some of the most important gTLDs (.com, .net, and .org), thus definitely establishing what could have been a non-profit public service as a money-making activity. ICANN therefore, even if it wanted (which clearly is not the case), would not be able to reverse this. Recently it managed to redelegate the .org gTLD to a non-profit especially created by ISOC – the Public Internet Registry (PIR) – but this gTLD remains open to anyone (as clearly stated in PIR's home page), instead of becoming the realm of non-profit groups worldwide.

At one of the Rome meeting's public forums with the Board, I asked for clarification regarding the fact that several ccTLDs in practice (from the user point of view at least) function like a gTLD (generic top level domain). In fact, Internet domains within these ccTLDs are sold for a profit to any taker, even if the prospective holder does not have any legal relationship with the corresponding country. Thus many ccTLDs are no longer identified with their countries on the Internet, having been sold to national or foreign companies for a profit. Some are supposed to be identified with some specific sectors of activity instead of countries, just like some sTLDs (sponsored gTLDs, like .aero for example), but in practice accept any registrant from anywhere in the world with a valid credit card.

As a very well known example, .tv is in practice a domain name suffix for the media industry (but not restricted to this industry), not the country of Tuvalu. São Tomé e Príncipe's .st registry Web site declares that any Internet user can hold a .st domain which, the main site page says, competes favorably with any gTLD.

At the other extreme of the ccTLD registry spectrum, the Brazilian registry, for example, does not allow individuals who or organizations which do not have a legal status in the country to use the .br domain. The service is operated on a non-profit basis. There are more significant details on the Brazilian case which are worth describing (see below).

My request for clarification to the ICANN Board and the public tried to pose the following questions: in practice, from the point of view of the Internet user who is shopping for a domain, what is the difference between those business-oriented country-specific domains open to any Internet user anywhere, and gTLDs? How could this loss of identity interfere in ccTLD representation at ccNSO? How could unified positions be sought if some registries are just there for profit while others are trying to preserve their ccTLDs as part of their national pool of ICT resources? What kind of dialogue and common ground can be established, say, between the Brazilian registry and the gTLD-like business-oriented ones, in the same supporting organization? Aren't some of the latter better represented in the already existing Generic Names Supporting Organization (GNSO)?

I did not ask, but should: have the decisions to open up the ccTLDs for profit and strip them of their country significance been submitted to public scrutiny in these countries?

The response to my request for clarification was, first, a careful, diplomatic reply from ICANN Chairman Vint Cerf, and then a flurry of nervous, sometimes even aggressive, reactions on the part of several ccTLD representatives, showing only that the issue is serious, is not resolved, and that the situation may not be getting better. I have even heard absurd "solutions" to the problem like proposing a new country-code domain name system to be held by governments based on the three-letter country code standard, instead of the current two-letter standard. Thus the current ones could be free to compete in the gTLD market.

A recent ccTLD survey by Michael Geist (commissioned by the ITU)[1] has covered a sample of 56 countries in all regions. The sample is a fair distribution of developed as well as developing countries. Results of the survey are interesting in several respects. One of them indicates that, whatever the trend towards more or less control of ccTLD registry management by the local government, registries run for profit either are or tend to move in the direction of becoming direct competitors with gTLDs, in a way that eventually sacrifices identification of a ccTLD with its country in favor of making money.

Geist elaborated a preliminary report on results of the survey (stating that some data was still coming and would be part of the final report), which has been criticized by CENTR – the mostly European consortium of 40 ccTLD registry operators – which sees in Geist's interpretation of his survey the "risk" of stimulating further government involvement in ccTLD governance[2]. It is a bit difficult to clearly establish CENTR's mission from the discourse of their representatives at the ICANN meeting in Rome – their emphasis on the importance of the "private sector" might indicate that defending business interests (which do not necessarily coincide with the public interest) in the ccTLD registry activity seems to be a most important part of their mission. Since they represent a very powerful voice in Internet governance politics, it is important to see how this will impact on the strategies carried out by ICANN's newly created ccNSO. In any case, Geist's sample included 54% of all CENTR members.

CENTR's criticism questions the validity of the sample's size (but does not explain why – samples may be quite small and still provide valid results for the entire population; Geist's sample may actually be quite large, at about 22% of all ccTLDs) and fears the report's conclusions as stimulating government control (which is not in Geist's report).

CENTR goes on to say that dominance of the private sector "...ensure[s] a stable, robust Internet which functions well..... [I]t also creates the best conditions for innovation and economical [sic] growth of countries." This is a trivial repetition of the same argument in defense of more business and less government which is heard in many instances every day.

However, there is a more serious (and potentially dangerous) statement in CENTR's reply to the Geist report. In associating more government presence in ccTLD governance with more

---

[1] Michael Geist, *Governments and country-code Top Level Domains: A Global Survey*, preliminary report on survey commissioned by the ITU, December, 2003.

[2] CENTR, *Some comments on Professor Michael Geist's "Government and country-code Top Level Domains: A global survey"*, available in *http://www.circleid.com/article/421_0_1_0_C/*. See also Geist's reply to CENTR in *http://www.circleid.com/article/424_0_1_0/*.

regulation (which is not necessarily true), CENTR states that "... if too strict regulation – on registering domain names nationally, for example, as pointed out by Professor Geist – prevents the citizen from accessing the Internet the way he wants to, he will use services from other countries. This is arguably not the best way to serve public interest." There is no proven relationship between a ccTLD being available only for nationals (or entities legally established as nationals, like the subsidiary of a multinational firm) and the need to seek domain registration abroad. On the other hand, opening up the ccTLD for international business certainly discourages national users – why would a Tuvalu citizen use .tv if he or she is not from the media industry?

Diversity is the rule, but Geist's survey provides a useful classification, which, however, may not capture all aspects of ccTLD governance and management. Angola's registry for example is operated by an academic entity, and due to a registry policy of charging very high prices for domain names, many Angola domain name users seek a gTLD domain instead. Brazil's ccTLD is an example of a government-controlled registry which is becoming far more representative of other social sectors and interest groups, as this paper tries to show.

These complex aspects of the ccTLD registries' realm cast, in my view, certain doubts about the possible common grounds within the newly created ccNSO.

Short history of Internet governance in Brazil

Brazil only established TCP/IP connections with the Internet in the United States in the beginning of the 1990s. Like other countries, in the 1980s Brazil sought to define network protocol standards for use by the federal government, and, through the State telecommunications monopoly at the time, Telebras, subscribed to the OSI/ISO standard.

The National Research and Education Network (RNP), a project of Brazil's Ministry of Science and Technology, led the process of introducing the Internet protocol despite strong opposition of Telebras. In this it was helped by a project led by an NGO – the Brazilian Institute of Social and Economic Analyses, IBASE – which led the pioneering UNCED '92 Internet project in Rio de Janeiro.

This project was developed in partnership with RNP and the Association for Progressive Communications (APC), and, since it became an official United Nations project for the conference, provided the necessary leverage to demand permanent connections to the Internet from Telebras. Thus two direct links to the Internet in the United States were activated just in time for the United Nations conference, and became the initial Brazil-US Internet links for research and education.

This was not only a key milestone for the development of the Internet in Brazil, but also marked the successful beginning of a significant working relationship between the research community and an independent NGO to build a strategic project. In fact, IBASE ran the first (and only until 1994) Brazilian Internet service provider open to the general public in partnership with RNP, thus breaking up the networking monopoly then in the hands of Telebras.

In the period between UNCED '92 and 1995 the basis for how Brazil would run the Internet was established – a process not without political and institutional difficulties, and also one in which RNP played a leading role. First, the unofficial understanding that the Internet, as a set of value-added services on top of physical telecommunications lines, did not fall under the legislation covering telecommunications became an official ruling, thus keeping the Internet beyond the reach of Telebras.

Secondly, at the end of 1994 it became evident to the government and the research community that the Internet would grow explosively and needed careful guidance. Again RNP and IBASE worked together and played a significant role in lobbying the ministries to form a national governance organization with representation of all interest groups.

As a result, the ministries of Communications and of Science and Technology agreed to form the Steering Committee for the Internet in Brazil (know by its acronym CGIbr) – a group of about 12 volunteers from the government, user community, service providers, business and academic communities, and telecommunications companies – which was officially installed in May 1995.

CGIbr's mission has since been to work out the coordination and integration of all Internet initiatives in Brazil as well as to manage domain names registration and IP numbers distribution. It is also part of its mission to promote digital inclusion in the country, to evaluate and recommend technical and operational standards and procedures, and to maintain Internet statistical data related to Brazil. CGIbr has created a subordinate technical organism (called Registro.br) which is the official .br registry (there are no registrars).

Furthering democracy in Internet governance

Since its beginning, CGIbr has established a clear policy which defines the .br ccTLD as an asset of the commons[3]. The guidelines have been fair and flexible, with minimal additional legislation and simple rules for registration.

The .br ccTLD has been considered by CGIbr as the identity of Brazil on the Internet, and its registry is a non-profit service in which all domain names cost the same (currently about US$10 per year) – domain registration fees are charged just to cover the annual operating and development costs of the .br domain governance system. Thus, a registrant must submit proof of legal status in the country (as identified by a national income tax registration number and documentation demonstrating the applicant has a physical address in Brazil).

Registrants do not get "instantaneous" domains, but get a domain environment which is far more secure than most gTLDs and many other ccTLDs. In fact, currently most Internet-based bank fraud activity in the country relies on a domain purchased from a gTLD or "loose" ccTLD registrar abroad. Frequently the real Web site of the fraud is a .com assigned "instantaneously" – you have a valid credit card, you take it – to a Mr. John Doe, with a fake post office box address, and hosted in a US or Eastern European service provider.

Clear rules apply for certain sectoral subdomains (only telecommunications companies, for instance, can use .net.br, only proven non-profit organizations can use .org.br, only TV broadcasters and cable companies can use .tv.br, and so on). To date, none of the gTLDs corresponding to these examples follow similar rules (not even .org).

Except for a few special cases (some research organizations and special management domains pertaining to CGIbr), the second level of the domain name must identify a sector or activity area which is predefined in a long list of subdomains approved (and updated from time to time) by the committee.

Brazil's registry has gained an international reputation as a very well managed and technically sophisticated operation, and today it is the technical headquarters of LACNIC, the Regional Internet Registry covering Latin America and the Caribbean, as well as the secondary DNS host to several other ccTLDs. The registry also maintains NBSO, a highly regarded Internet security response team.

---

[3] "Commons" here is used according to the concepts developed by David Bollier, *Silent Theft – The Private Plunder of our Common Wealth,* New York: Routledge, 2003, referring to common goods for the benefit of all which should be kept out of reach of private business enclosures.

Regionally, CGIbr has played a key role in the protracted process leading to LACNIC's recognition by ICANN, and is represented in several instances of ICANN's structure. Currently, there are more than 600,000 domains registered and active, growing at a rate of about 20,000 per month.

However, in this process there has been a serious shortcoming. CGIbr has no legal institutional status. Although the intention from the beginning has been to run it as a public interest civil society organization with government representation, only at the end of 2002 efforts to propose an institutional formalization started to materialize.

Until now, however, its formal operations are run as a project of the state of São Paulo's Research Foundation, FAPESP, including financial administration of the funds obtained with domain distribution. Legally, the foundation can decide what to do with the money, and might block any spending proposal from CGIbr which does not fit its rules (which, incidentally, demands for the most part that the money be spent in the state of São Paulo).

This has been an administrative nightmare for CGIbr. As a result, several initiatives have been kept dormant while the CGIbr has about US$30 million in cash (accumulated over nearly seven years) under FAPESP's control.

Another hurdle is that, since FAPESP had hosted most Internet infrastructure services, including Brazil's largest Internet exchange point (IEP), it assumed responsibility for deciding how to run these services. The committee managed to remove from FAPESP control over the registry system, but not over its IEP. In 2002, FAPESP decided unilaterally to convert the IEP from a non-profit service into a business operation, and sold it to a Miami-based company (Terremark). Thus, today Brazil's strategic exchange point is operated by a United States company.

There is also the problem of representation. Until the beginning of 2004, the federal government took charge of nominating every CGIbr board member, including the private sector, academic and user community representatives. In the meantime, a campaign by some NGOs led by the Information Network for the Third Sector (Rits) with strong support from RNP and the academic community pressed for transparency in governance, legitimacy in representation and for the formalization of a civil society organization to establish a new basis for the committee – a campaign to effectively democratize Internet governance in the country.

With the election of President Lula, members of the campaign were invited to present their case in a meeting with future government officials at the end of 2002, and, in February 2003, a full proposal was delivered to the government.

During 2003 a very slow process of discussions within the government took place, and finally, on April 2, 2003, it issued a ruling nominating a new interim committee with a new representation structure, now focusing on social sectors and sectoral interest groups – there was no longer space for a representative of the elusive "user community" for example – much along the lines proposed by the campaign.

One of the tasks of the new committee, besides continuing its original mission tasks, was to establish the details and schedule for the constituencies to elect their members to the committee. Another task was to propose the new institutional structure. Officially, this interim committee would end its mandate after delivering the requested proposals to the federal government. However, it continued to function to guarantee the basic operations of the .br registry.

In September 2004, the federal government issued a decree officially reinstating the CGIbr board members. The proposals were finally approved by the new government in the beginning of 2004, and in March the election guidelines were approved by the interim committee and submitted to public scrutiny.

Regarding the proposal for a new institutional structure, a non-profit organization called NIC.BR was created in the beginning of 2003 by members of the old CGIbr at the end of their mandate. This structure is now being analysed by the board to become a public interest non-profit organization. The CGIbr board will also become the managing board for the new organization, and all functions now delegated to FAPESP will be absorbed by the new organization. Ideally the new organization will be in place once the electoral process is concluded.

This will crown a long-term effort by leading NGOs and members of the Internet community in Brazil to make sure that Internet governance in the country secures assets of the commons as such (including the .br ccTLD), achieves as much democratic representation in its governing structure as possible, and operates and continues to develop its services on a non-profit, public interest basis, while guaranteeing top-level technical performance in the realm of domain names and addresses, as well as secure and optimized operation of the network.

The new institution will have the opportunity to use surplus income to develop research activities supporting digital inclusion strategies and technical development of the Internet in the country, as well as to deepen its technical, institutional and political relationships with similar bodies internationally.

Forming akin ccTLD constituencies?

It becomes clearly evident that the Brazilian example of Internet governance is far distanced on several counts from many other ccTLD registries and corresponding national policies. This casts doubt on the strategic possibilites for developing common policies in the ccTLD realm through bodies such as the ccNSO.

Just like in international politics there are groups of countries getting together for the defence of specific interests (like the G-20 and so on), a scenario might be devised of a group of countries agreeing on forms of democratic and sovereign Internet governance (like Brazil's) getting together to defend their specific positions.

Finally, it is clear that this form of governance could go "up the ladder" in the ICANN pyramid. RIRs could become far more representative of all social sectors and interest groups in their regions, for example – however, the usual practice is to have RIR board members drawn mostly from governments and companies in a top-down nomination process.

Recent proposals to seek alternatives to the ICANN pyramidal structure center around a network model run by an international consortium of ccTLDs, progressively rendering the current ICANN structure as less relevant, maybe dedicated only to cater to gTLDs in the future[4]. Given the divergent interests in the ccTLD universe, this might be extremely difficult to achieve at the present, but, depending on the growing awareness of public opinion in their countries regarding the importance of this process, it could move in that direction in the future.

---

[4] Kim G. von Arx (Canadian Internet Registration Authority) and Gregory R. Hagen (University of Ottawa), *Sovereign Domains - A Declaration of Independence of ccTLDs from Foreign Control,* paper submitted to the Workshop on Member States' experiences with ccTLDs, Geneva: March, 2003, ITU.

BRIDGING THE DIGITAL DIVIDE: DELIVERING INTERNET AND INFORMATION SOCIETY GOVERNANCE THROUGH LOCAL EMPOWERMENT[1] [2]

Khaled Fattal, Multilingual Internet Names Consortium

I. Who, Why, When?

A. The Multilingual Internet Names Consortium (MINC)

MINC is a non-profit, non-governmental, international organization. It focuses on the promotion of multilingualization of Internet names, including Internet domain names and keywords; internationalization of Internet names standards and protocols; and technical coordination and liaison with other international bodies. MINC is composed of organizational and individual members from industry, academia, research, government, investment, and international organizations from every corner of the world. MINC represents over 4.5 billion people through its language communities and is constantly working to bring each and every one of these individuals an Internet that they can access, understand, and contribute to in their own native language.

---

[1] A Proposal to the Secretary-General of the United Nations, Mr. Kofi. Annan, March 25, 2004

[2] This document has been edited specifically for the United Nations ICT Task Force Global Forum on Internet Governance Publication. To view the original document, please visit http://www.unicttaskforce.org/perl/documents.pl?id=1323.

With its December 2002 restructuring, MINC has recommitted itself to the four fundamental prerequisites to the establishment of a global Internet: language standards, interoperability testing, global cooperation, and local empowerment. MINC is the leader in language standards development. Its working groups develop legitimate language tables in multiple variants derived from the local regions themselves. Once developed, MINC uses its ground-breaking interoperability testing to ensure all elements of the Internet work well together thus guaranteeing the stability and integrity of the system. To deliver multilingualization effectively, MINC bridges the divide between local communities and international bodies through the Coordination Method. Because coordination is vital to multilingualization, MINC issues invitations to all network information centers and country-code Top Level Domains (ccTLDs) to participate in the development of a global Internet. But above all, MINC believes in directly involving non-English speakers to take charge in the creation of their Internet. Using the technical and linguistic experts of their language regions, MINC empowers local regions to have control over their own destiny and help them in their development of their own languages/scripts based on already agreed international standards and protocols.

MINC strongly believes that the delivery of a multilingual Internet is a moral mission in which every person, no matter their language, has a right to participate in the Information Society. MINC is committed to bridging the digital divide and will do everything within its power to establish a multilingual Internet.

B. What is Multilingualization?[3]
Multilingualization is the process of making the Internet accessible to all peoples in their own native languages, no matter what an individual's language may be.

Currently, Internet domain names and URLs can only be written in two formats: full English, or part English and part local language. The latter format is often referred to as Internationalized Domain Names (IDN). Despite the beliefs of many, the mixing of English with local languages to create Internet domain names and URLs has failed to incorporate non-English speaking communities into the Information Society. Instead, this half-and-half format has disenfranchised droves of individuals who do not know English. This is because the Internet, as it stands now, is really no more than a set of language-based intranets with the English being the most dominant and well known. Below is a visual representation of what is incorrectly referred to as the global Internet. The overlapping areas of a local languages and English, e.g. Chinese and English, represents those citizens who are able to use English in

---

[3] A multilingual Internet, .ML, and ML.ML are synonymous – an Internet infrastructure in which domain names and URLs can be written fully in the local native languages without any mixing with English letters or ASCII.

surfing the Internet. The local language areas outside of the shared regions represent the remaining part of that language group's population that does not possess any knowledge of the English language and hence is left outside of the current root system. Only English speakers are able to fully participate in the current Internet.

Figure 1

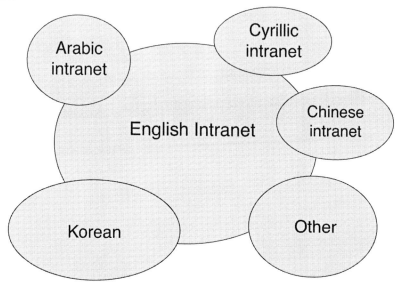

Unlike a set of language-based intranets, a truly global Internet is based on multilingual domain names in which URLs appear fully in the local language. A graphic representation of a truly multilingual global Internet where access to information is not restricted by language barriers and where all are within the same root system appears below.

Figure 2

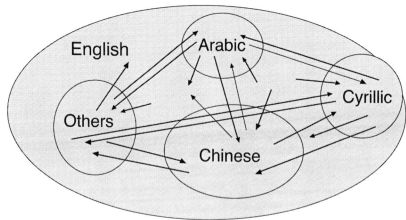

There are two ways to create this multilingual Internet: 1) teach English to over 4.5 billion non-English speaking peoples distributed across the world, or 2) incorporate the world's various languages and language variations into the Internet's infrastructure through multilingualization.

Approximately 80% of the world's population is composed of non-English speakers. If we do not multilingualize the Internet soon, the digital divide will only grow and these people may be permanently excluded, alienated, and disenfranchised from the Information Society.

C. Purpose of this Proposal – to Establish a Truly Global, Multilingual Internet

- Bridge the digital divide by fostering the creation of "a people-centered, inclusive and development-oriented Information Society, where everyone can create, access, utilize and share information and knowledge, enabling individuals, communities and peoples to achieve their full potential in promoting their sustainable development and improving their quality of life, premised on the purposes and principles of the Charter of the United Nations and respecting fully and upholding the Universal Declaration of Human Rights."[4]

- Realize the goal of a culturally relevant, global, multilingual Internet as mandated and agreed to by the endorsers of the World Summit on the Information Society (WSIS) Declaration of Principles and Plan of Action.

- Overcome the language barriers currently barring non-English-speaking peoples from fully participating in the Internet phenomenon.

D. Timing of this Proposal – Opportunity and Urgency

On December 12, 2003, all stakeholders of WSIS agreed that the Internet of the future must be founded on multilingualization.[5] With such broad consensus, there is no better time than the present to pursue real progress in the creation of a linguistically accessible and culturally relevant Internet.

MINC is now able and ready to begin Internet multilingualization. Through concrete steps and actions, as detailed by this proposal, MINC can establish a viable multilingual Internet while maintaining the safety and integrity of the system.

---

[4] World Summit on the Information Society (WSIS) Declaration of Principles: Building the Information Society (December 12, 2003), section A.1.

[5] WSIS Declaration, sections B.48, B.52, B.53; AND WSIS Plan of Action, sections B.6i, C.13d, C.23g, C.23.o.

A multilingual Internet, as mandated by the WSIS Declaration, is a prerequisite to any form of Internet governance that encourages and operates within the Information Society.

II. How? – Project to Multilingualize the Internet
A. Action Plan – Steps towards Multilingualization

- Create a multilingual Internet that allows for the participation of all peoples no matter their native language; that allows for the creation of websites with Internet domain names written in Internet users' own native languages; and that allows for the enjoyment of these empowering advances in a multilingual system which operates within the current root structure.

- Fashion legitimate standards and language tables – the key ingredients to a multilingual Internet. Ensure that these standards and tables are drafted by the peoples of each respective native language region, and by experts from these said regions, in accordance with internationally recognized standards such as the Internet Engineering Task Force (IETF) standards on IDN and MINC's visionary standards and policies concerning linguistic and cultural relevance. Utilize MINC's unique interoperability mechanism to guarantee the mutual internal compliance of each standard with every other standard.

- Continue and build upon the progress MINC has already made in its working language groups over many years. In the last six months alone, these groups have produced two new language standards, Russian and Georgian, as well as the first Request For Comments (RFC) for an Arabic standard with another to follow shortly. These accomplishments were achieved by the efforts of unpaid volunteers.

- Ensure future progress is made in the development of language standards by retaining the services of experts through paid employment. Paid employment will allow these experts to focus singularly on the task of developing language standards and thus increase the speed and scale of language standard production.

- Begin the development of standards for six to ten languages (already identified) immediately and simultaneously. Currently completed languages standards and their tables will be integrated into the project to maximize the inclusiveness of interoperability testing.

- Continue cooperation with the general manager of the Internet Assigned Numbers Authority ("IANA") and other world authorities on Internet governance within MINC's four commissions investigating areas for data gathering, research, and coordination in

Multilingual Multiscript domain names.[6] This cooperation is vital to the development of ML.ML as no single point of authority has the resources to achieve multilingualization alone. MINC recognizes and celebrates the role of cooperation in multilingualization and thus champions the coordination method over the single point of authority method. Under this cooperation method, MINC and the international community requires the enthusiastic support of individual communities, businesses, governments, and the United Nations to bridge the digital divide.

• Test interoperability of standards within a mock environment that simulates the current root – this process will ensure the safety, security, and integrity of the current root structure. Deploy ML.ML within the current root server system – not outside of it – once testing is complete and safety is assured.

• Take satisfaction in delivery of a truly Multilingual Internet following the implementation of ML.ML by the authorities running the root system function.

B. Specific Tasks – Making it Happen

• Launch an experimental IDN governance model to test the:

a) Administration of IDN ML.ML;

b) Administration of Unicode namespace allocation (analogous to the Regional Internet Registries' (RIR) IP address space allocations);

c) Root server network for ML.ML;

d) Shared registry services;

e) Distributed registrars for ML.ML;

f) Language modality, script modality, and country modality for delegations of specific i-gTLDs;

g) Governance process as an overlay to this IDN governance model involving the current key players such as ICANN, ITU, MINC, and the UnitedNations.

• Operate an experimental root server network ML.ML to test the operational issues pertaining to the governance models; and report on the technical feasibility and technical aspects of such a governance model.

---

[6] For more information on MINC's four commissions investigating the impact of MINC's, WSIS's, ITU's, and United Nation's Internet governance processes on IDN development, see http://www.minc.org/events/kl2004/papers/minc-commissions.ppt .

- Coordinate, integrate, and extend appropriate Internet technologies to deliver secure ML.ML transactions in multiple formats, i.e. mobile technology.

- Issue invitations for applications for ML.ML TLDs and gTLDs.

- Simulate delegation of shared registry services and distributed registrars for language, script, and country modality.

- Identify issues for dispute resolution and arbitration in conjunction with the World Intellectual Property Organization (WIPO) with whom MINC has been coordinating.

- Report to the UnitedNations on the findings at specific intervals during this two year project.

C. ML.ML/gTLD Authorization – Concerns with ICANN's Single Point of Authority Method

A single organization will not be able to successfully run ML.ML/TLD or gTLD authorization using the single point of authority method as ICANN has done with gTLDs in English, also commonly known as ASCII. Instead, ML.ML/TLD and gTLD authorization should be a function of coordinated efforts where an organization leads cooperation instead of dictates functions. Although the single point of authority approach has been accepted in ASCII, such an approach in ML.ML would almost certainly fail.

No organization alone, including MINC and ICANN, possesses all the knowledge, resources, or staff required to successfully perform the important role of .ML/gTLD authorization on behalf of the global community.

Single point authority, represented by ICANN, has already failed to make significant progress in ML.ML. Especially since the IETF standards came out over a year and a half ago, ICANN's lack of progress in .ML has frustrated non-English speaking communities. In defense of ICANN, it lacks the experience and staff to make progress in this area. Nor was multilingualization a high priority for ICANN as they have been focusing on internal reforms and while they are setting up satellite offices outside the United States. Additionally, common sentiments have often been repeated citing ICANN's inability to form meaningful bonds with the world's non-English speaking communities as the reason for ICANN's lack of progress in full multilingualization. Because of ICANN's poor relationships with these digitally disenfranchised communities, these communities will find any attempt by ICANN to assume the role of de facto single authority for ML.ML as lacking their recognition and authority and reject it outright.

The primary role of the organization in charge of ML.ML/gTLD authorization is to decide whether a proposed gTLD does or does not meet the requirement of serving the region or community it is designed to serve. Such an organization must possess equal or greater knowledge of that region or community in comparison to the knowledge of those proposing these new .ML gTLDs, which is an impossible task. Without such an equal or greater knowledge, the organization's decision will not be accepted, respected, and seen as authoritative. ICANN's gTLD approval process in English or ASCII places the burden of knowledge on the proposer, asking him/her to "prove his/her case". The purpose of this method is to educate ICANN on the issues before them and thus indicates their lack of local issue understanding.

The international community feels that ICANN has failed to make significant progress in the delivery of ML.ML. In recent years, many other objections have been raised from the international community and their organizations, local regional experts, and governments about ICANN's legitimacy and interests. Very often their anchor argument hinges on the fact that ICANN's authority is derived from a Memorandum of Understanding (MoU) with the Department of Commerce of the United States government. Many believe that ICANN's US government mandate does not authorize this or any US corporation to act on behalf of the entire international community without being granted authority in this area from the international community. Furthermore, it is widely believed that ICANN's ties to the United States government raise questions about conflicts of interest which need to be addressed and cannot be ignored.

D. ML.ML/gTLD Authorization - MINC and the Coordination Method

MINC is uniquely qualified to lead the coordination necessary to the success of ML.ML/gTLD authorization – a key component of multilingualization. MINC has broad experience in multilingualization and has championed a global Internet for years longer than many similar organizations have even existed. MINC's bottom-up organization and its relationships with local regions and communities through its working language groups will allow it to effectively implement the most effective strategy in ML.ML/gTLD authorization: *the coordination method.*

MINC will make coordination with local regions central to the process of multilingual gTLD authorization. Local regions will take the commanding role in deciding, for themselves, the appropriateness and priority of .ML/gTLD applications. One possible format would allow a maximum number of language-based gTLDs per language or language variant the first year, i.e. three to five ML gTLDs. And then two deadlines per year for submission of further applications for ML.ML gTLDs thereafter. With our proposed coordination format, the local regions know that they will be authorized the set number of .ML gTLDs creating a framework in which they can exercise their own choices. The criteria they have to meet are to ensure that the most suitable gTLDs for that region are chosen and that these gTLDs meet or exceed the technical, linguistic and cultural standards set by MINC – standards that are higher and more stringent than those of any other technical body in existence, including the IETF. Local regions would coordinate their choosing of proposed gTLDs with MINC through ongoing reviews and consultations before, during, and after the approval and deployment of localized gTLDs. Unlike the current apply, wait, and pray method used for English gTLDs, MINC's coordination method would directly include and actively involve the proposing region in every step of the authorization process. MINC's coordination method will replace despair, anxiety, and resentment with true empowerment.

MINC is committed to local empowerment through decentralized decision making. Under the coordination method, local regions decide which multilingual gTLDs are to be deployed while MINC ensures .ML gTLD interoperability and concurrence with standards. MINC further provides policy and localized dispute resolution mechanisms. When a ML.ML gTLD has met the technical requirements and MINC is satisfied that all the criteria have been met, MINC will deliver a recommendation on behalf of the proposed .ML/gTLD to IANA and the Root Sever System Advisory Committee (RSSAC) for immediate deployment. MINC plans to coordinate the approval process between local communities, IANA, and the RSSAC – all within a framework of transparent and specific milestones.

Local empowerment provides the surest path to successful .ML/gTLD authorization. The coordination method places local empowerment in the center of .ML/gTLD authorization not only incorporating local regions, but also respecting their rights and their representations in order to achieve a multilingual Internet accessible, relevant, and enthusiastically accepted by all.

III. To What Effect? – Consumer and Commercial Benefits of Multilingualization
A. Consumer and Commercial Participation – Resultant Commercial Benefits
In order to guarantee long-term growth in the use and expansion of a multilingual Internet, short-, medium- and long-term plans must be committed to encourage consumer/citizen participation in the global Internet. As ML.ML gTLDs are deployed, those who had previously been excluded from Internet-related business opportunities because of linguistic barriers will now be able to enjoy new Internet-related commercial benefits.

The above-mentioned plan must also encourage the development of new applications, software, and services to enhance the utility of a multilingual Internet.[7]

---

[7] In pursuance with WSIS Declaration, section B.51.

B. Emergence of New Markets from the Realization of a Multilingual Internet

The deployment of ML.ML will foster the emergence of new, untapped markets. A multilingual Internet will create new opportunities for the development of applications, email, web services, enhanced multilingual search engines, etc. targeted at localized .ML gTLDs.[8]

These applications will have a "snowball" effect by creating further opportunities in the development of other applications and services to complement the original products. In this way, a multilingual Internet will open up new markets to those who had previously been excluded from them because of language barriers.

Citizens' participation in these markets will encourage awareness of and participation in Internet governance by creating vested interests in the way governments may regulate the Internet.

C. A Bigger Market than Previously Assumed – Correcting ML.ML Market Misconceptions

There exists a misconception that the ML.ML market will be of little value because .ML deployment is based on the transliteration of the current gTLDs, like .info, .com, and .org. This is not completely accurate and drastically undervalues the ML.ML market.

In reality, full ML.ML deployment will create a demand for new applications produced for use with new, native language-based gTLDs. These new gTLDs will exist in addition to transliterations and will be unique to the needs and functions of each language's local community.[9]

MINC estimates that six to twelve months after the full deployment of ML.ML, transliterations will account for only 30% of gTLDs whereas 70% will be localized, new gTLDs. In other words, for every .com transliteration into Arabic, two new additional Arabic gTLDs, specific to the needs of that Arabic market, can be expected. This is a very conservative estimate.

With MINC planning to immediately start the simultaneous development of six to ten languages, the ML.ML market could potentially be huge. It is reasonable to assume that the deployment of six languages will result in twelve new localized ML.ML/gTLDs; twenty if MINC completes ten languages. Furthermore, these .ML/gTLDs are in addition to the transliteration equivalent in .ML/gTLDs per language. For example, seeing that there are roughly 300 million Arabs and 1.5 billion Arabic script users, one could reasonably expect

[8] In pursuance with WSIS Plan of Action, section B.6i.

[9] In pursuance with WSIS Declaration, section B.53; and WSIS Plan of Action, section C.11h.

approximately 500,000 new domain names sold per each new .ML Arabic gTLD in the first year alone. This is, in fact, a rather conservative estimate considering the number of possibilities that exist for a domain name written completely in Arabic. Furthermore, when the transliteration of the current ASCII gTLDs, like .com and .org, are accounted for, the market potential only increases.

D. Commercial Institutions – Incentives to Invest in Local Empowerment and Development

While this project looks to empower local communities allowing them to take charge of their futures, it will simultaneously work on a platform that is congruent with the current existing infrastructures. Support for this proposal will positively reflect on supporting commercial institutions and depict them as champions of local empowerment and development. Local consumers and citizens are likely to view these institutions as noble liberators. In this way, commercial support for this project will go very far towards ensuring consumer loyalty in burgeoning markets as well as enhance corporate image.

E. The Project's Accelerating Effect on the Deployment of ML.ML

With its focus on the establishment of a multilingual Internet, this project will accelerate the United Nations' efforts to deploy ML.ML as this deployment is a crucial step in the multilingualization of the Internet – a process agreed to in the December 2003 WSIS declaration, which is now a United Nations mandate.

IV. How Much? – Funding, Conclusion, and Call to Arms

A. Final Reasons Why the United Nations should Commit to this Proposal

This proposal establishes a clear, detailed, actionable path towards the realization of Internet multilingualization where no such path has previously existed. Observers will witness in the Global Forum of the United Nations the transparent accomplishment of a global Internet accessible to all.

This proposal represents, develops, establishes, and promotes fundamental aspirations of the United Nations – local empowerment, respect for the right and ability of local regions to make their own decisions in the pursuit of their own self-interests, equal access to all, freedom of information, and the breaking down of barriers between peoples, while ensuring the safety and integrity of the system.

The commitment to this proposal sends a clear message to all that the unnecessary and unjustified delays in bringing the global phenomenon of the Internet to the non-English speaking peoples of the world are unacceptable and can no longer be justified and tolerated.

This proposal looks to clearly identify the current structure's shortcomings, complement the achievements made by ICANN and others, identify pitfalls not to be adopted and repeated in multilingualization, effectively address those areas which previous organizations have been unable or have failed to address, and provide a valid path to achieving this noble goal.

The creation of a multilingual Internet benefits all involved parties but most importantly brings in the regions which have been left out and disenfranchised because they have no knowledge of English, and places them back at the heart of the Internet, a revolutionary tool that can assist in much needed enlightenment to those regions. It will require a spirit of cooperation and coordination which only the United Nations can foster and to which the peoples of the world look up and count on to provide this leadership.

B. Contact MINC and Support Multilingualization

Although MINC has been championing the cause of a truly multilingual Internet for many years against tremendous odds, and while it is a non-profit organization, MINC cannot multilingualize the Internet alone. The world requires the enthusiastic support of individuals, communities, governments, businesses, organizations, and the United Nations. The multilingualization of the Internet is a noble and moral purpose and we call on you to join us in our quest to form the Information Society. If you wish to help bridge the digital divide or have any questions or comments, please write to Khaledfattal@aol.com. And remember, everyone stands to benefit from a multilingual Internet.

GOVERNANCE OF IP-BASED NEXT GENERATION NETWORKS: A NEW ASPECT OF INTERNET GOVERNANCE
Rainer Händel, Siemens Munich

What Next Generation Network means

The current discussion of Internet governance, stimulated by the recent World Summit on the Information Society (WSIS), has mainly addressed "classical" Internet issues such as IP address and domain name management, anti-spam and anti-cybercrime measures, etc. IP-based networks are being evolved, however, to a new concept dubbed NGN, which stands for *Next Generation Networks*.

What is an NGN? There has been a lengthy debate on its definition in standardization organizations which is not yet finished. A first impression of NGN can be given by the following characterization:

> *Next Generation Networks* (NGNs) can be seen as an evolution from PSTN and IP networks to a *unified public network for electronic communications based on IP*.

This concept also impacts "governance" and market regulation: Where today's market regulation is focusing on voice services, future regulatory approaches and sectoral legal requirements will have to deal with electronic communications in a broader sense.

Definition of NGN according to ITU

ITU-T Study Group 13 (SG 13) has recently given the following definition of an NGN (TD 28 [GEN], Geneva, February 3-12, 2004):

> *"A Next Generation Network (NGN) is a packet-based network able to provide services including Telecommunication Services and able to make use of multiple broadband, QoS-enabled transport technologies and in which service-related functions are independent from underlying transport-related technologies. It offers unrestricted access by users to different service providers. It supports generalized mobility which will allow consistent and ubiquitous provision of services to users."*

With the further explanation:

> "The NGN can be defined by the following fundamental characteristics:

- Packet-based transfer;
- Separation of control functions among bearer capabilities, call/session, and application/service;
- Decoupling of service provision from network, and provision of open interfaces;
- Support for a wide range of services, applications and mechanisms based on service building blocks (including real time/streaming/non-real time services and multi-media);
- Broadband capabilities with end-to-end QoS and transparency;
- Interworking with legacy networks via open interfaces;
- Generalized mobility;
- Unrestricted access by users to different service providers;
- A variety of identification schemes which can be resolved to IP addresses for the purposes of routing in IP networks;
- Unified service characteristics for the same service as perceived by the user;
- Converged services between Fixed/Mobile;
- Independence of service-related functions from underlying transport technologies;
- *Compliant with all regulatory requirements, for example concerning emergency communications and security/privacy, etc."*

It should be noted that the next generation *mobile* networks (third generation mobile) also deploy IP techniques.

There is a strong tendency towards *convergence* of fixed and mobile networks and also of carrier and enterprise networks in the sense that services and applications should become more and more independent of the underlying network infrastructure. This grants certain mobility features even to fixed network users.

NGN key issues

From a manufacturer's viewpoint, the following key requirements can be stated:

- Multiservice networks need harmonized interfaces and defined protocols, whereby standardization should remain a transparent, market-driven process. We prefer open *international/global standards to support global markets.*

- Various requirements are no longer specified by the law; they are market-driven. Quality of service is a good example of a market request.

- Siemens as a global player has to be aware of legal and regulatory differences in different states. *We strongly support all efforts to make legal and regulatory approaches for NGNs as harmonized as possible worldwide* and as a consequence make market regulation predictable, transparent, effective, stable and secure.

- We ask for appropriate market regulation: Just as much market regulation as absolutely necessary!

- The European Union's New Regulatory Framework is a good example for a road ahead to a technologically neutral approach for regulating Next Generation Networks:

  o Next Generation Networks realized as unified public networks will definitely be of another quality than today's Internet. NGNs will not only offer Voice over IP functionalities but a wide variety of electronic communication services. In the past, the European Union was of the opinion that Voice over IP does not fulfil all of the quality requirements that had been outlined for voice telephony and could therefore, from a regulatory standpoint, not be considered as being covered by the voice telephony definition. The new legislation (the so-called New Regulatory Framework) does not set a specific regulation for switched voice anymore. *With the new regulatory framework the distinction between switched and packet-based networks and related services is no longer relevant,* as "technological neutrality" and "electronic communications" are now the catch phrases to be interpreted. Electronic communication networks and electronic communication services are facing the same regulations, no matter which technology they are using. The only thing that is still possible (just as in the previous legal framework) is to make a regulatory distinction between publicly available services and services that are not publicly available.

o "Classical" telephony services and comparable services offered over scalable and reliable NGNs that meet defined quality of service requirements will be treated equally.

In general the New Regulatory Framework does *not* cover *content regulation*. But there are several principles addressed within European Union regulations:

- Media pluralism;
- Cultural and linguistic diversity;
- Protection of user and consumer rights;
- Maximum benefit for end-users/stimulation of consumer confidence;
- Freedom of expression;
- Impartiality;
- Social inclusion;
- Protection of minors;
- Access for disabled users (choice, price, quality);
- Proper functioning of the single market (internal market).

These principles surely have to be obeyed, and industry has committed itself to contributing accordingly.

Specific NGN requirements

NGNs are definitely more than the next version of Internet implementation. They are not meant to replace the current Internet. They use IP techniques such as IP addressing, and therefore there will be mutual impact. NGNs will however offer access to the Internet as one service among many others, whose choice is up to the network operators', service providers' and users' wishes.

In any case, NGNs must meet the following (mainly legal and regulatory) requirements:

- High reliability, network integrity and availability, Quality of Service;
- Security and safety of the state in general (lawful interception) have to be granted by NGNs and must be a part of the NGN market offer;
- Network availability in cases of disaster (availability of services in the case of force majeure and catastrophic network breakdown);

- Access to emergency services (including calls to the local emergency number, e.g. 112 in Europe);

- Providing operators of emergency services with access to caller location information;

- Data protection and privacy issues are becoming more important (e.g. in billing) from the customer's point of view and have to be considered in NGNs (data protection rules in the communications sector must be technologically neutral and reliable);

- Carrier selection, carrier pre-selection and interconnection are persisting requirements whereby interfaces towards traditional and Next Generation Networks have to be provided;

- NGN service operators must be granted access to numbering resources (pressure on national numbering plans is to be expected). Unique numbers and a comprehensive scheme for number allocation and number portability are therefore key challenges.

Conclusions

A new generation of communication networks is about to be implemented which is based on both Internet techniques and traditional carrier-grade telecommunication networking and service offering. Such networks will have to fulfil the same stringent regulatory requirements as today's public telecommunication networks. The issue of *NGN governance should be included in the ongoing discussion of Internet governance.* Mutual impact of NGN and Internet in terms of technological and regulatory development can be expected.

NGNs offer a common network infrastructure for many communication services and applications. This reduces capital and especially operational costs compared with maintaining several dedicated networks for telephony, data, etc. Owing to this synergy effect, the NGN is a promising networking technology which can also be used to build a cost-effective network infrastructure in regions with sparse telecommunication density, thus helping to bridge the digital divide between developed and developing countries.

Identifying governance requirements for NGNs should therefore be in the interest of all countries which wish to enhance their communications infrastructure and improve access to both Internet and traditional telecommunication services.

comment

E-NATIONS, THE INTERNET FOR ALL
Tony Hain and Patrick Grossetete, Cisco Systems; Jim Bound, NAv6TF; Latif Ladid, IPv6 Forum[1]

Introduction

The robust address space available with IPv6 permits nodes, homes, and devices, as typical Internet use models, to have more than one address, of different scopes, for different reasons. Using this advantage of IPv6, the authors provide a view of address allocation, in which we compare the ratio of address space per country and population depicting one to five addresses per consumer.

Certainly few of the original IP protocol designers envisaged the "e-turmoil" of the end of the 20th century and the quick adoption of the Internet Protocol (IP) as *the* application convergence layer in many industry segments, outside its historic IT environment.

Today, despite the recent economic turndown, the worldwide Internet economy is a reality. As an example, data from Forrester Research projects growth for the European Union from the 2001 figure of €77 billion to €2.2 trillion in 2006. Growing adoption of the Internet by consumers – also referred to as Internet users – drives several markets such as home devices, mobile wireless equipment, transportation, media and others to introduce a new generation of products that embed the IP protocol.

---

[1] Reviewed by Richard Jimmerson and Ray Plzak, ARIN

Although a business model and its acceptance by society may still need to be defined for many of these products, it is anticipated that with global connectivity, which is different from global access to the network, a network may want to keep some privacy. This is a foundation for business-to-business (B-to-B), business-to-consumer (B-to-C) and consumer-to-consumer (C-to-C) services, and the inherent evolutionary trend is to push the services towards the edge of the network, where a particular device needs to be reached, served or monitored. It must be also noticed that recent deployment of new broadband access technologies such as Ethernet-to-the-home, WiFi, and SDSL enable symmetric communications from end-users sites.

"IN 2005, ALL SONY PRODUCTS WILL BE IPV6-ENABLED"

Mario Tokoro, Corporate Executive Vice President, Co-CTO and President of Network & Software Technology Centre at Sony Corporation

February 12, 2003 *http://www.ipv6style.jp/en/interviews/20030212/index.shtml*

Before any large scale adoption and deployment can begin and be successful, an evaluation of the Internet's capacity to support the model is clearly mandatory. But, it must be acknowledged that any major change will take years to achieve. So considering 5-10 years as a potential schedule to an update, it is not too soon to begin in 2004.

Endless debates have already been published regarding the number of global IPv4 addresses that are either dependent on the proponents' view of allocated/unallocated, used/unused, with/without H-Ratio address space, but so far most if not all of these addresses were consumed by the IT industry. Strict allocation control of the IPv4 address space is the currently accepted behaviour, but this does not look at an innovative model to enable every country without distinction of its population or economy to become a member of the e-Nation.

Today, only an Internet "client-to-server" architecture, where the primary assumption is that an end-user only gets connected when accessing the network, allows Internet service providers to provision access with a ratio superior to 1:1 [generally from 1:2 to 1:15], which can be deployed on a large scale. This is clearly not the model of the consumer electronics, mobile wireless phone, and automobile industries, which are considering IPv6 for their devices and applications. To serve all this equipment, "server-to-client" and "peer-to-peer" models for use must be affordable to anyone.

A different look at the today's IPv4 address space assignment may consider other criteria such as per country delegation versus population, requirements to reach massmarkets, and future growth of the population. The goal of this paper is to collect accurate numbers about the current status of the 221 /8 IPv4 networks and to provide a different vision about the allocation.

Looking at the Numbers

- According to the United Nations the earth's population is estimated to be 6.3 billion. Even without considering the H-ratio, the IPv4 32-bit address space is inadequate to support one-third of this population. Whether the Internet is an open model depends on the country you are living in.

- The United Nations expects the world's population to increase by 2.6 billion during the next 47 years, from 6.3 billion in 2002 to 8.9 billion in 2050. The Internet architecture has to cope with the evolution of the population. But once again, with the H-ratio the IPv4 address space cannot address 50% of the population. Is that an issue? Once again, it depends on the country you live in.

- The earth's population is growing by 79 million people per year. The growth ratio of Internet users must consider the evolution of the population as well.

- A technology is considered as reaching a massmarket size when its penetration rate reaches at least 20%. From our study, only 36 countries have reached this stage out of 208, 4 others being near this threshold. Given this assumption, it means that IPv4 has not reached massmarket deployment. Since, only 17.3% of the countries have substantially adopted IPv4, and those countries represent less than 15% of the total global population.

- In 2003, 71 countries out of 208 have an IPv4 global address space assignment ratio of 1 or more addresses, and not using the H-ratio per Internet user. Although IPv4 global address space is available from the Registry, it looks like already 139 countries have to deploy Network Address Translation (NAT) to satisfy the needs of their population. This statistic does not imply that countries with enough addresses are not deploying NAT.

- IP as an application convergence layer has a clear impact on the way addresses are required. Several statements were made regarding the need of at least five or more IP address per user to match the projected equipment needs for IPv6, e.g. mobile phone, TV, digital camera, car, and associated services for deployment. If only five addresses per home are considered, in 2003, only five countries have enough IPv4 global address assignment to enable such use of the Internet Protocol. This projection does not even consider the H-ratio, which will increase the ratio value to build operational Internet infrastructures by an order of magnitude. In any case, just looking at a ratio of 1/1 or 5/1 is far from the real numbers.

- To illustrate the previous section, let us consider the public mobile wireless industry as an example. Today, GSM and other digital technologies have reached more than 1.2 billion subscribers all over the world. Next generation 3G telephony and multimedia networks of wireless devices embed an IP stack to enable Internet applications and services to become mobile. If we only consider 50% of the current subscriber population, an additional 37 /8 network is required to offer an always-on capability. As the next generations of devices will tend to support several data link technologies, e.g. WLAN plus cellular, taking advantage of Mobile IPv6 to allow roaming between them, two IPv6 addresses as Home Address plus Care of Address must be provisioned per device, increasing the /8 requirements to 74. This is without considering the additional subscribers forecast, the infrastructure to be deployed. Or a potential 100% subscriber adoption rate.

Conclusion

The success of the Internet Protocol (IP) is built on an open and global model. The Internet economy is a reality that reaches all nations around the world and none want to be isolated, not even the less-developed nations as they clearly see a chance to improve their economy and education. IPv6 is a stable protocol that can sustain the growth of the Internet to enable a global *e-Nation*. The Internet Protocol version 4 or version 6 have no political or *balkanization* rules in their definition. IP technologies have to evolve to accommodate new challenges posed by these numbers; this will take several years to be achieved, but the authors see IPv6 as the best proposal to serve the future generations of children that will grow up using the Internet.

* * * * *

About the North American IPv6 Task Force

The *North American IPv6 Task Force* (NAv6TF) is a sub-chapter of the *IPv6 Forum* dedicated to the advancement and propagation of *IPv6* (Internet Protocol, version 6) in the North American continent. Comprised of individual, rather than corporate, membership the NAv6TF mission is to provide technical leadership and innovative thought for the successful integration of IPv6 into all facets of networking and telecommunications infrastructure, present and future. Through its continued facilitation of technical and business case whitepapers, IPv6-centric conferences, IPv6 test and interoperability events, and collaboration with IPv6 task forces from around the globe, the NAv6TF will strive to be the guiding force for IPv6 adoption in the United States and Canada. http://www.nav6tf.org/index.html

stakeholder perspective

UNDERSTANDING TELECOMMUNICATION NETWORK TRENDS
International Telecommunication Union (ITU)[1] [2]

1. Mobile and Internet: Two Innovations

Like most technology-driven industries, the telecommunication sector has historically been characterized by steady growth punctuated by an occasional leap forward, usually when a new technology is introduced. This historical pattern has repeated in the development of every new communications network technology, beginning with telegraph in the 1840s, the telephone in the 1870s, radio-telegraphy or "wireless" in the 1890s, radio broadcasting in the 1920s, television broadcasting in the 1950s, geostationary satellite communications in the 1960s, computer communications in the 1970s, optical communications in the 1980s, and the Internet

---

[1] ITU, 2004 - All rights reserved - International Telecommunication Union (ITU), Geneva

[2] **Disclaimer**: Denominations and classifications employed in this publication do not imply any opinion on the part of the International Telecommunication Union concerning the legal or other status of any territory or any endorsement or acceptance of any boundary. Where the designation "country" appears in this publication, it covers countries and territories.

Acknowledgements: The text of this report was prepared by a team from the ITU Strategy and Policy Unit, the ITU Telecommunication Development Bureau and the ITU Telecommunication Standardization Bureau.

The views expressed in this report are those of the authors and do not necessarily reflect the opinions of ITU or its membership.

A revised version of this report will be submitted to ITU Council 2004 for their review.

and mobile communications in the 1990s. For the last 139 years, the ITU has adapted to and embraced these evolutions in communications technologies.

In the latter part of the twentieth century, the almost simultaneous arrival of two major innovations—mobile phones and the Internet—not only changed the face of communications, but also gave fresh impetus for economic growth (see Figure 1).

The origins of the mobile communications industry date from the licensing of analogue cellular communications services in the early 1980s. As recently as 1990, there were only 11 million subscribers worldwide, but the introduction of digital services in the early 1990s, combined with competitive service provision and a shift to prepaid billing, spurred rapid growth in demand. At the end of 2003, there were over 1.35 billion mobile subscribers worldwide, compared with 1.2 billion fixed-line users (see Section 7).

The origins of the Internet go back to 1969, but it was in the early 1990s, with the development of the World Wide Web and graphical browsers, that the Internet really took off as a commercial undertaking. By the end of 2001, the Internet had passed the half billion user mark. Although the "dot.com" boom of the late 1990s proved to be short-lived, the Internet itself has continued to grow, adding more users and new applications.

Figure 1: Growth of mobile and Internet users

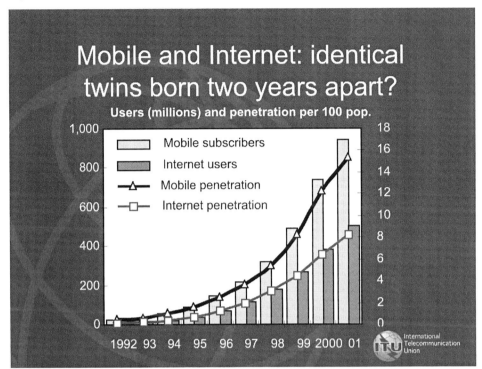

Source: ITU

As Figure 1 shows, the two industries have exhibited remarkably similar growth patterns since the start of the 1990s, but with a lag of about two years. The level of penetration of the Internet at the end of 2001 (8.2 users for every 100 inhabitants, worldwide) is almost identical to the penetration of mobile phones at the end of 1999. This two year lag might be explained by the fact that the formative moments in the growth of these industries occurred just under two years apart: digital cellphones were launched commercially on 1 July 1991 (by Radiolinja, in Finland), while graphical web browsers were launched commercially in April 1993.

2. Mobile: from 2G to 3G
Major stages in the technological development of mobile telecommunications are commonly described in terms of "generations". "First-generation" (1G) mobile technology refers to the analogue cellular systems that first appeared in the late 1970s and early 1980s. This phase of development was characterized by a wide range of different systems, many of which became popular in one or two countries only. "Second generation" (2G) technology refers to today's digital cellular systems (first deployed at the start of the 1990s), such as GSM (Global System

for Mobile Communications), PDC (Personal Digital Communications), TDMA (Time Division Multiple Access), and CDMA (Code Division Multiple Access).

While 2G networks were developed under a number of proprietary, regional and national standards, "third generation systems" (3G), were developed from the outset on the global stage, during the 1990s, under the leadership of the International Telecommunication Union (ITU) under the IMT-2000 (International Mobile Telecommunications) banner. Much effort has gone into the development of a single interoperable global standard for 3G systems, in order to avoid the market fragmentation that had very much characterized the 1G and 2G worlds.

3. 3G Systems or IMT-2000

It was in the mid-1980s that the ITU began its work on IMT-2000. The ITU's 1992 World Radio Conference (WRC) identified the 2 GHz band for the global deployment of IMT-2000. Eight years later, the 2000 WRC allocated additional spectrum for 3G services in three frequency bands: one below 1 GHz, another at 1.7 GHz (where many second-generation systems currently operate) and a third band in the 2.5 GHz range.

This effectively gave a green light to the mobile industry worldwide to start deploying IMT-2000 networks and services. Many economies, such as Australia, Hong Kong, China, and most European countries, have allocated spectrum for 3G, although, still in 2004, few services have been made commercially available. The countries that have begun deploying 3G services include Japan, the Republic of Korea, Brazil, Canada, United States and the United Kingdom.

Despite concerted global efforts at standardization, there remain different approaches to 3G technology. The major industrialized economies were unable to agree on a single standard. The result was an IMT-2000 standard with a number of "flavours", that is to say five possible radio interfaces based on three different access technologies (FDMA, TDMA and CDMA). Thus far, the vast majority of industry attention has been directed towards the CDMA technology, and in particular Wideband CDMA or W-CDMA (known in Europe as UMTS) and CDMA2000 (including CDMA2000 1x). Thus far, national license allocation has been limited to these two radio technologies, although China is licensing a third technology, TDSCDMA.

4. The Internet in Transition

The Internet has also been under significant transformation, particularly since the early 1990s. Fifteen years ago, prior to the web, the Internet was primarily focused on academic and research use, was primarily North American-based, not for profit, and used mostly for email and file transfer. With the invention of the World Wide Web in Geneva at CERN[3] in the early

---

[3] http://www.cern.ch/

1990s, the Internet became accessible to a much wider range of users. During the early and mid-1990s there was significant growth throughout OECD countries and increasing privatization of its backbone. The mid- to late-1990's witnessed the rise and fall of "dot.com" mania and with it the belief that the Internet was a suitable platform to subsume all existing telecommunication networks and services.

Despite the boom and bust (which is surprisingly common with most new communications technologies)[4], digital convergence will continue, albeit not as fast as many of us had imagined. For example, there is ongoing standardization to provide integration and interoperability of IP-based and PSTN network services and applications. The telephone network (both fixed and mobile) and the Internet are likely to converge into what some people refer to as "Next Generation Networks" or "NGN". The NGN is characterized by the following fundamental characteristics:[5]

- Packet-based transfer;
- Separation of control functions among bearer capabilities, call/session, and application/service;
- Decoupling of service provision from network, and provision of open interfaces;
- Support for a wide range of services, applications and mechanisms based on service building blocks (including real time/streaming/non-real time services and multi-media);
- Broadband capabilities with end-to-end QoS and transparency;
- Interworking with legacy networks via open interfaces;
- Generalized mobility;
- Unrestricted access by users to different service providers;
- A variety of identification schemes which can be resolved to IP addresses for the purposes of routing in IP networks;
- Unified service characteristics for the same service as perceived by the user;
- Converged services between Fixed/Mobile;
- Independence of service-related functions from underlying transport technologies;
- Compliant with national regulatory requirements, for example concerning emergency communications, security and privacy.

---

[4] See "The history of communications and its implications for the Internet" by Andrew Odlyzko, University of Minnesota.

[5] http://www.itu.int/ITU-T/studygroups/com13/ngn2004/working_definition.html

5. Mobile and Internet Demographic Trends

When the ITU started publishing statistical indicator reports on the development of telecommunications in different regions of the world in 1993, Asia-Pacific accounted for just one-quarter of the world's fixed telephone lines and around one-sixth of mobile users. In the last few years, the region has emerged as the world's largest telecommunication market (see Figure 2). It is also the only region to have increased its market share significantly, adding more than one new telephone user every second for the last decade.

The Asia-Pacific region now has the largest share of Internet and mobile users as well as leading in advanced Internet technologies such as broadband access and mobile data. The Republic of Korea and Hong Kong, China, are the top two economies in the world in terms of broadband Internet penetration. In mobile Internet technologies, Japan and the Republic of Korea were the first two nations to launch third generation cellular networks commercially. These exploits combined with a large potential for growth based on population demographics corroborate the view that the global telecommunications epicentre has shifted permanently from North America and Western Europe to the Asia-Pacific region.

Figure 2: Global Distribution of mobile and Internet users

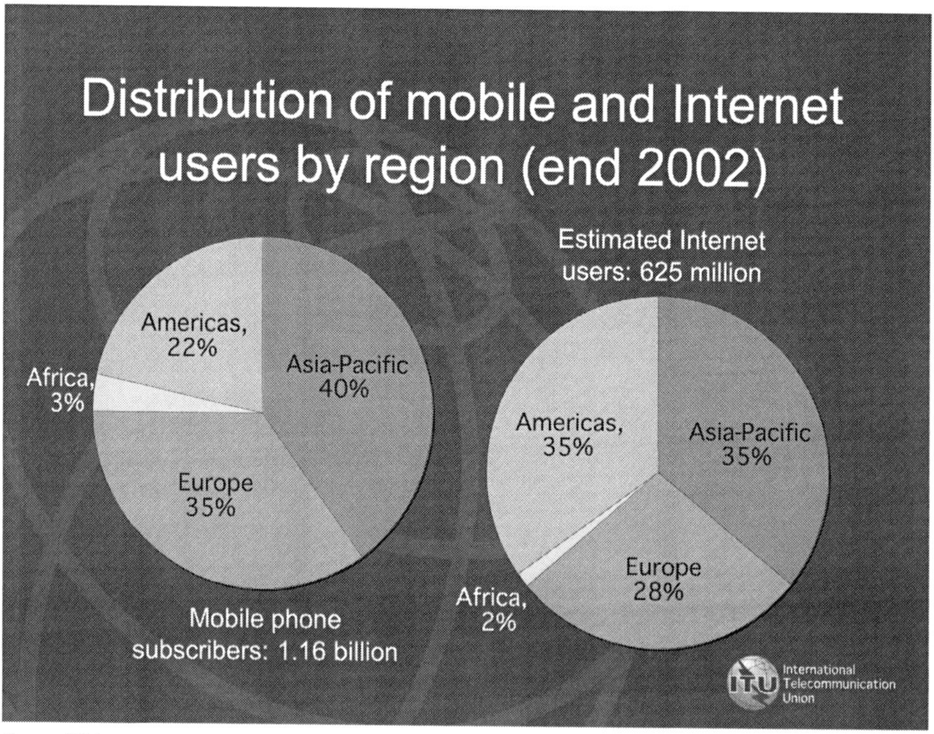

Source: ITU

6. Internet Connectivity Trends

Figure 2 also demonstrates that Africa still very much lags the rest of the world in both mobile and Internet penetration. Large disparities in access to the Internet exist, particularly for developing countries. It is widely recognized that one reason is the high costs of international circuits for Internet connectivity between least developed countries and Internet backbone networks. A number of initiatives are under way to address this problem. These include consideration of new models for financial exchanges among operators as well as efforts to facilitate the creation of traffic aggregation within localities, countries or regions in developing countries in order to avoid the sending of this traffic over satellite or cable links used for intercontinental traffic—for example between Africa and Europe or North America. The latter would aim to maximize the retention of local and national traffic within these regions and thus reduce the dependence on international communications links. To give a sense of the scale of the problem, over 75% of Internet traffic in Europe remains intra-regional compared with only 1% in regions like Africa (see Figure 3). The ITU's Telecommunication Standardization Sector Study Group 3 and the ITU Telecommunication Development Sector are particularly active in exploring solutions.

Figure 3: Global Distribution of Backbone Capacity (2001)

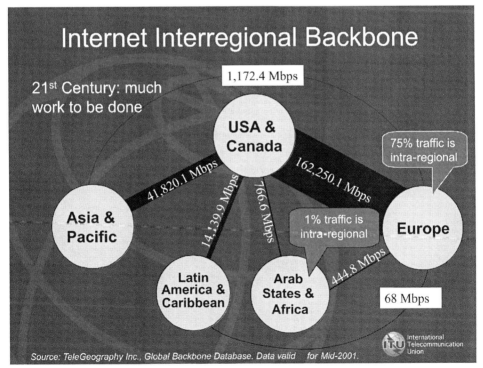

7. Mobile Overtakes Fixed

The year 2002 marked an historic turning point in the history of telephony, for it was the year when mobile subscribers overtook fixed-line subscribers worldwide (see Figure.4).[6] The rise of mobile telephony to overtake fixed lines has brought with it many implications, but perhaps the most significant impact is on access, both to basic telecommunication services, and to information and communication technologies (ICT), as a tool for economic and social development. This is partly because cellular networks can be built faster than fixed-line networks and can cover geographically challenging areas. Mobile services have served to boost competition, and prepaid models have opened access to mobile cellular for those who would otherwise not qualify for telephone subscription plans.

In countries where mobile communications constitute the primary form of access, increased exchange of information on trade or health services is contributing to development goals; in countries where people commonly use both fixed-line and mobile communications, the personalized traits of the mobile phone are changing social interaction.

Increasingly, mobile is not only overtaking fixed, but also substituting for it: in such cases, users have a mobile phone only and have no fixed-line subscription. In developed countries, this may be through choice. In developing ones, it may be the only possibility for individuals to have their own phone. This has created a whole new set of paradigms for users, regulators and providers alike. It is important to note that while there may be a similar percentage of mobile-only users in countries as diverse as, for example, Finland and Uganda, the reasons for this are very different and so are the implications.

As most of the legislative foundations of today's telecom regulatory frameworks were articulated and predicated on the concept of increasing basic fixed line telephony density and dealing with incumbent monopolies, the growth of mobile has significant impact on policy and regulation outlooks. Issues include issues of spectrum and numbering management, universal service policies, competition policy and interconnection for mobile communications, international roaming, pricing and billing models, privacy, and consumer and data protection.

---

[6] At the end of 2003, the ITU estimated that there were over 1.35 billion mobile subscribers worldwide, compared with only 1.2 billion fixed-line users. A recent workshop examined the social and human considerations relating to the rapid development of mobile technology. See http://www.itu.int/osg/spu/ni/futuremobile/index.html.

Figure 4: Global fixed lines and mobile subscribers, millions

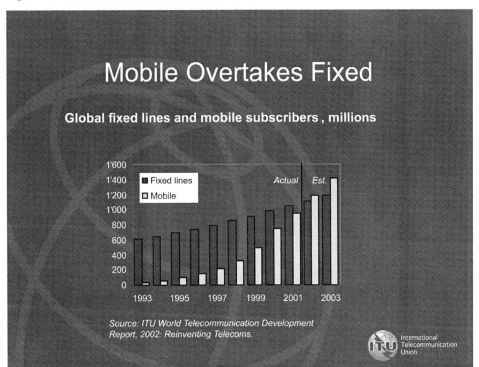

8. Mobile Internet

It requires no great leap of the imagination to believe that the convergence of mobile communications and the Internet will produce something big, perhaps even the mythical "sum that is bigger than its parts". If this view is accepted, the convergence of mobile communications and the Internet (as well as with RFID type technologies – see Section 2.9) is likely to produce major innovations.

The major Asian economies are the clear first movers, with Japan and Korea being the first to actually deploy mobile Internet services (see Figure 5). Although the experience of Japan and Korea would suggest the huge potential of the mobile Internet, the high hopes for 3G have been somewhat dampened by the slump of recent years in the telecommunication sector as a whole, as well as evidence that some mobile markets are reaching saturation. Many operators in countries that have yet to initiate 3G deployments are taking a more gradual or cautious approach, concentrating their efforts on new multimedia-type applications over existing 2G platforms. Many are choosing to upgrade their systems to support higher data transmission speeds needed for images. This approach may be a useful way to "test the waters" for 3G, or to exploit more fully the potential of 2.5G technologies without the need to invest heavily in new 3G networks.

Figure 5: Mobile Internet users as percentage of total mobile users

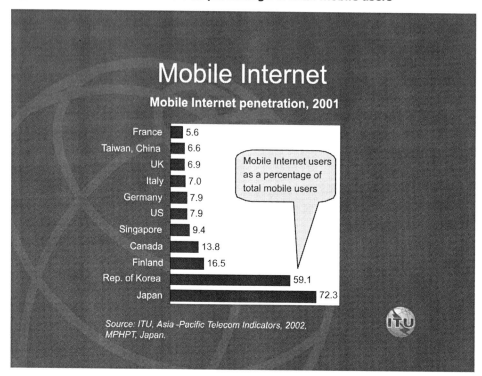

9. Ubiquitous Networks

The next trend over the horizon beyond mobile Internet is called *ubiquitous networking* or *pervasive networks*. This involves the use of radio frequency identification (RFID) technologies and their integration with other information and communications technologies, which has dramatically accelerated in the last few years with rapid reductions in microchip size and cost. This portends the possibility of a new totally new class of computing and communications recognized in the national IT strategies of Japan and Korea, two clear conceptual leaders in the field.

This development, aided by rapid advances in antennae technologies, will enable tiny microchips to be implanted in physical objects and from these perceive conditions in the real world which includes the ability to detect a diverse range of real world information such as, *inter alia,* the identity of a person, the current location, temperature and humidity levels, when a product was made and by whom it was made. Some suggest this is a new revolution, which might be called the "Internet of things". While much activity, particularly in Europe and the United States, has concentrated on RFID technologies in the context of product management or a replacement for Universal Product Codes, the Asia-Pacific vision of ubiquitous networks is very much broader. A glimpse of what a future ubiquitous networking environment might look like is the communications environment portrayed in the recent film "Minority Report" (albeit a somewhat negative one).

At the recent ITU TELECOM World 2003, Professor Ken Sakamura of Tokyo University, widely considered to be one of the "godfathers" of the concepts behind ubiquitous networking, said that while he was delighted to see the growing interest in the technology, there were a significant number of policy and regulatory issues that must be first addressed. He cited examples of companies with plans to insert RFID tags into millions of products that they distribute and manage. This has given rise to increasing concerns about the security, privacy and the societal aspects of this technology. As an example, at a recent workshop on RFID privacy issues at MIT, a large number of civic organizations jointly issued a statement of their deep concerns about the rapid application of RFID chip technology to consumer products, which they see as a potential invasion of privacy.

10. Fixed Wireless Technologies

In 2002, wireless LAN technology became a bright spot in the beleaguered telecommunication market. Wireless LANs can effectively be used to share Internet access from a broadband connection over 100 metres, although they are also being used increasingly as methods of providing broadband access over longer distances in rural areas. This is accomplished by increasing power levels of the equipment, using specialized antennae, and ensuring line-of-sight access. Of all WLAN technologies, the most popular and widely known is IEEE 802.11b, commonly referred to as "Wi-Fi".

Several factors have contributed to what is becoming the phenomenal growth of wireless LANs: a steep drop in prices, the mobility benefits of wireless connectivity, off-the-shelf availability, and easy installation. The combination of inexpensive equipment and easy installation has also made wireless LANs particularly attractive for rural connectivity. Many projects around the world are looking for ways to use wireless LAN technology to bridge the last mile. The ITU Telecommunications Development Sector, to cite just one example, is in the process of implementing three pilot projects to determine the performance of WLANs for provision of community access for rural areas of Bulgaria, Uganda and Yemen. Wireless LAN is also being rolled out in many rural areas of other developed economies.

One fast-growing use of WLANs is the provision of wireless hotspots in public areas such as airports, conference halls, and cafés, offering high-speed wireless Internet connections to users. Beyond the "hotspot" concept, several businesses are even looking into ambitious plans to develop a patchwork network of wireless LAN connections across entire countries. Zamora, a Spanish town with a population of 65,000, already boasts 75 per cent Wi-Fi coverage.

The IEEE also recently standardized 802.16, commonly known as WiMAX, as a new fixed-wireless standard that uses a point-to-multipoint architecture. The initial version (802.16) was developed to meet the requirements for broadband wireless access systems operating between 10 and 66 GHz. A recent amendment (802.16a) does the same for systems operating between 2 and 11 GHz. WiMAX equipment should be able to transmit between 32-56 km with maximum data rates close to 70 Mbit/s.

While other fixed wireless technologies have had great difficulty with interoperability, the WiMAX technical working group is seeking to replicate the success of Wi-Fi by following its development and certification processes. First, the WiMAX working group included leading companies in many industries whose clout in their individual markets would help promote a common standard.[7] Second, the WiMAX Forum is similar to the very successful Wi-Fi forum which offers a "stamp of approval" that equipment will interoperate with other certified products, further helping to create a single common standard.[8]

11. Birth of Broadband

Another technology is emerging that promises to provide a unifying platform for three converging industrial sectors: computing, communications and broadcasting. That technology is "broadband". Because of the nature of broadband (you have to use it to understand the benefits it offers), market take-off typically requires a critical mass of users. Currently, around one in every ten Internet subscribers worldwide has a dedicated broadband connection (see Figure 6, top chart), though many more share the benefits of high-speed Internet access, for instance, through a local area network (LAN), at work or at school. The world leader for broadband is the Republic of Korea (Figure 6, lower chart), which is around three years ahead of the global average in terms of converting Internet users to broadband. There, a critical mass was attained as early as 2000, when prices fell below US$ 25 per month; from which point onwards take-off was rapid (see Figure 6, bottom chart). Currently, over 93 per cent of Internet subscribers in Korea use broadband.

---

[7] The WiMAX forum has detailed information on 802.16 at: http://wimaxforum.org/tech/tech.asp.

[8] The ITU recently approved Sector Membership for the IEEE in its Radiocommunication Sector (ITU-R) which means that the IEEE can be a direct contributor to standards and other documents developed by ITU-R.

Figure 6: Broadband as percentage available to Internet users and penetration, by technology

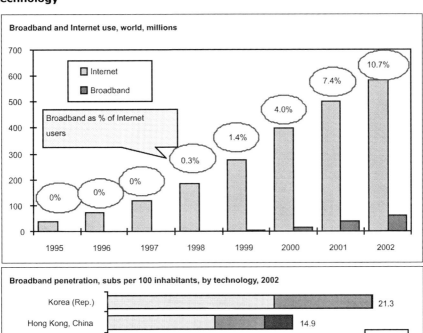

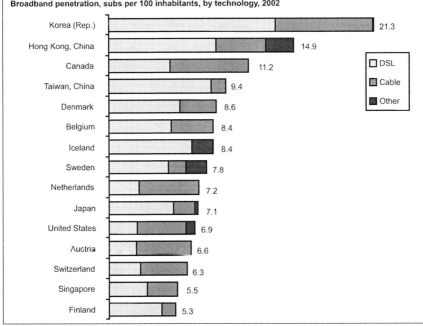

Source: ITU World Telecommunication Indicators Database.

Around the world, there were around 63 million "broadband" subscribers at the start of 2003 compared with 1.13 billion fixed-line users and 1.16 billion mobile phone users. Broadband users enjoy a range of service speeds from 256 kbit/s up to 100 Mbit/s. The number of subscribers is growing rapidly, with a 72 per cent increase during 2002. Digital subscriber line (DSL) is currently the most commonly deployed platform, followed by cable modems, Ethernet local area networks (LAN), fixed-wireless access, wireless LANs (WLAN), satellite and other technologies. The overwhelming majority of today's users are in the developed world. However, even among the 30 member countries of the Organisation for Economic Co-operation and Development (OECD), there remain large disparities, not only in service availability but also in terms of quality of access and price per Mbit/s. In developing countries, as broadband becomes cheaper, and wireless technologies evolve, broadband adoption may help countries to "leapfrog" traditional telephony technologies, as already has been proven in a number of development initiatives.

12. Telecommunication Sector Reform

A vast majority of countries worldwide have reformed, or are in the process of reforming, their telecommunication sectors through the review and adoption of new legislation to adapt to the rapidly changing communication environment. They have done so by opening some market segments, if not all, to competition, allowing private participation, and establishing a national regulatory authority. As of mid-2003, 123 countries worldwide recognized the importance of establishing a regulatory authority to foster competition in the information and communication (ICT) sectors in a fair and transparent fashion. As the development of ICTs is making the convergence of different types of network platforms and services a reality, more and more countries are responding either by merging their telecommunication and broadcasting regulatory authorities or improving coordination between various agencies involved in the ICT sector. Additional functions and tasks are required from regulators as a result of convergence, liberalization and market growth, including dispute resolution and consumer protection. At the same time, regional initiatives are taking place worldwide to harmonize national ICT legislative frameworks and work together toward the ultimate goal of providing universal access if not universal service to all citizens of the world.

This liberalization of telecommunication markets through the introduction of competition is also changing the way countries approach universal access and service policies. This is due, in part, to the fact that services are being provisioned at a more rapid pace, prices are falling and new and innovative services are being introduced.

Today a robust national telecommunication infrastructure has become much more important than a platform for voice: it is the fundamental underpinning layer of networked economies and information societies. As a result, the development of advanced ICT networks is now a key policy objective for most governments around the world. Not only are these networks seen as an important determinant of national competitiveness in an increasingly globalized knowledge economy, they are also seen as offering new opportunities in areas such as education, health and social advancement.

All policy makers and regulators, both established and new, are struggling to address changes resulting from convergence of the information and communication (ICT) sectors. One result is a serious re-examination of existing regulatory models and new approaches to convergence regulation. For example, the European Union's new telecommunication regulatory framework, adopted in March 2002, represents an attempt to move away from technology-specific and service-specific legislation. It attempts to proactively address convergence regulation issues by focusing more on market definitions related to competition law rather than embedding technology-specific definitions in legislation. It will be an interesting model to watch evolve as it is implemented by EU member states and tested by real-world issues.

13. Where Are We Heading?

Those familiar with the history of telecommunications know that predicting the future is notoriously difficult: technologies take time to mature and business models take time to evolve. For example, Alexander Graham Bell originally thought the telephone would be used for broadcasting. The reality is that it took over thirty years to find the "killer application" for the telephone: person-to-person communications.

We also forget that history tends to repeat itself. The invention of the telegraph was perceived, in many ways, as far more of a revolution than the Internet was during the last 10-15 years. Although it is hard to believe now, it was a technology that gripped the imagination of the mid-19th century. That is because for the first time in history, a communication means was available that was divorced from physical transportation. Exchanging messages suddenly took minutes instead of months. It was an invention that was described in the same glowing terms as the Internet: it was the "annihilation of space and time". And it had to be built from scratch. While the Internet was essentially built on top of the global telephone network infrastructure, the physical infrastructure for the telegraph was built from nothing. This required massive business investments and there were a great number of technical and business failures along the way. One example is demonstrated by the early days of submarine cables. According to one historian: "Of the 17,700 kilometers of cable laid by 1861, only 4,800 worked and the rest were lost". However, eventually the problems were solved and 20 years later, about 150,000 kilometers of submarine telegraph cables were in place and working.

Mobile communications and the Internet were the two major demand drivers for telecommunication services in the last decade of the twentieth century. Combine the two – mobile Internet – and this may suggest the major demand driver of the first decades of the twenty-first century. It is easy to envision a migration of traditional PSTNs to combined mobile and IP-based networks, and the potential integration of telecommunications, broadcasting, publishing and other media functions into these networks. This view suggests a future in which past divisions between "vertical" network structures would progressively be transformed into "horizontal" divisions between different network layers, in which everything ultimately would be connected through mobile broadband ubiquitous networks.

Section 6
THE WAY AHEAD

INFORMAL SUMMARY OF THE GLOBAL FORUM ON INTERNET GOVERNANCE (NEW YORK, MARCH 25-26, 2004)
United Nations Information and Communication Technologies Task Force

The Global Forum on Internet Governance, organized by the United Nations Information and Communication Technologies Task Force, was designed as a contribution to a process of consultations that would lead to the establishment by the United Nations Secretary-General of a working group on Internet governance, as requested by the Geneva phase of the World Summit on the Information Society in December 2003.

The Forum attracted participation of more than 300 representatives of all stakeholders, including key leaders of the Internet community, governments of major developed and developing countries at the policy-making level, and senior executives from the private sector, civil society and academia[1]. Most notable was the active involvement of the leaders of the Internet community.

---

[1] For the list of participants, visit http://www.unicttaskforce.org/perl/documents.pl?id=1296. About 35 per cent of participants represented governments (of which nearly 60 per cent were from developed countries and over 40 per cent were from developing countries and countries with economy in transition), 22 per cent were from civil society organizations and academia, 18 per cent – from the private sector, international organizations were represented by 14 per cent of participants, and the Internet community constituted 11 per cent of all registered participants.

The main features of the meeting were its open, participatory and interactive character, its focus on the substance of the issues rather than on institutional interests, and a broadly shared emphasis on finding common approaches and perspectives. The Forum did not, of course, resolve all problems related to Internet governance, but its deliberations brought about a significant advance towards a broadly shared agreement on most promising approaches to major outstanding issues.

In terms of its substantive outcome, the Global Forum succeeded in identifying important areas where commonalities existed, as well as in outlining workable approaches to issues that remained controversial. There was broad consensus on some baseline principles that should guide the evaluation of governance mechanisms and their future evolution and development. This became possible through a genuine dialogue between those who argue that the Internet is working well and should be left alone, and those who point to the many shortcomings of the current arrangements and advocate some form of global management of the medium. As a result, the Forum produced a broad agreement on several major areas where there was a clear and urgent need for international cooperation in developing globally acceptable solutions: spam, network security, privacy, and information security. The Secretary-General's call to be creative in managing, promoting and protecting the Internet struck wide resonance in the debate.

The Global Forum was organized in a format of plenary sessions and several concurrent break-out sessions[2]. The first three sessions helped identify in broad terms the key points to be addressed by the Forum. Break-out sessions on the afternoon of March 25 afforded an opportunity for an interactive discussion in smaller groups on the wide range of Internet Governance issues. The plenary session on the morning of March 26 examined areas of common understanding that had emerged as well as issues that would merit more deliberation at subsequent meetings.

The plenary meetings were broadcast live on the Internet and are available as archived audio files on the website of the ICT Task Force[3].

The following is an informal summary of proceedings of the Forum.

---

[2] Please see the Programme of the Global Forum here:
  http://www.unicttaskforce.org/sixthmeeting/agenda.html

[3] http://www.unicttaskforce.org/sixthmeeting

March 25, 2004

Opening Session

The Global Forum was opened by the Chairman of the Task Force, who thanked the Secretary-General of the United Nations for his consistent support for the Task Force and also for his recent decision to extend the mandate of the Task Force until the end of 2005, which would enable the Task Force to continue contributing to the follow-up to the first phase of the WSIS and to the preparations for the second phase in Tunis. The Chairman stressed that the Global Forum was intended to contribute to the process of world-wide consultations on Internet governance that the Secretary-General would launch in the coming months. The Global Forum would focus on identifying areas of commonalities in approaches and policies and in trying to build bridges where different opinions existed.

The Secretary-General of the United Nations addressed the Global Forum. He welcomed the organization of the Forum as a timely initiative. The Secretary-General said that Internet governance issues were numerous and complex, but the world had a common interest in ensuring the security and dependability of this new medium. Equally important was the need to develop inclusive and participatory models of governance. The Secretary-General referred to the request by the WSIS to set up a working group on Internet governance and noted that the views emerging from the Global Forum as well as from other deliberations would help identify issues for future consultations. Once these consultations had taken place, he would establish the working group, which would be open, transparent and inclusive of all stakeholders. These same principles of openness and inclusiveness would also apply to the Task Force on Funding that the WSIS had asked to create. This Task Force, which would be set up shortly, would review the adequacy of current funding approaches and consider new funding mechanisms that might strengthen the efforts to bridge the digital divide. The Secretary-General called upon participants to not forget the larger task, notably implementing the WSIS Plan of Action in its entirety. He assured the Global Forum of the United Nations' commitment to this effort. He concluded by urging participants to keep in mind, during their deliberations, the paramount goal of contributing to the cause of human development.

The Vice-President of the Economic and Social Council made brief opening remarks on behalf of the President of ECOSOC. He underscored that the Global Forum provided a unique opportunity to focus attention on the development angle of Internet governance and other ICT policy issues, and on ways for developing countries to harness the power of the Internet.

Dr. Vinton Cerf, one of the founders of the Internet, offered additional thoughts on the term "Internet governance" and the task that the Secretary-General had set before the Working Group on that subject. He emphasized that the very openness of the Internet design had contributed greatly to its evolution as participants in its use, operation and development had been able to contribute fresh ideas for new applications and functionality. He suggested that if there was a need to govern, the focus should be more on the use or abuse of the networks, and less on operation, except where technical rules dictated adherence to standards to assure the stability and integrity of the system. Dr. Cerf stressed that it was apparent that the use of the Internet could contribute to the achievement of the MDGs. Partnerships among the public and the private sector, academia and civil society as well as major players in the Internet space could contribute greatly to the goals of the ICT Task Force and to the charge given to the Working Group on Internet Governance. Dr. Cerf referred to the saying: "If it ain't broke, don't fix it" and "First, do no harm" and cautioned that one should strive not to stifle the innovation and freedom to create that the Internet offered.

Session I: Setting the Stage (Issues and Institutions)

Session I set the stage for the subsequent discussions by updating the meeting on the follow-up to WSIS and providing brief reports on the relevant outcomes of events on Internet governance that had taken place over the past few weeks.

In his opening remarks, the Chair expressed the hope that all sessions of the Global Forum would address issues from the development perspective, bearing in mind the needs of developing countries and ensuring that the benefits of the Internet contributed to the cause of human development.

The Forum then heard a series of brief presentations on the origins of the mandate on Internet governance, and on relevant activities held elsewhere prior to the Global Forum. A summary outline of substantive issues relevant to the topic of the Forum was also presented.

 Switzerland's e-envoy described the range of Internet governance issues as formulated by the Geneva phase of the WSIS and addressed the modalities of the process ahead, in particular regarding a working group on Internet governance. He stressed that all stakeholders and all relevant intergovernmental and other international organizations would have to be given equal access to the work of the group. It should be small but representative, inclusive, open and participatory, which could be achieved through a two- or three- layered approach. Developing countries needed to be given the possibility of making their voice heard. Their full and meaningful participation in this process would be essential. There was also a need for efforts aimed at capacity-building among developing countries, to allow them to defend their interests effectively. It was also stated that the Working Group on Internet Governance would have to deal with concerns that had been expressed during the WSIS preparations. There were two schools of thought: On the one hand there was a school calling for multilateral cooperation under the United Nations framework and on the other, there were those who were content with the status quo. The discussions during the WSIS process so far had focused on a narrow definition of Internet governance, but there might be some merit in starting with a definition as broad as possible and then narrowing it down and focusing on some priority issues. The working group could only be successful if all stakeholders recognized themselves in its final report.

The Honorary Chairman of the International Chamber of Commerce briefed the Forum on the outcome of the ICC special advisory committee meeting in Paris on February 24, 2004 to formulate an input for the Secretary-General's consultations on Internet governance. He summarized the key messages to the Secretary-General's working group from the business community: focus on governance issues today instead of reopening issues previously decided; don't target those areas already addressed by experts; concentrate on problems where all agree concrete action is necessary; and focus on areas where government intervention is necessary, but allow self-regulation a chance to work. He further expressed the ICC's position that the working group should be a steering committee rather than a prescriptive body and that it should focus on identifying gaps in current governance work and suggesting which stakeholders and which bodies be responsible for addressing those gaps using existing organizations consistent with their current mandates.

A representative of the International Telecommunications Union informed the Forum that the report on the ITU workshop in Geneva on February 26-27, 2004 would be finalized shortly. He further stated that ITU was an important element in the "grand collaboration" that was referred to earlier, and that the ITU was keen to see further participation of developing countries.

The President and CEO of ICANN briefly reported on the outcome of ICANN meetings in Rome on March 5-6, 2004. There were numerous subsidiary meetings of various constituencies on the practical problems facing the technical coordination function. He emphasized the fact that ICANN meetings are open to all stakeholders, and that, in order to facilitate participation, they are rotated through five regions and are also available online through video streaming.

The highlights of the on-line forum on Internet governance that took place on the WSIS-on-line platform were presented to the participants. Along four threads of discussion – the different dimensions of Internet governance, the actors, the concerns and the general process – there were several issues that emerged. These included concerns over jurisdiction and scope, in addition to technical and political dimensions. Spam was identified by online discussion participants as one of the most pressing issues and as an ideal test case through which a basis could be laid for addressing other issues. It was agreed that it would be useful to map relevant issues and to identify agencies, experts, panels and groups involved in this work. Approach to

Internet governance should be layered and adaptive as the network itself is. Electronic means for consultations should be used as much as possible to facilitate wide participation.

To help frame the substantive discussion, participants heard an outline of baseline propositions on definitional matters, institutional attributes and key political issues. It was asserted that "governance" is neither inherently good nor bad but rather refers to shared rules, procedures and programs that give rise to expectations and practices, assign roles to participants and shape their interactions. To illustrate, the speaker gave examples of issues and institutions encompassed by the heterogeneous and distributed array of governance that shape Internet infrastructure and the transactions and content it conveys. The problem with the diversity of mechanisms that govern the Internet is that expertise is fragmented among many domains, institutions and organizations, both directly and indirectly related to the medium. The speaker reiterated the approach that governance should first be thought of broadly and that the most important areas for focus should be selected by consensus.

Following the presentations, the meeting engaged in an interactive dialogue. Internet governance was recognized to be a multifaceted concept and that actors had a tendency to look at it differently depending upon their individual vantage points. It was mentioned that even the definition of Internet Governance was subject of debate. Participants underscored that they were ready to support the work of the working group that would be set up by the Secretary-General. There was agreement that the concerns of all stakeholders, including developing countries, should be considered in the WSIS process leading up to Tunis. Frequent reference was made to the importance of using ICT to promote development. Developing country representatives stressed the challenge of investing their scarce funds in Internet infrastructure when they had other immediate needs such as traditional infrastructure and other demands on their national budgets. The legitimacy, rather than the effectiveness, of the existing system of Internet governance was called into question by some speakers from developing countries. It was also suggested that what developing countries needed in this regard, was some kind of a participatory multilateral mechanism to reassure them that their legitimate interests related to the Internet will be reliably protected. The United Nations was mentioned as the body best capable to represent the interests of developing countries.

Several speakers stressed the need for international cooperation to develop globally acceptable solutions on such problems as spam, network security, privacy and information security.

Session II: Stakeholders Baseline: Accumulated concerns, perspectives, and exploring how we can cooperation

Session II was an occasion for the opinions and perspectives of various stakeholder groups in attendance to be presented with a view to identifying areas of agreement and areas for further discussion. The Chair introduced the session by reporting on the outcome of the recent meeting of European Union members and accession countries convened under Ireland's presidency to establish a common position on Internet governance. A vigorous discussion followed, in which many Forum participants presented their varying viewpoints on Internet governance.

Many speakers suggested that the present mechanisms could be improved. It was repeated in several interventions that there was no need to set up a new body to address all Internet governance and related issues under a single umbrella. Rather, existing disparate organizations and regional and national efforts that govern many aspects of the Internet should be drawn together and rationalized, including through capturing and applying best practices. It was noted, too, that Internet governance was inextricably linked to the larger issue of globalization.

Several speakers noted a perceived lack of "legitimacy" of the existing governance environment because of the exclusion of many stakeholders, notably from developing countries, NGOs and civil society. It was suggested that the Regional Nodes and Networks of the United Nations ICT Task Force could be used as effective tools for engaging developing countries in the governance process. Developing country representatives noted that they would require financial support in order to be able to fully and effectively participate in any governance process.

Some speakers believed that NGOs were restricted from participating in some parts of the WSIS process and, more generally, from having an impact on agenda-setting and decision-making on the larger governance discussion. This could be redressed by increasing participation in the governance process and extending "ownership" to developing countries and civil society.

The Internet was characterized several times as a kind of "global public utility" to be enjoyed by all and one that could serve a major role in promoting economic and social development and facilitating the attainment of the Millennium Development Goals. Consequently, it is in the world's interest to apply governance mechanisms that do not stifle its continued development, but rather promote a stable, open and inclusive Internet and ensure its continued growth and technical innovation. UNESCO emphasized the need to safeguard key values such as freedom of expression and openness throughout the Internet governance discussion and to ensure that any modifications to the current system preserve the free flow of knowledge and prevent censorship and government control.

It was observed that as governance issues moved toward transactions and content (away from technical considerations), local standards, laws and values would become more pertinent and that their heterogeneity would complicate the ability to develop and implement a global governance regime. Some interventions asserted that, rather than a global regime, governance should be a bottom-up process, addressing local issues through local action, and conforming to national law.

The business community emphasized its preference for self-regulation. One organization representing the private sector asserted that compliance costs of regulation were bad for business and, consequently, bad for communities, and urged that whatever regulation may be instituted should be seamless and coordinated globally.

Several speakers expressed their support for the work of the ICT Task Force and commended its multi-stakeholder composition. It was noted that, even within stakeholder groups, there were a diverse range of perspectives. Some speakers argued that there was an imbalance in power and influence among those groups. However, it was suggested that overlapping areas of interest between groups could serve as "launch pads" for further work.

Proposals[4]:

- It was suggested that an international root server convention combined with the formation of an intergovernmental committee or council could solve the problem surrounding ccTLDs and the mistrust of ICANN;

- It was proposed to develop a matrix of all issues of Internet governance, including gaps and concerns, which are addressed by various institutions.

Session III: Guiding Principles: A checklist for Internet governance

This session heard interventions suggesting and discussing the merits of principles that could guide the Internet governance debate. The speakers noted the complexity and broad impact of Internet governance mechanisms and therefore advocated a concerted, collaborative effort by all stakeholders. Governance mechanisms must be open and inclusive of representatives from all stakeholder groups, in addition to being transparent and democratically accountable. Content should be culturally and linguistically relevant. Technical standards on languages ought to be rapidly developed.

---

[4] All recommendations and proposals contained in this Summary are reproduced as formulated during the sessions. These proposals were not fully discussed at the Global Forum, nor was consensus necessarily reached. Neither the United Nations ICT Task Force nor the Global Forum have endorsed these recommendations. They are included in the informal Summary to fully reflect the range of opinions presented at the Forum.

Some speakers stressed that governance should be pursued on the principle of subsidiarity, with decisions taken and governance imposed at the lowest possible levels; others suggested that a coherent, global regime was preferable.

Representatives of some of the Internet standard-setting bodies believed that they were actively working to involve different stakeholder groups and representatives of developing countries. However, representatives from civil society and some developing countries raised examples of ways in which they are currently prevented from making an effective contribution, including through meetings conducted only or primarily in English, a lack of domestic funds to cover attendance costs coupled with insufficient external financial support, denial of full access to meetings or voting rights in decision-making processes, and insufficient capacity-building and outreach efforts.

Proposal:

- Verisign proposed to make funding available to improve participation by developing countries in meetings in order to make processes more accessible and transparent to technologists around the world, including through video conferencing or virtual meetings

Break-out Sessions

All break-out groups had a lively and stimulating discussion reflecting different perspectives (governments, international institutions, private sector and civil society)[5]. The sessions helped to deepen the discussions on a wide range of Internet governance issues by benefiting from contributions from a large group of participants. They made concrete recommendations on issues that needed to be further addressed by the United Nations ICT Task Force and by the Working Group on Internet Governance once it is set up by the Secretary-General, and identified areas of complementarity, commonality of interests and perspectives and convergence among stakeholders. All groups looked at the issues relating to Internet governance from a broad development perspective and stressed the important role of ICTs in supporting sustainable development and the MDGs.

Each group acknowledged the complexity of addressing the issues related to the dynamic and still rapidly evolving system. Participants agreed that Internet infrastructure is multi-layered and involves the interests of multiple stakeholders. The challenges associated with applying the sort of equity principles listed in the Forum agenda to diverse global governance mechanisms were

---

[5] Out of fifteen officials (chair, moderator and rapporteur) of the breakout sessions, eight were from developing countries, five from developed countries, and two from international organizations. They represented the civil society and academia (eight), Internet community, the private sector and international organizations (two each) and government (one).

identified. Many participants stressed in particular that the continued growth and functionality of the Internet is dependent on the level of trust and confidence in the system at both the technical and legal levels.

All sessions examined the ability of developing countries to be meaningfully and effectively involved in Internet governance. Issues of representation, participation, transparency, accountability, language and technical barriers to access were identified as major factors limiting their impact. At one group it was suggested that Internet governance should be thought of in terms of "institutional design" in order to be tractable. Awareness, training and capacity-building were seen as vital to improving quantity and quality of developing country participation.

Regarding ICANN's role in governance, at least in one instance, participants in a break-out session could not reconcile their opposite perspectives on that issue. Some asserted that the organization suffers from fundamental problems of legitimacy, accountability and representation of diverse stakeholder interests, while others argued that these issues are exaggerated and that ICANN is making progress in enhancing its responsiveness to the range of stakeholder interests.

The need for balance in governance emerged from each of the sessions. Most participants advocated finding a middle ground between informal, self-regulatory mechanisms and restrictive, hard regulations. It was stressed that balance must also be found amongst the role of government, reliance on technology and individual choice. In the area of intellectual property rights (IPR), a proper balance must be struck between the need to protect IP assets and the danger of limiting access to intellectual goods through strict regulations. The tension between the rights of the individual to privacy and the rights of companies to enforce their property rights was also noted, as well as that between security and civil liberties.

The cross-border dimensions of the Internet were mentioned by many as contributing to the complexity of deliberations, and the issues of jurisdiction and burden of cost on developing countries surfaced within the various sessions. Discussions on jurisdiction recurred many times, having implications on the protection of privacy, speech, human rights and consumers as well as e-commerce, electronic-contracting and intellectual property, all of which transcend borders. It was agreed that this issue required further consideration. Some participants also argued that the business models for Internet connectivity should ensure symmetry in the settlement of revenue and cost flows between developing and developed countries in order to be sustainable. It was noted that technical development has significantly lowered connectivity costs and increased connectivity capabilities and that the digital "real gap" had been reduced.

However, some participants underlined the importance of finding ways to further lower the cost to developing countries.

The issue of access was discussed at some length. One break-out group differentiated between two types: universal access (service) and universal inclusiveness (user access). The role of government in providing service in areas where the private sector has no incentive to provide coverage was discussed. To achieve greater inclusiveness, local language and transcription (speech-to-text) technology needed further attention. The Group on under-addressed issues suggested that linguistic diversity should be approached at both the global and local level, and that solutions should be local and should address technical, financial, content and capacity-building aspects.

Participants referred to e-commerce as a new way of conducting regular commerce and, thus, governance should build on existing mechanisms and structures governing commercial transactions, adapting the legal framework to e-trade and to ensure consumer protection. Some called for a set of best practices and information sharing on combating fraud and protecting customers. Participants argued that strong human rights and consumer protection and personal privacy would contribute to the flourishing of e-commerce. Warnings were voiced against over-regulating or over-legislating, urging global regulation to be used only when strictly necessary. Societies that transact primarily in cash required alternatives to current e-commerce that depends mainly upon credit cards. Taxation of e-commerce was discussed, acknowledging the impact of lost revenue and concern that it may hinder growth.

Participants noted the important roles that UNCTAD and the WTO are playing in capacity-building and education in helping developing countries raise the volume of e-commerce. The importance of the impacts of the pending classification of digital products as goods versus services was highlighted. Model legal instruments are being elaborated by international institutions, including the OECD and UNCITRAL. It was observed that the developed world agenda is driving regulatory development and reform and that it is not a priority in developing countries.

Participants of the Transactions and Content sessions identified a strong need for education surrounding the differences between e-signatures and digital signatures, and noted that governments need to be technology-neutral when implementing these schemes. International norms on such authentication mechanisms would be beneficial and facilitate the roll-out of the technology and remain an important policy issue. It was observed that the impact of e-signature and digital signatures on e-commerce was, so far, inconclusive. There was broad and strong interest expressed in network security in terms of commerce as well as privacy and data integrity. Several speakers emphasized the need to take a proactive approach to assess the vulnerability of the Internet infrastructure and to develop modalities for greater cooperation.

The topic of privacy received substantial attention. Participants noted that different value systems and standards throughout the world currently translate into an uneven level of protection of privacy. Participants suggested that universal standards be developed and implemented through international dialogue, perhaps building on OECD guidelines, the Convention on Civil and Private Rights, and other agreed-upon language that appears in human rights legislation. One participant noted that, rather than discussing only how to defend human rights online, we should view the Internet as a tool for fulfilling human rights, such as the right to freedom of expression, and that we must preserve and further utilize its ability to do so.

Divergent viewpoints on intellectual property rights were expressed within some of the break-out sessions. A key debate centered on whether or not the governments should be relied upon to provide protection of privacy, or whether technology was a more reliable source of protection. Regardless, there was a broad agreement that the current IPR regime needed reform. It was noted that no action on IPR was expected from the WSIS Declaration of Principles, though the Plan of Action does refer to multiple software development business models and recognizes that copyright protection is independent of any model.

One break-out group linked freedom of speech and basic human rights to the promotion of enterprise and economic growth, explaining that a competitive marketplace cannot exist without the free flow of information, that strong data and privacy protection promotes confidence in e-commerce. Strict IP regimes, it was argued, could restrict creativity and innovation and stifle free speech. New models are emerging which could be supported by governments, such as the "creative commons", open content, free and open source software, and the open publication of research. Government's role to step in when user and consumer protection and human rights protection measures break-down was noted, although it was emphasized that consumers should retain their freedom of choice. Caution against legislating in a patchwork style was expressed. Participants recognized the various alternative dispute resolution initiatives that have been developed and stated the need to raise awareness of these initiatives and to support them.

Spam was identified as the scourge of the Internet. Sixty percent of email traffic is spam, which significantly interferes with the Internet capacity of developing countries. Spam was identified as a "legal, moral and societal issue" that calls for both a technical and government solution and as a "culturally-invasive" phenomenon that "eats away our infrastructure." It was agreed that this problem requires urgent, coordinated action and international cooperation.

Groups cautioned against "reinventing the wheel" and duplicating the functions of existing agencies and standards bodies in developing a coherent Internet governance regime. It was reiterated that the "best governance is the governance that governs least". Participants in one group asserted that user/consumer needs/demands should drive policy-making and that nation states are not necessarily the most appropriate actors in the context of the Internet. Some argued for global solutions, some preferred experimentation at national levels, while others advocated applying the principle of subsidiarity. Most agreed on the desirability of building on existing arrangements and institutions. Groups agreed that broader participation is needed, along with more research, awareness and capacity building. Work was suggested to take place at a regional level and for institutional design to be examined to identify the make-up of who current participants. Break-out sessions identified areas where international collaboration could add value such as controlling spam and ensuring security.

Some participants noted a need for an international forum in which developing countries can discuss issues on their national development of the Internet. It was suggested that the United Nations may be able to provide a "home" to issues which do not already have obvious forums.

During the break-out sessions, participants came out with a number of proposals and recommendations addressed to the United Nations ICT Task Force:

On Internet Infrastructure

- Clarify the concerns of developing countries and continue to address the challenge of internationalization, including promoting and supporting inclusive participation;
- Facilitate human resource capacity building, particularly in technical disciplines;
- Undertake education and awareness-raising programs in issues relating to Internet development;
- Explore ways to facilitate dialogue and consideration on network security, paying particular attention to:

    o Raising awareness;
    o Sharing information about and among existing initiatives;
    o Assisting developing countries in assessing their vulnerabilities and taking necessary responses;

- Play a role in improving procedural aspects of collective management issues in Internet governance by fostering dialogue and promoting information sharing. As an example, a study and dialogue were proposed on how people participate in the existing organizations dealing with Internet issues and how participation in these organizations can be improved in terms of transparency, accountability, and participation of "non-dominant stakeholders" (developing countries, CSOs).

On Transactions and Content

- Serve as a participatory forum for the exchange of information and learning in the area of Internet governance and development in which developing countries can discuss and interact as they begin to engage with the digital economy and the information society and where they can receive help with laws, regulations, best practices, etc;
- Monitor and report on right of access to content and on freedom of speech;
- Support the development of local content in native languages and encourage speech-to-text initiatives;
- Create awareness and education about digital signatures and electronic signatures;
- Provide awareness and education about the UNCITRAL process and work on e-contracting;
- Support trade in digital goods and services through education and awareness-raising of the benefits of liberalization;
- Raise awareness of the need for more law enforcement to combat fraud and develop an assembly of best practices in consumer protection;
- Raise awareness of and support initiatives on alternative dispute resolution.

Some recommendations were directed to other actors:

- The ITU should address interconnection agreements in a more open, multi-stakeholder forward-looking manner;
- Deployment of IPv6 should be fostered;
- ICANN should continue its reform efforts to increase representation of all stakeholders, enhance its neutrality and accountability;
- Experts within the WTO should continue their important work in regard to trade in digital goods and services;
- Countries are urged to update laws so that there is equivalent consumer protection in the on-line world as in the off-line world;
- UNCTAD and WTO could play an important role in helping in capacity building and education in developing countries to raise the level of their involvement in e-commerce.

There were also some general recommendations on how the Internet governance debate should be structured:

- Avoid duplication of actions and do not "reinvent the wheel" when addressing Internet governance issues;
- Engage in further consultation and consideration regarding network security;
- Promote broad participation in the ongoing discussion, particularly of developing countries;
- Promote more research and research networks;
- Increase capacity-building efforts;

- Promote working at the regional level;

- Examine institutional design (e.g., who participates, etc.);

- Create a set of "filters" to consider whether global governance is needed and then examine whether these issues are not being dealt with by others;

- Help to overcome the language barrier by addressing technical, financial, content and capacity-building aspects at both the global and local levels;

- Promote investment in Internet infrastructure in order to expand Internet service and access;

- Encourage symmetry in the settlement of revenue and cost flows between developing and developed countries in the context of Internet connectivity infrastructure;

- Focus on finding solution for the issue of spam.

March 26, 2004

Session IV: The Way Ahead
The session consolidated the discussions about the follow-up to WSIS and Internet governance that had taken place in the previous sessions and the break-out meetings, identified issues on which there appeared to be a consensus, as well as those that required further dialogue, and attempted to make recommendations for actions.

Representatives of the two host WSIS host countries spoke on the follow-up of the Geneva phase and the preparation for Tunis. The representative of the Swiss Government addressed the meeting on "The Way to Tunis: From first to second phase". He called on all participants to work intensively to prepare for Tunis, where the focus will be on the implementation of the WSIS Plan of Action. He stressed that the private sector has a key role in this undertaking and expressed his hope that business will play a more active part in the second phase. Suggesting that financial assistance to bring countries online was necessary before the governance discussion became relevant to them, the speaker named activities being undertaken to address the issue of funding that had also emerged unresolved from the Summit in Geneva. On Internet governance, he advised that its definition should be neither too restrictive nor too wide and warned that, except for some common underlying principles, it may vary from region to region. He also cautioned against trying to govern or regulate what already works or what cannot be governed or regulated, but rather urged actors to focus on those public policy issues in which it makes the most sense to intervene, such as spam. He concluded by stating his intention to support Tunisia throughout the second phase of the WSIS.

A representative of Tunisia reaffirmed her country's full engagement in the WSIS process and its efforts to help build a people-centered, development-oriented information society. She described some of the actions the Tunisian government has undertaken in the preparation process and announced that a date has been set at the end of June for the first PrepCom. She emphasized that the second WSIS phase will be characterized by a holistic nature, complementarity with the first phase, and inclusiveness. The focus will be on implementing the Geneva Plan of Action, with the intention of increasing the awareness of relevant actors and expanding their contributions to the effort. Two documents are expected to be adopted: a political text and an operational one, consisting of inter-regional action plans naming concrete actions to help bridge the digital divide and to put ICTs at the service of development. Anticipating the conclusions that the Secretary-General's Working Group on Internet Governance will submit, the speaker stated the intention of the Tunis meeting to facilitate defining its scope, identifying relevant issues and building a common understanding of the roles of the various actors. She expressed her hope that consensus on the topic might emerge at Tunis and urged all stakeholders to participate at the highest possible level, especially the media and civil society. She acknowledged that specific measures to help civil society representatives from developing countries participate may have to be devised.

The Moderators from the previous days' break-out sessions then presented their summary reports. Following the statements, the Chairman reiterated that this meeting was not a negotiating forum and that it was not intended to produce a formal definition or formulation by its conclusion.

From the reports, the Chair observed a general support of negotiations that are on-going within the specialized organizations and approval of ICANN's move to greater inclusion. There was a desire to avoid "reinventing the wheel" and to build on existing structures. Spam was identified as a "quick win", an opportunity to be a test case for cooperation among stakeholders. Capacity building on technical and policy issues, as well as logistical assistance, were necessary to ensure effective participation and to empower actors to take an active part in the dialogue. A challenge remains to find a system that improves transparency and legitimacy while preserving the creativity and entrepreneurship that has allowed the Internet to take its current form. The Chairman affirmed that the United Nations ICT Task Force has a role in facilitating dialogue on the governance issue and that recommendations on Task Force activities developed from the break-out sessions would be presented at its Sixth Meeting on Saturday, March 27. He also noted that the written report on Forum's conclusions would be submitted to the Secretary-General as input for his Working Group on Internet Governance.

During the lively and productive discussion that followed the Chairman's reflections, there was general recognition of progress made on the complex issue of Internet governance. It was affirmed that the Forum was useful, particularly in achieving a level of understanding of what was meant by "governance" greater than that which prevailed at the end of the first phase of WSIS. It was generally agreed that governance is broader than the technical administration of the DNS and IP addresses, although the discussion will continue to determine the precise boundaries. A practical, pragmatic approach to addressing governance issues was recommended. There was overwhelming agreement to support the Secretary-General's working group on the subject.

One delegate urged that the Secretary-General's working group start where Geneva ended and not reopen issues that have been concluded. Another speaker reminded the meeting that some issues raised at the Forum, including multilingualism, were part of the agreed Plan of Action from the Geneva phase of WSIS and that the scope of the group's deliberation should remain focused only on governance issues.

One of the challenges identified during the debate was how to assure inclusiveness amidst the multiplicity of stakeholders. Speakers underscored the need to widen the multi-stakeholder nature of the process including through increasing dialogue among all key actors. Money and distance must not be a barrier to participation, and suggestions were made that the Internet itself should be used more vigorously as a means by which to engage developing countries and other stakeholder groups with limited resources.

There was also agreement that the Internet should be multilingual in order to achieve wider participation. A representative from the Multilingual Internet Names Consortium (MINC) informed the meeting of the work his organization has undertaken in order to make this technically possible and asserted that it may be realized sooner than commonly thought. Multilingualism must also be incorporated into the forums and meetings on governance, and steps must be taken to promote presentations and contributions in a wider range of languages.

It was noted that additional concrete steps and increasing commitments were needed to ensure the equal participation of developing countries. Special efforts were needed through capacity building and education to level out the playing field. The Least Developed Countries and countries emerging from conflict required special attention in this regard. Technical developments needed to be shared with developing countries. Illustrating action being taken to address this need, a representative from the Inter-American Development Bank brought to the attention of participants a technical cooperation project for the Latin American and Caribbean region undertaken in collaboration with UNDESA, ICA and OED for the organization and implementation of a series of sub-regional and regional meetings to strengthen the region's planning and decision-making capability in the area of ICT for development and e-governance.

Some participants expressed concern over the effect of brain drain, Internet engineers leaving developing countries for more lucrative opportunities. Another issue remaining to be addressed was how Internet governance, or the lack of it, constrains ICT for development. The peaceful use of technology needed also to be ensured.

Some speakers cautioned against radical change in Internet governance as this could have a potentially destabilizing effect. They believed that change be permitted to evolve rather than utilizing a "big bang" approach. The ingenuity of the Internet stemmed from the fact that simultaneously "no one and everyone" were in charge and that it has grown quickly because it has not required governance. The Internet had been built around simple standards using a bottom-up approach, with individual choice guiding its evolution. What was needed, said several speakers, was a governance system in the hands of individual users that minimized the need for governance.

Proposals advanced during the discussion:

- The United Nations ICT Task Force should contribute to efforts to identify the best organization(s) to deal with each of the issues that are related to Internet governance, to catalogue existing sources of excellence, as well as to collect and disseminate knowledge and identify best practices and existing gaps, to assign roles to the various stakeholders, and mobilize resources to ensure as wide a participation as possible;

- The ICT Task Force should compile and make available a compendium of meetings and events on Internet governance issues;

- The ICT Task Force should produce a "road map" which should attempt to identify future developments as well as the expected time span for such developments;

- The Secretariat that will be created to support the Secretary-General's Working Group on Internet Governance could be a clearing house for all related Internet governance conferences, activities, researches and best practices. This information could be available to all through a virtual, online library. All institutions and organizations acting in the field could be urged to link to it, producing a decentralized and ongoing effort to bring together knowledge on the subject;

- Two concrete outcomes to emerge from the Secretary-General's Working Group on Internet Governance ought to be: 1) a consolidated international regime, principles and values that would guarantee openness and a presence for developing countries on the Internet; and 2) an explicit institutional arrangement that would guarantee that ccTLDs will not be removed from root zone files without authorization from the affected country;

- Governments should establish scholarship funds to facilitate the participation of developing country representatives in the meetings of the Internet Engineering Task Force;

- Future meetings and summits should use several working languages as a way to facilitate the involvement of under-represented stakeholders from non-English-speaking parts of the world.

Closing Session

Mr. Robert E. Kahn, President & CEO, Corporation for National Research Initiatives CNRI, delivered a closing address. He congratulated the participants of the Global Forum for achieving a remarkable level of consensus.

He recalled the roles researchers had played in developing the Internet. The way in which the standards and the social structures that supported those standards were developed – through the contributions of a number of different bodies and many individuals and organizations that fueled a bottom-up, grass-roots process of coming to consensus within the technical community – was very different from the way standards are developed by other standards bodies.

As the Internet has matured and reliance on it for all kinds of activities has expanded, prudence and caution dictated a more deliberate approach for the future. The speaker referred to the long time it has taken to deploy IPv6 as an example of the caution that now pervades the Internet landscape. He noted a lack of researchers at the Global Forum and expressed his belief that it was time for the research community to resume a central presence on the Internet stage, but that it would be shared with many others, for there are some issues that cannot be solved by the technical community alone, and others for which the choice of technology is not really relevant. In this regard, he stressed the importance of coordination with the international community in dealing with matters like cyber-terrorism and suggested that this is an area where the convening power of the ICT Task Force may be particularly helpful.

He described the public policy challenges the world will face in making substantive change to the Internet in the future and stated that there are no clear answers at this time. The Internet has many of the attributes of the evolution of society itself and, like society, the Internet will need to evolve along many different dimensions. He stated his hope that it becomes accessible to all citizens of the world.

Mr. Kahn proposed that:

- The research and technical community regains a central role in shaping the further evolution of the Internet in recognition of the importance of innovation and technological development to its future growth; and

- The convening power of the United Nations ICT Task Force may be helpful in broadly coordinating the international community to deal with transnational threats such as cyber-terrorism.

The Deputy Secretary-General of the United Nations delivered a closing statement on behalf of the United Nations. She congratulated the Forum on accomplishing its goals and moving the discussion on Internet governance in a positive direction. She listed a number of issues where a need for international cooperation to develop globally acceptable solutions was deemed necessary and recalled several conclusions that the meeting had reached in regards to basic principles that should underlie the governance discussion. She welcomed the call to develop a matrix of all issues of Internet governance addressed by multilateral institutions and stated that this would be helpful to the Secretary-General in advancing the agenda on these issues. She also thanked the Forum for its readiness to support the work of both the Working Group on Internet Governance and the Task Force on Funding that will be set up by the Secretary-General. She announced that a secretariat to support the Secretary-General's working group is being established and that on March 25, 2004 Mr. Kummer was appointed its head.

The Chairman of the United Nations ICT Task Force stated that the Forum's recommendations would be taken up by the United Nations ICT Task Force. He recalled some key points made throughout the meeting, including the distinction between "government" and "governance", the challenge of being inclusive, and the imperative of addressing the developmental aspects of the issue. He concluded that there is a need for a new social construct, a new type of governance, namely that of "global polity", and that this task necessitated better coordination between institutions. Geopolitical, economic and environmental issues needed to be tackled through a multi-stakeholder dialogue.

INITIAL RESULTS OF THE ONLINE FORUM ON INTERNET GOVERNANCE
Bertrand de La Chapelle, wsis-online.net

Wsis-online.net is the community platform serving all actors implementing the WSIS Action Plan. During the months of February and March 2004, at the solicitation of the United Nations Department of Economic and Social Affairs (DESA) and the United Nations ICT Task Force, wsis-online hosted an Online Forum on Internet Governance in the perspective of the Global Forum organized on March 25, 2004.

The objective of this open and inclusive consultation process was to allow all interested stakeholders to post and make visible views on this issue and to feed an iterative process in view of the creation of the United Nations Secretary-General Working Group decided at the Geneva Summit.

The consultation was organized around four threads:

- the various dimensions of Internet governance
- what are the concerned stakeholders for each of them?
- what are the concerns for each issue?
- contributions on how the future WG should be organized

More than 80 contributions were submitted in about 5 weeks. Beyond their diversity, they mostly addressed three elements:

- the nature of Internet governance and in particular the relations between Internet governance and the Internet architecture;
- the need to map the various issues to address and those who already address them;
- suggestions for the United Nations Secretary-General Working Group consultation process itself.

The present summary report outlines the main comments, without specific attribution.

I – ON INTERNET GOVERNANCE
Is Internet Governance a technical or political issue?

Both dimensions are considered interrelated and it is important to identify the respective impacts of decisions from one sphere on the other. Comments like: "politicians should not be allowed to make decisions with technological consequences without consulting the techies" and "the technical may immediately follow once there is an agreement on the political" (for example for spam) illustrate this challenge.

Still, the interrelationship between political and technical aspects does not mean there cannot be a distinction between the two dimensions but rather demands to map where they interact.

How much governance is needed?

At this preliminary stage, participants in the consultation wanted less to provide definitive answers than to outline the main questions facing the international community.

One comment asked: "How little governance can we get away with in the next 25 years?" And another recalled that: "The Internet was the most unmanaged project on content and the most disciplined one in technological infrastructure."

A widespread desire seems to be to find a balance between a light approach to regulation and the need for some sort of rules:

- "As little governance as possible"*BUT* "Need for rules more uniform and efficient across national boundaries"
- "Effective efficient management needs means to define rules and control responses"

In particular, it was mentioned that "countries are not required to manage their networks in the same way but any impact on the overall operation and usage of the global network does require cooperation and interaction between countries and national bodies". This distinction introduces a notion of responsibility of individual actors, including governments, for the impact they may have on the global network.

A broader question is whether there should be "worldwide rules or softer regimes of cooperation and coordination", knowing the answer may vary depending on the issue.

Inspiration from the Internet architecture itself

Beyond content, comments also addressed the methodological dimension, outlining the inspiration Internet governance could take from the Internet architecture itself. In substance, the question is: can the governance of the network work like the network itself? The main ideas were:

- the architecture of the Internet being layered – its governance should probably be as well;
- there is a need to "extend the spirit of cooperation on which the Internet was founded to all bodies now involved in it";
- Internet issues should be addressed using the tools the Internet provides, with actors "meeting electronically and through video-conference", as Internet-related bodies have always done.

Last but not least, the Internet Protocol was able to withstand time because of its flexibility. Similarly, Internet governance should not only allow us to address present issues but also those that may emerge in the future.

II – ON RELEVANT POLICY ISSUES

Broad or narrow definition of Internet governance

Many comments relate to the question of whether there should be a narrow or broad understanding of the expression "Internet governance":

- the Internet (underlying framework for electronic communications) or the applicable layers (such as the World Wide Web)?
- a narrow definition (for instance the domain name system and ICANN) allows focus, but the United Nations Secretary-General Working Group mandate seems to imply a broader approach (as indicated by the expression "policy issues").

Tentative distinctions were also suggested:

- governance OF the Internet (narrow) vs. governance ON the Internet (broader);
- running the Internet vs. the impact of the Internet on society (legal, social, economic);

- ICT governance in general (including broadcast regulation for instance);
- Information Society governance.

Some comments insist the best way to define Internet governance is actually to identify the most pressing issues first ("how do you eat an elephant? One bite at a time") and create a sort of taxonomy or mapping.

It is also suggested to start with one specific issue that could serve as a template for addressing others. Spam in particular is considered as an emblematic "global nuisance", typically meshing multiple dimensions, both technical and legal, and requiring coordinated action between a wide diversity of players. For some, solving this immediate problem could "lay the basis for other governance issues".

Mapping the relevant issues

Several comments related to the diversity of issues to address and listed the most urgent. In most cases, actors do not agree on how the issue should be addressed or what solution should be provided. But they may agree at least that it should be put on the agenda as an issue of common concern or interest. Many of them are indeed mentioned in the WSIS Plan of Action. The most frequently mentioned issues are related to the following themes:

Infrastructure:	Technology related issues (hardware, software, standards, protocols) and Security (servers and messages)
Resource management:	the Domain Names system in general, the role of ICANN and its relationship to the US government, the role and content of the "distribution master", regional root servers, the digital divide on address allocation (equitable allocation of IP addresses, IPv6), internationalized domain names, the management of ccTLDs and sovereignty; a "root server convention was suggested"
Financial:	taxation (of Internet traffic, of e-commerce), cost of connectivity – particularly in developing countries, Internet exchange centres, peering/interconnection costs
Content-related issues:	cybercrime, pornography, legality of electronic messages, activity of information providers (respecting information users), intellectual property rights (and effective dissemination of knowledge), protection of privacy

More original issues were raised, like statistical data unification and gathering, or the connection of Internet governance with sustainable development (for instance environmental governance like disposal of electronic waste).

Mapping who already does what

Internet governance is not starting from a white page. There is "already governance on parts of what we call the Internet (for instance the underlying telephone infrastructure in part, some content …)".

Therefore, a "mapping exercise" is needed to allow identification of the numerous existing working groups, experts, panels, agencies, programmes… on the respective issues. "At least a central body on what rules and processes are already in place and how individuals, organizations and governments may interact within those rules and processes is required."

It could be one of the first tasks of the future United Nations Secretary-General Working Group to identify the existing regimes for the various issues.

III – ON THE UNITED NATIONS SECRETARY-GENERAL WORKING GROUP ITSELF

Finally, some comments addressed the future methodology of the United Nations Secretary-General Working Group, around three aspects:

The need for a clear methodological framework for this process:

- "Clearly defined goals and outcomes for the United Nations Secretary-General Working Group"
- "Process has to be very much structured, with clear objectives, procedures and time frames"
- "The wider the consultation process, the more management it seems to require"
- Subsidiarity/Transparency/Participatory processes/Accountability

The diversity of actors that have to be involved

Gender and regional balance (geopolitical diversity) was mentioned as well as diversity of personal and cultural background, and age: "young business people as well as young hackers".

As for civil society, a question is how to represent not only existing users but also those who do not use the Internet yet, but should not be excluded.

Last but not least, the development dimension should be brought into the picture, and some even suggested it should become a fourth item in the United Nations Secretary-General

Working Group mandate. Participation of developing countries and particularly of their civil society actors appears as a major challenge. In a completely different tone, the question was raised whether Internet governance (and the WSIS process in general) should really be the main priority for developing countries, in light of the numerous challenges they are already facing.

The methodology of the Working Group itself

Should the United Nations Secretary-General Working Group be a formal group composed by all stakeholders working on a report or (and?) an informal process collecting ideas through expert meetings and online consultations? A comment explicitly mentioned the objective of "creating a consortium and not another panel of stand-alone experts".

Drawing lessons from various existing Internet bodies, some suggested in this perspective an interactive and iterative process of successive input gathering, drafting, consultation, draft refining and final endorsement, combining a broad consultation base and a more limited drafting group.

CONCLUSION

The first conclusion of this exercise was the willingness of actors to engage in it, even in such a limited time frame, and the interest of online tools for setting up the "open and inclusive process" mentioned by the WSIS Plan of Action.

Other clear results can be summarized as follows:

- a preference towards a broad understanding of the notion of Internet governance, rather than a narrow one, limited to the Domain Name System;

- the utility of first listing the different issues at stake and mapping the corresponding activities of existing relevant actors, rather than trying to start with an abstract definition exercise of this complex notion;

- the need for the United Nations Secretary-General Working Group to conduct an iterative consultation process rather than limiting itself to being a close expert body.

PREPARATIONS FOR THE TUNIS PHASE OF WSIS

Faryel Mouria-Beji, Tunisian Internet Agency and ENSI-University of Tunis

The short period that will lead us to the Tunis phase of the World Summit on the Information Society, which will be held from November 16 to 18, 2005, will indeed be full of challenges. I believe that all concerned parties and stakeholders must exert all efforts to meet these challenges, and to make sure that the people-centred, inclusive and development-oriented information society, as stated in the Declaration of Principles and Plan of Action adopted in Geneva, is moving along the desired path.

The Tunisian Government has been actively preparing to host this important event. Tunisia established a national organizing committee composed of all stakeholders and parties concerned (Ministries, national organizations, civil society, private companies, etc.). Another committee has been set up that will focus on the logistical aspects.

Special Cabinet meetings, some of them chaired at the highest level, are being held on a regular basis. These meetings focus on the organizational aspects of this international event and the different stages of preparation. A special web site devoted to the WSIS has been set up by the Tunisian Government and is now accessible in the French, English and Arabic languages. Furthermore, numerous consultations are taking place on a regular basis between Tunisian ministers and high-level officials with the United Nations, the International Telecommunication Union (ITU), the Swiss Government as the host of the first phase, as well as with other Governments.

Tentative dates for holding the first Prepcom for the Tunis phase have been set, and two meetings of the Prepcom are expected. In addition, regional conferences are expected to be held as well as thematic meetings. I insist on the word "expected", since consultations continue in this regard.

At the initiative of the Government of Tunisia and the ITU, an informal preparatory meeting was held in Tunis from March 2 to 3, 2004. It was a meeting which in a way launched the preparatory process of the Tunis phase.

Members of the Bureau of the Prepcom, which is under the chairmanship of Mr. Samassekou from Mali, the International Bureau for Civil Society, the International Chamber of Commerce, and other stakeholders took part in this brainstorming meeting, which focused on the implementation of the Geneva outcome and its follow-up, and discussed the preparations of the Tunis phase, including its structure, outcome, and the nature of the documents to be adopted.

During this brainstorming session, participants reiterated some basic principles regarding how to approach the second phase of the Summit, namely:

- the holistic character of the Summit and its framework;
- the interaction, complementarity and synergy between its two phases;
- its inclusive character associating all stakeholders (Governments, international organizations, civil society and the private sector).

Implementation of Geneva Plan of Action

Participants exchanged views on ways and means to implement the Plan of Action adopted at the Geneva phase of WSIS. Important questions were raised and can be summarized as follows:

- "Who will implement what" in the areas identified in the Plan of Action, and how do we get that information?
- How to increase awareness of all actors and urge them to get involved in this new phase?
- The implementation of the Plan of Action will extend beyond Tunis (at least up to 2015); what is the role of the Tunis phase in this regard?

Participants examined the different components of the implementation of the Plan of Action:

- the implementation process itself;

- documentation for the process;
- follow-up and coordination;
- review and appraisal of the results achieved with the definition of possible indicators (to measure the commitment of all stakeholders).

Discussions also focused on the Summit Declaration of Principles. Participants raised questions pertaining to:

- the operational elements of this Declaration and how to deal with them;
- the linkages between the thematic and regional approaches in the implementation process;
- availability and mobilisation of the means of implementation, particularly those related to the financial resources;
- complementarity between international, regional and national components.

Expected Outcome of the Second Phase of WSIS

As far as the outcome of the Tunis phase is concerned, the dominant view was that the Tunis summit should adopt two documents: a political document, the nature of which had yet to be agreed upon; and an operational document in the form of an agenda encompassing, *inter alia*, regional action plans.

Participants emphasized that the Tunis phase should come up with concrete initiatives at all levels to bridge the digital divide and to place information and communications technologies (ICT) at the service of development. In this vein, "partnerships for solidarity and sustainable development" was suggested as a possible general theme for the Tunis phase.

Participants also highlighted the need to promote complementarity between the regional and the thematic dimensions. The concept of digital solidarity was reaffirmed along with other aspects such as technology transfer, financing, adequate resources, and capacity building, all of which are of course essential to bridge the digital divide.

The scope of the Tunis phase and the *modus operandi* for the period 2005-2015 was also debated, as well as the interlinkages with the objectives of the Millennium Declaration and other fundamental issues in the international arena.

Of course, in addition to the expected recommendations of the upcoming meetings of the Prepcom, the Tunis phase will have on its agenda the reports of the working groups on

Internet governance and on the proposed digital solidarity fund, to be set up by the Secretary-General of the United Nations.

ICT constitutes a primary national priority and an important tool to achieve economic and social development in most developing countries. The holding of the second phase of the World Summit on the Information Society in Tunisia, a developing country taking a leading role in this field, adds to the importance and the significance of the event.

We look forward to working with all concerned parties to meet the challenges ahead, particularly the challenge of ensuring that the determination and commitment of the international community to shape an information society accessible to all are translated into concrete actions.

As the host country, Tunisia is fully committed at the highest level to ensuring the success of the second phase of WSIS. It will play a key role in the process in close cooperation with the United Nations and the International Telecommunication Union. We will endeavour during the process leading to Tunis to put our experience and all our efforts at the disposal of all stakeholders, in order to help iron out any difficulties and achieve consensus. We count on all countries to participate actively in the preparatory process and in the Summit itself. We would like also to recall Resolutions 56/183 and 57/238 of the General Assembly which, *inter alia*, called on all States to contribute to the trust fund established by ITU to support the preparations for and the holding of the Summit. Financing will indeed be one of the challenges the international community will have to face in this regard.

Finally, I wish to reiterate the importance given by the Government of Tunisia to the constructive participation of all components of the international community, including civil society and the media, in accordance with the established procedures. Special measures to help civil society from developing countries participate actively in the preparatory process leading to the second phase in Tunis and in the Summit itself may have to be devised. We hope that all stakeholders, governmental and non-governmental, will be represented at the highest level possible. We are also looking forward to seeing a stronger presence of the private sector in Tunis.

The Tunisian Mission remains ready for any further exchange of views with all delegations and with the Secretariat of the United Nations during the period leading to Tunis.

ANNEXES

ABOUT THE CONTRIBUTORS

Karl Auerbach is Chief Technology Officer at InterWorking Labs in Scotts Valley, California. He was formerly a senior researcher in the Advanced Internet Architecture group in the Office of the Chief Strategy Officer at Cisco Systems, and he has also been a member of the Board of Directors of ICANN. In addition to his technical work, Mr. Auerbach has been an attorney in California since 1978. He is a member of the Intellectual Property Section of the California State Bar and he has been named as a Yuen Fellow of Law and Technology at the California Institute of Technology and Loyola Law School of Los Angeles. Mr. Auerbach has been working on Internet technology since the early 1970s. He has been a long-time member of the Internet Engineering Task Force (IETF). He founded both Epilogue Technology Corporation and Empirical Tools and Technologies, Inc., and he has been closely involved with several other startups.

Carlos A. Afonso is co-founder of the Brazilian Institute of Social and Economic Analyses (Ibase) and the Association for Progressive Communications (APC). From 1995 to 1997, and during 2003-2004, Mr. Afonso was a member of the Steering Committee of the Brazilian Internet. Since 1998 he has been Planning and Strategy Director of the Information Network for the Third Sector (Rits), Rio de Janeiro, Brazil, and currently he is also the Secretary of the board of Ibase and board member of the Brazilian Interdisciplinary AIDS Association (Abia). He is GNSO council member in representation of ICANN's Non Commercial Users Constituency (NCUC) and is also serving as NGO representative in the interim Board of CGIbr. He has been working as an international consultant for several international organizations on ICT and human development. Mr. Afonso holds a Masters degree in Economics, York University, Toronto, with doctoral studies in Social and Political Thought at the same university.

Zoë Baird is President of the Markle Foundation. Ms. Baird's career spans business, government, and academia. She previously served as a Senior Vice President and General Counsel of Aetna, Inc.; a senior visiting scholar at Yale Law School; counselor and staff executive at General Electric; and a partner in the law firm of O'Melveny & Myers. She also served in the administrations of Presidents Carter and Clinton, and is currently a member of the Technology & Privacy Advisory Committee, which advises regarding the Defense Department's use of technology to fight terrorism.

Jim Bound works at Hewlett Packard Corporation as HP Fellow and is a Network Technical Director within the Enterprise UNIX (HP-UX) Division's Network and Security Lab Engineering Group. Mr. Bound was a member of the Internet Protocol Next Generation (IPng) Directorate within the Internet Engineering Task Force (IETF). He has been a key designer and implementer of IPv6, and contributor and co-author of IPv6 specifications. Mr. Bound is the founder, CTO and member of the Board of Directors of the IPv6 Forum, and he is also the Chair of the North American IPv6 Task Force. Mr. Bound is a pioneer member of the Internet Society, and member of the Institute of Electrical and Electronics Engineers (IEEE). He has been working in the field of networking as engineer and architect since 1978, and is a subject matter expert for IPv6 and network-centric technology to government and industry.

Vinton G. Cerf is Senior Vice President of Technology Strategy and was previously Senior Vice President of Architecture and Technology for MCI. Widely known as one of the "Fathers of the Internet," Mr. Cerf is the co-designer of the TCP/IP protocols and the architecture of the Internet. Prior to rejoining MCI in 1994, he was Vice President of the Corporation for National Research Initiatives (CNRI). As Vice President of MCI Digital Information Services from 1982-1986, he led the engineering of the first commercial email service to be connected to the Internet. During his tenure from 1976-1982 with the United States Department of Defense's Advanced Research Projects Agency (DARPA), Mr. Cerf played a key role leading the development of Internet and Internet-related data packet and security technologies. Mr. Cerf serves as Chairman of the Board of ICANN; is Honorary Chairman of the IPv6 Forum; and serves on several national, state and industry committees focused on cyber-security. He has served as founding President of the Internet Society from 1992-1995, and in 1999 he served a term as Chairman of the Board. In addition, Mr. Cerf sits on the Board of Directors and is a fellow for several corporations and institutions. He is a recipient of numerous awards and commendations in connection with his work on the Internet. Mr. Cerf holds a Bachelors of Science degree in Mathematics from Stanford University and Masters of Science and Ph.D. degrees in Computer Science from UCLA.

Kenneth Neil Cukier is a writer for *The Economist* specializing in technology and public policy issues. From 2002 to 2004, he was a Research Fellow at the National Center for Digital Government at Harvard University's Kennedy School of Government, where he worked on a book about the history of Internet governance. Mr. Cukier has also held posts as the Technology Editor of the *Asian Wall Street Journal* in Hong Kong; a commentator for CNBC Asia; and the European Editor in London of *Red Herring* magazine. From 1992 to 1996 he worked at the *International Herald Tribune* in Paris. His work has also appeared in *The New York Times*, *The Washington Post* and *The Financial Times*, among others. He has served as a commentator on technology matters for CBS, CNN, NPR and the BBC.

Pierre Dandjinou is currently Regional Policy Advisor at ICT for Development, SURF, West Africa. Previously Mr. Dandjinou served as Director of Infocom Services, a consultancy firm operating from Cotonou, Benin and Libreville, Gabon. As a Programme Officer for the United

Nations Development Programme (1997-2000) Mr. Dandjinou coordinated the Africa node of the Sustainable Development Networking Programme (SDNP). He is involved with many IT-related initiatives on the continent, and is a member of various Advisory Committees including AfriNIC, the African nascent Internet registry; the At-Large Study Committee (ALSC) of ICANN; and the Global Internet Policy Initiative (GIPI). He also currently chairs the Research and Outreach Committee of the Advisory Committee of the PIR, the .Org Registry.

Bertrand de La Chapelle, an entrepreneur and a diplomat, is a co-animator of the OpenWSIS Initiative since its founding in December 2002. A former advisor to the French Minister for European Affairs, co-founder of Virtools and former member of the G8 DOT Force, he devoted two years in 2001-2002 to the study of multi-stakeholder mechanisms for global governance. Mr. de La Chapelle is a graduate of Ecole Polytechnique (1981), Institut d'Etudes Politiques de Paris (1983) and an alumni of Ecole Nationale d'Administration (1986).

William J. Drake is Senior Associate at the International Centre for Trade and Sustainable Development and President of Computer Professionals for Social Responsibility (CPSR). He is also a research associate of the Institute for Tele-Information at Columbia University and a member of the Social Science Research Council Network on IT Governance and Civil Society. Mr. Drake has been affiliated with many other universities, societies and research institutes and has authored several publications. He is a member of the editorial boards of the journals *Telecommunications Policy* and *Info*. He received his M.A., M.Phil, and Ph.D. in Political Science from Columbia University, New York.

Raúl Echeberría is Computer and Telecommunication Advisor at Uruguay's National Institute of Agricultural Research and E-commerce consultant to Portal@gro.com, which is implementing the first electronic cattle market in Latin America. In addition, Mr. Echeberría is Chairman of the Interim Board of LACNIC, the emerging regional internet registry for Latin America and the Caribbean, Interim Chairman of ENRED, the Latin American Network Forum, and a participant in the Internet Society and the IETF. He holds a degree in Computer Science from the Universidad de la Republica, Uruguay, and a Masters Degree in Information Technologies from the Universitario Autonomo del Sur, Uruguay.

Khaled Fattal is CEO of International Business Enterprises (IBE) Limited, Chairman and CEO of Multilingual Internet Names Consortium (MINC), and President of Waqalat Arbitration Center in New Delhi, India. He is also a founding member of Arabic Internet Names Consortium (AINC) and is its Acting Executive Director. Mr. Fattal brings experience from the IT industry as well as the financial sector where he worked with major banking institutions in the United States and top Fortune 500 multinationals specializing in fast moving consumer goods. He has specialized expertise in market development across continents, especially the Middle East, Europe, North America and the Far East. Mr. Fattal holds a Bachelors degree in Business Administration, International Finance and Marketing from University of Southern California, and a Masters degree in International Business from California State University at Los Angeles.

José María Figueres is Senior Managing Director of the World Economic Forum, Switzerland. He is also the Chairperson for the UN ICT Task Force and a member of the Board of Directors for the World Resources Institute (WRI). He was the Minister of Agriculture, Minister of Foreign Trade, President for San Cristobal Agroindustrial Group and General Manager for Fibers of Central America. He serves on the Dean's Alumni Leadership Council for Harvard's Kennedy School of Government. Prior to joining the World Economic Forum, he was the President of Costa Rica from 1994 to 1998. Mr. Figueres was educated at United States Military Academy where he graduated with an Engineering degree and at Harvard University where he obtained his MPA.

Michael Geist is the Canada Research Chair of Internet and E-commerce Law at the University of Ottawa and serves as Technology Counsel to Osler, Hoskin & Harcourt LLP. He has obtained a Bachelor of Laws degree from Osgoode Hall Law School in Toronto, Master of Laws degrees from Cambridge University in the United Kingdom and Columbia Law School in New York City, and a Doctorate in Law from Columbia Law School. Mr. Geist has written numerous academic articles and government reports on the Internet and law. He is a member of Canada's National Task Force on spam, a columnist on technology law issues for the Toronto Star, and the author of the textbook *Internet Law in Canada* (Captus Press).

Patrick Grossetete is a Senior Product Manager at Cisco Systems and is responsible for a suite of Cisco IOSR software technologies including IPv6. Mr. Grossetete is a member of the IPv6 Forum Technical Directorate and manages Cisco's participation in the Forum. He has more than 20 years experience in the networking industry. Mr. Grossetete has a degree in Computer Technology from the Control Data Institute, Paris, France.

Tony Hain is currently a Technical Leader with Cisco Systems focusing on IPv6. In addition to providing guidance to the various internal product teams, he has also been co-chair of the IETF Working Group developing IPv6 Transition tools. His IETF participation since 1987 included a term on the Internet Architecture Board from 1997 - 2001. As an IPv6 Forum Fellow, Mr. Hain is currently serving as Technology Director on the North American IPv6 Task Force Steering Committee. Prior to joining Cisco in 2001, he spent five years at Microsoft where his roles included Program Manager for IPv6, as well as Network Analyst for the CIO's office. Prior to Microsoft, he was the Associate Network Manager for the United States Department of Energy's Internet effort, ESnet.

Rainer Händel works within the Siemens Information and Communication Networks Group as a Director of Standards Coordination. In 1978 Mr. Händel joined Siemens where he was engaged in software development for switching systems, in concepts and standardization of broadband networks, and in the analysis of the liberalization and deregulation of telecommunication markets. From October 1994 until the end of 1995, he was a member of the Planning Board of the German Foreign Office in Bonn with a focus on the societal impact of new information and communication technologies. Mr. Händel has been a long-time, active member of several international standardization organisations such as ITU and ETSI and is the author of several technical articles and a book on broadband networking. Mr. Händel is an elected member of the ICANN Nomination Committee. He holds a Doctorate in Physics from the University of Erlangen-Nürnberg.

International Chamber of Commerce (ICC) is the largest, most representative business organization in the world. Its thousands of member companies in over 130 countries have interests spanning every sector of private enterprise. A world network of national committees keeps the ICC International Secretariat in Paris informed about national and regional business priorities. The United Nations, the World Trade Organization, and many other intergovernmental bodies, both international and regional, are kept in touch with the views of international business through ICC. ICC forges internationally agreed rules and standards that companies adopt voluntarily and that can be incorporated in binding contracts. The ICC Commission on E-Business, IT and Telecoms (EBITT) formulates policies and provides an industry interface on ICT issues.

International Telecommunication Union (ITU) is an international organization within the United Nations System where governments and the private sector coordinate global telecommunication networks and services. Its membership includes 189 countries and over 500 private members from the telecommunication, broadcasting and information technology sectors. The Union produces a range of authoritative information resources, including the flagship publication *World Telecommunication Development Report* (WTDR), which provides a comprehensive overview of an industry in full transition, and the *Tele-communication Regulatory Survey*, an annual survey conducted by the Telecommunication Development Bureau, which monitors world telecommunication reform and serves as the basis of a regulatory database offering vital information for governments reforming their telecommunication sector. The Union's standardization activities, which have helped foster the growth of new technologies such as mobile telephony and the Internet, are now being put to use in defining the building blocks of the emerging global information infrastructure, and designing advanced multimedia systems which handle a mix of voice, data, audio and video signals.

Internet Society (ISOC) is a global non-profit membership organization founded in 1991 to provide leadership in Internet-related standards, education, and policy issues. ISOC works together with members and partner organizations to increase understanding and awareness of how the Internet's stability, open nature and global reach can be developed and maintained for the benefit of people everywhere. ISOC encourages broad participation in the processes that make the Internet work and is the organizational home of the Internet Engineering Task Force (IETF).

Robert E. Kahn is Chairman, CEO and President of the Corporation for National Research Initiatives (CNRI), which he founded in 1986 after a thirteen-year term at the United States Defense Advanced Research Projects Agency (DARPA). He worked on the technical staff at Bell Laboratories and then became an Assistant Professor of Electrical Engineering at MIT. At technical research and development firm Bolt, Beranek, and Newman, Mr. Kahn was responsible for the system design of the Arpanet, the first packet-switched network. In 1972 he moved to DARPA and subsequently became Director of DARPA's Information Processing Techniques Office (IPTO). Mr. Kahn conceived the idea of open-architecture networking. He is a co-inventor of the TCP/IP protocols and was responsible for originating DARPA's Internet Program. Mr. Kahn also coined the term National Information Infrastructure (NII) in the mid-1980s, which later became more widely known as the Information Super Highway. In his recent work, Mr. Kahn has been developing the concept of a digital object architecture as a key middleware component of the NII. Mr. Kahn is a member of several institutions, organizations and committees engaged in ICT issues. He is a recipient of numerous awards and commendations and has received several honorary degrees. Mr. Kahn earned M.A. and Ph.D. degrees from Princeton University in 1962 and 1964 respectively.

Daniel Karrenberg currently serves the RIPE NCC as Chief Scientist. In the 1990s Mr. Karrenberg led the establishment of the RIPE NCC, the first of the Regional Internet Registries. He has helped to shape Internet address space distribution policy, transferring both policy development and implementation to the region. He also brought the second DNS root name server to Europe in 1997. In the 1980s Mr. Karrenberg helped to build EUnet and led the effort to transition it to Internet protocols, making EUnet the first pan-European ISP and bringing Internet connections to many places in and around Europe.

Norbert Klein created the first dial-up internet connection from Cambodia in 1994. He established the .kh country domain in 1996 and administered it until 1998. In 1999, Mr. Klein joined the Non-Commercial Constituency of the ICANN. He has made various international presentations on problems of the Digital Divide. Since 2000 he was involved with the standardization of the Khmer script on computers, until the Khmer UNICODE standard was finalized in 2002. At present he is promoting a Khmer Open Source Initiative to create a full range of UNICODE-based Open Source applications. Mr. Klein has been a member of the Conseil d'Orientation of the "Institut des Nouvelles Technologies de l'Information et de la Formation" of the Francophonie since 2003. Mr. Klein regularly advises the Director of the NGO Open Forum of Cambodia and is editor of a weekly press review of the Khmer language press - in English and in Khmer.

Wolfgang Kleinwächter is a Professor for International Communication Policy and Regulation at the Department for Media and Information Sciences of the University of Aarhus, Denmark. As co-founder of the WSIS Civil Society Internet Governance Caucus, he was also a member of the WSIS Civil Society Bureau since 2002. From 1994 to 1998 Mr. Kleinwächter was the Chairman of the Management Board of the Inter-Regional Information Society Initiative of the European Commission in Brussels and coordinated the regional "Saxonian Information Initiative" (SII) of the government of the Free State of Saxony in Germany. Since 1997 he was involved in numerous activities on Internet governance, starting with the IAHC and ICANN. Mr. Kleinwächter has studied Communication, International Law and International Relations at the University of Leipzig and holds Bachelors, Masters and Ph.D. degrees. He has authored more than 100 international publications.

Markus Kummer is a career diplomat who has been appointed by the Secretary-General of the United Nations to head the Secretariat of the Working Group on Internet Governance. As a member of the Swiss delegation he chaired several negotiating groups at the first phase of the WSIS, including the group on Internet governance. Since 2002 he held the position as eEnvoy of the Swiss Foreign Ministry in Bern. From 1998 to 2002 he served as Head of Unit in the Secretariat of the European Free Trade Association (EFTA). In 1998 he had a special assignment with the Swiss Mission in Geneva as co-coordinator for the organization of the Second Session of the WTO Ministerial Conference. During a previous posting at the same Mission, between 1993 and 1996, he was in charge of matters related to UNCTAD and the International Trade Center (UNCTAD/WTO). Mr. Kummer has been working for the Swiss Foreign Ministry since 1979.

Latif Ladid is the President of IPv6 Forum, a Trustee of the Internet Society, the Chair of the European Commission IPv6 Task Force and the Vice Chair of the North American IPv6 Task Force and the SuperComm EntNET. Mr. Ladid is a researcher on multiple European Commission Next Generation Technologies IST Projects. He is also a member of 3GPP(2) PCG, IEC Executive Committee and ITU-T Informal.

Patrice Lyons is currently in practice in Washington, D.C. at the Law Offices of Patrice Lyons, Chartered. As Senior Legal Counsel to the Corporation for National Research Initiatives (CNRI) for over ten years, Ms. Lyons has been involved in the analysis of a wide range of legal and regulatory issues relating to the development of the Internet including trademark and licensing matters. Ms. Lyons' interest in the application of copyright and related bodies of law to new technical developments began upon graduation from Georgetown University Law Center (J.D. 1969), when she attended Columbia University Law School (1969-70) as the Burton Memorial Fellow in copyright and communications studies. While serving as a Legal Officer in the Copyright Division of UNESCO (Paris, France; 1971-76), she participated in the preparation of the Convention relating to the distribution of programme-carrying signals transmitted by space satellite. She was a Senior Attorney in the Office of General Counsel of the United States Copyright Office, Library of Congress (1976-87). Ms. Lyons then served as a partner in the communications law firm of Haley, Bader & Potts (1987-90). She is a member of the Bars of the United States Supreme Court, New York State and the District of Columbia.

Don MacLean is an independent consultant on national and international ICT-related policy, strategy and governance issues, based in Ottawa, Canada. His national work has included projects on the e-economy, e-government, policies and strategies for achieving universal access to broadband networks and services. His international work has included projects on supporting the creation of e-strategies in developing countries; strengthening developing country participation in international ICT decision-making; reforming international governance institutions; and contributing to the WSIS and other initiatives to close the digital divide. Mr. MacLean served as Head of Strategic Planning and External Affairs at the International Telecommunication Union from 1992-99. Prior to joining the ITU he held a number of senior policy and planning positions in the Canadian Department of Communications.

Veni Markovski was the founder and CEO of Bulgaria's second Internet Service Provider, BOL.BG, and is founding Chair of the Board of the Internet Society – Bulgaria. He currently serves as the Bulgarian country coordinator for the Global Internet Policy Initiative, chairs the Bulgarian President's IT Advisory Committee for Bulgaria and the Board of the IT Development Association, and is helping the Bulgarian Parliamentary Committee on Transport and Telecommunications. Mr. Markovski has been an active advocate for reform of laws and regulations governing the Internet. He was a member of the Civil Society Bureau to the World Summit on the Information Society and is a member of the Board of Computer Professionals for Social Responsibility. A frequent contributor to ICANN, Mr. Markovski also served as a Chair of ICANN's Membership Implementation Task Force in 2000.

John Mathiason is Adjunct Professor of International Relations at the Maxwell School of Citizenship and Public Affairs of Syracuse University where he teaches in the area of international public sector and NGO management. He is also Program Manager for International Education and Distance Learning. He has been Managing Director of Associates for International Management Services, a consulting company that uses the Internet extensively for its work in improving international public and not-for-profit management. Mr. Mathiason has also been an Adjunct Professor of Public Administration at the Robert Wagner Graduate School of Public Service of New York University. His Internet-related research centers on the role of the Internet in the management of the international public sector and the role of the international public and non-governmental sector in the governance of the Internet. He also works on issues related to Internet accessibility for persons with disabilities, with an emphasis on international norms and policies favoring accessibility. He was a career staff member of the United Nations Secretariat for over 25 years and holds a Ph.D. in Political Science from the Massachusetts Institute of Technology.

Lee W. McKnight is an Associate Professor in the School of Information Studies, Syracuse University. He is also a Research Associate Professor of Computer Science at Tufts University; a Research Affiliate of the Program on Internet and Telecoms Convergence at MIT; and President of Marengo Research. Previously Mr. McKnight was an Associate Professor and Director of the Edward R. Murrow Center at the Fletcher School of Law and Diplomacy, Tufts University; Research Affiliate at the MIT Center for Technology, Policy and Industrial Development; and Founder of the Internet Telephony Consortium. Mr. McKnight received a B.A. magna cum laude from Tufts University in 1978, an M.A. from the School of Advanced International Studies, Johns Hopkins University, in 1981 and a Ph.D. in 1989 from MIT.

Faryel Mouria-Beji is President and Chief Executive Officer of the Tunisian Internet Agency and Professor Researcher at ENSI-University of Tunis.

Milton Mueller is a Professor at the School of Information Studies, Syracuse University. He is co-Director and founder of the Convergence Center and Senior Associate at the Global Affairs Institute, Maxwell School of Citizenship and Public Affairs. He has conducted scholarly research on telecommunications and information policy since 1982. His research focuses on property rights, institutions and regulation in telecommunication and information industries. He has authored 5 books and over 30 refereed journal articles and book chapters on public policy issues in telecommunications and Internet and is on the international editorial boards of *Telecommunications Policy* and *Info. The Journal of Policy, Regulation and Strategy for Telecommunication, Information and Media*. Mr. Mueller received his B.A from Columbia College, Chicago and M.A. and Ph.D. from the University of Pennsylvania, Annenberg School.

George Sadowsky is Executive Director of the Global Internet Policy Initiative (GIPI) and also serves as Senior Technical Adviser for USAID's dot-GOV program. He has worked as an applied mathematician and a programmer, and has headed computing centers at the Brookings Institution, Northwestern University and New York University. At the United Nations

Secretariat, he backstopped technical assistance projects and worked in about 50 developing countries. He has been a consultant to multiple international institutions and governmental offices, and has served on boards of several corporations. Mr. Sadowsky has served on the Board of the Internet Society for seven years, where he headed a group of ISOC volunteers who defined and conducted the ISOC Developing Country Network Training Workshops from 1993 through 2001. He has written and lectured extensively on ICT and development. He received an A.B. degree in Mathematics from Harvard College and Masters and Ph.D. degrees in Economics from Yale University.

United Nations Conference on Trade and Development (UNCTAD) aims at the development-friendly integration of developing countries into the world economy. UNCTAD is the focal point within the United Nations for the integrated treatment of trade and development and the interrelated issues in the areas of finance, technology, investment and sustainable development. The application of ICT to business and trade represents a unique opportunity for developing countries, and UNCTAD thus emphasizes the role of ICTs for business. In addition to its current activities in a number of ICT applications, UNCTAD addresses a selection of other ICT-related activities, including those that would enable developing countries to take full advantage of free and open-source software, promote e-tourism, e-business and e-finance, and assist them in developing national e-strategies and building capacity to monitor ICT developments at the national level.

United Nations Economic Commission for Africa (UNECA) is the regional arm of the United Nations in Africa. Its mandate is to support the economic and social development of its 53 Member States, foster regional integration, and promote international cooperation for Africa's development. ECA, working with key partners, has assisted over 28 African countries in developing ICT national strategies for accelerating their socio-economic development and is also working with a number of these countries to embark on implementation programmes. It also supports the development of sectoral and village level strategies, and liaises with the regional economic communities to develop regional plans.

United Nations Economic and Social Commission for Western Asia (UNESCWA) promotes economic and social development through regional and subregional cooperation and integration and serves as the main general economic and social development forum within the United Nations system for the Western Asia region. It formulates and promotes development assistance activities and projects commensurate with the needs and priorities of the region and acts as an executing agency for relevant operational projects. It has an Information and Communication Technology Division which aims to increase the capabilities of Member States in harnessing information and communications technologies for their development. In this respect, it provides support to the development of ICT policies, infrastructure, and applications, and raises awareness with regard to the potential of ICTs in promoting sustainable development and enabling ESCWA countries to integrate into the global economy.

United Nations Information and Communication Technologies (ICT) Task Force was launched by Secretary-General Kofi Annan in 2001 to mobilize information and communication technologies in the service of development. Task Force members – representing governments, the private sector, civil society, non-profit foundations and mulitlateral organizations – have focused on leveraging ICT for achieving the Millennium Development Goals by 2015. Utilizing a decentralized approach that allows for broad participation, it has developed multistakeholder networks in all major regions and across several thematic areas in its efforts to build human capacity, mobilize resources and promote collaborative initiatives.

Stefaan Verhulst is the Chief of Research at the Markle Foundation. Previously Mr. Verhulst was the Founder and Director of the Programme in Comparative Media Law and Policy (PCMLP) at Oxford University, as well as Senior Research Fellow at the Centre for Socio Legal Studies. In addition, he was the UNESCO Chairholder in Communications Law and Policy for the United Kingdom. Before his move to Oxford in 1996, he had been a lecturer on communications law and policy issues in Belgium and founder and co-director of the International Media and Info-comms Policy and Law studies (IMPS) at the School of Law, University of Glasgow. Mr. Verhulst has served as consultant to various international and national organizations including the Council of Europe, European Commission, UNESCO, UNDP, USAID and DFID. Mr. Verhulst has published several publications, and he is also the founder and editor of the *International Journal of Communications Law and Policy* and the *Communications Law in Transition Newsletter.*

Raúl Zambrano is Senior ICT-for-Development Policy Advisor at the United Nations Development Programme (UNDP). He joined UNDP in 1993 and has worked there as programme manager for the Sustainable Development Networking Programme (SDNP) which supported the development of Internet activities in over 40 developing countries. With vast country knowledge and experience, he has worked on global issues and supported global forums such as ICANN, the G8 Dot Force and the United Nations ICT Task Force. He has also worked with the Global Internet Policy Initiative, supported the creation of national mechanisms to manage ccTLDs on an open and participatory basis, and promoted the participation of developing countries in the various Internet governance forums.

ACRONYMS AND INTERNET REFERENCES

ADB	Asian Development Bank – www.adb.org
AFDB	African Development Bank – www.afdb.org
AFNOG	Africa Network Operators' Group – www.afnog.org
APC	Association for Progressive Communications – www.apc.org
APEC	Asia-Pacific Economic Cooperation – www.apec.org
APNG	Asia Pacific Networking Group – www.apng.org
APNIC	Asia Pacific Network Information Centre – www.apnic.net
APRICOT	Asia Pacific Regional Internet Conference on Operational Technologies – www.apricot.net
APT	Asia-Pacific Telecommunity – www.aptsec.org
ARIN	American Registry for Internet Numbers – www.arin.net
ASEAN	Association of Southeast Asian Nations – www.aseansec.org
ASTA	Anti-Spam Technical Alliance
ATIS	Alliance for Telecommunications Industry Standards – www.atis.org
ATU	African Telecommunications Union – www.atu-uat.org
BTS	United States Bureau of Transportation Statistics – www.bts.gov
ccNSO	Country Code Names Supporting Organization – http://ccnso.icann.org
CENTR	Council Of European National Top-Level Domain Registries – www.centr.org
CEPT	European Conference of Postal and Telecommunications Administrations – www.cept.org
CERN	European Organization for Nuclear Research – www.cern.ch
CERT/CC	CERT Coordination Centre – www.cert.org
CGIbr	Comitê Gestor da Internet no Brasil – www.cg.org.br
CIS	Center for Internet Security – www.cisecurity.org
CITEL	Inter-American Telecommunication Commission (Organization of American States) – www.citel.oas.org
COE	Council of Europe – www.coe.int
CompTIA	Computing Technology Industry Association – www.comptia.org
DISA	Data Interchange Standards Association – www.disa.org
DoC	United States Department of Commerce – www.doc.gov
EDIFICE	European B2B Forum for the Electronic Industry – www.edifice.org
ENISA	European Network and Information Security Agency
ETNO	European Telecommunications Network Operators' Association – www.etno.be
ETSI	European Telecommunications Standardization Institute – www.etsi.org

EU	European Union – www.europa.eu.int
FAPESP	Fundação de Amparo à Pesquisa do Estado de São Paulo – www.fapesp.br
FIRST	Forum of Incident Response and Security Teams – www.first.org
FTC	United States Federal Trade Commission – www.ftc.gov
GAC	ICANN's Government Advisory Committee – www.icann.org/committees/gac
GBDe	Global Business Dialogue on Electronic Commerce – www.gbde.org
GNSO	Generic Names Supporting Organization – www.gnso.icann.org
IAB	Internet Architecture Board – www.iab.org
IADB	Inter-American Development Bank – www.iadb.org
IANA	Internet Assigned Numbers Authority – www.iana.org
IBASE	Instituto Brasileiro de Análises Sociais e Econômicas – www.ibase.br
ICANN	Internet Corporation for Assigned Names and Numbers – www.icann.org
ICC	International Chamber of Commerce – www.iccwbo.org
ICPEN	International Consumer Protection and Enforcement Network – www.imsnricc.org
ICRA	Internet Content Rating Association – www.icra.org
IDRC	International Development Research Centre – www.idrc.ca
IEEE	Institute of Electrical and Electronics Engineers – www.icee.org
IESG	Internet Engineering Steering Group – www.ietf.org/iesg.html
IETF	Internet Engineering Task Force – www.ietf.org
ILETS	International Law Enforcement Telecommunications Seminar
ISC2	International Systems Security Certification Consortium Inc. – www.isc2.org
ISO	International Organization for Standardization – www.iso.org
ISOC	Internet Society – www.isoc.org
ISSA	Information Systems Security Association – www.issa.org
ITA	International Trademark Association – www.inta.org
ITAA	Information Technology Association of America – www.itaa.org
ITU	International Telecommunication Union – www.itu.int
LACNIC	Latin American and Caribbean Internet Addresses Registry – www.lacnic.net
MIT	Massachusetts Institute of Technology – www.mit.edu
MINC	Multilingual Internet Names Consortium – www.minc.org
NANOG	North American Network Operators' Group – www.nanog.org
NATIA	National Technical Investigators' Association – www.natia.org
NBSO	NIC BR Security Office, Brazilian Computer Emergency Response Team – www.nbso.nic.br

NEPAD	New Partnership for Africa's Development – www.nepad.org
NICI	Nijmegen Institute for Cognition and Information – www.nici.kun.nl
NSF	National Science Foundation – www.nsf.gov
OASIS	Organization for the Advancement of Structured Information Standards – www.oasis-open.org
OECD	Organisation for Economic Co-operation and Development – www.oecd.org
PIR	Public Interest Registry – www.pir.org
Registro.br	.br Internet registry – www.registro.br
RIAA	Recording Industry Association of America – www.riaa.com
RIPE NCC	Réseaux IP Européens Network Co-ordination Centre – www.ripe.net
RITS	Rede de Informações para o Terceiro Setor – www.rits.org.br
RNP	Rede Nacional de Ensino e Pesquisa – www.rnp.br
SANOG	South Asian Network Operators Group – www.sanog.org
SilkNOG	Network Operators Group for countries participating in the Virtual Silk Highway – see www.silkproject.org
TECF	Trusted Electronic Communication Forum – www.tecf.org
TIA	Telecommunications Industry Association – www.tiaonline.org
TTC	Telecommunication Technology Committee (Japan) – www.ttc.or.jp
UN/CEFACT	United Nations Centre for Trade Facilitation and Electronic Business – www.unece.org/cefact
UNCITRAL	United Nations Commission on International Trade Law – www.uncitral.org
UNCTAD	United Nations Conference on Trade and Development – www.unctad.org
UNDP	United Nations Development Programme – www.undp.org
UNESCO	United Nations Educational, Scientific and Cultural Organization – www.unesco.org
W3C	World Wide Web Consortium – www.w3.org
WCO	World Customs Organization – www.wcoomd.org
WIPO	World Intellectual Property Organisation – www.wipo.org
WTO	World Trade Organization – www.wto.org,

GLOSSARY

3G: *Third-generation mobile network or service.* Generic name for mobile network/service based on the IMT-2000 family of global standards.

Always-on: Devices remain connected to the Internet when powered up, rather than establishing temporary connections (e.g. dial-up). Because devices need a unique IP address continuously, the rise in always-on devices demands more IP address space.

ARPANET: *Advanced Research Projects Agency Network.* The precursor to the Internet. Developed in the late 60's and early 70's by the United States Department of Defense as an experiment in wide-area-networking that would survive a nuclear war.

ASCII: *American Standard Code for Information Interchange.* Worldwide standard for representing ordinary text (the upper and lower-case Latin letters, numbers, punctuation, etc.) as a stream of binary numbers.

ATM: *Asynchronous transfer mode.* A transmission mode in which the information is organized into cells; it is asynchronous in the sense that the recurrence of cells from an individual user is not necessarily periodic.

Bandwidth: The range of frequencies available to be occupied by signals. In analogue systems it is measured in terms of Hertz (Hz) and in digital systems in bits per second (bit/s). The higher the bandwidth, the greater the amount of information that can be transmitted in a given time. High bandwidth channels are referred to as "broadband" which typically means 1.5-2.0 Mbit/s or higher.

Bit (binary digit): A bit is the primary unit of electronic, digital data. Written in base-2, binary language as a "1" or a "0".

Bit/s: *Bits per second.* Measurement of the transmission speed of units of data (bits) over a network. Also kbit/s: kilobits (1,000) per second; Mbit/s: megabits (1,000,000) per second, and Gbit/s: Gigabits (1,000,000,000) per second.

Broadband access: High-speed Internet connection technologies. Transmission capacity with sufficient bandwidth to permit combined provision of voice, data and video, with no lower limit.

Browser: Application that retrieves world wide web documents specified by URLs from an HTTP server on the Internet. Displays the retrieved documents according to the Hypertext Markup Language (HTML).

Cable modem: A technology that allows high-speed interactive services, including Internet access, to be delivered over a cable TV network.

ccTLD: *country-code Top Level Domain.*

CDMA: *Code division multiple access.* A technology for digital transmission of radio signals based on spread spectrum techniques where each voice or data call uses the whole radio band and is assigned a unique code.

CDMA2000: *Code division multiple access 2000.* A third-generation digital cellular standard based on Qualcomm technology. One of the IMT-2000 "family" of standards.

Cellular: A mobile telephone service provided by a network of base stations, each of which covers one geographic cell within the total cellular system service area.

Channel: One of a number of discrete frequency ranges utilized by a base station to transmit and receive information from cellular terminals (such as mobile handsets).

Circuit-switched connection: A temporary connection that is established on request between two or more stations in order to allow the exclusive use of that connection until it is released. At present, most voice networks are based on circuit-switching, whereas the Internet is packet-based. See also *Packet-based.*

Client-server: A communication model where connections are initiated one-way, from clients to servers.

Connectivity: The capability to provide, to end-users, connections to the Internet or other communication networks.

Digital: Representation of voice or other information using digits 0 and 1. The digits are transmitted as a series of pulses. Digital networks allow for higher capacity, greater functionality and improved quality.

DNS: *Domain name system.* Used to map between Internet domain names (e.g. www.ipv6forum.org) and IP addresses (for use by the network).

DSL: *Digital subscriber line.* (See also *SDSL.*)

E-commerce: *Electronic commerce.* Term used to describe transactions that take place online where the buyer and seller are remote from each other.

Email: *Electronic mail.* The exchange of electronic messages between geographically dispersed locations.

End-to-end model: Devices communicating on the Internet do so directly without any intervening translation devices; such devices fate-share their connection.

End-user: The individual or organization that originates or is the final recipient of information carried over a network (i.e. the consumer).

Ethernet: A protocol for interconnecting computers and peripheral devices at high speed. Recently Gigabit Ethernet has become available which enables speeds up to 1 Gbit/s.

Ethernet can run on several types of wiring including: twisted pair, coaxial, and even fiber optic cable.

FDMA: *Frequency division multiple access.* A cellular technology that has been used in the first-generation analogue systems (i.e. NMT, AMPS, and TACS).

Fixed line: A physical line connecting the subscriber to the telephone exchange. Typically, fixed-line network is used to refer to the PSTN to distinguish it from mobile networks.

Frequency: The rate at which an electrical current alternates, usually measured in Hertz (see *Hz*). It is also used to refer to a location on the radio frequency spectrum, such as 800, 900 or 1,800 Mhz.

G8: Group of eight major industrial nations (Japan, Russia, U.K., France, Italy, Germany, USA, and Canada).

GATS: *General Agreement on Trade in Services.*

gTLD: *Generic top level domain,* such as .com or .museum.

Hotspot: An access point to a wireless local area network (WLAN). Hotspots are areas where wireless data can be sent and received, and Internet access is provided to wireless devices. For example, a laptop computer can be used to access the Internet in a hotspot provided in an airport or hotel.

H-ratio: Used to measure the limited efficiency of Internet address allocation procedures. Often referred to when discussed about the limitations of the current Internet protocol and about the need to move to IPv6 as the number of computers connected to Internet is increasing.

Hyperlink: An electronic link in an electronic document that, typically through clicking, provides access to another place in the same document or in another document.

Hz: *Hertz.* The frequency measurement unit equal to one cycle per second.

ICT: *Information and Communication Technologies.*

IDN: *International Domain Name.*

IMT-2000: *International Mobile Telecommunications-2000.* Third-generation (3G) "family" of mobile cellular standards approved by ITU. For more information see the website at: http://www.itu.int/imt.

Incumbent: The major network provider in a particular country, often a former State-owned monopoly.

Internet: Interconnected global networks that use the Internet protocol (see *IP*).

Internet backbone: The high-speed, high capacity lines or series of connections that form a major pathway and carry aggregated traffic within the Internet.

Interoperability: The ability of two devices, usually from different vendors, to work together.

IP: *Internet Protocol.* The underlying technology by which all Internet data communication is carried out.

IP telephony: *Internet protocol telephony.* IP telephony is used as a generic term for the conveyance of voice, fax and related services, partially or wholly over packet-based, IP-based networks. (See also *VoIP.*)

IPv4: *Internet Protocol version 4.* The current protocol.

IPv6: *Internet Protocol version 6.* The new protocol.

IPR: *Intellectual property rights.* Copyrights, patents and trademarks giving creators the right to prevent others from using their inventions, designs or other creations. The ultimate aim is to act as an incentive to encourage the development of new technology and creations, which will eventually be available to all. The main international agreements are the World Intellectual Property Organization's (WIPO) *Paris Convention for the Protection of Industrial Property* (patents, industrial designs, etc.), the *Berne Convention for the Protection of Literary and Artistic Works* (copyright), and the World Trade Organization's (WTO) *Agreement on Trade-Related Aspects of Intellectual Property Rights* (TRIPS).

ISP: *Internet service provider.* ISPs provide end-users access to the Internet. *Internet Access Providers* (IAPs) may also provide access to other ISPs. ISPs may offer their own proprietary content and access to online services such as email.

IT: *Information Technology.*

ITR: *Information Technology Research.*

IXPs: *Internet Exchange Points.*

LAN: *Local area network.* A computer network that spans a relatively small area. Most LANs are confined to a single building or group of buildings. However, one LAN can be connected to other LANs over any distance via telephone lines and radio waves. A system of LANs connected in this way is called a wide-area network (WAN). (See also *WLAN.*)

Local loop: The system used to connect the subscriber to the nearest switch. It generally consists of a pair of copper wires, but may also employ fiber-optic or wireless technologies.

Main telephone line: Telephone line connecting a subscriber to the telephone exchange equipment. This term is synonymous with the term *fixed line.*

Mercosur: *Mercado Común del Sur.* A free trade agreement between Argentina, Brazil, Paraguay and Uruguay.

Mobile: As used in this report, the term refers to mobile cellular systems and to mobile phones.

MOU: *Memorandum of Understanding.*

NAFTA: *North American Free Trade Agreement.* For NAFTA secretariat see www.nafta-sec-alena.org.

NAT: *Network address translation.* Allow multiple computers to connect to the Internet via a limited number of global IPv4 addresses. Restricts end-to-end principle of the Internet.

NGN: *Next Generation Network.*

Packet: Block or grouping of data that is treated as a single unit within a communication network.

Packet-based: Message-delivery technique in which packets are relayed through stations in a network. (See also *Circuit-switched connection.*)

Peer-to-peer: Communication model in which client devices may communicate directly, initiating the data exchange in either direction, without a server system.

Penetration: A measurement of access to telecommunications, normally calculated by dividing the number of subscribers to a particular service by the population and multiplying by 100. Also referred to as *teledensity* (for fixed-line networks) or *mobile density* (for cellular ones), or *total teledensity* (fixed and mobile combined).

Pervasive computing: A concept that describes a situation in which computing capability is embedded into numerous different devices around the home or office (e.g. refrigerators, washing machines, cars, etc.). Also referred to as *ubiquitous computing. Pervasive communications* implies that the microchips in these devices are also able to communicate, for instance their location and status.

Phishing: The practice of impersonating someone or something trusting in order to convince unknowing victims to give out their passwords and other personal or sensitive information.

Protocol: A set of formal rules and specifications describing how to transmit data, especially across a network.

PSTN: *Public switched telephone network.* The public telephone network that delivers fixed telephone service.

QoS: *Quality of service.* A measure of network performance that reflects the quality and reliability of a connection. QoS can indicate a data traffic policy that guarantees certain amounts of bandwidth at any given time, or can involve traffic shaping that assigns varying bandwidth to different applications.

RFC document: The document format used by the IETF to describe Internet standards.

RFID: *Radio frequency identification.* A system of radio tagging that provides identification data for goods in order to make them traceable. Typically used by manufacturers to make goods such as clothing items traceable without having to read bar code data for individual items.

RIRs: *Regional Internet Registries.*

Root server: A central name server that stores authoritative data for the very top-level domains. For example, a root server knows which name servers hold authoritative information for .com, .fr, .org, etc. The number of root servers is currently limited to 13. (See also *Server.*)

SDSL: *Symmetrical DSL.* A proprietary North American DSL standard.

Server: (1) A host computer on a network that sends stored information in response to requests or queries. (2) The term server is also used to refer to the software that makes the process of serving information possible.

Spectrum: The radio frequency spectrum of hertzian waves used as a transmission medium for cellular radio, radiopaging, satellite communication, over-the-air broadcasting and other services.

TCP: *Transmission control protocol.* A transport layer protocol that offers connection-oriented, reliable stream services between two hosts. This is the primary transport protocol used by TCP/IP applications.

Teledensity: Number of main telephone lines per 100 inhabitants. (See *Penetration.*)

TLD: *Top Level Domain.* Such as '.org', '.com', '.ch', '.uk'.

Total teledensity: Sum of the number of fixed lines and mobile phone subscribers per 100 inhabitants. (See *Penetration.*)

TRIPS: WTO's Agreement on Trade-Related Aspects of Intellectual Property Rights.

Ubiquitous computing: A term that reflects the view that future communication networks will allow seamless access to data, regardless of where the user is. See *Pervasive computing.*

UDRP: *Uniform Dispute Resolution Policy.*

UMTS: *Universal mobile telecommunications system.* The European term for third-generation mobile cellular systems or IMT-2000 based on the W-CDMA standard. For more information see the UMTS Forum website at: http://www.umts-forum.org/.

Unicode: A character set encoding standard that aims eventually to provide universal way of encoding characters of all the scripts of the world.

Universal access: Refers to reasonable telecommunication access for all. Includes universal service for those that can afford individual telephone service and widespread provision of public telephones within a reasonable distance of others.

VAT: *Value-added tax.*

VoIP: *Voice over Internet Protocol.* A generic term used to describe the techniques used to carry voice traffic over IP. (See also *IP telephony.*)

W-CDMA: *Wideband code division multiple access.* A third-generation mobile standard under the IMT-2000 banner, first deployed in Japan. Known as UMTS in Europe. (See also *CDMA.*)

Whois: (1) A searchable Internet database maintained by registries and registrars. Contains information about Internet users, hosts, networks, networking organizations and domain names. (2) Set of rules that describes the application used to access the database.

Wi-Fi: *Wireless fidelity.* A mark of interoperability among devices adhering to the 802.11b specification for Wireless LANs from the Institute of Electrical and Electronics Engineers (IEEE). However, the term Wi-Fi is sometimes mistakenly used as a generic term for wireless LAN.

WiMAX: Fixed wireless standard that allows for long-range wireless communication at 70 Mbit/s over 50 kilometers. It can be used as a backbone Internet connection to rural areas.

Wireless: Generic term for mobile communication services which do not use fixed-line networks for direct access to the subscriber.

WLAN: *Wireless local area network.* Also known as *Wireless LAN.* A wireless network whereby a user can connect to a local area network (LAN) through a wireless (radio) connection, as an alternative to a wired local area network.

WSIS: (United Nations) *World Summit on the Information Society.* The first phase of WSIS took place in Geneva (hosted by the Government of Switzerland) from December 10-12, 2003. The second phase will take place in Tunis (hosted by the Government of Tunisia), from November 16-18, 2005. For more information see: http://www.itu.int/wsis.